TExES Chemistry 7-12
240 Teacher Certification Exam

By: Sharon A. Wynne, M.S.

XAMonline, Inc.
Boston

Copyright © 2018 XAMonline, Inc.
All rights reserved. No part of the material protected by this copyright notice may be reproduced or utilized in any form or by any means, electronic or mechanical, including photocopying, recording or by any information storage and retrievable system, without written permission from the copyright holder.

To obtain permission(s) to use the material from this work for any purpose including workshops or seminars, please submit a written request to:

XAMonline, Inc.
21 Orient Avenue
Melrose, MA 02176
Toll Free 1-800-301-4647
Email: info@xamonline.com
Web www.xamonline.com

Library of Congress Cataloging-in-Publication Data
Wynne, Sharon A.

    TExES Chemistry 7–12 (240): Teacher Certification / Sharon A. Wynne.
    ISBN 978-1-60787-653-3

1. Chemistry 7 – 12   2. Study Guides.   3. TExES
4. Teachers' Certification & Licensure.   5. Careers

Disclaimer:
The opinions expressed in this publication are the sole works of XAMonline and were created independently from the National Education Association, Educational Testing Service, or any State Department of Education, National Evaluation Systems or other testing affiliates.

Between the time of publication and printing, state specific standards as well as testing formats and website information may change that is not included in part or in whole within this product. XAMonline developed the sample test questions and the questions reflect similar content as on real tests; however, they are not former tests. XAMonline assembles content that aligns with state standards but makes no claims nor guarantees teacher candidates a passing score. Numerical scores are determined by testing companies such as NES or ETS and then are compared with individual state standards. A passing score varies from state to state.

Printed in the United States of America
TExES: Chemistry 7– 12 (240)
ISBN: 978-1-60787-653-3

TEACHER CERTIFICATION STUDY GUIDE

ABOUT THE TEST

The Texas Examination of Educator Standards (TExES) test for Field 240: Chemistry 7–12 measures the content knowledge required of an entry-level Chemistry teacher in Texas public schools.

ORGANIZATION OF THE TExES TEST FRAMEWORK

The test framework is based on the educator standards for Chemistry. The content covered is organized into broad areas of content called domains. Each domain covers one or more of the educator standards for this field. Within each domain, the content is further defined by a set of competencies which are further broken down into various skills.

The complete list of domains, competencies, and skills appears in the Table of Contents for this guide.

TEST FRAMEWORK FOR FIELD 240: CHEMISTRY 7—12

Domain I: Scientific Inquiry and Processes – approx. 24% of the test
Domain II: Matter and Energy – approx. 41% of the test
Domain III: Chemical Reactions – approx. 23% of the test
Domain IV: Science Learning, Instruction, and Assessment – approx. 12% of the test

---

The Chemistry 7–12 test is designed to include 80 scorable multiple-choice items and approximately 10 nonscorable items. Your final scaled score will be based only on scorable items. The nonscorable multiple-choice items are pilot tested by including them in the test in order to collect information about how these items will perform under actual testing conditions. Nonscorable test items are not considered in calculating your score, and they are not identified on the test.

Calculators. Scientific calculators will be provided at the test administration site. See the TExES registration bulletin for the brand and model of the calculator that will be available.

Physical Constants. A set of physical constants will be provided in your test booklet.

Periodic Table of the Elements. A Periodic Table of the Elements will be provided in your test booklet.

CHEMISTRY 7-12

TEACHER CERTIFICATION STUDY GUIDE

TABLE OF CONTENTS

DOMAIN I. SCIENTIFIC INQUIRY AND PROCESSES – 24%

COMPETENCY 001 THE TEACHER UNDERSTANDS HOW TO SELECT AND MANAGE LEARNING ACTIVITIES TO ENSURE THE SAFETY OF ALL STUDENTS AND THE CORRECT USE AND CARE OF NATURAL RESOURCES, MATERIALS, EQUIPMENT, AND TECHNOLOGIES 1

Skill 1.1 Uses current sources of information about laboratory safety, including safety regulations and guidelines for the use of science facilities, materials, and equipment 1

Skill 1.2 Recognizes potential safety hazards in the laboratory and in the field and knows how to prevent accidents and apply procedures, including basic first aid, for responding to accidents 5

Skill 1.3 Employs safe practices in planning and implementing all instructional activities and designs and implements rules and procedures to maintain a safe learning environment 5

Skill 1.4 Understands procedures for selecting, maintaining, and safely using chemicals, tools, technologies, materials, specimens, and equipment, including procedures for the recycling, reuse, and conservation of laboratory resources 17

Skill 1.5 Knows how to use appropriate equipment and technology (e.g., Internet, spreadsheet, calculator) for gathering, organizing, displaying, and communicating data in a variety of ways (e.g., charts, tables, graphs, diagrams, written reports, oral presentations) 22

Skill 1.6 Understands how to use a variety of tools, techniques, and technology to gather, organize, and analyze data and how to apply appropriate methods of statistical measures and analysis ... 28

Skill 1.7 Knows how to apply techniques to calibrate measuring devices and understands concepts of precision, accuracy, and error with regard to reading and recording numerical data from scientific instruments 30

Skill 1.8 Uses the International System of Units (i.e., metric system) and performs unit conversions within and across measurement systems 33

TEACHER CERTIFICATION STUDY GUIDE

COMPETENCY 002 THE TEACHER UNDERSTANDS THE NATURE OF SCIENCE AND THE PROCESS OF SCIENTIFIC INQUIRY 40

Skill 2.1 Understands the nature of science, the predictive power of science, and limitations to the scope of science (i.e., the types of questions that science can and cannot answer) 40

Skill 2.2 Knows the characteristics of various types of scientific investigations (e.g., descriptive studies, controlled experiments, comparative data analysis) and how and why scientists use different types of scientific investigations 45

Skill 2.3 Understands principles and procedures for designing and conducting a variety of scientific investigations, with emphasis on inquiry-based investigations, and understands how to communicate and defend scientific results 47

Skill 2.4 Understands how logical reasoning, verifiable observational and experimental evidence, and peer review are used in the process of generating and evaluating scientific knowledge 50

Skill 2.5 Understands the relationship, similarities, and differences between science and technology 51

COMPETENCY 003 THE TEACHER UNDERSTANDS THE ROLE OF MATHEMATICS AND THE UNIFYING CONCEPTS COMMON TO ALL SCIENCES 53

Skill 3.1 Knows the characteristics and general features of systems; how properties and patterns of systems can be described in terms of space, time, energy, and matter; and how system components and different systems interact 53

Skill 3.2 Understands how to identify potential sources of error in an investigation, evaluate the validity of scientific data, and develop and analyze different explanations for a given scientific result 54

Skill 3.3 Knows how to apply and analyze the systems model (e.g., interacting parts, boundaries, input, output, feedback, subsystems) across the science disciplines 56

Skill 3.4	Understands how shared themes and concepts (e.g., systems, order, and organization; evidence, models, and explanation; change, constancy, and measurements; evolution and equilibrium; form and function) provide a unifying framework in science	58
Skill 3.5	Understands how models are used to represent the natural world and how to evaluate the strengths and limitations of a variety of scientific models (e.g., physical, conceptual, mathematical)	58
Skill 3.6	Understands the importance of mathematics to science and applies scientific conventions and mathematical methods (e.g., significant figures, scientific notation, dimensional analysis, statistical analysis, algebraic manipulation)	60

COMPETENCY 004 THE TEACHER UNDERSTANDS THE HISTORY OF SCIENCE, HOW SCIENCE IMPACTS THE DAILY LIVES OF STUDENTS, AND HOW SCIENCE INTERACTS WITH AND INFLUENCES PERSONAL AND SOCIETAL DECISIONS 61

Skill 4.1	Understands the historical development of science, key events in the history of science, and the contributions that diverse cultures and individuals of both genders have made to scientific knowledge	61
Skill 4.2	Knows how to use examples from the history of science to demonstrate the changing nature of scientific theories and knowledge (i.e., that scientific theories and knowledge are always subject to revision in light of new evidence)	68
Skill 4.3	Knows that science is a human endeavor influenced by societal, cultural, and personal views of the world and knows that decisions about the use and direction of science are based on factors such as ethical standards, economics, and personal and societal biases and needs	69
Skill 4.4	Understands the application of scientific ethics to the conducting, analyzing, and publishing of scientific investigations	70
Skill 4.5	Applies scientific principles, probability, and risk/benefit analysis to analyze the advantages of, disadvantages of, or alternatives to a given decision or course of action	71

TEACHER CERTIFICATION STUDY GUIDE

Skill 4.6 Understands the role science can play in helping to resolve personal, societal, and global issues (e.g., population growth, disease prevention, resource use) 72

DOMAIN II. MATTER AND ENERGY 41%

COMPETENCY 005 THE TEACHER UNDERSTANDS THE CHARACTERISTICS OF MATTER 80

Skill 5.1 Differentiates between physical and chemical properties and changes of matter 80

Skill 5.2 Explains the structure and properties of solids, liquids, and gases 80

Skill 5.3 Identifies and analyzes properties of substances (i.e., elements and compounds) and mixtures 87

Skill 5.4 Identifies elements and isotopes by atomic number and mass number 88

Skill 5.5 Understands the structure, significance, and history of the periodic table 89

COMPETENCY 006 THE TEACHER UNDERSTANDS THE STRUCTURE AND CHARACTERISTICS OF ATOMS 90

Skill 6.1 Models the atom in terms of protons, neutrons, and electron clouds 90

Skill 6.2 Understands atomic orbitals and electron configurations and describes the relationship between electron energy levels and atomic structure 91

Skill 6.3 Analyzes relationships among electron energy levels, photons, and atomic spectra 97

Skill 6.4 Applies the concept of periodicity to predict the physical and chemical properties of an element 102

Skill 6.5 Understands the historical development of atomic theory 111

TEACHER CERTIFICATION STUDY GUIDE

COMPETENCY 007 THE TEACHER UNDERSTANDS THE PROPERTIES OF GASES 115

Skill 7.1 Understands interrelationships among temperature, moles, pressure, and volume of gases contained within a closed system 115

Skill 7.2 Analyzes data obtained from investigations with gases in a closed system and determines whether the data are consistent with the ideal gas law 120

Skill 7.3 Applies the gas laws (e.g., Charles' law, Boyle's law, combined gas law, Avogadro's law) to predict gas behavior in a variety of systems 121

Skill 7.4 Applies Dalton's law of partial pressure in various systems, as in collecting a gas over water 122

Skill 7.5 Understands the relationship between Kinetic Molecular Theory and the ideal gas law 122

Skill 7.6 Knows how to apply the ideal gas law to analyze mass relationships between reactants and products in chemical reactions involving gases 123

COMPETENCY 008 THE TEACHER UNDERSTANDS PROPERTIES AND CHARACTERISTICS OF IONIC AND COVALENT BONDS 125

Skill 8.1 Relates the electron configuration of an atom to its chemical reactivity 125

Skill 8.2 Compares and contrasts characteristics of ionic and covalent bonds 126

Skill 8.3 Applies the "octet" rule to construct Lewis structures 128

Skill 8.4 Identifies and describes the arrangement of atoms in molecules, ionic crystals, polymers, and metallic substances 130

Skill 8.5 Understands the influence of bonding forces on the physical and chemical properties of ionic and covalent substances 131

Skill 8.6 Identifies and describes intermolecular and intramolecular forces 135

TEACHER CERTIFICATION STUDY GUIDE

Skill 8.7	Uses intermolecular forces to explain the physical properties of a given substance	135
Skill 8.8	Applies the concepts of electronegativity, electron affinity, and oxidation state to analyze chemical bonds	138
Skill 8.9	Evaluates energy changes in the formation and dissociation of chemical bonds	138
Skill 8.10	Understands the relationship between covalent bonding, hybridization, and molecular geometry	144

COMPETENCY 009 THE TEACHER UNDERSTANDS AND INTERPRETS CHEMICAL NOTATION AND CHEMICAL EQUATIONS 152

Skill 9.1	Identifies elements, ions, and compounds using scientific nomenclature	152
Skill 9.2	Uses and interprets symbols, formulas, and equations in describing interactions of matter and energy in chemical reactions	166
Skill 9.3	Understands mass relationships involving percent composition, empirical formulas, and molecular formulas	176
Skill 9.4	Interprets and balances chemical equations using conservation of atoms, mass, and charge	178
Skill 9.5	Understands mass and mole relationships in chemical equations	180
Skill 9.6	Solves stoichiometric problems including limiting reagents, reaction yield, and percent yield	182

COMPETENCY 010 THE TEACHER UNDERSTANDS TYPES AND PROPERTIES OF SOLUTIONS 186

Skill 10.1	Analyzes factors that affect solubility (e.g., temperature, pressure, polarity of solvents and solutes)	186
Skill 10.2	Identifies characteristics of saturated, unsaturated, and supersaturated solutions	189
Skill 10.3	Determines the molarity, molality, and percent composition of aqueous solutions	190

TEACHER CERTIFICATION STUDY GUIDE

Skill 10.4   Analyzes precipitation reactions and derives net ionic equations 195

Skill 10.5   Analyzes the colligative properties of solutions (e.g., vapor-pressure lowering, osmotic pressure changes, boiling-point elevation, freezing-point depression) 196

Skill 10.6   Understands the properties of electrolytes and explains the relationship between concentration and electrical conductivity ... 203

Skill 10.7   Analyzes models to explain the structural properties of water and evaluates the significance of water as a solvent in living organisms and the environment 204

COMPETENCY 011 THE TEACHER UNDERSTANDS ENERGY TRANSFORMATIONS THAT OCCUR IN PHYSICAL AND CHEMICAL PROCESSES 206

Skill 11.1   Analyzes the energy transformations that occur in phase transitions 206

Skill 11.2   Solves problems in calorimetry (e.g., determining the specific heat of a substance, finding the standard enthalpy of formation and reaction of substances) 206

Skill 11.3   Applies the law of conservation of energy to analyze and evaluate energy exchanges that occur in exothermic and endothermic processes 206

Skill 11.4   Understands thermodynamic relationships among spontaneous reactions, entropy, enthalpy, temperature, and Gibbs free energy 206

DOMAIN III. CHEMICAL REACTIONS 23%

COMPETENCY 012 THE TEACHER UNDERSTANDS CHEMICAL KINETICS AND EQUILIBRIUM 213

Skill 12.1   Analyzes factors (e.g., temperature, pressure, concentration, catalysts) that influence the rate of a chemical reaction 213

Skill 12.2   Solves problems involving rate laws and determines the rate law of a reaction from experimental data 218

Skill 12.3   Understands principles of chemical equilibrium 224

TEACHER CERTIFICATION STUDY GUIDE

Skill 12.4 Solves problems involving principles of chemical equilibrium 226

Skill 12.5 Identifies the chemical properties of a variety of common household chemicals (e.g., baking soda, bleach, ammonia) in order to predict the potential for chemical reactivity 231

COMPETENCY 013 THE TEACHER UNDERSTANDS ACIDS, BASES, AND THEIR REACTIONS 233

Skill 13.1 Identifies the general properties of and relationships among acids, bases, and salts 233

Skill 13.2 Identifies acids and bases using models of Arrhenius, Brønsted-Lowry, and Lewis 234

Skill 13.3 Differentiates between strong and weak acids and bases 236

Skill 13.4 Applies the relationship between hydrogen ion concentration and pH for acids and bases 238

Skill 13.5 Understands and analyzes acid-base equilibria and buffers 242

Skill 13.6 Analyzes and applies the principles of acid-base titration 244

Skill 13.7 Analyzes neutralization reactions based on the principles of solution concentration and stoichiometry 250

Skill 13.8 Describes the effects of acids and bases in the real world 250

COMPETENCY 014 THE TEACHER UNDERSTANDS OXIDATION AND REDUCTION REACTIONS 251

Skill 14.1 Determines the oxidation state of ions and atoms in compounds 251

Skill 14.2 Identifies and balances oxidation and reduction reactions 252

Skill 14.3 Uses reduction potentials to determine whether a redox reaction will occur spontaneously 257

Skill 14.4 Explains the operating principles of electrochemical cells and the process of electroplating metals 258

Skill 14.5 Analyzes applications of oxidation and reduction reactions from everyday life (e.g., combustion, corrosion, electroplating, batteries) 261

TEACHER CERTIFICATION STUDY GUIDE

COMPETENCY 015 THE TEACHER UNDERSTANDS NUCLEAR FISSION, NUCLEAR FUSION, AND NUCLEAR REACTIONS 263

Skill 15.1 Uses models to explain radioactivity and types of radioactive decay (i.e., alpha, beta, gamma) 263

Skill 15.2 Interprets and balances equations for nuclear reactions 264

Skill 15.3 Compares and contrasts fission and fusion reactions 265

Skill 15.4 Knows how to use the half-life of radioactive elements to study real-world problems (e.g., carbon dating, radioactive tracers).....269

Skill 15.5 Identifies various issues associated with using nuclear energy (e.g., medical, commercial, environmental) 271

DOMAIN IV. SCIENCE LEARNING, INSTRUCTION, AND ASSESSMENT 12%

COMPETENCY 016 THE TEACHER UNDERSTANDS RESEARCH-BASED THEORETICAL AND PRACTICAL KNOWLEDGE ABOUT TEACHING SCIENCE, HOW STUDENTS LEARN SCIENCE, AND THE .ROLE OF SCIENTIFIC INQUIRY IN SCIENCE INSTRUCTION 274

Skill 16.1 Knows research-based theories about how students develop scientific understanding and how developmental characteristics, prior knowledge, experience, and attitudes of students influence science learning 274

Skill 16.2 Understands the importance of respecting student diversity by planning activities that are inclusive by selecting and adapting science curricula, content, instructional materials, and activities to meet the interests, knowledge, understanding, abilities, and experiences of all students, including English Language Learners and students with special needs 275

Skill 16.3 Knows how to plan and implement strategies to encourage student self-motivation and engagement in their own learning (e.g., linking inquiry-based investigations to students' prior knowledge, focusing inquiry-based instruction on issues relevant to students, developing instructional materials using situations from students' daily lives, fostering collaboration among students) 276

TEACHER CERTIFICATION STUDY GUIDE

Skill 16.4 Knows how to use a variety of instructional strategies to ensure all students comprehend content-related texts, including how to locate, retrieve, and retain information from a range of texts and technologies 277

Skill 16.5 Understands the science teacher's role in developing the total school program by planning and implementing science instruction that incorporates schoolwide objectives and the statewide curriculum as defined in the Texas Essential Knowledge and Skills (TEKS)..279

Skill 16.6 Knows how to design and manage the learning environment (e.g., individual, small-group, whole-class settings) to focus and support student inquiries and to provide the time, space, and resources for all students to participate in field, laboratory, experimental, and nonexperimental scientific investigation 280

Skill 16.7 Understands the rationale for using active learning and inquiry methods in science instruction and understands how to model scientific attitudes such as curiosity, openness to new ideas, and skepticism..281

Skill 16.8 Knows principles and procedures for designing and conducting an inquiry-based scientific investigation (e.g., making observations; generating questions; researching and reviewing current knowledge in light of existing evidence; choosing tools to gather and analyze evidence; proposing answers, explanations, and predictions; communicating and defending results)..282

Skill 16.9 Knows how to assist students with generating, refining, focusing, and testing scientific questions and hypotheses 284

Skill 16.10 Knows strategies for assisting students in learning to identify, refine, and focus scientific ideas and questions guiding an inquiry-based scientific investigation; to develop, analyze, and evaluate different explanations for a given scientific result; and to identify potential sources of error in an inquiry-based scientific investigation..285

Skill 16.11 Understands how to implement inquiry strategies designed to promote the use of higher-level thinking skills, logical reasoning, and scientific problem solving in order to move students from concrete to more abstract understanding 286

CHEMISTRY 7-12 xi

TEACHER CERTIFICATION STUDY GUIDE

Skill 16.12　Knows how to guide students in making systematic observations and measurements 287

Skill 16.13　Knows how to plan learning activities in a way that uncovers common misconceptions, allows students to build upon their prior knowledge, and challenges them to expand their understanding of science 289

COMPETENCY 017　THE TEACHER KNOWS HOW TO MONITOR AND ASSESS SCIENCE LEARNING IN LABORATORY, FIELD, AND CLASSROOM SETTINGS 290

Skill 17.1　Knows how to use formal and informal assessments (e.g., projects, laboratory reports and field journals, rubrics, portfolios, student profiles, checklists) of student performance and products to evaluate student participation in and understanding of inquiry-based scientific investigations 290

Skill 17.2　Connects assessment to instruction in the science curriculum (e.g., designing assessments to match learning objectives, using assessment results to inform instructional practice) 291

Skill 17.3　Knows the importance of monitoring and assessing students' understanding of science concepts and skills on an ongoing basis by using a variety of appropriate assessment methods (e.g., performance assessment, self-assessment, peer assessment, formal/informal assessment) 293

Skill 17.4　Understands the purposes and characteristics of and uses various types of assessment in science, including formative and summative assessments, and the importance of limiting the use of an assessment to its intended purpose 294

Skill 17.5　Understands strategies for assessing students' prior knowledge and misconceptions about science and how to use these assessments to develop effective ways to address these misconceptions 296

Skill 17.6　Understands characteristics of assessments, such as reliability, validity, and the absence of bias in order to evaluate assessment instruments and their results 297

Skill 17.7　Understands the role of assessment as a learning experience for students and strategies for engaging students in meaningful self-assessment and peer assessment 298

TEACHER CERTIFICATION STUDY GUIDE

Skill 17.8 Recognizes the importance of selecting assessment instruments and methods that provide all students with adequate opportunities to demonstrate their achievements 300

Skill 17.9 Recognizes the importance of clarifying teacher expectations and student achievement by sharing evaluation criteria and assessment results with students and other appropriate educational stakeholders. 301

Sample Test 302

Answer Key 323

Rationales with Sample Questions 324

TEACHER CERTIFICATION STUDY GUIDE

GREAT STUDY AND TESTING TIPS!

What to study in order to prepare for the subject assessments is the focus of this study guide but equally important is *how* you study.

You can increase your chances of truly mastering the information by taking some simple, but effective steps.

STUDY TIPS:

1. Some foods aid the learning process. Foods such as milk, nuts, seeds, rice, and oats help your study efforts by releasing natural memory enhancers called CCKs (*cholecystokinin*) composed of *tryptophan*, *choline*, and *phenylalanine*. All of these chemicals enhance the neurotransmitters associated with memory. Before studying, try a light, protein-rich meal of eggs, turkey, and fish. All of these foods release the memory enhancing chemicals. The better the connections, the more you comprehend.

Likewise, before you take a test, stick to a light snack of energy boosting and relaxing foods. A glass of milk, a piece of fruit, or some peanuts all release various memory-boosting chemicals and help you to relax and focus on the subject at hand.

2. Learn to take great notes. A by-product of our modern culture is that we have grown accustomed to getting our information in short doses (i.e., TV news sound bites or USA Today style newspaper articles).

Consequently, we've subconsciously trained ourselves to assimilate information better in neat little packages. If your notes are scrawled all over the paper, it fragments the flow of the information. Strive for clarity. Newspapers use a standard format to achieve clarity. Your notes can be much clearer through use of proper formatting. A very effective format is called the *"Cornell Method."*

> Take a sheet of loose-leaf lined notebook paper and draw a line all the way down the paper about 1-2" from the left-hand edge.
>
> Draw another line across the width of the paper about 1-2" up from the bottom. Repeat this process on the reverse side of the page.

Look at the highly effective result. You have ample room for notes, a left hand margin for special emphasis items or inserting supplementary data from the textbook, a large area at the bottom for a brief summary, and a little rectangular space for just about anything you want.

TEACHER CERTIFICATION STUDY GUIDE

3. Get the concept then the details. Too often we focus on the details and don't gather an understanding of the concept. However, if you simply memorize only dates, places, or names, you may well miss the whole point of the subject.

A key way to understand things is to put them in your own words. If you are working from a textbook, automatically summarize each paragraph in your mind. If you are outlining text, don't simply copy the author's words.

Rephrase them in your own words. You remember your own thoughts and words much better than someone else's, and subconsciously tend to associate the important details to the core concepts.

4. Ask Why? Pull apart written material paragraph by paragraph and don't forget the captions under the illustrations.

Example: If the heading is "Stream Erosion," flip it around to read "Why do streams erode?" Then answer the questions.

If you train your mind to think in a series of questions and answers, not only will you learn more, but it also helps to lessen the test anxiety because you are used to answering questions.

5. Read for reinforcement and future needs. Even if you only have 10 minutes, put your notes or a book in your hand. Your mind is similar to a computer; you have to input data in order to have it processed. *By reading, you are creating the neural connections for future retrieval.* The more times you read something, the more you reinforce the learning of ideas.

Even if you don't fully understand something on the first pass, *your mind stores much of the material for later recall.*

6. Relax to learn so go into exile. Our bodies respond to an inner clock called biorhythms. Burning the midnight oil works well for some people, but not everyone.

If possible, set aside a particular place to study that is free of distractions. Shut off the television, cell phone, and pager and exile your friends and family during your study period.

If you really are bothered by silence, try background music. Light classical music at a low volume has been shown to aid in concentration over other types. Music that evokes pleasant emotions without lyrics is highly suggested. Try just about anything by Mozart. It relaxes you.

CHEMISTRY 7-12

7. Use arrows not highlighters. At best, it's difficult to read a page full of yellow, pink, blue, and green streaks. Try staring at a neon sign for a while and you'll soon see that the horde of colors obscures the message.

A quick note, a brief dash of color, an underline, and an arrow pointing to a particular passage is much clearer than a horde of highlighted words.

8. Budget your study time. Although you shouldn't ignore any of the material, *allocate your available study time in the same ratio that topics may appear on the test.*

TEACHER CERTIFICATION STUDY GUIDE

TESTING TIPS:

1. Get smart, play dumb. Don't read anything into the question. Don't make an assumption that the test writer is looking for something other than what is asked. Stick to the question as written and don't read extra things into it.

2. Read the question and all the choices *twice* before answering the question. You may miss something by not carefully reading, and then re-reading, both the question and the answers.

If you really don't have a clue as to the right answer, leave it blank on the first time through. Go on to the other questions, as they may provide a clue as to how to answer the skipped questions.

If later on, you still can't answer the skipped ones . . . *Guess.* The only penalty for guessing is that you *might* get it wrong. Only one thing is certain; if you don't put anything down, you will get it wrong!

3. Turn the question into a statement. Look at the way the questions are worded. The syntax of the question usually provides a clue. Does it seem more familiar as a statement rather than as a question? Does it sound strange?

By turning a question into a statement, you may be able to spot if an answer sounds right, and it may also trigger memories of material you have read.

4. Look for hidden clues. It's actually very difficult to compose multiple-foil (choice) questions without giving away part of the answer in the options presented.

In most multiple-choice questions you can often readily eliminate one or two of the potential answers. This leaves you with only two real possibilities and automatically your odds go to fifty-fifty for very little work.

5. Trust your instincts. For every fact that you have read, you subconsciously retain something of that knowledge. On questions that you aren't really certain about, go with your basic instincts. **Your first impression on how to answer a question is usually correct.**

6. Mark your answers directly on the test booklet. Don't bother trying to fill in the optical scan sheet on the first pass through the test.

Just be very careful not to mis-mark your answers when you eventually transcribe them to the scan sheet.

7. Watch the clock! You have a set amount of time to answer the questions. Don't get bogged down trying to answer a single question at the expense of 10 questions you can more readily answer.

Periodic Table of the Elements

Group	1 IA	2 IIA	3 IIIB	4 IVB	5 VB	6 VIB	7 VIIB	8	9 VIIIB	10	11 IB	12 IIB	13 III IIIA	14 IV IVA	15 V VA	16 VI VIA	17 VII VIIA	18 VIII VIIIA
1	hydrogen 1 H 1.0079																	helium 2 He 4.002
2	lithium 3 Li 6.941	beryllium 4 Be 9.0122											boron 5 B 10.811	carbon 6 C 12.011	nitrogen 7 N 14.007	oxygen 8 O 15.999	fluorine 9 F 18.998	neon 10 Ne 20.18
3	sodium 11 Na 22.990	magnesium 12 Mg 24.305											aluminum 13 Al 26.982	silicon 14 Si 28.086	phosphorus 15 P 30.974	sulfur 16 S 32.065	chlorine 17 Cl 35.453	argon 18 Ar 39.94
4	potassium 19 K 39.098	calcium 20 Ca 40.078	scandium 21 Sc 44.956	titanium 22 Ti 47.867	vanadium 23 V 50.942	chromium 24 Cr 51.996	manganese 25 Mn 54.938	iron 26 Fe 55.845	cobalt 27 Co 58.933	nickel 28 Ni 58.693	copper 29 Cu 63.546	zinc 30 Zn 65.409	gallium 31 Ga 69.723	germanium 32 Ge 72.64	arsenic 33 As 74.922	selenium 34 Se 78.96	bromine 35 Br 79.904	krypton 36 Kr 83.79
5	rubidium 37 Rb 85.468	strontium 38 Sr 87.62	yttrium 39 Y 88.906	zirconium 40 Zr 91.224	niobium 41 Nb 82.906	molybdenum 42 Mo 95.94	technetium 43 Tc [98]	ruthenium 44 Ru 101.07	rhodium 45 Rh 102.91	palladium 46 Pd 106.42	silver 47 Ag 107.87	cadmium 48 Cd 112.41	indium 49 In 114.82	tin 50 Sn 118.71	antimony 51 Sb 121.76	tellurium 52 Te 127.60	iodine 53 I 126.90	xenon 54 Xe 131.29
6	cesium 55 Cs 132.91	barium 56 Ba 137.33	57-71 *	hafnium 72 Hf 178.49	tantalum 73 Ta 180.95	tungsten 74 W 183.84	rhenium 75 Re 186.21	osmium 76 Os 190.23	iridium 77 Ir 192.22	platinum 78 Pt 195.08	gold 79 Au 196.97	mercury 80 Hg 200.59	thallium 81 Tl 204.38	lead 82 Pb 207.2	bismuth 83 Bi 208.98	polonium 84 Po [209]	astatine 85 At [210]	radon 86 Rn [222]
7	francium 87 Fr [223]	radium 88 Ra [226]	89-103 **	rutherfordium 104 Rf [261]	dubnium 105 Db [262]	seaborgium 106 Sg [266]	bohrium 107 Bh [264]	hassium 108 Hs [277]	meitnerium 109 Mt [268]	darmstadtium 110 Ds [271]	roentgenium 111 Rg [272]							

*Lanthanoids	lanthanum 57 La 138.91	cerium 58 Ce 140.12	praseodymium 59 Pr 140.91	neodymium 60 Nd 144.24	promethium 61 Pm [145]	samarium 62 Sm 151.96	europium 63 Eu 151.96	gadolinium 64 Gd 157.25	terbium 65 Tb 158.93	dysprosium 66 Dy 162.50	holmium 67 Ho 164.93	erbium 68 Er 167.2	thulium 69 Tm 168.93	ytterbium 70 Yb 173.04	lutetium 71 Lu 174.97
**Actinoids	actinium 89 Ac [227]	thorium 90 Th 232.04	protactinium 91 Pa 231.04	uranium 92 U 238.03	neptunium 93 Np [237]	plutonium 94 Pu [244]	americium 95 Am [243]	curium 96 Cm [247]	berkelium 97 Bk [247]	californium 98 Cf [251]	einsteinium 99 Es [252]	fermium 100 Fm [257]	mendelevium 101 Md [258]	nobelium 102 No [259]	lawrencium 103 Lr [262]

Atomic mass values from IUPAC review (2001): http://www.iupac.org/reports/periodic_table/

TEACHER CERTIFICATION STUDY GUIDE

DOMAIN I.   **SCIENTIFIC INQUIRY AND PROCESSES**

COMPETENCY 001   **THE TEACHER UNDERSTANDS HOW TO SELECT AND MANAGE LEARNING ACTIVITIES TO ENSURE THE SAFETY OF ALL STUDENTS AND THE CORRECT USE AND CARE OF NATURAL RESOURCES, MATERIALS, EQUIPMENT, AND TECHNOLOGIES**

Skill 1.1   **Uses current sources of information about laboratory safety, including safety regulations and guidelines for the use of science facilities, materials, and equipment**

CHEMICAL PURCHASE, USE, AND DISPOSAL

- Inventory all chemicals on hand at least annually. Keep the list up-to-date as chemicals are consumed and replacement chemicals are received.
- If possible, limit the purchase of chemicals to quantities that will be consumed within one year and that are packaged in small containers suitable for direct use in the lab without transfer to other containers.
- Label all chemicals to be stored with date of receipt or preparation and have labels initialed by the person responsible.
- Generally, bottles of chemicals should not remain:
  - Unused on shelves in the lab for more than one week. Move these chemicals to the storeroom or main stockroom.
  - Unused in the storeroom near the lab for more than one month. Move these chemicals to the main stockroom.
- Check shelf life of chemicals. Properly dispose of any out-dated chemicals.
- Ensure that the disposal procedures for waste chemicals conform to environmental protection requirements.
- Do not purchase or store large quantities of flammable liquids. Fire department officials can recommend the maximum quantities that may be kept on hand.
- Never open a chemical container until you understand the label and the relevant portions of the MSDS.

CHEMICAL STORAGE PLAN FOR LABORATORIES

- Chemicals should be stored according to hazard class (ex. flammables, oxidizers, health hazards/toxins, corrosives, etc.).
- Store chemicals away from direct sunlight or localized heat.
- All chemical containers should be properly labeled, dated upon receipt, and dated upon opening.
- Store hazardous chemicals below shoulder height of the shortest person working in the lab.

CHEMISTRY 7-12   1

- Shelves should be painted or covered with chemical-resistant paint or chemical-resistant coating.
- Shelves should be secure and strong enough to hold chemicals being stored on them. Do not overload shelves.
- Personnel should be aware of the hazards associated with all hazardous materials.
- Separate solids from liquids.

Below are examples of chemical groups that can be used to categorize storage. Use these groups as examples when separating chemicals for compatibility. Please note: reactive chemicals must be more closely analyzed since they have a greater potential for violent reactions. Contact Laboratory Safety if you have any questions concerning chemical storage.

ACIDS

- Make sure that all acids are stored by compatibility (ex. separate inorganics from organics).
- Store concentrated acids on lower shelves in chemical-resistant trays or in a corrosives cabinet. This will temporarily contain spills or leaks and protect shelving from residue.
- Separate acids from incompatible materials such as bases, active metals (ex. sodium, magnesium, potassium) and from chemicals which can generate toxic gases when combined (ex. sodium cyanide and iron sulfide).

BASES

- Store bases away from acids.
- Store concentrated bases on lower shelves in chemical-resistant trays or in a corrosives cabinet. This will temporarily contain spills or leaks and protect shelving from residue.

FLAMMABLES

- Approved flammable storage cabinets should be used for flammable liquid storage.
- You may store 20 gallons of flammable liquids per 100 sq.ft. in a properly fire separated lab. The maximum allowable quantity for flammable liquid storage in any size lab is not to exceed 120 gallons.
- You may store up to 10 gallons of flammable liquids outside of approved flammable storage cabinets.
- An additional 25 gallons may be stored outside of an approved storage cabinet if it is stored in approved safety cans not to exceed 2 gallons in size.

- Use only explosion-proof or intrinsically safe refrigerators and freezers for storing flammable liquids.

PEROXIDE-FORMING CHEMICALS

- Peroxide-forming chemicals should be stored in airtight containers in a dark, cool, and dry place.
- Unstable chemicals such as peroxide-formers must always be labeled with date received, date opened, and disposal/expiration date.
- Peroxide-forming chemicals should be properly disposed of before the date of expected peroxide formation (typically 6-12 months after opening).
- Suspicion of peroxide contamination should be immediately investigated. Contact Laboratory Safety for procedures.

WATER-REACTIVE CHEMICALS

- Water-reactive chemicals should be stored in a cool, dry place.
- Do not store water-reactive chemicals under sinks or near water baths.
- Class D fire extinguishers for the specific water-reactive chemical being stored should be made available.

OXIDIZERS

- Make sure that all oxidizers are stored by compatibility.
- Store oxidizers away from flammables, combustibles, and reducing agents.

TOXINS

- Toxic compounds should be stored according to the nature of the chemical, with appropriate security employed when necessary.
- A "Poison Control Network" telephone number should be posted in the laboratory where toxins are stored. Color-coded labeling systems that may be found in your lab are shown below:

Hazard	Color Code
Flammables	Red
Health Hazards/Toxins	Blue
Reactives/Oxidizers	Yellow
Contact Hazards	White
General Storage	Gray, Green, Orange

Please Note: Chemicals with labels that are colored and striped may react with other chemicals in the same hazard class. See MSDS for more information. Chemical containers which are not color-coded should have hazard information on the label. Read the label carefully and store accordingly.

DISPOSAL OF CHEMICAL WASTE

Schools are regulated by the Environmental Protection Agency, as well as state and local agencies, when it comes to disposing of chemical waste. Check with your state science supervisor, local college or university environmental health and safety specialists, and the Laboratory Safety Workshop for advice on the disposal of chemical waste. The American Chemical Society publishes an excellent guidebook, *Laboratory Waste Management, A Guidebook* (1994).

The following are merely guidelines for disposing of chemical waste.

You may dispose of hazardous waste as outlined below. It is the responsibility of the generator to ensure hazardous waste does not end up in ground water, soil, or the atmosphere through improper disposal.

1. **Sanitary Sewer** - Some chemicals (acids or bases) may be neutralized and disposed to the sanitary sewer. This disposal option must be approved by the local waste water treatment authority prior to disposal. This may not be an option for some small communities that do not have sufficient treatment capacity at the waste water treatment plant for these types of wastes. Hazardous waste may NOT be disposed of in this manner. This includes heavy metals.

2. **Household Hazardous Waste Facility** - Waste chemicals may be disposed through a county household hazardous waste facility (HHW) or through a county contracted household hazardous waste disposal company. Not all counties have a program to accept waste from schools. Verify with your county HHW facility that they can handle your waste prior to making arrangements.

3. **Disposal Through a Contractor** - A contractor may be used for disposal of waste chemicals. Remember that you must keep documentation of your hazardous waste disposal for at least three years. This information must include a waste manifest, reclamation agreement or any written record which describes the waste and how much was disposed, where it was disposed and when it was disposed. Waste analysis records must also be kept when it is necessary to make a determination of whether waste is hazardous. **Any unknown chemicals should be considered hazardous!**

TEACHER CERTIFICATION STUDY GUIDE

Skill 1.2 **Recognizes potential safety hazards in the laboratory and in the field and knows how to prevent accidents and apply procedures, including basic first aid, for responding to accidents**

See Skill 1.3 below.

Skill 1.3 **Employ safe practices in planning and implementing all instructional activities and designs and implements rules and procedures to maintain a safe learning environment**

The following is a summary of the requirements for chemical laboratories:

1) A dousing shower and eye-wash with a floor drain are required where students handle potentially dangerous materials.

2) Accessible fully-charged fire extinguishers of the appropriate type and fire blankets must be present if a fire hazard exists.

3) There must be a master control valve or switch accessible to and within 15 feet of the instructor's station for emergency cut-off of all gas cocks, compressed air valves, water, or electrical services accessible to students. Valves must completely shut off with a one-quarter turn. This master control is in addition to the regular main gas supply cut-off, and the main supply cut-off must be shut down upon activation of the fire alarm system.

4) A high capacity emergency exhaust system with a source of positive ventilation must be installed, and signs providing instructions must be permanently installed at the emergency exhaust system fan switch.

5) Fume hoods must contain supply fans that automatically shut down when the emergency exhaust fan is turned on

6) Rooms and/or cabinets for chemical storage must have limited student access and ventilation to the exterior of the building separate from the air-conditioning system. The rooms should be kept at moderate temperature, be well-illuminated, and contain doors lockable from the outside and operable at all times from the inside. Cabinet shelves must have a half-inch lip on the front and be constructed of non-corrosive material.

7) Appropriate caution signs must be placed at hazardous work and storage areas.

Therefore, all chemistry laboratories should be equipped with the following safety equipment. Both teachers and students should be familiar with the operation of this equipment.

FIRE EXTINGUISHER

Fire extinguishers are rated for the type of fires they will extinguish. Chemical laboratories should have a combination ABC extinguisher along with a type D fire extinguisher. If a type D extinguisher is not available, a bucket of dry sand will do. Make sure you are trained to use the type of extinguisher available in your setting.

- **Class A** fires are ordinary materials like burning paper, lumber, cardboard, plastics etc.

- **Class B** fires involve flammable or combustible liquids such as gasoline, kerosene, and common organic solvents used in the laboratory.

- **Class C** fires involve energized electrical equipment, such as appliances, switches, panel boxes, power tools, hot plates and stirrers. Water is usually a dangerous extinguishing medium for class C fires because of the risk of electrical shock unless a specialized water mist extinguisher is used.

- **Class D** fires involve combustible metals, such as magnesium, titanium, potassium and sodium as well as pyrophoric organometallic reagents such as alkyllithiums, Grignards and diethylzinc. These materials burn at high temperatures and will react violently with water, air, and/or other chemicals. Handle with care!!

- **Class K** fires are kitchen fires. This class was added to the NFPA portable extinguishers Standard 10 in 1998. Kitchen extinguishers installed before June 30, 1998 are "grandfathered" into the standard.

Some fires may be a combination of these! Your fire extinguishers should have ABC ratings on them. These ratings are determined under ANSI/UL Standard 711 and look something like "3-A:40-B:C." Higher numbers mean more firefighting power. In this example, the extinguisher has a good firefighting capacity for Class A, B and C fires. NFPA has a brief description of UL 711 if you want to know more.

EYEWASH

In the event of an eye injury or chemical splash, use the eyewash immediately.

Help the injured person by holding their eyelids open while rinsing. Rinse copiously and have the eyes checked by a physician afterwards.

FIRE BLANKET

A fire blanket can be used to smother a fire. However, use caution when using a fire blanket on a clothing fire. Some fabrics are polymers that melt onto the skin. Use of a safety shower is the best method for extinguishing clothing on fire.

SAFETY SHOWER

Use a safety shower in the event of a chemical spill or fire. Pull the overhead handle and remove clothing that may be contaminated with chemicals, to allow the skin to be rinsed.

EYE PROTECTION

Everyone present must wear eye protection whenever anyone in the laboratory is performing any of the following activities:

1) Handling hazardous chemicals
2) Handling laboratory glassware
3) Using an open flame.

Safety glasses do not offer protection from splashing liquids. Safety glasses appear similar to ordinary glasses and may be used in an environment that only requires protection from **flying fragments**. Safety glasses with side-shields offer additional protection from **flying fragments approaching from the side**.

CHEMISTRY 7-12

Safety goggles offer protection from both flying fragments and splashing liquids. **Only safety goggles** are suitable for eye protection where **hazardous chemicals** are used and handled. Safety goggles with no ventilation (type G) or with indirect ventilation (type H) are both acceptable. Goggles should be marked "Z87" to show they meet federal standards.

SKIN PROTECTION

Wear gloves made of a material known to resist penetration by the chemical being handled. Check gloves for holes and the absence of interior contamination. Wash hands and arms and clean under fingernails after working in a laboratory.

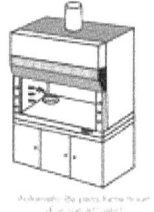

Wear a lab coat or apron. Wear footwear that completely covers the feet.

VENTILATION - USING A FUME HOOD

A fume hood carries away vapors from reagents or reactions you may be working with. Using a fume hood correctly will reduce your personal exposure to potentially harmful fumes or vapors. When using a fume hood, keep the following in mind:

- Place equipment or reactions as far back in the hood as is practical. This will improve the efficiency of fume collection and removal.

- Turn on the light inside the hood using the switch on the outside panel, near the electrical outlets.

- The glass sash of the hood is a safety shield. The sash will fall automatically to the appropriate height for efficient operation and should not be raised above this level, except to move equipment in and out of the hood. Keep the sash between your body and the inside of the hood. If the height of the automatic stop is too high to protect your face and body, lower the sash below this point. Do not place your head inside a hood or climb inside a hood.

- Wipe up all spills immediately. Clean the glass of your hood if a splash occurs.

- When you are finished using a hood, lower the sash to the level marked by the sticker on the side.

WORK HABITS

- Never work alone in a laboratory or storage area.
- Never eat, drink, smoke, apply cosmetics, chew gum or tobacco, or store food or beverages in a laboratory environment or storage area.
- Keep containers closed when they are not in use.
- Never pipet by mouth.
- Restrain loose clothing and long hair and remove dangling jewelry.
- Tape all Dewar flasks with fabric-based tape.
- Check all glassware before use. Discard it if chips or star cracks are present.
- Never leave heat sources unattended.
- Do not store chemicals and/or apparatus on the lab bench or on the floor or aisles of the lab or storage room.
- Keep lab shelves organized.
- Never place a chemical, not even water, near the edges of a lab bench.
- Use a fume hood that is known to be in operating condition when working with toxic, flammable, and/or volatile substances.
- Never put your head inside a fume hood.
- Never store anything in a fume hood.
- Obtain, read, and be sure you understand the MSDS (see below) for each chemical that is to be used before allowing students to begin an experiment.
- Analyze new lab procedures and student-designed lab procedures in advance to identify any hazardous aspects. Minimize and/or eliminate these components before proceeding. Ask yourself these questions:
    - What are the hazards?
    - What are the worst possible things that could go wrong?
    - How will I deal with them?
    - What are the prudent practices, protective facilities and equipment necessary to minimize the risk of exposure to the hazards?
- Analyze close calls and accidents to eliminate their causes and prevent them from occurring again.
- Identify which chemicals may be disposed of in the drain by consulting the MSDS or the supplier. Clear one chemical down the drain by flushing with water before introducing the next chemical.
- Preplan for emergencies:
    - Keep the fire department informed of your chemical inventory and its location.
    - Consult with a local physician about toxins used in the lab and ensure that your area is prepared in advance to treat victims of toxic exposure.
    - Identify devices that should be shut off if possible in an emergency.
    - Inform your students of the designated escape route and alternate route.

SUBSTITUTIONS

- When feasible, substitute less hazardous chemicals for chemicals with greater hazards in experiments.
- Dilute substances when possible instead of using concentrated solutions.
- Use lesser quantities instead of greater quantities in experiments when possible.
- Use films, videotapes, computer displays, and other methods rather than experiments involving hazardous substances.

LABEL INFORMATION

Chemical labels contain safety information in four parts:

1) There will be a signal word. From most to least potentially dangerous, this word will be "Danger!" "Warning!" or "Caution."
2) Statements of hazard (e.g., "Flammable," "May Cause Irritation") follow the signal word. Target organs may be specified.
3) Precautionary measures are listed such as "Keep away from ignition sources" or "Use only with adequate ventilation."
4) First aid information is usually included, such as whether to induce vomiting and how to induce vomiting if the chemical is ingested.

CHEMICAL HAZARD PICTORIAL

Several different pictorials are used on labels to indicate the level of a chemical hazard. The most common is the **"fire diamond" NFPA (National Fire Prevention Association) pictorial** shown below. A zero indicates a minimal hazard and a four indicates a severe risk. Special information includes if the chemical reacts with water, **OX** for an oxidizer, **COR ACID** for a corrosive acid, and **COR ALK** for a corrosive base. The "Health" hazard level is for **acute toxicity only**.

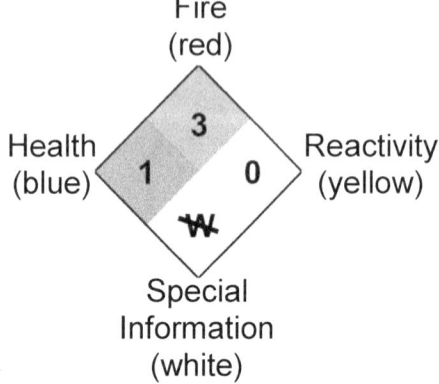

Pictorials are designed for **quick reference in emergency situations**, but they are also useful as minimal summaries of safety information for a chemical. They are not required on chemicals you purchase, so it's a good idea to add a label pictorial to every chemical you receive if one is not already present. **The entrance to areas where chemicals are stored should carry a fire diamond label** to represent the materials present.

PROCEDURES FOR FLAMMABLE MATERIALS: MINIMIZE FIRE RISK

The vapors of a flammable liquid **or solid** may travel across the room to an ignition source and cause a fire or explosion.

- Store flammables in an approved safety cabinet. Store in safety cans if possible.
- Minimize volumes and concentrations used in an experiment with flammables.
- Minimize the time containers are open.
- Minimize ignition sources in the laboratory.
- Ensure that there is good air movement in the laboratory before the experiment.
- Check the fire extinguishers and be certain that you know how to use them.
- Tell the students that the "Stop, Drop, and Roll" technique is best for a clothing fire outside the lab, but in the lab they should walk calmly to the safety shower and use it. Practice this procedure with students in drills.
- A fire blanket should not be used for clothing fires because clothes often contain polymers that melt onto the skin. Pressing these fabrics into the skin with a blanket increases burn damage.
- If a demonstration of an exploding gas or vapor is performed, it should be done behind a safety shield using glass vessels taped with fabric tape.

PROCEDURES FOR CORROSIVE MATERIALS: MINIMIZE RISK OF CONTACT

Corrosive materials **destroy or permanently change living tissue** through chemical action. **Irritants** cause inflammation due to an immune response but not through chemical action. The effect is usually reversible but can be severe and long lasting. **Sensitizers** are irritants that cause no symptoms after the first exposure but may cause irritation during a later exposure to the same or a different chemical.

- Always store corrosives below eye level.
- Only diluted corrosives should be used in pre-high school laboratories and their use at full-strength in high school should be limited.
- Dilute corrosive materials by slowly and carefully **adding them to water**. Adding water to a concentrated acid or base can cause rapid boiling and splashing.
- Wear goggles and face shield when handling hazardous corrosives. The face, ears, and neck should be protected.
- Wear gloves known to be impervious to the chemical. Wear sleeve gauntlets and a lab apron made of impervious material if splashing is likely.
- Always wash your hands after handling corrosives.

- Splashes on skin should be flushed with flowing water for 15 minutes while a doctor is called.
- If a corrosive material is splashed on the clothing:
  - First use the safety shower with clothing on.
  - Remove all clothing while under the safety shower including shoes and socks. This is no time for modesty.
  - Stay under the shower for 15 minutes while a doctor is called.
- Splashes in eyes should be dealt with as follows:
  - Go to the eyewash fountain within 30 seconds.
  - Have someone else hold the eyelids open with thumb and forefinger and use the eyewash.
  - Continuously move the eyeballs during 15 minutes of rinsing to cleanse the optic nerve at the back of the eye. A doctor should be called.

PROCEDURES FOR TOXIC MATERIALS: MINIMIZE EXPOSURE

Toxic effects are either **chronic** or **acute**. Chronic effects are seen after repeated exposures or after one long exposure. Acute effects occur within a few hours at most.

- Use the smallest amount needed at the lowest concentration for the shortest period of time possible. Weigh the risks against the educational benefits.
- Be aware of the five different routes of exposure:

  1) Inhalation – the ability to smell a toxin is not a proper indication of unsafe exposure. Work in the fume hood when using toxins. Minimize dusts and mists by cleaning often, cleaning spills rapidly, and maintaining good ventilation in the lab.
  2) Absorption through intact skin – always wear impervious gloves if the MSDS indicates this route of exposure.
  3) Ingestion.
  4) Absorption through other body orifices such as ear canal and eye socket.
  5) Injection by a cut from broken contaminated glassware or other sharp equipment.

- Be aware of the first symptoms of overexposure described by the MSDS. Often these are headache, nausea, and dizziness. Get to fresh air and do not return until the symptoms have passed. If the symptom returns when you come back into the lab, contact a physician and have the space tested.
- Be aware of whether vomiting should be induced in case of ingestion.
- Be aware of the recommended procedure in case of unconsciousness.

PROCEDURES FOR REACTIVE MATERIALS: MINIMIZE INCOMPATIBILITY

Many chemicals are **self-reactive**. For example, they explode when dried out or when disturbed under certain conditions or they react with components of air. These materials generally **should not be allowed into the high school**. Other precautions must be taken to minimize reactions between **incompatible pairs**:

- Store fuels and oxidizers separately.
- Store reducing agents and oxidizing agents separately.
- Store acids and bases separately.
- Store chemicals that react with fire-fighting materials (i.e., water or carbon dioxide) under conditions that minimize the possibility of a reaction if a fire is being fought in the storage area.
- MSDSs list other incompatible pairs.
- <u>Never</u> store chemicals in alphabetical order by name.
- When incompatible pairs must be supplied to students, do so under direct supervision with very dilute solutions and/or small quantities.

MATERIAL SAFETY DATA SHEET (MSDS) INFORMATION

Many chemicals have a mixture of toxic, corrosive, flammable, and reactive risks. The **Material Safety Data Sheet** or **MSDS** for a chemical contains detailed safety information beyond that presented on the label. This includes acute and chronic health effects, first aid and firefighting measures, what to do in case of a spill, and ecological and disposal considerations.

The MSDS will state whether the chemical is a known or suspected carcinogen, mutagen, or teratogen. A **carcinogen** is a compound that causes cancer. A **mutagen** alters DNA with the potential of causing cancer or birth defects in children not yet conceived. A **teratogen** produces birth defects and acts during fetal development.

There are many parts of an MSDS that are not written for the layperson. Their level of detail and technical content may be difficult for many people outside the fields of toxicology and industrial safety to understand. According to the safety manual of the American Chemical Society available on the internet (http://www.acs.org/content/dam/acsorg/about/governance/committees/chemical safety/publications/chemical-safety-manual-teachers.pdf an MSDS places "an over-emphasis on the toxic characteristics of the subject chemical."

In a high school chemistry lab, the value of an MSDS is in the words and not in the numerical data it contains, but some knowledge of the numbers is useful for comparing the dangers of one chemical to another. Numerical results of animal toxicity studies are often presented in the form of **LD_{50} values**. These represent the **dose required to kill 50% of animals** tested.

Exposure limits via inhalation may be presented in three ways:

1) PEL (Permissible Exposure Limit) or TLV-TWA (Threshold Limit Value-Time Weighted Average). This is the maximum permitted concentration of the airborne chemical in volume parts per million (ppm) for a **worker exposed 8 hours daily**.
2) TLV-STEL (Threshold Limit Value-Short Term Exposure Limit). This is the maximum concentration permitted for a 15-minute exposure period.
3) TLV-C (Threshold Limit Value-Ceiling). This is the concentration that should never be exceeded at any moment.

http://hazard.com/msds/index.php contains a large database of MSDSs. http://www.ilpi.com/msds/ref/demystify.html contains a useful "MSDS demystifier." Cut and paste an MSDS into the web page, and hypertext links will appear to a glossary of terms.

FACILITIES AND EQUIPMENT

- Use separate labeled containers for general trash, broken glass, and for each type of hazardous chemical waste — ignitable, corrosive, reactive, and toxic.
- Keep the floor area around safety showers, eyewash fountains, and fire extinguishers clear of all obstructions.
- Never block escape routes.
- Never prop open a fire door.
- Provide safety guards for all moving belts and pulleys.
- Instruct everyone in the lab on the proper use of the safety shower and eyewash fountain (see corrosive materials above). Most portable eyewash devices cannot maintain the required flow for 15 minutes. A permanent eyewash fountain is preferred.
- If contamination is suspected in the breathing air, arrange for sampling to take place.
- Regularly inspect fire blankets, if present, for rips and holes. Maintain a record of inspection.
- Regularly check safety showers and eyewash fountains for proper rate of flow. Maintain a record of inspection.
- Keep up-to-date emergency phone numbers posted next to the telephone.
- Place fire extinguishers near an escape route.
- Regularly maintain fire extinguishers and maintain a record of inspection. Arrange with the local fire department for training of teachers and administrators in the proper use of extinguishers.
- Regularly check fume hoods for proper airflow. Ensure that fume hood exhaust is not drawn back into the intake for general building ventilation.
- Secure compressed gas cylinders at all times and transport them only while secured on a hand truck.

- Restrict the use and handling of compressed gas to those who have received formal training.
- Install chemical storage shelves with lips. Never use stacked boxes for storage instead of shelves.
- Only use an explosion-proof refrigerator for chemical storage.
- Have appropriate equipment and materials available in advance for spill control and cleanup. Consult the MSDS for each chemical to determine what is required. Replace these materials when they become outdated.
- Provide an appropriate supply of first aid equipment and instruction on its proper use.

ADDITIONAL COMMENTS: TEACH SAFETY TO STUDENTS

- Weigh the risks and benefits inherent in lab work, inform students of the hazards and precautions involved in their assignment, and involve students in discussions about safety before every assignment.
- If an incident happens, it can be used to improve lab safety via student participation. Ask the student involved. The student's own words about what occurred should be included in the report.
- Safety information supplied by the manufacturer on a chemical container should be seen by students who actually use the chemical. If you distribute chemicals in smaller containers to be used by students, copy the hazard and precautionary information from the original label onto the labels for the students' containers. Students interested in graphic design may be able to help you perform this task. Labels for many common chemicals may be found here: http://www.ehs.cornell.edu/labels/rtk_requestlabel.cfm.
- Organize a student safety committee whose task is to conduct one safety inspection and present a report. A different committee may be organized each month or every other month.

ADDITIONAL COMMENTS: GENERAL

- Any chemical can be hazardous. The way it is used determines the probability of harm.
- Every person is individually and personally responsible for the safe use of chemicals.
- If an accident might happen, it will eventually happen. Proper precautions will ensure the consequences are minimized when it does occur.
- Accidents are often predicted by one or more **close calls** in which nobody is injured and no property is damaged but something out of the ordinary occurs. Examples might be a student briefly touching a hot surface and saying "Ouch!" with no injury, two students engaged in horseplay, or a student briefly removing safety goggles to read a meniscus level.

ELIMINATE THE CAUSE OF A CLOSE CALL TO PREVENT A FUTURE ACCIDENT.

Also see:
http://www.labsafety.org/40steps.htm,
http://www.flinnsci.com/Sections/Safety/safety.asp,
and the American Chemical Society safety publications listed under References.

Today's chemistry teachers must not only act responsibly, they must also be prepared to prove to others how they acted responsibly. Here are a few ideas you can use in your classroom to document that you are a responsible chemistry teacher.

SAFETY CONTRACTS

Safety contracts are a good way to establish the importance of safe work habits. A student safety contract is a detailed listing of all of the rules in force in the chemistry laboratory. Review the safety contract with your students and have them sign and date it. Students should then take the contract home so their parents or guardians can review and sign the contract as well. This will establish a good understanding of how important it is to follow all the classroom safety rules. Most science departments have general safety contracts that you can use or modify.

LESSON PLANS

In your daily lesson plans you need to document that you discussed with your students the safety rules that applied to the experiments they were doing on each day. Your lesson plans make up a personal journal that documents all of the activities you have done in class for the entire school year. Safety rules must be reinforced every time a laboratory experiment is done with your students.

SAFETY POSTERS

Commercial safety posters can be purchased that reinforce the most important safety rules, such as wearing your goggles and aprons, no horseplay, and notifying your instructor whenever there has been an accident. These posters can be placed in strategic locations around the chemistry laboratory.

GOGGLE POLICY

There is only one policy on goggles that needs to be enforced. "Any time chemicals, glassware, or heat are used, you must wear your laboratory goggles. No exceptions!"

CHEMICAL HAZARD TERMS

Many chemistry experiments include terms like corrosive, flammable, oxidizer, reducer, etc. in the safety instructions. Make sure your students understand the meaning of these terms.

DOCUMENTATION OF SAFETY VIOLATIONS

Whenever a safety violation occurs, it is a good idea to write down the name of the student and the safety violation that occurred on that day in your lesson plan. Have the student sign your plan book documenting his or her violation.

A prudent attitude toward dealing with hazards in the laboratory is characterized by a determination to make every effort to be informed about risks and reduce them to a minimum while recognizing that the notion of "zero risk" in laboratory settings (or any other workplace) is an impossible ideal.

If you can reasonably foresee the consequences of what you are about to do, or are not about to do, you will be held responsible. Begin to implement some of the ideas suggested. Safety contracts, lesson plans, safety posters, a firm goggle policy, definition of terms, and documentation of safety violations will all go a long way in demonstrating that you are a responsible chemistry teacher.

Information regarding legislation and national guidelines is available from a number of sources. Consult your state science supervisor, the American Chemical Society, and the National Science Teachers Association for information. A good print source of current regulations is found in *Prudent Practices in the Laboratory: Handling and Disposal of Chemicals* (1995) published by the National Academies Press (available through amazon.com).

Skill 1.4 **Understands procedures for selecting, maintaining, and safely using chemicals, tools, technologies, materials, specimens, and equipment, including procedures for the recycling, reuse, and conservation of laboratory resources**

See also Skill 1.3 above for safety procedures.

The descriptions and diagrams in this skill are included to help you identify basic equipment and techniques used in a chemistry lab. They are not meant as a guide to perform the techniques in the lab.

HANDLING LIQUIDS

A **beaker** (below left) is a cylindrical cup with a notch at the top. Beakers are often used for making solutions. An **Erlenmeyer** flask (below center) is a conical flask. A liquid in an Erlenmeyer flask will evaporate more slowly than in a beaker and is easier to swirl about. A **round-bottom flask** (below right) is also called a Florence flask. It is designed for uniform heating, but requires a stand to keep it upright.

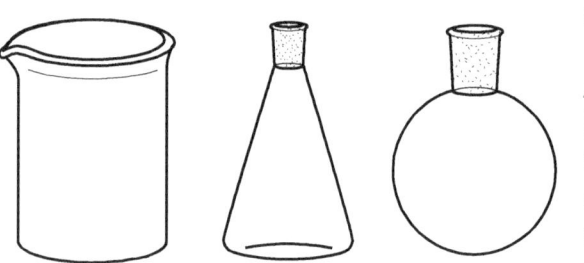

A **test tube** has a rounded bottom and is designed to hold and heat small volumes of liquid. A **Pasteur pipet** is a small glass tube with a long thin capillary tip and a latex suction bulb, and is used for transferring small amounts of liquid from one container to another.

A **crucible** is a cup-shaped container made of porcelain or metal for holding chemical compounds when heating them to very high temperatures. A **watch glass** is a concave circular piece of glass that is usually used as surface for evaporating liquids and observing precipitates or crystallization. A **Dewar flask** is a double walled vacuum flask with a metallic coating to provide good thermal insulation and short term storage of liquid nitrogen.

FITTING AND CLEANING GLASSWARE

If a thermometer, glass tube, or funnel must be threaded through a stopper or a piece of tubing and it won't fit, either make the hole larger or use a smaller piece of glass. Use soapy water or glycerol to lubricate the glass before inserting it. Hold the glass piece as close as possible to the stopper during insertion. It's also good practice to wrap a towel around the glass and the stopper during this procedure. **Never apply undue pressure**.

Glassware sometimes contains **tapered ground-glass joints** to allow direct glass-to-glass connections. A thin layer of joint **grease** must be applied when assembling an apparatus with ground-glass joints. Too much grease will contaminate the experiment, and too little will cause the components to become tightly locked together. Disassemble the glassware with a **twisting** motion immediately after the experiment is over.

Cleaning glassware becomes more difficult with time, so it should be cleaned soon after the experiment is completed. Wipe off any lubricant with paper towel moistened in a solvent like hexane before washing the glassware. Use a brush with lab soap and water. Acetone may be used to dissolve most organic residues. Spent solvents should be transferred to a waste container for proper disposal.

HEATING

A **hot plate** (shown below) is used to heat Erlenmeyer flasks, beakers and other  containers with a flat bottom. Hot plates often have a built-in **magnetic stirrer**. A **heating mantle** has a hemispherical cavity that is used to heat round-bottom flasks. A **Bunsen burner** is designed to burn natural gas. Bunsen burners are useful for heating high-boiling point liquids, water, or solutions of non-flammable materials. They are also used for bending glass tubing. Smooth boiling is achieved by adding **boiling stones** to a liquid.

BOILING AND MELTING POINT DETERMINATION

The **boiling point** is determined by heating a liquid along with a boiling stone in a clamped test tube with a clamped thermometer positioned just above the liquid surface and away from the tube walls. The thermometer measures the temperature of the vapor above the liquid, which is at the same temperature as the liquid while boiling. The highest constant-value temperature reading after boiling is achieved is the boiling point.

The **melting point** is determined by placing a pulverized solid in a capillary tube and using a rubber band to fasten the capillary to a thermometer so that the sample is at the level of the thermometer bulb. The thermometer and sample are inserted into a **Thiele tube** filled with mineral or silicon oil. The Thiele tube has a sidearm that is heated with a Bunsen burner to create a flow of hot oil. This flow maintains an even temperature during heating. The melting point is read when the sample turns into a liquid. Many **electric melting point devices** are also available that heat the sample more slowly to give more accurate results. These are also safer to use than a Thiele tube with a Bunsen burner.

CENTRIFUGATION

A **centrifuge** separates two immiscible phases by spinning the mixture (placed in a **centrifuge tube**) at high speeds. A **microfuge** or microcentrifuge is a small centrifuge. The weight of material placed in a centrifuge must be balanced, so if one sample is placed in a centrifuge, a tube with roughly an equal mass of water should be placed opposite the sample.

FILTRATION

The goal of **gravity filtration** is to remove solids from a liquid and obtain a liquid without solid particulates. Filter paper is folded, placed in a funnel on top of a flask, and wetted with the solvent to seal it to the funnel. Next the mixture is poured through, and the solid-free liquid is collected from the flask.

The goal of **vacuum filtration** is usually to remove liquids from a solid to obtain a solid that is dry. An **aspirator** or a **vacuum pump** is used to provide suction through a rubber tube to a **filter trap**. The trap is attached to a **filter flask** (shown to the right) by a second rubber tube. The filter flask is an Erlenmeyer flask with a thick wall and a hose barb for the vacuum tube. Filter flasks are used to filter material using a **Büchner funnel** (shown to the right) or a smaller **Hirsch funnel**. These porcelain or plastic funnels hold a circular piece of filter paper. A single-hole rubber stopper supports the funnel in the flask while maintaining suction.

MIXING

Heterogeneous reaction mixtures in flasks are often mixed by **swirling**. To use a magnetic stirrer, a bar magnet coated with Teflon called a flea or a **stir bar** is placed in the container, and the container is placed on the stirrer. The container should be moved and the stir speed adjusted for smooth mixing. Mechanical stirring paddles, agitators, vortexers, or rockers are also used for mixing.

DISTILLATION

Liquids in solution are often separated based on their **boiling point differences**. During simple **distillation**, the solution is placed in a round-bottom flask called the **distillation flask** or **still pot**, and boiling stones are added. The apparatus shown below is assembled (note that clamps and stands are not shown), and the still pot is heated using a heating mantle.

While boiling, hot vapor escapes through the **distillation head**, enters the **condenser**, and is cooled and condensed back to a liquid. The vapor loses its heat to water flowing through the outside of the condenser. The condensate or **distillate** falls into the **receiving flask**. The apparatus is open to the atmosphere through a vent above the receiving flask. The distillate contains a higher concentration of the liquid with the lower boiling point. The less volatile liquid reaches a high concentration in the still pot. Head temperature is monitored during the process. Distillation may also be used to remove a solid from a pure liquid by boiling and condensing the liquid into the receiving flask.

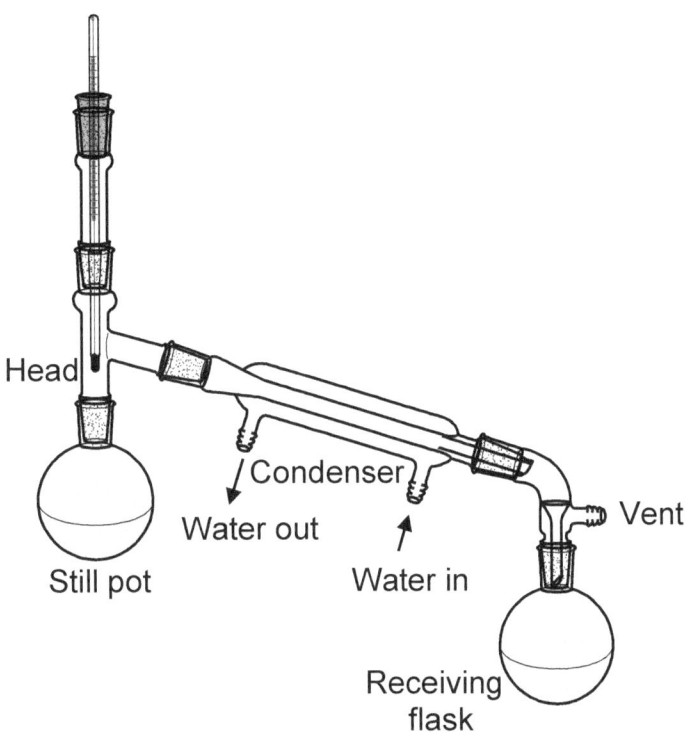

DECANTING

When a coarse solid has settled at the bottom of a flask of liquid, **decanting** the solution simply means pouring out the liquid and leaving the solid behind.

EXTRACTION

Compounds in solution are often separated based on their **solubility differences**. During **liquid-liquid extraction** (also called **solvent extraction**) a second solvent immiscible to the first is added to the solution in a **separatory funnel** (shown at right). Usually one solvent is nonpolar and the other is a polar solvent like water. The two solvents are immiscible and separate from each other after the mixture is shaken to allow solute exchange. One layer contains the compound of interest, and the other contains impurities to be discarded. The solutions in the two layers are separated from each other by draining liquid through the stopcock.

Skill 1.5   Knows how to use appropriate equipment and technology (e.g., Internet, spreadsheet, calculator) for gathering, organizing, displaying, and communicating data in a variety of ways (e.g., charts, tables, graphs, diagrams, written reports, oral presentations)

Scientists use a variety of tools and technologies to perform tests, collect and display data, and analyze relationships. Examples of commonly used tools include computer-linked probes, spreadsheets, and graphing calculators.

Scientists use computer-linked probes to measure various environmental factors including temperature, dissolved oxygen, pH, ionic concentration, and pressure. The advantage of computer-linked probes, as compared to more traditional observational tools, is that the probes automatically gather data and present it in an accessible format. This property of computer-linked probes eliminates the need for constant human observation and manipulation.

Scientists use spreadsheets to organize, analyze, and display data. For example, conservation ecologists use spreadsheets to model population growth and development, apply sampling techniques, and create statistical distributions to analyze relationships. Spreadsheet use simplifies data collection and manipulation and allows the presentation of data in a logical and understandable format.

Graphing calculators are another technology with many applications to science. For example, biologists use algebraic functions to analyze growth, development and other natural processes. Graphing calculators can manipulate algebraic data and create graphs for analysis and observation. In addition, biologists use the matrix function of graphing calculators to model problems in genetics. The use of graphing calculators simplifies the creation of graphical displays including histograms, scatter plots, and line graphs. Scientists can also transfer data and displays to computers for further analysis. Finally, scientists connect computer-linked probes, used to collect data, to graphing calculators to ease the collection, transmission, and analysis of data.

Usually, data are initially organized into tables, spreadsheets, or databases. However, trends or patterns in data can be difficult to identify using tables of numbers. For example, the table below presents carbon dioxide concentrations taken over many years atop the Mauna Loa Observatory in Hawaii.

Atmospheric CO_2 concentrations at Mauna Loa (Carbon Dioxide Information Analysis Center (CDIAC))

Year	Jan.	Feb.	March	April	May	June	July	Aug.	Sept.	Oct.	Nov.	Dec.	Annual
1958	--	--	315.71	317.45	317.50	--	315.86	314.93	313.19	--	313.34	314.67	--
1959	315.58	316.47	316.65	317.71	318.29	318.16	316.55	314.80	313.84	313.34	314.81	315.59	315.98
1960	316.43	316.97	317.58	319.03	320.03	319.59	318.18	315.91	314.16	313.83	315.00	316.19	316.91
1961	316.89	317.70	318.54	319.48	320.58	319.78	318.58	316.79	314.99	315.31	316.10	317.01	317.65
1962	317.94	318.56	319.69	320.58	321.01	320.61	319.61	317.40	316.26	315.42	316.69	317.69	318.45
1963	318.74	319.08	319.86	321.39	322.24	321.47	319.74	317.77	316.21	315.99	317.07	318.36	318.99
1964	319.57	--	--	--	322.23	321.89	320.44	318.70	316.70	316.87	317.68	318.71	--
1965	319.44	320.44	320.89	322.13	322.16	321.87	321.21	318.87	317.81	317.30	318.87	319.42	320.03
1966	320.62	321.59	322.39	323.70	324.07	323.75	322.40	320.37	318.64	318.10	319.79	321.03	321.37
1967	322.33	322.50	323.04	324.42	325.00	324.09	322.55	320.92	319.26	319.39	320.72	321.96	322.18
1968	322.57	323.15	323.89	325.02	325.57	325.36	324.14	322.11	320.33	320.25	321.32	322.90	323.05
1969	324.00	324.42	325.64	326.66	327.38	326.70	325.89	323.67	322.38	321.78	322.85	324.12	324.62
1970	325.06	325.98	326.93	328.13	328.07	327.66	326.35	324.69	323.10	323.07	324.01	325.13	325.68
1971	326.17	326.68	327.18	327.78	328.92	328.57	327.37	325.43	323.36	323.56	324.80	326.01	326.32
1972	326.77	327.63	327.75	329.72	330.07	329.09	328.05	326.32	324.84	325.20	326.50	327.55	327.46
1973	328.54	329.56	330.30	331.50	332.48	332.07	330.87	329.31	327.51	327.18	328.16	328.64	329.68
1974	329.35	330.71	331.48	332.65	333.09	332.25	331.18	329.40	327.44	327.37	328.46	329.58	330.25
1975	330.40	331.41	332.04	333.31	333.96	333.59	331.91	330.06	328.56	328.34	329.49	330.76	331.15
1976	331.74	332.56	333.50	334.58	334.87	334.34	333.05	330.94	329.30	328.94	330.31	331.68	332.15
1977	332.92	333.42	334.70	336.07	336.74	336.27	334.93	332.75	331.58	331.16	332.40	333.85	333.90
1978	334.97	335.39	336.64	337.76	338.01	337.89	336.54	334.68	332.76	332.54	333.92	334.95	335.50
1979	336.23	336.76	337.96	338.89	339.47	339.29	337.73	336.09	333.91	333.86	335.29	336.73	336.85
1980	338.01	338.36	340.08	340.77	341.46	341.17	339.56	337.60	335.88	336.01	337.10	338.21	338.69
1981	339.23	340.47	341.38	342.51	342.91	342.25	340.49	338.43	336.69	336.85	338.36	339.61	339.93
1982	340.75	341.61	342.70	343.56	344.13	343.35	342.06	339.82	337.97	337.86	339.26	340.49	341.13
1983	341.37	342.52	343.10	344.94	345.75	345.32	343.99	342.39	339.86	339.99	341.16	342.99	342.78
1984	343.70	344.51	345.28	347.08	347.43	346.79	345.40	343.28	341.07	341.35	342.98	344.22	344.42
1985	344.97	346.00	347.43	348.35	348.93	348.25	346.56	344.69	343.09	342.80	344.24	345.56	345.90
1986	346.29	346.96	347.86	349.55	350.21	349.54	347.94	345.91	344.86	344.17	345.66	346.90	347.15
1987	348.02	348.47	349.42	350.99	351.84	351.25	349.52	348.10	346.44	346.36	347.81	348.96	348.93
1988	350.43	351.72	352.22	353.59	354.22	353.79	352.39	350.44	348.72	348.88	350.07	351.34	351.48
1989	352.76	353.07	353.68	355.42	355.67	355.13	353.90	351.67	349.80	349.99	351.30	352.53	352.91
1990	353.66	354.70	355.39	356.20	357.16	356.22	354.82	352.91	350.96	351.18	352.83	354.21	354.19
1991	354.72	355.75	357.16	358.60	359.34	358.24	356.17	354.03	352.16	352.21	353.75	354.99	355.59
1992	355.98	356.72	357.81	359.15	359.66	359.25	357.03	355.00	353.01	353.31	354.16	355.40	356.37
1993	356.70	357.16	358.38	359.46	360.28	359.60	357.57	355.52	353.70	353.98	355.33	356.80	357.04
1994	358.36	358.91	359.97	361.26	361.68	360.95	359.55	357.49	355.84	355.99	357.58	359.04	358.88
1995	359.96	361.00	361.64	363.45	363.79	363.26	361.90	359.46	358.06	357.75	359.56	360.70	360.88
1996	362.05	363.25	364.03	364.72	365.41	364.97	363.65	361.49	359.46	359.60	360.76	362.33	362.64
1997	363.18	364.00	364.57	366.35	366.79	365.62	364.47	362.51	360.19	360.77	362.43	364.28	363.76
1998	365.32	366.15	367.31	368.61	369.30	368.87	367.64	365.77	363.90	364.23	365.46	366.97	366.63
1999	368.15	368.86	369.58	371.12	370.97	370.33	369.25	366.91	364.60	365.09	366.63	367.96	368.29
2000	369.08	369.40	370.45	371.59	371.75	371.62	370.04	368.04	366.54	366.63	368.20	369.43	369.40
2001	370.17	371.39	372.00	372.75	373.88	373.17	371.48	369.42	367.83	367.96	369.55	371.10	370.89
2002	372.29	372.94	373.38	374.71	375.40	375.26	373.87	371.35	370.57	370.10	371.93	373.63	372.95

However, more often than not, the data are then compiled into graphs or charts. Graphs help scientists visualize and interpret variations and patterns in data. Depending on the nature of the data, there are many types of graphs that may be useful. Bar graphs, pie charts and line graphs are just a few methods used to pictorially represent numerical data.

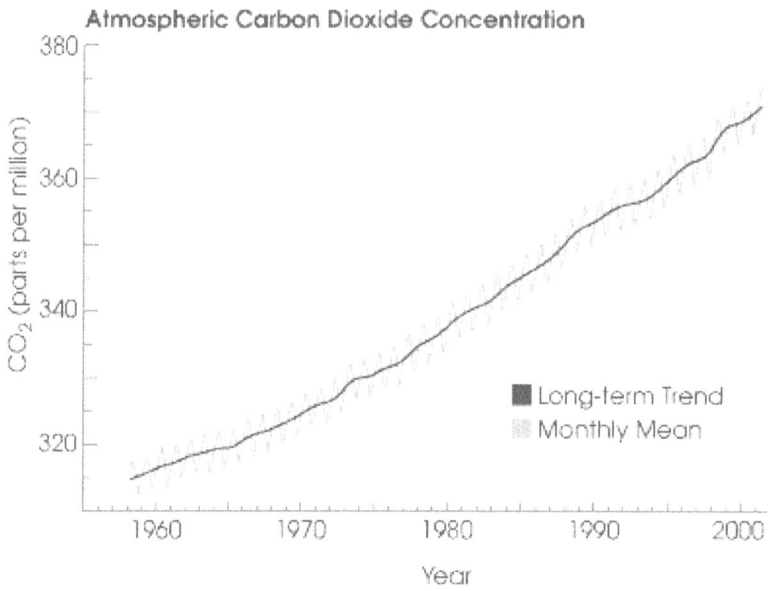

Atmospheric CO_2 measured at Mauna Loa. This is a famous graph called the Keeling Curve (courtesy NASA).

For example, in the graph above the x-axis represents time in units of years and the y-axis represents CO_2 concentration in units of parts per million (ppm). The best fit line (solid dark line) shows the trend in CO_2 concentration during the time period shown. This steady upward-sloping line indicates an overall trend of increasing CO_2 concentration between 1958 and 2002.

However, the light blue line, which indicates monthly mean CO_2 levels, shows a periodic variation in CO_2 concentrations during each year. This periodic variation is accounted for by seasonal effects. In the spring and summer, deciduous trees and plants undergo increased photosynthesis and remove more CO_2 from the atmosphere in the Northern Hemisphere than in the fall and winter.

The interpretation of data and the construction and interpretation of graphs are central practices in science. Graphs are effective visual tools which relay information quickly and reveal trends easily. While there are several different types of graphical displays, extracting information from them can be described in three basic steps.

1. **Describe the graph:** What does the title say? What is displayed on the x- and y-axes, including the units? Notice any symbols used and check for a legend or explanation.

2. **Describe the data:** Identify the range of data. Are patterns reflected in the data?

3. **Interpret the data:** How do patterns seen in the graph relate to other variables? What conclusions can be drawn from the patterns?

There are seven basic types of graphs and charts:

COLUMN GRAPHS

Column graphs consist of patterned rectangles displayed along a baseline called the x-category or the horizontal axis. The height of the rectangle represents the amount of the variable shown on the y-axis. Column graphs best show:
• changes in data over time (short time series)
• comparisons of several items (relationship between two series).

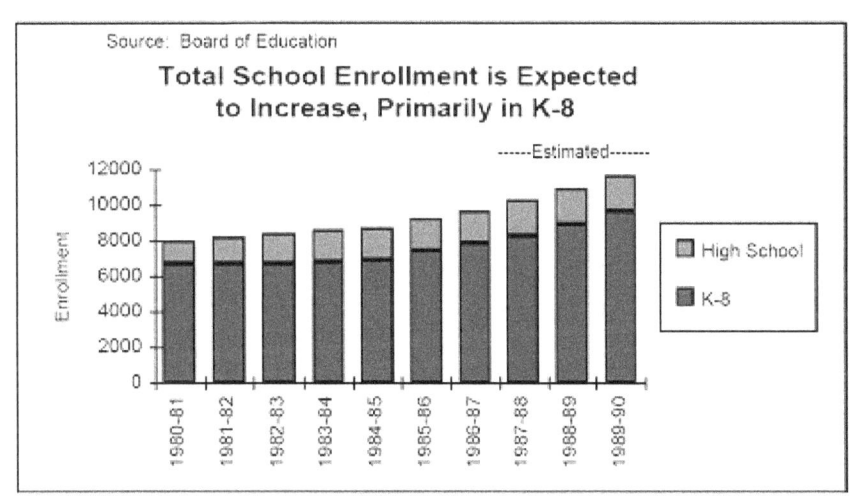

BAR GRAPHS

Bar graphs are column graphs in which the rectangles are arranged horizontally. The length of each rectangle represents its value. Bar graphs are sometimes referred to as histograms.

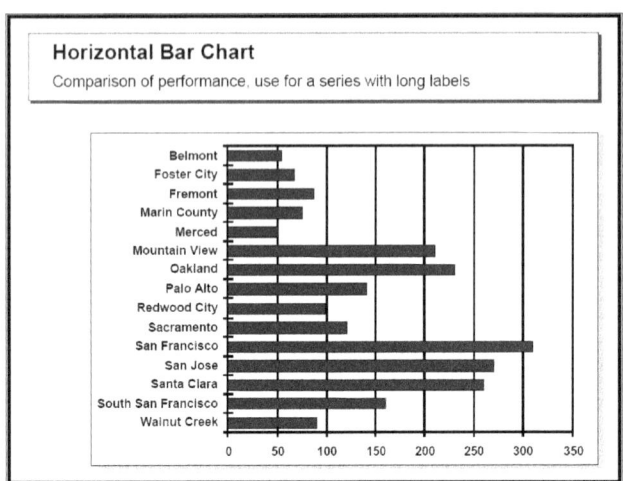

Bar graphs are good for looking at differences amongst similar things. If the data are a time series, a carefully chosen column graph is generally more appropriate but bar graphs can be used to vary a presentation when many column graphs of time series are used. One advantage of bar graphs is that there is greater horizontal space for variable descriptors because the vertical axis is the category axis.

LINE GRAPHS

Line graphs show data points connected by lines; different series are given different line markings (for example, dashed or dotted) or different tick marks. Line graphs are useful when the data points are more important than the transitions between them. They are best at showing long series' of data points, general trends, or changes over time.

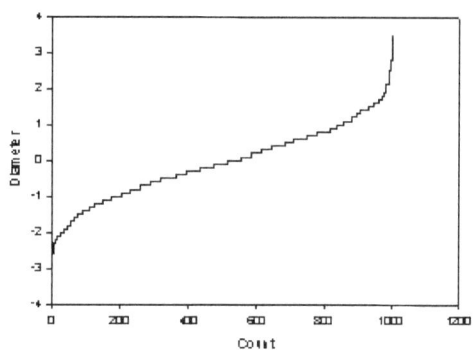

AREA CHARTS

Area charts show the relative contributions over time that each data series makes to a whole picture and are "stacked line graphs" in the sense that the variables are added together (e.g., principal + interest = total payment). Unlike line graphs, the space between lines is filled with shadings to emphasize variation among the variables over time. Thus, the scale provides accurate measurements only for the lowest part of the graph. This can cause misinterpretation if not fully understood. If reasonable, consider putting the "flattest" graph on the bottom.

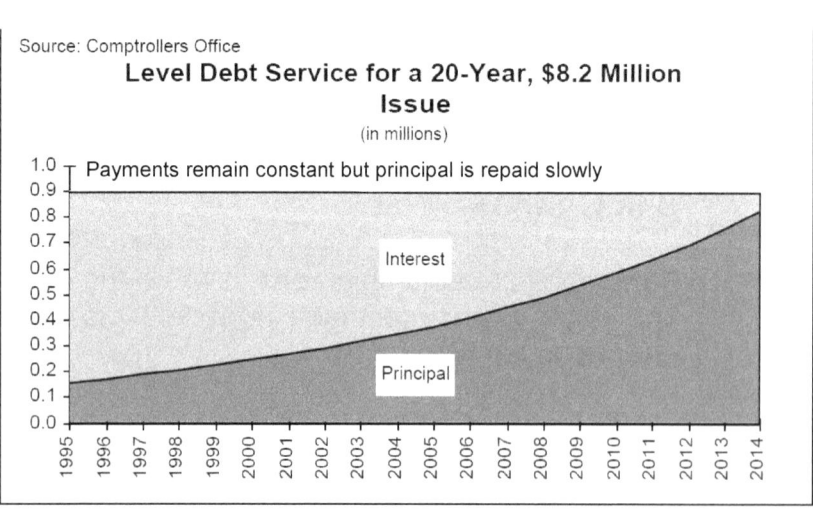

Scatter Plots

A scatter plot is the simplest type of graph. It simply plots the data points against their values, without adding any connecting lines, bars or other features. The first variable is measured along the x-axis and the second along the y-axis. Scatter plots show possible relationships between two variables. The purpose of the graph is to try to decide if some partial or indirect relationship—a correlation—exists. In some cases, a regression line may be drawn through the scatter plot to illustrate a possible correlation.

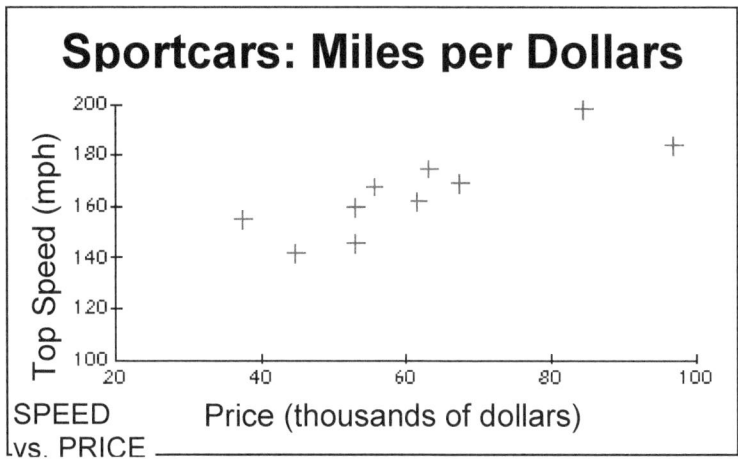

Pie Charts

A pie chart is a circle with radii connecting the center to the edge. The area between two radii is called a slice. Data values are proportionate to the angle between the radii.

Pie charts best show parts of a whole. Be careful not to include too many slices, as this may result in a cluttered graph. Six slices are typically as many as can be handled on one pie.

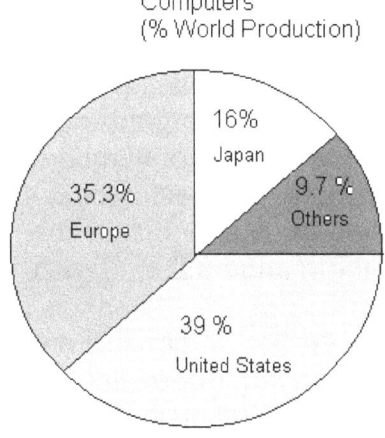

Skill 1.6 Understands how to use a variety of tools, techniques, and technology to gather, organize, and analyze data and how to apply appropriate methods of statistical measures and analysis

To more easily manage large amounts of data, statistical measures are employed to characterize trends in the data. In many systems, the data fit a **normal distribution,** which has a concentration of data points in the center and two equally sized tails (the ends of the distributions).

This type of distribution looks like this:

A distribution is considered **skewed** if one tail is larger than the other. To further characterize distributions, a variety of statistical measures are used. The following are the most commonly used statistical measures:

Arithmetic Mean: The arithmetic mean is the same as the average of a distribution - the sum of all the data points divided by the number of data points. The arithmetic mean is a good measure of the central tendency of roughly normal distributions, but may be misleading in skewed distributions. In cases of skewed distributions, other statistics such as the median or geometric mean may be more informative.

Geometric Mean: The geometric mean is a better representation of the central tendency of a log-normal distribution or a distribution with a very wide range. The geometric mean is found by multiplying all the values together, then taking the nth root of the result, where n is the number of data points.

Median: The median is the middle of a distribution: half the scores are above the median and half are below it. Unlike the mean, the median is not highly sensitive to extreme data points. This makes the median a better measure than the mean for finding the central tendency of highly skewed distributions. The median is determined by organizing the data points from lowest to highest. When there is an odd number of numbers, the median is simply the middle number. For example, the median of 2, 4, and 7 is 4. When there is an even number of numbers, the median is the mean of the two middle numbers. Thus, the median of the numbers 2, 4, 7, and 12 is (4+7)/2 = 5.5.

Percentile: Percentiles are similar to a median, but may represent any point in the data set. For example, the 90th percentile represents that point at which 90% of the data points are below that value and 10% of the data points are above that value. Quartiles, representing the 25th, 50th, and 75th percentiles of a data set, are often used to describe a distribution.

Mode: The mode is the most frequently occurring data point in a distribution and is used as a measure of central tendency. The advantage of the mode as a measure of central tendency is that its meaning is obvious. However, the mode is greatly subject to sample fluctuations and so is not recommended for use as the only measure of central tendency. Additionally, many distributions have more than one mode. Note also that **in the case of a perfectly normal distribution, the mean, median, and mode are identical**.

Variance: The variance is used to give a measure of the variability in a distribution. It is computed as the average squared deviation of each number from its mean. For example, for the numbers 1, 2, and 3, the mean is 2 and the variance (σ^2) is:

$$\sigma^2 = [(1-2)^2 + (2-2)^2 + (3-2)^2]/3 = 0.667$$

Standard deviation: Like variance, standard deviation is a measure of the spread of the distribution, but it is the more commonly used statistic. The standard deviation is simply the square root of the variance.

Note that the standard deviation can be used to compute the percentile rank associated with a given data point (if the mean and standard deviation of a normal distribution are known). In such a normal distribution, about 68% of the data points are within one standard deviation of the mean and about 95% of the data points are within two standard deviations of the mean.

Skill 1.7   Knows how to apply techniques to calibrate measuring devices and understands concepts of precision, accuracy, and error with regard to reading and recording numerical data from scientific instruments

A measurement is **precise** when individual measurements of the same quantity agree with one another. A measurement is **accurate** when they agree with the true value of the quantity being measured. An accurate measurement is **valid**. We get the right answer. A precise measurement is **reproducible**. We get a similar answer each time. These terms are related to **sources of error** in a measurement.

Precise measurements are near the **arithmetic mean** of the values. The arithmetic mean is the sum of the measurements divided by the number of measurements. The arithmetic mean is commonly called the **average**. It is the **best estimate** of the quantity based on the measurements taken.

Random error results from **limitations in equipment or techniques**. **Random error decreases precision**. Remember that all measurements reported to a proper number of significant digits contain an imprecise final digit to reflect random error.

Systematic error results from **imperfect equipment or technique**. **Systematic error decreases accuracy**. Instead of a random error with random fluctuations, there is a biased result that on average is too large or small.

Example: An environmental engineering company creates a solution of 5.00 ng/L of a toxin and distributes it to four toxicology labs to test their protocols. Each lab tests the material 5 times. Their results are charted as points on the number lines below. Interpret these data in terms of precision, accuracy, and type of error.

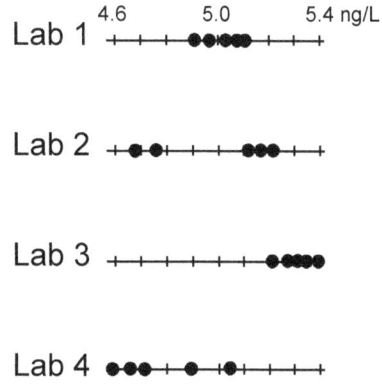

Solution: Results from Lab 1 are both accurate and precise when compared to results from the other labs. Results from Lab 2 are less precise than those from Lab 1. Lab 2 seems to use a protocol that generates a greater random error. However, the mean result from Lab 2 is still close to the known value. Lab 3 returned results that were about as precise as Lab 1 but inaccurate compared to Labs 1 and 2. Lab 3 most likely uses a protocol that yields a systematic error. The data from Lab 4 are both imprecise and inaccurate. Systematic and random errors are larger than for Lab 1.

Significant figures or **significant digits** are the digits indicating the **precision of a measurement**. There is uncertainty **only** in the last digit.

Example: You measure an object with a ruler marked in millimeters. The reading on the ruler is found to be about 2/3 of the way between 12 and 13 mm. What value should be recorded for its length?

Solution: Recording 13 mm does not give all the information that you found. Recording $12 \frac{2}{3}$ mm implies that an exact ratio was determined. Recording 12.666 mm gives more information than you found. A value of 12.7 mm or 12.6 mm should be recorded because there is uncertainty only in the last digit.

There are five rules for determining the **number of significant digits** in a quantity:

1) All nonzero digits are significant and all zeros between nonzero digits are significant.

   Example: 4.521 kJ and 7002 u both have four significant digits.

2) Zeros to the left of the first nonzero digit are not significant.

   Example: 0.0002 m contains one significant digit.

3) Zeros to the right of a non-zero digit and the decimal point are significant.

   Example: 32.500 g contains five significant figures.

4) The significance of numbers ending in zeros that are not to the right of the decimal point can be unclear, so **this situation should be avoided** by using scientific notation or a different decimal prefix. Sometimes a decimal point is used as a placeholder to indicate the units-digit is significant. A word like "thousand" or "million" may be used in informal contexts to indicate that the remaining digits are not significant.

   Example: 12000 Pa would be considered to have five significant digits by many scientists, but in the sentence, "The pressure rose from 11000 Pa to 12000 Pa," it almost certainly has only two. "12 thousand Pa" only has two significant digits, but 12000. Pa has five, indicated by the decimal point. The value should be represented as 1.2×10^4 Pa (or 1.2000×10^4 Pa). The best alternative would be to use 12 kPa or 12.000 kPa.

5) Exact numbers have no uncertainty and contain an infinite number of significant digits. These relationships are **definitions**. They are not measurements.

    Example: There are exactly 1000 L in one cubic meter.

There are four rules for **rounding off significant digits**:

1) If the leftmost digit to be removed is a four or less, then round down. The last remaining digit stays as it was.

    Example: Round 43.4 g to two significant digits. **Answer:** 43 g.

2) If the leftmost digit to be removed is a six or more, then round up. The last remaining digit increases by one.

    Example: Round 6.772 g to two significant digits. **Answer:** 6.8 g.

3) If the leftmost digit to be removed is a five that is followed by nonzero digits, then round up. The last remaining digit increases by one.

    Example: Round 18.502 g to two significant digits. **Answer:** 19 g.

4) If the leftmost digit to be removed is a five followed by nothing or by only zeros, force the last remaining digit to be even. If it is odd then round up by increasing it by one. If it is even (including zero) then it stays as it was.

    Examples: Round 18.50 g and 19.5 g to two significant digits.
    Answers: 18.50 g rounds off to 18 g and 19.5 g rounds off to 20 g.

There are three rules for **calculating with significant digits**:

1) For multiplication or division, the result has the same number of significant digits as the term with the least number of significant digits.

    Example: What is the volume of a compartment in the shape of a rectangular prism 1.2 cm long, 2.4 cm high and 0.9 cm deep?

    Solution: Volume = length x height x width

Volume = 1.2 cm × 2.4 cm × 0.9 cm = 2.592 cm³ (as read on a calculator)

Round to one digit because 0.9 cm has only one significant digit.

Volume = 3 cm³

2) For addition or subtraction, the result has the same number of digits after the decimal point as the term with the least number of digits after the decimal point.

Example: Volumes of 250.0 mL, 26 μL, and 4.73 mL are added to a flask. What is the total volume in the flask?

Solution: Only identical units may be added to each other, so 26 μL is first converted to 0.026 mL.

Volume = 250.0 mL + 0.026 mL + 4.73 mL = 254.756 mL (calculator value)

Round to one digit after the decimal because 250.0 mL has only one digit after the decimal. Volume = 254.8 mL.

3) For multi-step calculations, maintain all significant digits when using a calculator or computer and <u>round off the final value to the appropriate number of significant digits after the calculation</u>. When calculating by hand or when writing down an intermediate value in a multi-step calculation, maintain the first insignificant digit. In this text, insignificant digits in intermediate calculations are shown in italics except in the examples for the two rules above.

Skill 1.8   Uses the International System of Units (i.e., metric system) and performs unit conversions within and across measurement systems

SI is an abbreviation of the French *Système International d'Unités* or the **International System of Units**. It is the most widely used system of units in the world and is the system used in science. The use of many SI units in the United States is increasing outside of science and technology. There are two types of SI units: **base units** and **derived units**. The base units are:

Quantity	Unit name	Symbol
Length	meter	m
Mass	kilogram	kg
Amount of substance	mole	mol
Time	second	s
Temperature	kelvin	K
Electric current	ampere	A
Luminous intensity	candela	cd

Amperes and candelas are rarely used in chemistry. The name "kilogram" occurs for the SI base unit of mass for historical reasons. Derived units are formed from the kilogram, but appropriate decimal prefixes are used with the word "gram."

Derived units measure a quantity that may be **expressed in terms of other units**. The derived units important for chemistry are:

Derived quantity	Unit name	Expression in terms of other units	Symbol (if any)
Area	square meter	m^2	
Volume	cubic meter	m^3	
	liter	$dm^3 = 10^{-3} m^3$	L or l
Mass	unified atomic mass unit	$(6.022 \times 10^{23})^{-1}$ g	u or Da
Time	minute	60 s	min
	hour	60 min = 3600 s	h
	day	24 h = 86400 s	d
Speed	meter per second	m/s	
Acceleration	meter per second squared	m/s^2	
Temperature*	degrees Celsius	K−273.15°	°C
Mass density	gram per liter	$g/L = 1 kg/m^3$	
Amount-of-substance concentration (molarity†)	molar	mol/L	M
Molality‡	molal	mol/kg	*m*
Chemical reaction rate	molar per second†	M/s = mol/(L•s)	
Force	newton	$m \cdot kg/s^2$	N
Pressure	pascal	$N/m^2 = kg/(m \cdot s^2)$	Pa
	standard atmosphere§	101325 Pa	atm
Energy, Work, Heat	joule	$N \cdot m = m^3 \cdot Pa = m^2 \cdot kg/s^2$	J
	nutritional calorie§	4184 J	Cal
Heat (molar)	joule per mole	J/mol	
Heat capacity, entropy	joule per kelvin	J/K	
Heat capacity (molar), Entropy (molar)	joule per mole kelvin	J/(mol•K)	
Specific heat	joule per kilogram kelvin	J/(kg•K)	
Power	watt	J/s	W
Electric charge	coulomb	s•A	C
Electric potential, electromotive force	volt	W/A	V
Viscosity	pascal second	Pa•s	
Surface tension	newton per meter	N/m	

*Temperature differences in kelvin are the same as in degrees Celsius. To obtain degrees Celsius from Kelvin, subtract 273.15 (see below).
†Molarity is considered to be an obsolete unit by some physicists.

‡Molality, *m*, is often considered obsolete. Differentiate *m* and meters (m) by context.
§These are commonly used non-SI units.

Decimal multiples of SI units are formed by attaching a **prefix** directly before the unit and a symbol prefix directly before the unit symbol. SI prefixes range from 10^{-24} to 10^{24}. Only the prefixes you are likely to encounter in chemistry are shown below:

Factor	Prefix	Symbol	Factor	Prefix	Symbol
10^9	*giga-*	G	10^{-1}	*deci-*	d
10^6	*mega-*	M	10^{-2}	*centi-*	c
10^3	*kilo-*	k	10^{-3}	*milli-*	m
10^2	*hecto-*	h	10^{-6}	*micro-*	μ
10^1	*deca-*	da	10^{-9}	*nano-*	n
			10^{-12}	*pico-*	p

Example: 0.0000004355 meters is 4.355×10^{-7} m or 435.5×10^{-9} m. This length is also 435.5 nm or 435.5 nanometers.

Example: Find a unit to express the volume of a cubic crystal that is 0.2 mm on each side so that the number before the unit is between 1 and 1000.

Solution: Volume is length x width x height, so this volume is $(0.0002 \text{ m})^3$ or 8×10^{-12} m³. Conversions of volumes and areas using powers of units of length must take the power into account. Multiply the factor in the chart above by the power of the unit to obtain the new exponent, as follows:

$$1 \text{ m}^3 = 10^3 \text{ dm}^3 = 10^6 \text{ cm}^3 = 10^9 \text{ mm}^3 = 10^{18} \text{ μm}^3$$

The length 0.0002 m is 2×10^2 μm, so the volume is also 8×10^6 μm³. This volume could also be expressed as 8×10^{-3} mm³, but none of these numbers are between 1 and 1000.

Expressing the volume in liters is helpful in cases like these. There is no power on the unit of liters, therefore:

$$1 \text{ L} = 10^3 \text{ mL} = 10^6 \text{ μL} = 10^9 \text{ nL}$$

Converting cubic meters to liters gives:

$$8 \times 10^{-12} \text{ m}^3 \times \frac{10^3 \text{ L}}{1 \text{ m}^3} = 8 \times 10^{-9} \text{ L}$$

The crystal's volume is 8 nanoliters (8 nL).

Example: Determine the ideal gas constant, R, in L•atm/(mol•K) from its SI value of 8.3144 J/(mol•K).

Solution: One joule is equal to one m³•Pa (see the table of SI units). Therefore:

$$8.3144 \, \frac{\text{m}^3 \bullet \text{Pa}}{\text{mol} \bullet \text{K}} \times \frac{1000 \text{ L}}{1 \text{ m}^3} \times \frac{1 \text{ atm}}{101325 \text{ Pa}} = 0.082057 \, \frac{\text{L} \bullet \text{atm}}{\text{mol} \bullet \text{K}}$$

Notice that both the initial quantity and the final value have five significant digits.

DIMENSIONAL ANALYSIS

Dimensional analysis is a structured way to convert units. It involves a conversion factor that allows the units to be cancelled out when multiplied or divided, as shown in the solution to the example above.

The following are the steps to converting one dimensional measurements:

1. Write the term to be converted (both number and unit): 6.0 cm = ? km
2. Write the conversion formula(s): 100 cm = 0.001 km
3. Make a fraction of the conversion formula such that:

    a. If the unit in step 1 is in the numerator, that same unit in step 3 must be in the denominator.
    b. If the unit in step 1 is in the denominator, that same unit in step 3 must be in the numerator.

    $$\frac{0.001 \text{ km}}{100 \text{ cm}} \quad \text{or} \quad \frac{100 \text{ cm}}{0.001 \text{ km}}$$

    Since the numerator and denominator are equal, the fraction must equal 1.

4. Multiply the term in step 1 by the fraction in step 3. Since the fraction equals 1, you can multiply by it without changing the size of the term.

5. Cancel units: $6.0 \, \cancel{\text{cm}} \times \dfrac{0.001 \text{ km}}{100 \, \cancel{\text{cm}}}$

6. Perform the indicated calculation, rounding the answer to the correct number of significant figures:

$$0.000060 \text{ km } or \text{ } 6.0 \times 10^{-5} \text{ km}$$

The process is nearly the same for two and three dimensional conversions, as shown in the following examples.

Example: How many cm^3 is $1 \text{ } m^3$?

Solution: Remember that $1 \text{ } m^3$ is really $1m \times 1m \times 1m$, and $100 \text{ cm} = 1m$. Substituting in the 100 cm for every meter the problem can be rewritten as
$100 \text{ cm} \times 100 \text{ cm} \times 100 \text{ cm}$ or $1 \text{ } m^3 = 1,000,000 \text{ } cm^3$ or $1 \times 10^6 \text{ } cm^3$.

Example: Convert $4.17 \text{ kg/}m^2$ to $\text{g/}cm^2$.

Solution: First convert from kg to g, using 1000 g = 1 kg as the conversion factor:

$$4.17 \text{ kg/}m^2 \times 1000 \text{ g}/1 \text{ kg} = 4170 \text{ g/}m^2$$

Then use 1 m = 100 cm to convert the denominator. Remember that m^2 is actually $m \times m$, and replacing m with 100 cm, m^2 becomes $100 \text{ cm} \times 100 \text{ cm}$
or $10,000 \text{ } cm^2$. The conversion factor for the denominator becomes $1 \text{ } m^2/10,000 \text{ } cm^2$:

$$4170 \text{ g/}m^2 \times 1 \text{ } m^2/10,000 \text{ } cm^2 = 0.417 \text{ g/}cm^2$$

Dimensional analysis can also be used to help solve mathematical problems.

Example: The density of gold is $19.3 \text{ g/}cm^3$. How many grams of gold would be found in $55 \text{ } cm^3$?

Solution: Using dimensional analysis, some unit must be made to cancel. The answer needs to be in grams, so the cm^3 needs to be cancelled out. Multiply or divide the units so that the cm^3 cancel. In this case the units part of the problem works out as follows:

$$\text{g/}cm^3 \times cm^3 = \text{g}$$

Now adding in the values from the problem, we get:

$$19.3 \text{ g/}cm^3 \times 55 \text{ } cm^3 = 1060 \text{ g of gold}$$

THE CELSIUS, FAHRENHEIT, AND KELVIN TEMPERATURE SCALES

The **Fahrenheit** (°F) non-metric temperature scale was proposed in 1724 by Gabriel Fahrenheit who was looking to improve upon Galileo's thermometer by changing from an enclosed gas to mercury. Mercury has a large uniform thermal expansion, does not adhere to the glass, and its silvery color makes it easy to read.
He calibrated his thermometer as follows:

> "Placing the thermometer in a mixture of sal ammoniac or sea salt, ice, and water a point on the scale will be found which is denoted as zero. A second point is obtained if the same mixture is used without salt. Denote this position as 30. A third point, designated as 96, is obtained if the thermometer is placed in the mouth so as to acquire the heat of a healthy man." (D. G. Fahrenheit, Phil. Trans. (London) 33, 78, 1724)

On his scale, he found the temperature of boiling water to be 212°. He adjusted the freezing point temperature for water to 32° so that the interval between freezing and boiling would be a rational number - 180°.

The **centigrade** scale, proposed about twenty years later, sets the freezing point of water at 0° and the boiling point of water at 100°. Anders Celsius reversed the scale when he proposed the **Celsius** scale. Both the centigrade and Celsius scales were designed to have 100 degrees between the boiling point temperature of water and its freezing point temperature at standard atmospheric pressure.

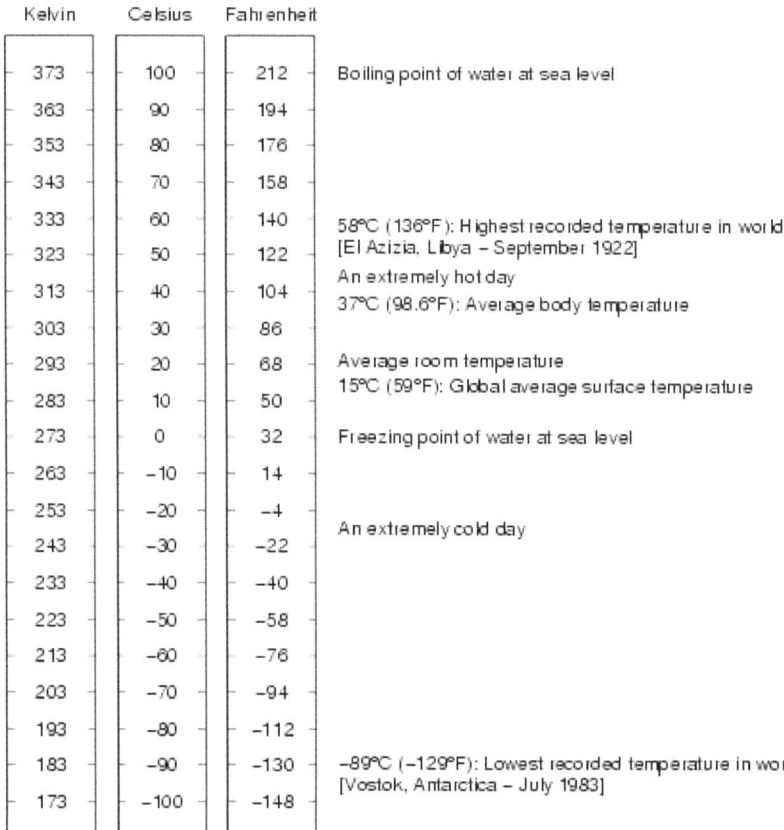

The use of the Celsius or Fahrenheit scale requires using negative numbers when measuring low temperatures. This proves to be inconvenient, so in the late 1800s Lord Kelvin suggested a new temperature scale. This temperature scale is based on absolute zero, the temperature at which a material has cooled to the point where it has no more heat to lose (or the point at which all molecular motion ceases). This temperature is the basis for the Kelvin scale and the value zero kelvin is assigned to it. At sea level, water freezes at around 273 K and boils at 373 K. Notice that there are still 100 degrees between the freezing and boiling point temperatures on the Kelvin scale. Temperatures on this scale are called **kelvins**, *not* degrees kelvin, kelvin is *not* capitalized, and the symbol (capital K) stands alone with no degree symbol.

In 1948 the 9th General Conference on Weights and Measures (CGPM) changed the name of the centigrade scale to the Celsius scale and adopted its use. The Celsius scale is now defined as follows:

1. The triple point of water is defined to be 0.01° C.

2. A degree Celsius equals the same temperature change as a degree on the ideal-gas scale, now called the **Kelvin scale**.

3. On the Celsius scale the boiling point of water at standard atmospheric pressure is 99.975° C in contrast to the 100° originally defined by the Centigrade scale.

Conversions between scales are simple but require a little math:

- To convert from Celsius to Fahrenheit, multiply by 1.8 and add 32:

$$°F = 1.8 \times °C + 32$$

From Fahrenheit to Celsius, subtract 32 and divide by 1.8:

$$°C = (°F - 32) / 1.8$$

- To convert from Celsius to Kelvin, add 273 (273.15 to be more exact) to the Celsius temperature: $K = °C + 273$

From Kelvin to Celsius, subtract 273 from the Kelvin temperature:

$$°C = K - 273$$

Common temperature comparisons

temperature	degree Celsius	degree Fahrenheit
symbol	°C	°F
boiling point of water	100.	212.
average human body temperature	37.	98.6

average room temperature	20. to 25.	68. to 77.
melting point of ice	0.	32.

TEACHER CERTIFICATION STUDY GUIDE

COMPETENCY 002   **THE TEACHER UNDERSTANDS THE NATURE OF SCIENCE AND THE PROCESS OF SCIENTIFIC INQUIRY**

Skill 2.1   **Understands the nature of science, the predictive power of science, and limitations to the scope of science (i.e., the types of questions that science can and cannot answer)**

Modern science began around the late 16th century with a new way of thinking about the world. Few scientists will disagree with Carl Sagan's assertion that "science is a way of thinking much more than it is a body of knowledge" (Broca's Brain, 1979). Science is a process of inquiry and investigation. It is a way of thinking and acting, not just a body of knowledge to be acquired by memorizing facts and principles. This way of thinking, the scientific method, is based on the idea that scientists begin their investigations with observations. From these observations they develop a hypothesis, which is further developed into a prediction. The hypothesis is challenged through experimentation and further observations and is refined as necessary. Science has progressed in its understanding of nature through careful observation, a lively imagination, and increasingly sophisticated instrumentation. Science is distinguished from other fields of study in that it provides guidelines or methods for conducting research, and the research findings must be reproducible by other scientists for those findings to be validated.

It is important to recognize that scientific practice is not always this systematic. Discoveries have been made that are serendipitous and others have been predicted based on theory rather than observation of phenomena. Einstein's theory of relativity was developed not from the observation of data but with a kind of mathematical puzzle. Only later were experiments able to be conducted that validated his theory.

The scientific method is a logical set of steps that a scientist goes through to solve a problem. The main purpose of using the Scientific Method is to eliminate, as much as possible, preconceived ideas, prejudices and biases by presenting an objective way to study possible answers to a question. Only by designing a way to study one variable at a time can each possible answer be ruled out or accepted for further study. While an inquiry may start at any point in this method and may not involve all of the steps, the overall approach can be described as follows:

MAKING OBSERVATIONS

Scientific questions frequently result from observation of events in nature or in the laboratory. An observation is not just a look at what happens. It also includes measurements and careful records of the event. Records could include photos, drawings, or written descriptions. The observations and data collection may provide answers, or they may lead to one or more questions. In chemistry, observations almost always deal with the behavior of matter.

Having arrived at a question, a scientist usually researches the scientific literature to see what is known about the question. Perhaps the question has already been answered, or another experimenter has found part of the solution. The scientist may want to test or reproduce the answer found in the literature. Or, the research might lead to a new question.

Sometimes the same observations are made over and over again and are always the same. For example, one can observe that daylight lasts longer in summer than in winter. This observation never varies. Such observations are called **laws of nature**. For example, one of the most important laws in chemistry was discovered in the late 1700s. Chemists observed that no mass was ever lost or gained in chemical reactions. This law became known as the law of conservation of mass. Explaining this law was a major topic of chemistry in the early 19th century.

DEVELOPING A HYPOTHESIS

If the question has not yet been answered, the scientist may prepare for an experiment by making a hypothesis. A hypothesis is a statement of a possible answer to the question. It is a tentative explanation for a set of facts and can be tested by experiments. Although hypotheses are usually based on observations, they may also be based on a sudden idea or intuition or a mathematical theory.

CONDUCTING AN EXPERIMENT

An experiment tests the hypothesis to determine whether it may be a correct answer to the question or a solution to the problem. Some experiments may test the effect of one thing on another under controlled conditions. Such experiments have two variables. The experimenter controls one variable, called the independent variable. The other variable, the *dependent variable*, shows the result of changing the *independent variable*.

For example, suppose a researcher wanted to test the effect of Vitamin A on the ability of rats to see in dim light. The independent variable would be the dose of Vitamin A added to the rats' diet. The dependent variable would be the intensity of light to which the rats respond. All other factors, such as time, temperature, age, water and other nutrients given to the rats, are held constant.

Chemists sometimes do short experiments "just to see what happens" or to see what a certain reaction produces. Often, these are not formal experiments. Rather they are ways of making additional observations about the behavior of matter.

When students are involved in designing experiments, they better understand what scientists are doing as well as the difficulty of designing appropriately controlled experiments. An ideal experiment at the high school level should not last more than 12-14 days.

COLLECTING DATA

In most experiments scientists collect *quantitative data*, which are data that can be measured with instruments. Quantitative data involves numbers and measurements against a standard. Those measurements may be taken at specified time intervals. They also collect *qualitative data*, descriptive information from observations other than measurements. Qualitative data includes any observations made with the senses of hearing or seeing such as a popping sound or a color change.

Interpreting data and analyzing observations are important parts of the scientific method. If data are not organized in a logical manner, incorrect conclusions can be drawn. Also, other scientists may not be able to follow or reproduce the results.

By placing data into charts and graphs, the scientist may see patterns or lack thereof. The scientist will also be able to understand if the experiment truly tested the hypothesis. Induction is drawing conclusions based on facts or observations. Deduction is drawing conclusions based on generalizations.

DRAWING CONCLUSIONS

Finally, a scientist must draw conclusions from the experiment. A conclusion must address the hypothesis on which the experiment was based. The conclusions state whether or not the data support the hypothesis. If not, the conclusion should state what the experiment did show. If the hypothesis is not supported, the scientist uses the observations from the experiment to make a new or revised hypothesis and plan new experiments.

Effective written communication is necessary to present the research to a teacher or to a scientific journal. Effective oral communication is needed to present the research to a group whether that group is a class or other scientists. Students must recognize that, in this age of communication, those who cannot communicate effectively will be left behind. Accordingly, the evaluation system of the use of the scientific method should make provision for communication skills and activities.

THE SCIENTIFIC METHOD

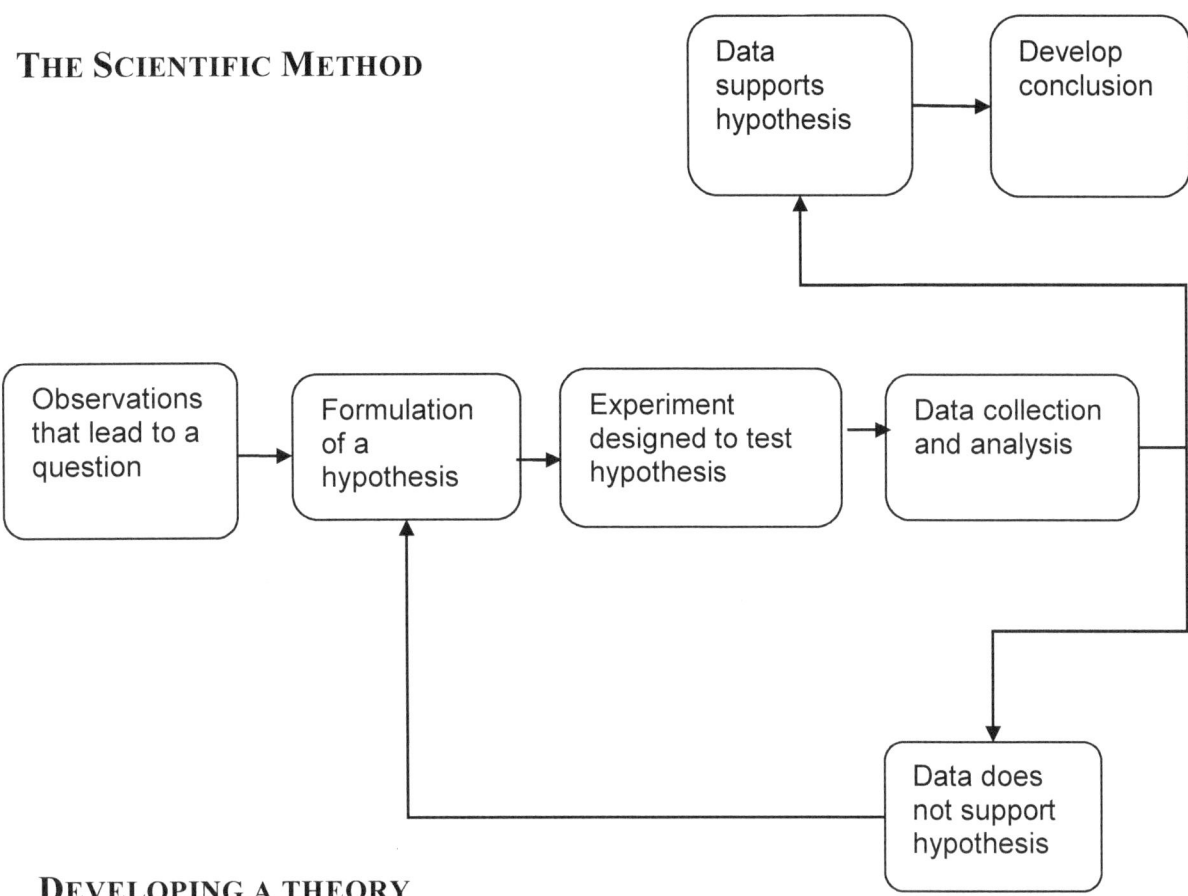

DEVELOPING A THEORY

When a hypothesis survives many experimental tests to determine its validity, the hypothesis may be developed into a **theory**. A theory explains a body of facts and laws that are based on the facts. A theory also reliably predicts the outcome of related events in nature. For example, the law of conservation of matter and many other experimental observations led to a theory proposed early in the 19th century. This theory explained the conservation law by proposing that all matter is made up of atoms which are never created or destroyed in chemical reactions, only rearranged. This atomic theory also successfully predicted the behavior of matter in chemical reactions that had not been studied at the time. As a result, the atomic theory has stood for 200 years with only minor modifications.

A theory also serves as a scientific **model**. A model can be a physical model made of wood or plastic, a computer program that simulates events in nature, or simply a mental picture of an idea. A model illustrates a theory and explains nature. For example, in your chemistry course, you will develop a mental (and possibly a physical) model of the atom and its behavior. Outside of science, the word theory is often used to describe an unproven notion. In science, theory means much more. It is a thoroughly tested explanation of things and events observed in nature.

A theory can never be proven true, but it can be proven untrue. All this requires is to demonstrate *one* exception to the theory.

THE LIMITS OF SCIENCE

Throughout history, different ways of knowing have complimented each other and have been used by all civilizations. Different fields of study require different skills, from mathematics and science to arts and crafts, from medicine and law to religion and philosophy.

There are four basic ways of knowing:

- From personal experience
- From a trusted source
- From intuition or inspiration
- From reason or logical thinking.

Science is a combination of observational experience, reason, and logical thinking. Religion flows from a trusted source along with inspiration, while philosophy comes from logical thinking.

Science, including the natural sciences of physics, biology and chemistry along with social sciences like psychology and sociology, uses the scientific method to establish a standard of proof. There is a well-established series of steps that must be followed, beginning with research and experimentation and leading to peer review and publication. These standards of proof make it more difficult for science to be manipulated for any length of time. For example, March of 1989 brought the announcement of cold fusion, a long sought after phenomenon that set the scientific community ablaze. However, this fire was extinguished quickly amidst accusations of fraud and incompetence after many other research teams unsuccessfully attempted to replicate the results. The authors' research was discredited by rushed publication of incomplete results as well as errors in their data interpretation.

In other areas of knowing, information is much more difficult to evaluate since the evidence used for study is open to wide interpretation. For the most part, other areas of study rely on personal experience for knowing. Religious knowing relies on information from religious texts, personal inspiration, or from a deity. It can come from a variety of translations, or it can come through prayer or meditation or association with other believers and followers. Philosophy is a belief accepted by a school or group and relies on public discourse for validation. Assessments of the same piece of literature can vary widely from one person to another. Learning about history uses primary and secondary sources, and again relies on a great deal of elucidation.

While no method for learning is more right than another, each different way of knowing is necessary to fill our senses and explain our world. They all work together to provide a full picture of the world in which we live. In general, one type of investigation is not appropriate for evaluating other ways of knowing. For example, science is not an appropriate way of investigating religious truths, while religion or philosophy may not be adequate means of investigating scientific phenomena.

Skill 2.2 Knows the characteristics of various types of scientific investigations (e.g., descriptive studies, controlled experiments, comparative data analysis) and how and why scientists use different types of scientific investigations

The design of chemical experiments must include every step needed to obtain the desired data. In other words, the design must be **complete** and it must include all required **controls**. These attributes are described further in Skill 2.3.

By definition, **qualitative** observations are descriptive in nature. For example, "the sample was yellow" is a descriptive statement and thus is an example of qualitative data. **Quantitative** data are measurements that are numerical in nature. "The sample had a mass of 1.15 grams" is a quantitative data point. Both types of observations have their place in scientific research.

QUALITATIVE ANALYSIS (DESCRIPTIVE STUDIES)

The objective of qualitative data analysis is a complete and detailed (though subjective) description, from which patterns or other useful information may be gained. For example, an ornithologist may observe individuals of a bird species over a period of time to identify the resources they need for food and shelter or to document mating behavior.

Qualitative analysis involves a continual interplay between theory and analysis. In analyzing qualitative data, we seek to discover patterns such as changes over time or possible causal links between variables. The main disadvantage of qualitative approaches to data analysis is that the results can not be extended to wider populations with the same degree of certainty that quantitative analyses can. This is because the findings of the research are not tested to discover whether they are statistically significant or due to chance.

Qualitative analysis is frequently used to study natural phenomena or activities that do not lend themselves as easily to quantitative analysis, such as the behavioral interactions of animals and people. In such cases, a qualitative analysis is often conducted prior to designing a more rigorous quantitative study.

In disciplines such as chemistry, which rely largely on quantitative approaches, qualitative observations are still very important and are nearly always recorded in laboratory notebooks alongside quantitative measurements. Qualitative information can be very important in developing hypotheses to explain unexpected results. For example, observations of color or texture changes during an experiment may identify impurities likely present in the reagents or overheating of the solution during a particular step.

QUANTITATIVE ANALYSIS

Analysis of quantitative data involves making detailed measurements, classifying features, counting them and constructing statistical models in an attempt to explain observations. These findings, then, can be generalized to a larger population or the ideal case, and direct comparisons can be made between two data sets so long as valid sampling and significance techniques have been used.

However, the picture of the data which emerges from quantitative analysis is less rich than that obtained from qualitative analysis. For statistical purposes, classifications must be strict. An item either belongs to class x or it doesn't. Quantitative analysis is therefore an *idealization* of the data in some cases. In addition, quantitative analysis tends to sideline rare occurrences. To ensure that certain statistical tests (such as chi-squared) provide reliable results, it is essential that minimum frequencies are obtained - meaning that categories may have to be collapsed into one another resulting in a loss of data richness. In addition, censoring of outliers may occur.

Basically, quantitative research is objective; qualitative is subjective. Quantitative research seeks explanatory laws; qualitative research aims at in-depth description. Quantitative research measures what it assumes to be a static reality in hopes of developing universal laws and is well suited to establishing cause-and-effect relationships. Qualitative research is an exploration of what is assumed to be a dynamic reality. It does not claim that what is discovered in the process is universal, and thus necessarily replicable.

Whether to choose a fundamentally quantitative or a qualitative design depends on the nature of the project, the type of information needed, the context of the study, and the availability of resources (time, money, and human). It is important to keep in mind that these are two different approaches, not necessarily polar opposites. In fact, elements of both designs can and should be used together in mixed-methods studies. In scientific disciplines such as chemistry, it is generally the norm to record at least some observations of both types.

Advantages of combining both types of data include:

1. Research development (one approach is used to inform the other, such as using qualitative research to develop an instrument to be used in quantitative research)
2. Increased validity (confirmation of results by means of different data types)
3. Complementarity (adding information, e.g., descriptions alongside measurements)
4. Providing additional resources for explaining unanticipated results or failed experiments.

Skill 2.3 **Understands principles and procedures for designing and conducting a variety of scientific investigations, with emphasis on inquiry-based investigations, and understands how to communicate and defend scientific results**

The design of chemical experiments must include every step needed to obtain the desired data. In other words, the design must be **complete** and it must include all required **controls**.

COMPLETE DESIGN

Familiarity with individual experiments and equipment will help you evaluate if anything is missing from the design. For data requiring a difference between two values, the experiment **must determine both values**. For data utilizing the ideal gas law, the experiment **must determine three values of P, V, n, or T** in order to determine the fourth, or **one value and a ratio of the other two** in order to determine the fourth. In general, whenever an equation is used to determine an unknown quantity, each of the other quantities in the equation must be measured or otherwise derived from the experiment.

Example: In a mercury manometer, the level of mercury in contact with a reaction vessel is 70.0 mm lower than the level exposed to the atmosphere. What additional information is required to determine the pressure in the vessel in kPa? Use the following conversion factors:

$$760 \text{ mm Hg} = 1 \text{ atm} = 101.325 \text{ kPa}$$

Solution: The barometric pressure is needed to determine vessel pressure from an open-ended manometer. A manometer reading is always a **difference** between two pressures. One standard atmosphere is 760 mm mercury, but on a given day at a given location, the actual ambient pressure may vary. If the barometric pressure on the day of the experiment is 104 kPa, the pressure of the vessel is:

$$104 \text{ kPa} + 70.0 \text{ mm Hg} \times \frac{101.325 \text{ kPa}}{760 \text{ mm Hg}} = 113 \text{ kPa}.$$

CONTROLS

Experimental **controls** prevent factors other than those under study from impacting the outcome of the experiment. A **test sample** in a controlled experiment is the unknown to be compared against one or more **control samples**. Control samples should be selected to be as identical to the test sample as possible in every way other than the one variable being tested.

A **negative control** is a control sample that is known to lack the effect. A **positive control** is known to contain the effect. Positive controls of varying strengths or concentrations are often used to generate a **calibration curve** (also called a **standard curve**).

For example, a scientist may wish to measure the level of arsenic in drinking water in a former mining area. A negative control would consist of water similar to that being tested that does not contain arsenic. This insures that there has been no cross-contamination during the experiment, and that the instruments are recording properly. Positive controls are also prepared consisting of water samples with increasing known concentrations of arsenic. The curve of concentration responses obtained is called a calibration curve, and is compared to past curves to ensure that the instrument is recording accurate and precise measurements across a wide concentration range.

When determining the concentration of a component in a mixture, an **internal standard** is a known concentration of a different substance that is added to the experimental sample. An **external standard** is a known concentration of the substance of interest. External standards are more commonly used. They are not added to the experimental sample; they are analyzed separately. These standards are frequently used to evaluate potential bias in the results, which may be caused by poor instrument calibration, interference from other compounds, or loss of the substance during sample pre-processing.

Example: A pure chemical in aqueous solution is known to absorb light at 615 nm. What controls would ideally be used with a spectrophotometer to determine the concentration of this chemical when it is present in a mixture with other solutes in an aqueous solution?

Solution: The other solutes may also absorb light at 615 nm. The ideal negative control would be an identical mixture with the chemical of interest entirely absent. Known concentrations of the chemical could then be added to the negative control to create positive controls (external standards) and develop a calibration curve of the spectrophotometer absorbance reading at 615 nm as a function of concentration. Replicate samples of each standard and of the unknown should be read.

Example: Ethanol is separated from a mixture of organic compounds by gas chromatography. The concentration of each component is proportional to its peak area. However, the chromatograph detector has a variable sensitivity from one run to the next. Is an internal standard required to determine the concentration of ethanol?

Solution: Yes. The variable detector sensitivity may only be accounted for by adding a known concentration of a chemical not found in the mixture as an internal standard to the experimental sample and control samples. The variable sensitivity of the detector will be accounted for by determining the ratio of the peak area for ethanol to the peak area of the added internal standard.

REPLICATE SAMPLES

Replicate samples characterize the degree of random error that is present. A mean may be taken of the results from replicate samples to obtain a best value, or replicate samples may be used in statistical testing to determine if one sample is likely part of the same population as another. If one replicate is obviously inconsistent with the results from other replicates, it may be discarded as an **outlier** and not counted as an observation when determining the mean. Discarding an outlier is equivalent to assuming the presence of a systematic error for that particular observation. In research, this must be done with great caution because some real-world behavior generates sporadically unusual results, and most natural populations contain occasional outliers.

EXPERIMENTAL BIAS

Experimental bias exists when a researcher favors one particular outcome over another in an experimental setup. In order to avoid bias, it is imperative to conduct each experiment under exactly the same conditions, including a *control* experiment with a known negative outcome. Additionally, in order to avoid experimental bias, a researcher must not "read" particular results into data.

An example of experimental bias is as follows. A researcher is timing mice as they move through a maze toward a piece of cheese. The experiment relies on the mouse's ability to smell the cheese as it approaches. If one mouse chases a piece of Cheddar cheese, while another chases Limburger (a cheese with a very strong odor), the Limburger mouse may have a large advantage over the Cheddar mouse because it can smell the cheese more easily. To remove the experimental bias from this experiment, the same cheese should be used for both mice.

SCIENTIFIC DEFENSIBILITY

The ability to defend scientific results relies not only on well-designed experiments, but on excellent documentation, the ability to communicate the experiment and results to other researchers, and their ability to replicate the results. Careful notes should be taken of the setup, conduct, and results of the experiment at the time the events are happening. These notes should be kept available in their original form. When writing up the results, enough detail should be provided of the experimental setup and controls to assure reviewers that appropriate measures were taken to ensure accuracy, precision, lack of interference, and reproducibility of the results. If the results allow for more than one possible conclusion (i.e., not all variables could be controlled), the conclusions drawn should include only those that can be fully justified by the results of the experiment and should recognize alternative possible hypotheses.

Skill 2.4 Understands how logical reasoning, verifiable observational and experimental evidence, and peer review are used in the process of generating and evaluating scientific knowledge

Modern science began around the late 16th century with a new way of thinking about the world. **Science is a process of inquiry and investigation**. It is a way of thinking and acting, not just a body of knowledge to be acquired by memorizing facts and principles. This way of thinking, the scientific method, is based on the idea that scientists begin their investigations with observations.

Science is distinguished from other fields of study in that it **provides guidelines or methods for conducting research.** Of utmost importance is that the results of scientific research be **reproducible**, not just by the original investigators, but by any other person performing the identical experiment. Ideally the scientific community all works together to advance knowledge of the natural world. The process of peer review is central to this ideal.

Peer review is the process by which scientific results produced by one group are subjected to the analysis of other experts in the field. In practice it is most often used by scientific journals. Scientists author manuscripts detailing their experiments, results, and interpretations and these manuscripts are distributed by the journal editors to other researchers in the field for review prior to publication. The authors must address the comments and questions of the reviewers and make appropriate revisions for their work to be accepted for publication. Peer review is also the process by which applications for research funds are evaluated and awarded. Peer review may also be used informally by groups of researchers or graduate students wishing to get an evaluation of their research prior to writing it up for publication.

Reviewers of scientific work are typically experts in the field, but it is important that they be objective in their evaluations because it is possible that the results under review may contradict the ideas of the reviewers. Peer review is typically done **anonymously** so that the identities of the reviewers remain unknown by the scientists submitting work for review. However, less formal peer review may occur through lunch seminars, presentations at scientific conferences, and other venues where comments and responses may be provided in person.

The goal of peer review is to "weed out" science not performed to appropriate standards. This typically means the scientific method has been employed but also state of the art technical procedures have been followed and the conclusions that are drawn are fully supported by the results. Therefore, the reviewer will determine whether proper controls were in place, enough replicates were performed, and that the experiments clearly address the presented hypothesis. The reviewer will scrutinize the interpretations and how they fit into what is already known in the field. Often reviewers will suggest that additional experiments be done to further corroborate presented conclusions.

Occasionally, new scientific results may contradict long held ideas in a particular field. In these cases, in-depth and objective peer review is highly important. Scientists must work together to determine whether the new evidence is correct and how it might change current theories. Typically, there is resistance to the overthrow of scientific theories and many, many experiments must be arduously validated before new, contradictory hypotheses are accepted. Unfortunately, scientists are still people and so can be stubborn and slow to change their ideas. Therefore, **acceptance of new scientific results, even when experiments have been correctly performed, often takes some time.**

Skill 2.5 Understands the relationship, similarities, and differences between science and technology

The union of science, technology, and mathematics has shaped the world we live in today. Science describes the world. It attempts to explain all aspects of how nature works, from our own bodies to the tiny particles making up matter, from the entire earth to the universe beyond. Science lets us know in advance what will happen when a cell splits or when two chemicals react. Yet, science is ever-evolving. Throughout history, people have developed and validated many different ideas about the processes of the universe. Frequently, the development of new technology used in conducting experiments allows for new information and theories to emerge.

Technology makes use of scientific knowledge to solve real-world problems. For example, science is used to study the flow of electrons but technology is required to channel the flow of electrons to create a supercomputer. **Basic research** generally refers to investigation of fundamental scientific principles. **Applied research** is oriented toward making use of basic research in technology development. Applied research is dependent on basic research, and both are necessary for technology advancement. Mathematics in turn provides the language that allows this knowledge to be communicated. It allows the creation of models for scientists to use in explaining natural phenomena and is also the language of technology and computers.

Chemistry is an everyday experience. Some facet of chemistry is involved in every aspect of our daily lives whether in the manufacture of the soaps and cosmetics one uses to get ready for the day, in the synthesis of the fabrics one wears, or in the production of the foods that are consumed daily.

Through the partnership of Chemistry and Biology, enormous advances in medicine and biotechnology have been made in the discovery of the molecular structure of the DNA molecule to the development of the field of medicinal chemistry. We have the ability to clone animals from a single adult cell and cure people of certain types of cancer. In the field of medicinal chemistry, scientists identify, synthesize, develop, and study chemicals to use for diagnostic tools and pharmaceuticals. Most tools in biotechnology originated from chemical technology, and with the continued partnership, better instruments and equipment will continue to be invented. With such developments, doctors can diagnose and treat patients more easily and with greater precision, so that we as a society are able to live longer and healthier lives.

The economy today is dependent upon the existence of technology. The job market changes as new technologies develop. For example, with the advent of computers, many trained workers in information science and technology are needed, moving our economy from a manufacturing-based economy to a knowledge-based economy. Industrial labs are being redefined or eliminated, creating a convergence between scientific disciplines and engineering and providing new entrepreneurial opportunities.

At the same time, advances in scientific knowledge and technology often present ethical dilemmas for society. Industrialization brings the consumption of great amounts of energy. This in turned creates environmental problems, contributes to global conflicts, and depletes natural resources. Scientific knowledge tells us there is oil as shale that we have not yet accessed. Technology developments may allow us to cost-effectively reach this oil and power our economy. At the same time, new technologies will emerge providing for alternative power supplies, such as wind farms or biofuels. New types of skills will be needed to support these new technologies and the job market; education and our society will shift in response.

COMPETENCY 003   THE TEACHER UNDERSTANDS THE ROLE OF MATHEMATICS AND THE UNIFYING CONCEPTS COMMON TO ALL SCIENCES

Skill 3.1   Knows the characteristics and general features of systems; how properties and patterns of systems can be described in terms of space, time, energy, and matter; and how system components and different systems interact

The study of the properties and behavior of systems as a whole is known as **systems theory**. It is a highly interdisciplinary field ranging from physics to philosophy. **A system is composed of parts or activities that work together to form a whole**. The most basic definition of a system is a configuration of parts joined together by various relationships. Systems theory places emphasis on the recognition of the structure of systems and the dependence of its components on one another, even if in a time-delayed fashion. Typically, **the whole has unique properties not possessed by the parts alone.** As a result, systems theory prioritizes characterizing the behavior of the system and not the individual parts. This is occasionally at odds with the more traditional approach to science in which components are isolated as much as possible for study.

Systems theory supports the notion that these isolated components do not behave in the same manner if they are removed from their system. For instance, an individual cell in a Petri dish does not behave in the same manner as it would within an organ inside a person. **In some systems, it is not possible to explain the behavior of the whole in terms of the behavior of the parts**. If you consider the English alphabet, you can see the manner in which each letter is largely meaningless on its own but when used to together the letters form words which convey much information. As another example, it is very difficult to predict the properties of water based on the elemental properties of hydrogen and oxygen. Properties of the whole that go beyond what can be readily predicted by studying the parts are called **emergent properties**.

Systems theory has grown to encompass physics, chemistry, biology, engineering, economics, sociology, political science, management, psychotherapy, and many other disciplines. Therefore, systems-based models have been applied to a wide variety of instances in which multiple components interact. These systems can become quite complex. For instance, consider the human body. To understand how food is used to make energy, studying a single cell from the wall of the small intestine might give you some information about how free nutrients are absorbed. But you must also understand how all the organs in the digestive system work together in sequence to digest the food.

Next, you would study the equally complex process by which energy in sugar is converted to ATP (adenosine triphosphate). Again, simply examining the mechanisms of addition of a phosphate group to ADP (adenosine diphosphate) would not give you a full picture of what is happening. Only when relationships between components in the systems and the relationships between the systems are clear can the entire process be understood. This illustrates that components of systems may be separated by space and time and a single system may interact with other systems to form an even more complex system.

There are certain recurring themes and overarching "rules" that seem to govern science, technology, and mathematics. Those overarching "rules" are the **natural laws**: the laws of gravity, inertia, conservation of energy and mass, and the various ways in which matter naturally behaves. Understanding chemistry is central to understanding these laws and, therefore, to understanding much of science, math and technology. Once one learns how to predict the physical and chemical properties of the elements, he can better predict the reactions of one element with another. Because reactions either need energy and emit energy, the study of chemistry leads to the study of energy transformations which borders on technology, and because those transformations conserve energy and mass, the mathematics must also be understood.

Skill 3.2   Understands how to identify potential sources of error in an investigation, evaluate the validity of scientific data, and develop and analyze different explanations for a given scientific result

See also Skill 1.7 for a discussion of precision and accuracy (and related errors), and Skills 2.3 and 2.4 for discussion of how scientific results are evaluated for validity.

There are many sources of error in a scientific investigation. Being aware of the many types of error that can occur helps researchers design good studies, explain unexpected results, formulate and evaluate alternative hypotheses, and conduct peer review. Several broad categories of errors include the following:

STUDY DESIGN

Errors in study design may include a poorly developed problem statement or hypothesis, improper selection of controls, not controlling enough variables or allowing for too many independent variables at once, and improper selection of materials, equipment, or analytical tools. If you are sampling a population, care needs to be taken that your sampling protocol will result in a sample that is representative of the population you are sampling, to the degree possible. The sample size and/or replication also must be large enough to provide sufficient statistical power for analyzing the results.

CONDUCT OF THE STUDY

Errors may occur if mistakes are made during the experiment, for example, miscalibration of an instrument, measuring incorrectly, setting the temperature too high, misreading an instrument, mislabeling a beaker, or mixing up reagents.

RANDOM AND SYSTEMATIC ERROR

Use of measuring techniques may lead to either random or systematic errors, as discussed in Skill 1.7. It is important to differentiate random measurement error from natural variability in a population, and to be aware of which of the two you are observing. For example, water should always boil at the same temperature under the same environmental conditions, and if you observe variations in the measured temperature, it is most likely due to random error in the measurement.

On the other hand, students have natural variation in their heights, and if you measure such a variation you can be sure that natural variability in the population is what you are observing. Most likely there is also some random error in the measurement, but it is much smaller than the natural variability. If the population you are working with is expected to have natural variability, it is helpful to know the expected magnitude of this variability compared with the magnitude of random error in your measurements to determine whether the random error is likely to interfere with interpretation of the data.

MANIPULATION OF THE DATA

Errors may arise during manipulation of the data once the experiment is over. For example, a number may be incorrectly transcribed from a lab sheet to a spreadsheet. An equation may be set up incorrectly or an error may be made during a calculation. Special care should be used when manipulating data in spreadsheets or databases, as many software programs have inherent errors in their data manipulation routines. For example, the most widely used spreadsheet programs are known to have errors in rounding, treatment of significant digits, and generation of random numbers, as well as certain statistical manipulations. Databases may also automatically convert number fields to other types of data, such as text or dates. All calculations performed by a computer should be spot-checked by hand to ensure that calculations are being performed as intended and that errors (such as rounding errors) are not being propagated through the calculations.

CONCLUSIONS

Data analysis is one of the steps in which conceptual errors can be easily introduced if the researcher is not completely objective and open to alternative hypotheses. Even if the results seem to support the initial hypothesis, the researcher should ask whether alternative hypotheses or explanations are possible, and carefully study all quantitative and qualitative data collected to determine which hypothesis is best supported by all the information gathered. If some aspect of the results doesn't seem to fit, it should be emphasized in the discussion to allow broader review of the issue. Often another researcher may be able to shed light on the seeming discrepancy, but only if it is mentioned and discussed.

PRESENTATION

One of the most important parts of conducting an experiment is presenting it to others. Care should be taken in the presentation to ensure that transcription errors are not introduced, tables and figures are labeled accurately and with complete units, and that the setup, conduct, and results of the study are accurately characterized.

VALIDATION OF RESULTS

In order to validate any scientific data, an experiment should be clearly documented and reproducible. Other researchers reviewing the study should be able to identify the steps taken to reduce all possible sources of error and should have access to the information needed to repeat the experiment. Original laboratory records and instrument print-outs should be archived by the researcher so that they can be made available if there are any questions that need to be investigated.

Skill 3.3   Knows how to apply and analyze the systems model (e.g., interacting parts, boundaries, input, output, feedback, subsystems) across the science disciplines

See also Skill 3.1 for an introduction to the systems model.

One of the key aspects of systems is that the various parts *interact*. **A system is not simply a conglomeration of the various parts, but a description of the relationship between these parts**. Thus, when we model systems, it is important that both the parts and their interactions are elucidated. We can use the system theory approach to examine a man-made system: a savings account. A more traditional view of a savings account would simply show how interest is accrued.

But a systems model might look more like this:

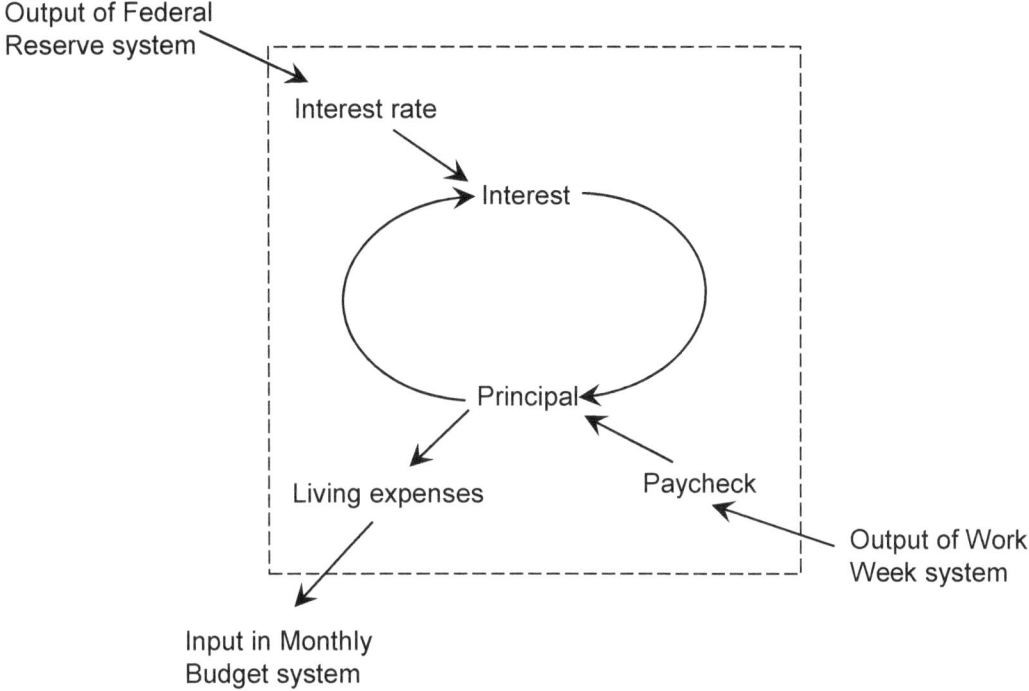

The dashed line encloses the savings account system and it is clear how the various components interact. The systems model makes it clear that principal doesn't simply grow forever; some principal is always lost to living expenses. We are also aware that each of these components belongs to other systems. **The system we have diagrammed provides outputs to and takes inputs from other systems**.

In the natural world, a similar level of complexity in interactions exists and ultimately requires an understanding of various scientific disciplines. For instance, if we wanted to fully explain an ecosystem, we would need to understand how climate (meteorology) and soil types (geology) influence the plant and animals (biology) that thrive and how they ultimately return nutrients to the environment (chemistry).

Our description of this ecosystem could become infinitely large as we include smaller and smaller subsystems within each system and feedback loops between these subsystems. At the same time, this ecosystem would be interacting with other ecosystems, and being acted on by large-scale effects such as weather, seasonal migrations of animals and birds, and human influences. When working with human or natural systems of such great complexity, it is important to define the boundaries of the system you are working with carefully.

Skill 3.4 **Understands how shared themes and concepts (e.g., systems, order, and organization; evidence, models, and explanation; change, constancy, and measurements; evolution and equilibrium; form and function) provide a unifying framework in science**

All fields of science strive to produce useful models of how the universe works. **Experimentation and the scientific method are used to create and test the accuracy of these models**. But it is not just the way in which science is performed that unites the various fields; the **theories that have emerged from these fields also demonstrate some commonality**.

Certain types of structures and relationships are seen throughout the universe. **Complex systems**, for instance, are seen in ants, ant-hills, economies, and modern energy infrastructures. The tendency of a system to achieve **equilibrium** is important whether we are observing chemical reactions or all the components in an ecosystem. The effect described by **chaos theory,** the creation of recognizable order from chaotic systems, has been observed throughout the sciences. In biology, understanding the forces of **evolution** is important whether considering a single biochemical pathway or an entire organism. Closely related is the recurring theme that the **structure** of biological subsystems is almost always a result of their **function**.

Recognizing these themes is highly important. First, sharing common concepts allows scientists working in disparate areas to recognize how they may be able to more quickly understand the world and **solve problems using cross-disciplinary approaches**. Second, these recurring structures provide a starting point from which we may **more accurately hypothesize explanations for various observations**. Thirdly, these common approaches provide scientists in widely divergent fields with a common language, methods of investigation, and means of communicating and validating data that are familiar even if the subject matter is not fully within their area of expertise.

Skill 3.5 **Understands how models are used to represent the natural world and how to evaluate the strengths and limitations of a variety of scientific models (e.g., physical, conceptual, mathematical)**

A scientific model is a set of ideas that describes a natural process. Models may be physical representations like a space-filling model of a molecule, they may be mathematical algorithms or complex software programs, or ideas expressed in the form of philosophy or mathematics.

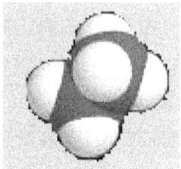

Whatever form they take, scientific models are based on what is known about the systems or objects at the time the models are constructed. Models usually evolve and are improved as scientific advances are made. Sometimes, a model must be discarded because new findings show it to be misleading or incorrect.

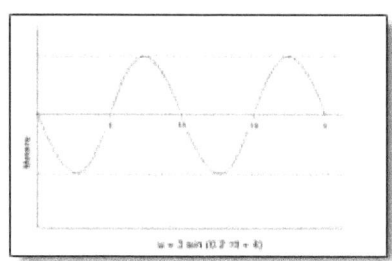

Models are developed in an effort to explain how things work in nature. Because models are not the "real thing," they can never accurately represent the system or object in all respects. The amount of detail that they contain depends upon how the model will be used as well as the sophistication and skill of the scientist doing the modeling. If a model has too many details left out, its usefulness may be limited. But too many details may make a model too complicated to be useful. So it is easy to see why models lack some features of the real system.

To overcome this difficulty, different models are often used to describe the same system or object. Scientists must then choose which model most closely fits the data and in some cases, which one is appropriate for the sophistication of the investigation itself. For example, there are many models of atoms. The "solar system" model is adequate for some purposes, because electrons have properties of matter. They have mass and charge and they are found in motion in the space outside the nucleus. However, a highly mathematical model based on the field of quantum mechanics is necessary when describing the energy (or wave) properties of electrons in the atom.

Scientific models are based on physical observations that establish some facts about the system or object of interest. Scientists then combine these facts with appropriate laws or scientific principles and assumptions to produce a model that mimics the behavior of the system or object to the greatest possible extent. It is on the basis of such models that science makes many of its most important advances, because such models provide a vehicle for making predictions about the behavior of a system or object. The predictions can then be tested as new measurements, technology or theories are applied to the subject. The new information may result in modification and refinement of the model, although certain issues may remain unresolved for years. The goal, however, is to continue to develop the model in such a way as to move it ever closer to a true description of the natural phenomenon. In this way, models are vital to the scientific process.

Skill 3.6 **Understands the importance of mathematics to science and applies scientific conventions and mathematical methods (e.g., significant figures, scientific notation, dimensional analysis, statistical analysis, algebraic manipulation)**

See Skill 1.7 for a discussion of significant digits and scientific notation, Skill 1.8 for a discussion of dimensional analysis, and Skill 1.6 for a discussion of descriptive statistics.

COMPETENCY 004 THE TEACHER UNDERSTANDS THE HISTORY OF SCIENCE, HOW SCIENCE IMPACTS THE DAILY LIVES OF STUDENTS, AND HOW SCIENCE INTERACTS WITH AND INFLUENCES PERSONAL AND SOCIETAL DECISIONS

Skill 4.1 Understands the historical development of science, key events in the history of science, and the contributions that diverse cultures and individuals of both genders have made to scientific knowledge

DEVELOPMENT OF MODERN CHEMISTRY

Chemistry emerged from two ancient roots: **craft traditions** and **philosophy**. The oldest ceramic crafts (i.e., pottery) known are from roughly 10,000 BC in Japan. **Metallurgical crafts** in Eurasia and Africa began to develop by trial and error around 4000-2500 BC resulting in the production of copper, bronze, iron, and steel tools. Other craft traditions in brewing, tanning, and dyeing led to many useful empirical ways to manipulate matter.

Ancient philosophers in Greece, India, China, and Japan speculated that all matter was composed of four or five elements. The Greeks thought that the four elements were fire, air, earth, and water. Indian philosophers and the Greek **Aristotle** also thought a fifth element—"aether" or "quintessence"—filled all of empty space. The Greek philosopher **Democritus** thought that matter was composed of indivisible and indestructible atoms. These concepts are now known as **classical elements** and **classical atomic theory**.

Before the emergence of the **scientific method**, attempts to understand matter relied on **alchemy**: a mixture of mysticism, best guesses, and supernatural explanations. Goals of alchemy included the transmutation of other metals into gold and the synthesis of an elixir to cure all diseases. Ancient Egyptian alchemists developed cement and glass. Chinese alchemists developed gunpowder in the 800s AD.

During the height of European alchemy in the 1300s, the philosopher **William of Occam** proposed the idea that when trying to explain a process or develop a theory, **the simplest explanation with the fewest variables is best**. This is known as **Occam's Razor**. European alchemy slowly developed into modern chemistry during the 1600s and 1700s. This began to occur after **Francis Bacon** and **René Descartes** described the scientific method in the early 1600s.

Robert Boyle was educated in alchemy in the mid-1600s, but he published a book called *The Skeptical Chemist* that attacked alchemy and advocated using the scientific method. He is sometimes called **the founder of modern chemistry** because of his emphasis on proving a theory before accepting it, but the birth of modern chemistry is usually attributed to Lavoisier. Boyle rejected the 4 classical elements and proposed the modern definition of an element. **Boyle's law** states that the volume of a gas is proportional to the reciprocal of pressure.

Blaise Pascal in the mid-1600s determined the relationship between **pressure** and the height of a liquid in a **barometer**. He also helped to establish the scientific method. The SI unit of pressure is named after him.

Isaac Newton studied the nature of **light**, the laws of **gravity**, and the **laws of motion** around 1700. The SI unit of force is named after him.

Daniel Bernoulli proposed the **kinetic molecular theory** for gases in the early 1700s to explain the nature of heat and Boyle's Law. At that time, heat was thought to be related to the release of a substance called *phlogiston* from combustible materials.

James Watt created an efficient **steam engine** in the 1760s-1780s. Later chemists and physicists would develop the theory behind this empirical engineering accomplishment. The SI unit of power is named after him.

Joseph Priestley studied various gases in the 1770s. He was the first to produce and drink **carbonated water**, and he was the first to isolate **oxygen** from air. Priestley thought oxygen was air with its normal phlogiston removed so it could burn more fuel and accept more phlogiston than natural air.

Antoine Lavoisier is called **the father of modern chemistry** because he performed **quantitative, controlled experiments**. He carefully weighed materials before and after combustion to determine that burning objects gain weight. Lavoisier formulated the rule that **chemical reactions do not alter total mass** after finding that reactions in a closed container did not cause the total weight to change. This disproved the phlogiston theory, and he named Priestley's substance oxygen. He demonstrated that air and water were not elements. He defined an element as a substance that could not be broken down further. He published the first modern chemistry textbook, *Elementary Treatise of Chemistry*. Lavoisier was executed in the Reign of Terror at the height of the French Revolution.

GAS LAWS IN THE 1700S AND 1800S

These contributions built on the foundation developed by Boyle in the 1600s.

Jacques Charles developed **Charles' law** in the late 1700s. This law states that gas volume is proportional to absolute temperature.

William Henry developed the law stating that gas solubility in a liquid is proportional to the pressure of gas over the liquid. This is known as **Henry's Law**.

Joseph Louis Gay-Lussac developed the gas law stating that gas pressure is directly proportional to absolute temperature. He also determined that two volumes of hydrogen react with one of oxygen to produce water and that other reactions occur with similar simple ratios. These observations led him to develop the **Law of Combining Volumes**.

Amedeo Avogadro developed the hypothesis that **equal volumes of different gases contain equal numbers of molecules** if the gases are at the same temperature and pressure. The proportionality between volume and number of moles is called **Avogadro's Law**, and the number of molecules in a mole is called **Avogadro's Number**. Both were posthumously named in his honor.

Thomas Graham developed **Graham's Law** of effusion and diffusion in the 1830s. He is called the father of **colloid chemistry**.

ELECTRICITY AND MAGNETISM IN THE 1700S AND 1800S

Benjamin Franklin studied electricity in the mid-1700s. He developed the concept of **positive and negative electrical charges**. His most famous experiment showed that lightning is an electrical process.

Luigi Galvani discovered **bioelectricity**. In the late 1700s, he noticed that the legs of dead frogs twitched when they came into contact with an electrical source.

In the late 1700s, **Charles Augustin Coulomb** derived mathematical **equations for attraction and repulsion** between electrically charged objects.

Alessandro Volta built the first **battery** in 1800 permitting future research and applications to have a source of continuous electrical current available. The SI unit of electric potential difference is named after him.

André-Marie Ampère created a mathematical theory in the 1820s for magnetic fields and electric currents. The SI unit of electrical current is named after him.

Michael Faraday is best known for his work in the 1820s and 1830s establishing that a moving magnetic field induces an electric potential. He built the first **dynamo** for electricity generation. He also discovered benzene, invented oxidation numbers, and popularized the terms **electrode**, **anode**, and **cathode**. The SI unit of electrical capacitance is named in his honor.

James Clerk Maxwell derived the **Maxwell Equations** in 1864. These expressions completely describe **electric and magnetic fields** and their interaction with matter. Also see Ludwig Boltzmann below for Maxwell's contribution to thermodynamics.

NINETEENTH CENTURY CHEMISTRY: CALORIC THEORY AND THERMODYNAMICS

Lavoisier proposed in the late 18th century that the heat generated by combustion was due to a weightless material substance called **caloric** that flowed from one place to another and was never destroyed.

In 1798, **Benjamin Thomson**, also known as **Count Rumford**, measured the heat produced when cannon were bored underwater and concluded that caloric was not a conserved substance because heat could continue to be generated indefinitely by this process.

In the 1820s, **Sadi Carnot** used caloric theory in developing theories for the **heat engine** to explain the engine already developed by Watt. Heat engines perform mechanical work by expanding and contracting a piston at two different temperatures.

Also in the 1820s, **Robert Brown** observed dust particles and particles in pollen grains moving in a random motion. This was later called **Brownian motion**.

Germain Henri Hess developed **Hess' Law** in 1840 after studying the heat taken up by or emitted from reactions composed of several steps.

James Prescott Joule determined the equivalence of heat energy to mechanical work in the 1840s by carefully measuring the heat produced by friction. Joule attacked the caloric theory and played a major role in the acceptance of **kinetic molecular theory**. The SI unit of energy is named after him.

William Thomson, 1st Baron of Kelvin (also called **Lord Kelvin**) recognized the existence of **absolute temperature** in the 1840s and proposed the temperature scale named after him. He failed in an attempt to reconcile caloric theory with Joule's discovery and caloric theory began to fall out of favor.

In the 1840s, **Hermann von Helmholtz** proposed that **energy is conserved** during physical and chemical processes, not heat as proposed in caloric theory.

Rudolf Clausius introduced the concept of **entropy** in the 1860s.

In the 1870s, **Ludwig Boltzmann** generalized earlier work by Maxwell, solving the **velocity or energy distribution among gas molecules** (the Maxwell-Boltzmann distribution).

In the 1870s, **Johannes van der Waals** was the first to consider **intermolecular attractive forces** in modeling the behavior of liquids and non-ideal gases.

Francois Marie Raoult studied colligative properties in the 1870s. He developed **Raoult's Law** relating solute and solvent mole fraction to vapor pressure lowering.

Jacobus van 't Hoff was the first to fully describe **stereoisomerism** in the 1870s. He later studied **colligative properties** and the impact of temperature on equilibria.

Josiah Willard Gibbs studied thermodynamics and statistical mechanics in the 1870s. He formulated the concept now known as **Gibbs free energy**, which determines whether or not a chemical process at constant pressure will spontaneously occur.

Henri Louis Le Chatelier described chemical **equilibrium** in the 1880s using **Le Chatelier's Principle**.

In the 1880s, **Svante Arrhenius** developed the idea of **activation energy**. He also described the dissociation of salts—including **acids and bases**—into ions. Before then, salts in solution were thought to exist as intact molecules and ions were mostly thought to exist as electrolysis products. Arrhenius also predicted that CO_2 emissions would lead to global warming.

In 1905, **Albert Einstein** created a **mathematical model of Brownian motion** based on the impact of water molecules on suspended particles. Kinetic molecular theory could now be observed under the microscope. Einstein's more famous later work on **relativity** may be applied to chemistry by correlating the energy change of a chemical reaction with extremely small changes in the total mass of reactants and products.

DISCOVERY AND SYNTHESIS: NINETEENTH CENTURY

Humphry Davy used Volta's battery in the early 1800s for **electrolysis of salt solutions**. He synthesized several pure elements using electrolysis to generate non-spontaneous reactions.

Jöns Jakob Berzelius isolated several elements, but he is best known for inventing modern **chemical notation** by using one or two letters to represent elements in the early 1800s.

Friedrich Wöhler isolated several elements, but he is best known for the chemical **synthesis of an organic compound** in 1828 using the carbon atom in silver cyanide. Before Wöhler, many had believed that a transcendent "life-force" was needed to make the molecules of life.

Justus von Liebig studied the chemicals involved in agriculture in the 1840s. He has been called the **father of agricultural chemistry**.

Louis Pasteur studied **chirality** in the 1840s by separating a mixture of two chiral molecules. His is better known in biology for discovering the germ theory of disease.

In the 1850s, **Henry Bessemer** developed the **Bessemer Process** for mass producing steel by blowing air through molten iron to oxidize impurities.

Friedrich August Kekulé von Stradonitz studied the chemistry of carbon in the 1850s and 1860s. He proposed the **ring structure of benzene** and the tetravalent nature of carbon.

Anders Jonas Ångström was one of the founders of the science of spectroscopy. In the 1860s, he found hydrogen and other **elements in the spectrum of the sun**. A non-SI unit of length equal to 0.1 nm is named for him.

Alfred Nobel invented the explosive **dynamite** in the 1860s and continued to develop other explosives. In his will he used his fortune to establish the **Nobel Prizes**.

Dmitri Mendeleev developed the first modern **periodic table** in 1869.

Also see Skill 6.5 for a discussion of the development of atomic theory in the 19th and 20th centuries.

DISCOVERY AND SYNTHESIS: TURN OF THE 20TH CENTURY

William Ramsay and **Lord Rayleigh** (John William Strutt) isolated the **noble gases**.

Wilhelm Konrad Röntgen discovered **X-rays**.

Antoine Henri Becquerel discovered **radioactivity** using uranium salts.

Marie Curie named the property radioactivity and determined that it was **a property of atoms** that did not depend on which molecule contained the element.

Pierre and Marie Curie utilized the properties of radioactivity to **isolate radium** and other radioactive elements. Marie Curie was the first woman to receive a Nobel Prize and the first person to receive two. Her story continues to inspire. See http://nobelprize.org/physics/articles/curie/index.html for a biography.

Frederick Soddy and **William Ramsay** discovered that **radioactive decay can produce helium** (alpha particles).

Fritz Haber developed the **Haber Process** for synthesizing ammonia from hydrogen and nitrogen using an iron **catalyst**. Ammonia is still produced by this method to make fertilizers, textiles, and other products.

Robert Andrew Millikan determined the **charge of an electron** using an oil-drop experiment.

Discovery and synthesis: 20th century

Gilbert Newton Lewis described **covalent bonds** as sharing electrons in the 1910s and the **electron pair donor/acceptor theory of acids and bases** in the 1920s. Lewis dot structures and Lewis acids are named after him.

Johannes Nicolaus Brønsted and **Thomas Martin Lowry** simultaneously developed the **proton donor/acceptor theory of acids and bases** in the 1920s.

In the 1920s, **Irving Langmuir** developed the science of **surface chemistry** to describe interactions at the interface of two phases. This field is important to heterogeneous catalysis.

Fritz London studied the electrical nature of chemical bonding in the 1920s. The weak intermolecular **London dispersion forces** are named after him.

Hans Wilhelm Geiger developed the **Geiger counter** for measuring ionizing radiation in the 1930s.

Wallace Carothers and his team first synthesized **organic polymers** (including neoprene, polyester and nylon) in the 1930s.

In the 1930s, **Linus Pauling** published his results on **the nature of the covalent bond**. Pauling electronegativity is named after him. In the 1950s, Pauling determined the α-helical structure of proteins.

Lise Meitner and **Otto Hahn** discovered **nuclear fission** in the 1930s.

Glenn Theodore Seaborg created and isolated several **elements larger than uranium** in the 1940s. Seaborg reorganized the periodic table to its current form.

James Watson and **Francis Crick** determined the double helical structure of DNA in the 1950s.

Neil Bartlett produced **compounds containing noble gases** in the 1960s, proving that they are not completely chemically inert.

Harold Kroto, **Richard Smalley**, and **Robert Curl** discovered the **buckyball (C_{60})** in the 1980s.

Skill 4.2   Knows how to use examples from the history of science to demonstrate the changing nature of scientific theories and knowledge (i.e., that scientific theories and knowledge are always subject to revision in light of new evidence)

The scientific method is defined as principles and procedures for the systematic pursuit of knowledge involving the recognition and formulation of a problem, the collection of data through observation and experiment, and the formulation and testing of hypotheses. This process is used to continually test existing theories and revise them over time. The scientific method is discussed in detail in Skill 2.1.

A **scientific theory** is used to explain an observation or a set of observations. It is generally accepted to be true, though no absolute proof exists. An important feature of a scientific theory is that there are no experimental observations to disprove it, and each piece of evidence that exists supports the theory as written. Theories can be revised over time to include the results of all experimental observations, or even discarded completely if new experimental evidence is accepted by the scientific community and entirely at odds with the original theory.

An example of a theory is the big bang theory. While there is no experiment that can directly test whether or not the big bang actually occurred, there is no strong evidence indicating otherwise.

Theories provide a framework to explain the known information of the time, but are subject to constant evaluation and updating. There is always the possibility that new evidence will conflict with a current theory. For example, the atomic model described in Skill 6.5 underwent many revisions over the centuries as new evidence and measurement techniques became available.

The following are some examples of theories that have been rejected because they are now better explained by current knowledge:

- Theory of spontaneous generation
- Inheritance of acquired characteristics
- The caloric theory

Below are some examples of theories that were initially rejected because they fell outside of the accepted knowledge of the time, but are well-accepted today due to advancement of science:

- The sun-centered solar system
- Warm-bloodedness in dinosaurs
- The germ theory of disease
- Continental drift

Laws of nature are descriptions of phenomena that so far as is known are invariable under the given conditions. If the truth of a statement is verified repeatedly in a reproducible way then it may be considered a law of nature. However, even laws of nature are subject to refinement, particularly as we study the behavior of matter in ever more minute detail. For example, most "laws" of classical mechanics still hold true in the general case, but break down at quantum levels, where relativity and quantum mechanics take over. To be more precise from a mathematical perspective, the laws of classical mechanics are actually special cases of special and general relativity. However, they apply to most real-world activities and are therefore still highly relevant.

Skill 4.3 **Knows that science is a human endeavor influenced by societal, cultural, and personal views of the world and knows that decisions about the use and direction of science are based on factors such as ethical standards, economics, and personal and societal biases and needs**

Science and society are interconnected. Important discoveries in science and technology influence society and have the potential to alter society. For example, the invention of the printing press caused a blurring of the classes and supported scientific endeavors. The printing press allowed inexpensive production of books so that common individuals, not just the wealthy, could access literary works. It became easier to learn to read and write, increasing the education level of all classes. It also became easier to dream of places, things, and worlds not yet discovered. Scientists could work from exactly the same book at the same time, allowing for fewer errors. The printing press also supported the scientific revolution, since scientists could communicate their research results with a larger community at faster rates. The printing press changed the way people thought and looked at their world.

At the same time, the needs of society drive the direction of scientific investigation. The fear that the world would be dominated by Hitler and his supply of powerful new weapons led the United States to begin developing its own atomic bomb. The need to end World War II strengthened the incentive for the Manhattan Project to be successful. On August 6, 1945 the world changed forever. The creation and use of the atomic bomb changed the way society existed. It also changed the direction of science. Would we have discovered nuclear power, the television and computer, nuclear medicine and all of the other discoveries that came from the work of the Manhattan Project scientists otherwise? Probably, but the pace and the development of such technologies might not have occurred so quickly.

The need for technological development drives science, and in turn discoveries in science influence society and allow new technologies to be developed. The first personal computers were mass-marketed by IBM and Apple in the late 1970s. The IBM 5100 had 16K of memory, a five-inch screen, and cost nearly $11,000 in 1975! A mere twenty-five years later, computers are everywhere and used for everything, with gigabytes of memory and monitors larger than some televisions. Why did computers develop so quickly? It was the interconnection between science, technology, and society.

Skill 4.4 Understands the application of scientific ethics to the conducting, analyzing, and publishing of scientific investigations

One form of scientific ethics is to be aware of the potential sources of error in an experiment, as discussed in Skill 3.2, and conduct research carefully to avoid such errors. This is important and a matter of ethics because all scientists build on the work of others. An error in one person's research may lead to incorrect conclusions that affect other scientists' research, and each scientist must accept a share of the responsibility for ensuring that the collective body of knowledge is accurate. For example, it was recently discovered that a computer model being used by one laboratory had transposed the arrangement of atoms in molecular structures to their mirror images. The published structures had already been relied upon by other researchers in the field for three years, and now many papers are having to be retracted and years of work redone. Had the original laboratory checked their computer model more carefully, this situation could have been avoided.

Scientists are expected to truthfully report the results of their experiments without fabricating data. Falsification of certain kinds of results has become easier with the advent of computer software that allows images to be manipulated. In the past decade, there has been an explosion of fraud in the scientific world. Some scientists feel great pressure to make important discoveries that will garner funding, further their career, or enable them to file a patent, and this clouds their judgment. However, scientists are forced to resign and forfeit their careers if they are found to have published false data. The consequences of fraud are expected to be severe, since other scientists worldwide will be utilizing their time and resources to build on the published work.

In most institutions, there are policies against scientists accepting gifts, honoraria, or payment from stakeholders in order to avoid a conflict of interest. Many scientific papers now include a disclosure paragraph stating whether any of the authors currently have any kind of relationship, monetary or otherwise, with a company or other entity that has an interest in the research presented. For example, if a paper is published with the latest experimental results on a new drug, the authors should be truly impartial scientists who have no relationship with the pharmaceutical company that invented the drug and do not stand to benefit financially from acceptance of the drug.

Skill 4.5 Applies scientific principles, probability, and risk/benefit analysis to analyze the advantages of, disadvantages of, or alternatives to a given decision or course of action

Individuals, on a daily basis, make judgments about risks and benefits as part of many decisions. For instance, a person may decide to spend one dollar on a lottery ticket because the potential benefit (millions of dollars in prize money) is great even though the chance of winning is small. Another person may decide that the potentially large pay-off is too unlikely to make it worth spending a dollar. **The science of risk-benefit analysis is simply a more formalized system to help make these decisions**. Many corporations employ risk/benefit analysis in determining future business strategies. Government also evaluates risks and benefits in many of its activities, such as deciding to approve a new drug or to carry out a manned space-flight mission.

Risk combines the probability of an event occurring and the results of that event occurring. For the risk assessment to be accurate, quantitative data are needed on both the probability and the magnitude of the effect. In the example of the lottery ticket above, both the amount of the possible loss ($1) and the probability of losing are known, based on information printed on the ticket. Similarly, the amount of the possible payoff is known, as well as the odds of winning. From this information, each person decides whether or not to take the risk based on the perceptions he or she has of the risk and reward involved. Persons or other entities seeking to avoid risk are said to be risk-averse, while those more comfortable with risk may be considered risk-tolerant or risk-seeking.

When companies are developing new products, this type of risk analysis is performed to determine what potential problems must be addressed; both the probability of an event and its impact must be considered. Therefore, if a certain malfunction is extremely unlikely but could cause consumer death, it must be remedied. Companies typically have an established **tolerance for risk**, usually based on financial considerations, but also taking into account reputation and other non-monetary values.

A simplified standard equation for calculating risk might look like this:

Risk = probability of accident x average cost of accident

We can use a similar technique to determine whether we should undertake a course of action that might have either a positive or a negative outcome. For instance, to determine whether an investment is worthwhile:

Risk/benefit = (probability of positive outcome x pay-off of positive outcome) − (probability of negative outcome x loss associated with negative outcome)

These calculations cannot actually tell someone what he or she should do; they only clarify the risk inherent in doing so. If a person were strictly risk-neutral, he or she would take the risk if the quantity above was positive and would not take the risk if the quantity above was negative. However, most of us are not strictly risk-neutral. We may be more or less risk-averse depending on the amount of money or danger involved and the seriousness of the outcome.

Risk assessment professionals may develop extremely complex models to determine the risks associated with scientific or engineering questions, for example, the risk associated with a chemical exposure or the risk of a dam failure. To perform these calculations, we **must have good data about probabilities**. These data come from properly performed scientific studies. There are some areas of science where the probabilities are not well-known, for example, in epidemiology. In these cases, safety factors are often added to risk assessment equations to account for the uncertainties involved, especially when the adverse effect being evaluated is severe, such as cancer or mortality.

Skill 4.6 **Understands the role science can play in helping to resolve personal, societal, and global issues (e.g., population growth, disease prevention, resource use)**

A baby born today in the United States is expected to live 30 years longer on average than a baby born 100 years ago. A significant contribution to this improvement has been made by the field of chemistry. The manufacture and distribution of vaccines and antibiotics, an increase in understanding human nutritional needs, and the use of fertilizers in agriculture have all played a role in improving the length and quality of human life. However, the benefits of these technologies are frequently accompanied by problems and significant risks that must be taken into account in evaluating their overall value to society.

NUTRITION: GENERAL

Chemistry and related technology helps **keep foods fresh** longer and **alters the molecules** in food. The thermochemistry of refrigeration helps food last longer.

Other technologies such as pasteurization, drying, salting, and the addition of preservatives all prevent microbial contamination by altering the composition of food. **Preservatives** are substances added to food to prevent the growth of microorganisms and the spoilage they cause. For example, potassium and sodium **nitrites** and **nitrates** are often used as preservatives for vegetables, fruits, and processed meats.

Physical separation techniques such as milling, centrifugation, and pressing give flour, oils, and juices that are used as ingredients. **Chemical techniques** are used to prepare fatty acids, amino acids, vitamins, and minerals that are used in nutritional supplements or to fortify processed foods. Some compounds in processed foods are removed intentionally or as an unintended consequence of processing. Other ingredients are added for a wide variety of reasons such as improving taste or decreasing the cost of production.

Eating too much processed food over time has a long history of **causing harm** because of the substances it lacks or contains. Whole, fresh food usually has a better nutritional value. For example, in the late 1800s many infants in the US developed **scurvy (vitamin C deficiency)** from drinking heat-treated milk that controlled bacterial infections but destroyed vitamin C. Local production of food with minimal time-to-market and proper preparation is a healthier approach to food safety than chemical modification and long-distance transport of the food, but processed food will remain popular for the foreseeable future because it is usually cheaper to buy, more profitable to sell, and more convenient to obtain, store, prepare and use.

NUTRITION: HYDROGENATION

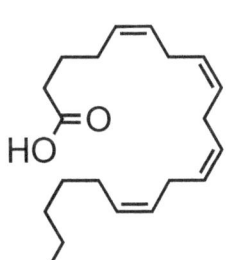

A benefit of chemical technology is the ability to manipulate the chemical structure of molecules. **Hydrogenation** uses a chemical reaction to convert unsaturated to saturated oils. Many plant oils are **polyunsaturated** with double bonds in the *cis-* form as shown at left. These molecules contain rigid bends in them. Complete hydrogenation creates a flexible straight-chain molecule that permits more area for London dispersion forces to form intermolecular bonds. The result is that **hydrogenation increases the melting point** of oils. Semi-solid fats are preferred for baking because the final product has a pleasing taste and texture in the mouth. Unfortunately, saturated fats are less healthy than *cis-* unsaturated fats because they promote obesity and heart disease.

Complete hydrogenation of the molecule above is shown below:

When the hydrogenation process does not fully saturate, it results in partially **hydrogenated** oil. Partial hydrogenation often creates a semi-solid fat in cases where complete hydrogenation would create a fat that is fully solid.

However, **partial hydrogenation** of cis-polyunsaturated fats results in **random isomerization**, creating a **mixture of *cis-* and *trans-*** forms. In the structure below, the molecule at the top of the page has been partially hydrogenated, resulting in the saturation of two double bonds. One of the two remaining *cis-* bonds has been converted to a *trans-* form:

Trans-fatty acids have a slight kink in them compared to *cis-* forms, and they rarely occur in food found in nature. Campaigns against saturated fat in the 1980s led to the increased use of partially hydrogenated oils. The health benefits of **monounsaturated fat** were promoted, but labels made no distinction between *cis-* and *trans-* forms. As a result, there has been an increase in consumption of *trans* fat. Unfortunately, it is now known that ***trans* fat is even less healthy than saturated fat**. Some nations have completely banned the use of partially hydrogenated oils. Food labels in the United States are required to list **total, saturated, and *trans*-fat content**. Fatty acids with one or more *trans* unconjugated double bonds are labeled as *trans* fat under this rule.

NUTRITION: IRRADIATION

Food may also be sterilized and preserved by **food irradiation**. **Gamma rays** from a sealed source of ^{60}Co or ^{137}Cs are used to **kill microorganisms** in over 40 countries. This process is less expensive than refrigeration, canning, or use of additives, and it **does not make food radioactive**.

Opponents of irradiation fear the risks involved in the **transport and use of nuclear materials** to build the facilities and to maintain them. A potential health risk in the food itself is the possibility that the radiation required to kill organisms may alter a biological molecule to produce a harmful by-product, but no evidence has been found of such a toxin. Another concern is that irradiation will lead to a permissive attitude about safe food-handling procedures that can lead to other types of contamination. Food irradiation is still under study in the United States to conclusively prove its safety, particularly for meats.

INDUSTRY

The *chemical industry* usually refers to **industries that manufacture chemicals**. But it could be argued that the impact of those chemicals and the ability to alter matter by chemical technology has **created tools that have improved the industrial production of nearly every substance**. Some divisions of the chemical industry include petrochemicals (chemicals produced from petroleum), oleochemicals (chemicals produced from biological oils and fats), agrochemicals (chemicals for agricultural use), pharmaceuticals, polymers, and paints. Chemical technology has impacted everything from testing and maintaining a clean water supply to the plastics used in cell phones.

These industries make up an entire **sector of the economy**. In the United States, about 900,000 people are employed in the chemical industry, and sales totaled about $500 billion in 2004.

http://pubs.acs.org/cen/coverstory/83/8302wcousa.html

Chemical engineering is the **application of chemistry** along with mathematics and economics to the process of converting raw materials or chemicals into more useful forms. In the development of a new chemical, a chemist typically discovers or **designs the compound** and synthesizes it for the first time. A chemical engineer will then take that information and the **design a process** to manufacture the chemical in the amount required for a useful application. The individual processes used by chemical engineers (such as distillation or solvent extraction) are called **unit operations**. All chemical engineers are trained in process design, but most work in a variety of other disciplines.

MEDICINE

In the field of **medicinal chemistry**, scientists identify, synthesize, develop, and study chemicals that are used as diagnostic tools and pharmaceuticals. **Pharmacology** is the study of how chemical substances interact with living systems. As biological knowledge has increased, the biochemical causes of many diseases have been determined and the field of pharmacology has grown tremendously.

Antibiotics are organic chemicals to **kill or slow the growth of bacteria**. Before antibiotics were available, infections were often treated with moderate levels of systemic poisons like strychnine or arsenic. Antibiotics **target the disease without harming the patient**, and they have saved millions of lives. Unfortunately, some bacteria in **antibiotic resistant strains** have developed defenses against these chemicals since they first became available over 60 years ago. New antibiotics are developed every year in an effort to continue suppressing bacterial diseases.

Biotechnology uses living organisms—often cells in a **fermentation tank** or **bioreactor**—to create useful molecules. The oldest examples are the use of yeast to make bread and beer. Since 1980, **genetic engineering** has been used to design **recombinant DNA** that produces **human protein** molecules in bioreactors using non-human cells. These molecules fight disease by elevating the levels of proteins produced naturally by the human body or by providing proteins that are missing due to genetic disorders. Most tools in biotechnology originated from chemical technology.

AGRICULTURE

Plants, like humans and animals, need adequate water, protection from disease, and certain nutrients to grow. In natural ecosystems, soil fertility is maintained at a sustainable level when the waste products derived from plants are returned to the soil. Human agriculture prevents this from occurring to the same degree, as not all parts of the plant are returned to the earth; some are harvested and sold, burned, or otherwise disposed of. **Fertilizers** are materials given to plants to **promote growth** and replace the missing nutrients. **Nitrogen, phosphorus, and potassium** are the most important elements in fertilizers.

There are many types of fertilizers, including natural materials like manure, seaweed, compost, and minerals. Plants that are able to utilize nitrogen from the atmosphere may also be grown in some seasons so their nitrogen is added to the soil. Many of these natural approaches are thousands of years old. In the 1800s, studies by **von Liebig** and others resulted in the worldwide transport of certain minerals and by-products of the steel industry as fertilizer.

A major breakthrough in the production of fertilizers using chemical processes was the **Haber process for ammonia production** in 1910:

$$N_2(g) + 3H_2(g) \leftrightarrow 2NH_3(g) \text{ over Fe catalyst.}$$

Millions of tons of ammonia are used worldwide each year to supply crops with nitrogen. Ammonia is either added to irrigation water or injected directly into the ground. Many other nitrogen fertilizers are synthesized from ammonia.

Phosphorus in fertilizers originates from phosphate (PO_4^{3-}) in mineral deposits. Potassium in fertilizers comes from evaporated ancient seabeds in the form of potassium oxide (K_2O).

Pesticides are used to control or kill organisms that harm crops, compete with humans for food, spread disease, or are considered a nuisance. Herbicides are pesticides that attack weeds, insecticides attack insects, and fungicides attack molds and other fungus. Sulfur was used as a fungicide in ancient times. The development and use of new pesticides has exploded over the last 60 years, but these pesticides are often poisonous to humans, fish, and wildlife.

Farming designed to **maximize productivity** is called **intensive agriculture**. Intensive fertilizer and pesticide use in combination with other farming techniques decreased the number of farm laborers needed and gave a growing world population enough to eat over the last 50 years. Intensification of agriculture in developing countries is known as the **green revolution**. These techniques were credited with saving a billion people from starvation in India and Pakistan alone.

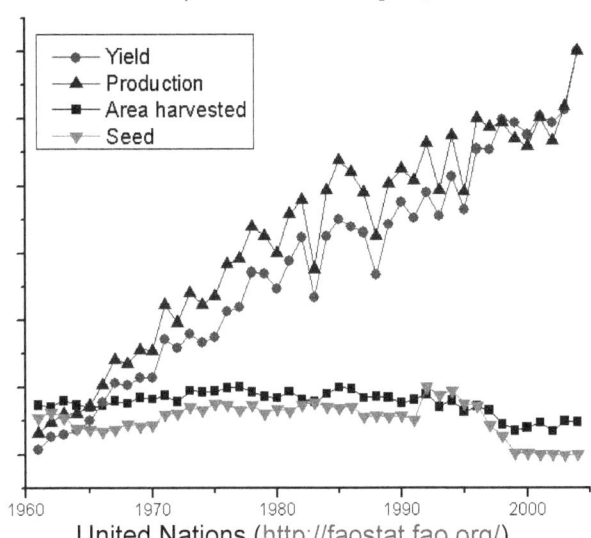

United Nations (http://faostat.fao.org/)

The **insecticide DDT** was widely used in the 1940s and 1950s and is responsible for **eradicating malaria from Europe and North America**. It quickly became the most widely used pesticide in the world. In the 1960s, it was discovered that DDT was responsible for widespread reductions in bird populations and causes birth defects in humans. DDT is now banned in many countries, but it is still used in developing nations to prevent diseases carried by insects. Unfortunately, its use in agriculture has often led to resistant mosquito strains that have hindered its effectiveness.

The **herbicide *Roundup*** kills all natural plants it encounters while breaking down in the environment within a few days, making it a relatively safe herbicide compared to more persistent compounds. It began to be used in the 1990s in combination with **genetically engineered crops** that include a gene intended to make the crop (and only the crop) resistant to the herbicide. This combination of chemical and genetic technology has been an economic success but it has raised many concerns about potential problems in the future should these crops hybridize with other strains and propagate the resistant gene.

ENVIRONMENT

Many chemical technologies that save lives or improve the quality of life in the short term have had a negative long-term impact on the environment and human health. Chemical **pollution** is often divided into gas, liquid, and solid waste materials. Additional technologies often exist remediate these effects and clean up pollution.

Most scientists believe the emission of **greenhouse gases** has already led to **global warming** due to an increase in **the greenhouse effect**. The greenhouse effect occurs when these gases in the atmosphere warm the planet by **absorbing heat** to prevent it from escaping into space. This is similar—but not identical—to what occurs in greenhouse buildings. Greenhouse buildings warm an interior space by preventing mixing with colder air outside. Most greenhouse gases such as water vapor occur naturally and are important for life to exist on Earth, but are being added to the atmosphere is much larger quantities by human activities.

Human production of **carbon dioxide** from combustion of fossil fuels has increased the concentration of this important greenhouse gas to its highest value since millions of years ago. The precise impact of these changes in the atmosphere is difficult to predict with certainty, but is likely to include a rise in sea level, an increase in extreme weather events, reduction of glaciers and snowpack, increasing drought, and changes in habitat and species distributions.

Rain with a pH less than 5.6 is known as **acid rain**. Acid rain is caused by burning fossil fuels (especially coal) and by fertilizers used in intensive agriculture. These activities emit sulfur and nitrogen in gaseous compounds that are converted to sulfur oxides and nitrogen oxides. These in turn create sulfuric acid and nitric acid in rain. Acid rain may also be created from gases emitted by volcanoes and other natural sources. Acid rain harms fish and trees and triggers the release metal ions from minerals into water that can harm people. It can also have destructive effects on building surfaces, statues, and sculptures.

The problem of acid rain in the United States has been addressed to some extent in recent decades by the use of **scrubbers** in coal burning power plants and **catalytic converters** in vehicles.

The **ozone layer** is a region of the stratosphere that contains higher concentrations of ozone (O_3) than other parts of the atmosphere. The ozone layer is important for human health because it **blocks ultraviolet radiation** from the sun, helping to protect us from skin cancer.

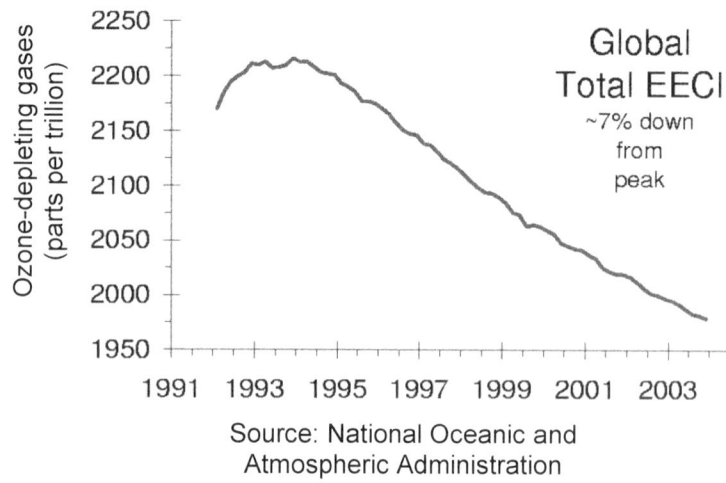

Research in the 1970s revealed that several gases used for refrigeration and other purposes were depleting the ozone layer. Many of these ozone-destroying molecules are short alkyl halides known as **chlorofluorocarbons** or **CFCs**. CCl_3F is one example of these compounds. The widespread use of ozone-destroying compounds was banned by an international agreement in the early 1990s. Other substances are used in their place such as CF_3CH_2F, a hydrofluorocarbon. Since that time the concentration of ozone-depleting gases in the atmosphere has been declining and **the rate of ozone destruction has been decreasing**. Many see this improvement as one of the most important positive examples of international cooperation to solve a global environmental issue. The story of these new refrigerants is found at http://www.chemcases.com/fluoro/index.htm.

TEACHER CERTIFICATION STUDY GUIDE

DOMAIN II. **MATTER AND ENERGY**

COMPETENCY 005 THE TEACHER UNDERSTANDS THE CHARACTERISTICS OF MATTER

Skill 5.1 Differentiates between physical and chemical properties and changes of matter

PHYSICAL PROPERTIES

A physical property of matter is a property that can be determined without inducing a chemical change. Melting point, boiling point, specific heat, hardness, density, and conductivity are all examples of physical properties. Any given element or chemical compound will have a unique set of physical properties and can be identified through these properties.

Matter may go through physical changes without any chemical modification of the elements or compounds that make up the matter. For example, a substance may be divided into smaller pieces without changing the nature of the substance. Matter may also go undergo phase changes among gas, liquid, and solid forms without changing its fundamental nature.

CHEMICAL PROPERTIES

The chemical properties of an element or compound are those that affect chemical reactions. For example, these include electronegativity, oxidation state, ionization potential, chemical structure, and type of chemical bonds.

Unlike a phase change, which is a change between two physical states (see Skill 5.2), a chemical change rearranges atoms to form a new molecule. The idea that chemical changes are due to the rearrangement of atoms in molecules formed the basis of Dalton's atomic theory.

CHANGES OF MATTER

See Skill 5.2 below for a detailed discussion of phase changes between states of matter (solids, liquids, and gases).

Skill 5.2 Explains the structure and properties of solids, liquids, and gases

Molecules have **kinetic energy** (they move around), and they also have **intermolecular attractive forces** (they are attracted to each other). The relationship between these two properties determines whether a collection of molecules will be a gas, liquid, or solid under various conditions of temperature and pressure.

A **gas** has an indefinite shape and an indefinite volume. The kinetic model for a gas is a collection of widely separated molecules, each moving in a random and free fashion, with negligible attractive or repulsive forces between them. Gases will expand to occupy a larger container so there is more space between the molecules. Gases can also be compressed to fit into a small container so the molecules are less separated.

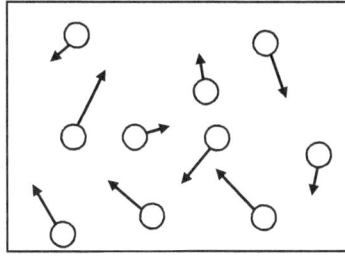

Diffusion occurs when one material spreads into or through another. Gases diffuse rapidly and easily move from one place to another.

A **liquid** assumes the shape of any container that it occupies and has a specific volume. The kinetic model for a liquid is a collection of molecules attracted to each other with sufficient strength to keep them close to each other but with insufficient strength to prevent them from moving around randomly. Liquids have a higher density and are much less compressible than gases because the molecules in a liquid are closer together. Diffusion occurs more slowly in liquids than in gases because the molecules in a liquid stick to each other and are not completely free to move.

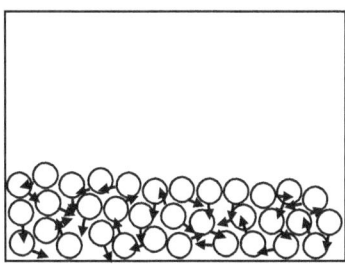

A **solid** has a definite volume and definite shape regardless of the container it is in. The kinetic model for a solid is a collection of molecules attracted to each other with sufficient strength to essentially lock them in place. Each molecule may vibrate, but it has an average position relative to its neighbors. If these positions form an ordered pattern, the solid is called **crystalline**. Otherwise, it is called **amorphous**.

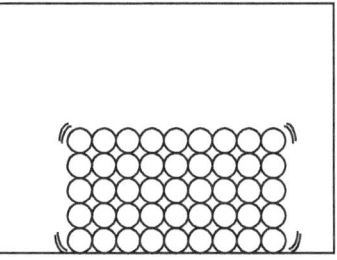

Solids have a high density and are almost incompressible because the molecules are very close together. Diffusion occurs extremely slowly because the molecules almost never alter their position.

Phase changes occur when the relative importance of kinetic energy and intermolecular forces is altered sufficiently for a substance to change its state.

In a solid, the energy of intermolecular attractive forces (such as ionic or covalent bonds) is much stronger than the kinetic energy of the molecules. As temperature increases in a solid, the vibrations of individual molecules grow more intense and the molecules spread slightly further apart, decreasing the density of the solid. (See the next skill for a full discussion of solids.)

In a liquid, the energy of intermolecular attractive forces (such as dipole-dipole and London dispersion forces) is about as strong as the kinetic energy of the molecules. Therefore, both play a role in the properties of liquids. Liquids will be discussed in detail later.

In a gas, the energy of intermolecular forces is much weaker than the kinetic energy of the molecules. Kinetic molecular theory is usually applied to gases.

The transition from gas to liquid is called **condensation** and from liquid to gas is called **vaporization**. The transition from liquid to solid is called **freezing** and from solid to liquid is called **melting**. The transition from gas to solid is called **deposition** and from solid to gas is called **sublimation**.

Heat removed from a substance during condensation, freezing, or deposition permits new intermolecular bonds to form, and heat added to a substance during vaporization, melting, or sublimation breaks intermolecular bonds. During these phase transitions, this **latent heat** is removed or added with **no change in the temperature** of the substance because the heat is not being used to alter the speed of the molecules or the kinetic energy when they strike each other or the container walls. Latent heat alters intermolecular bonds.

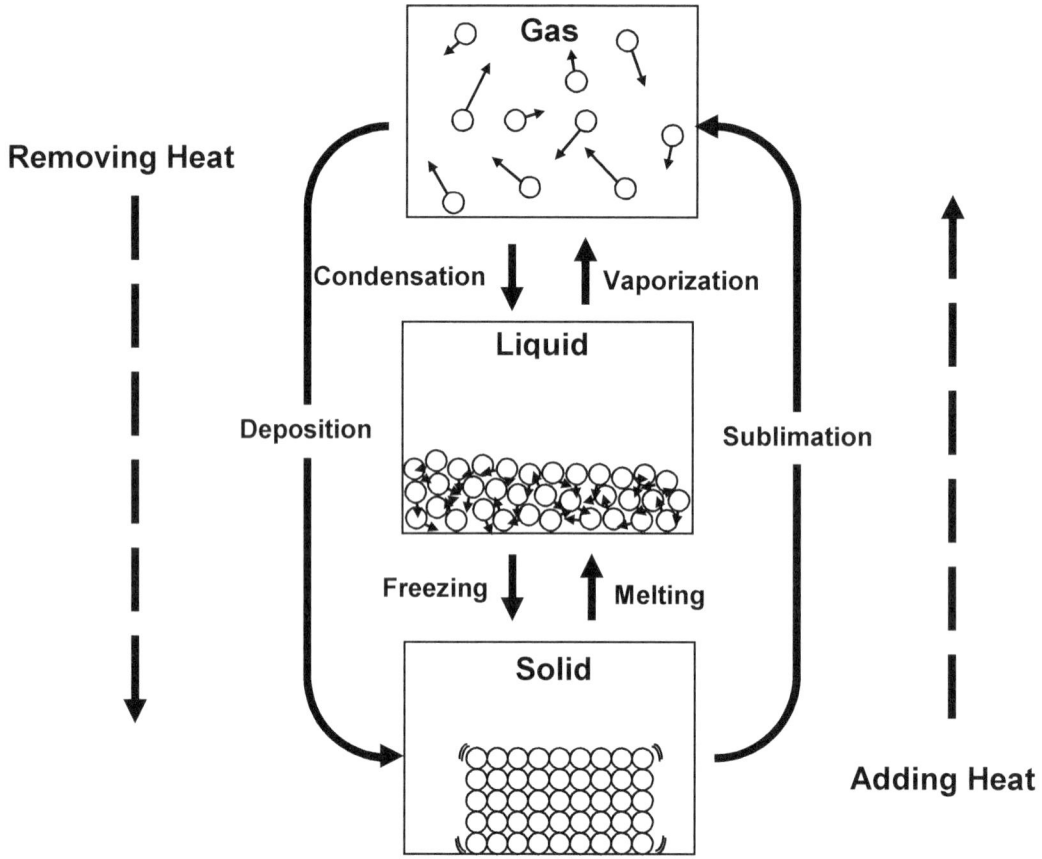

If a time graph was made of a pure substance being heated or cooled, it would look something like this graph for the heating of water. Different changes are taking place during each interval on the graph.

When the system is heated, energy is transferred into it. In response to the energy it receives, the system changes, either by increasing its temperature or changing phase.

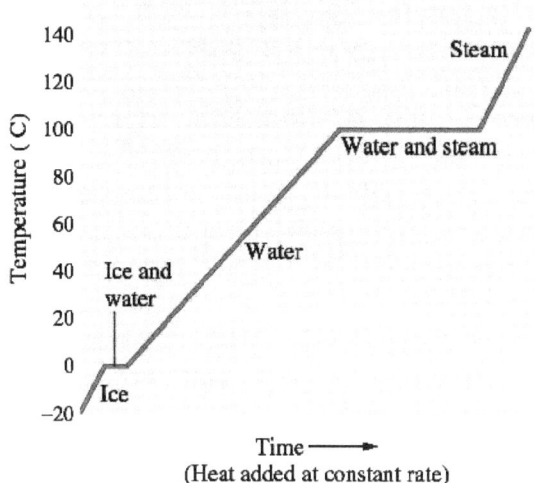

During the interval marked A on the graph below, energy is being absorbed by the water molecules to increase the temperature to water's melting point, 0° C. The slope of the line for this interval shows the increase in temperature and is related to the heat capacity of the substance.

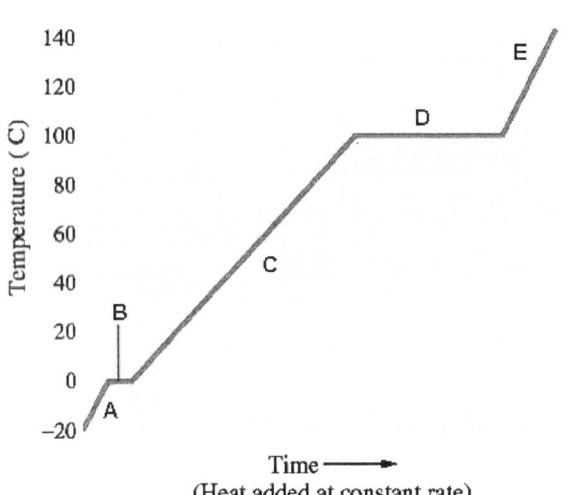

During the interval marked B on the graph, energy is still being added to the water but the temperature remains the same, at 0° C or water's melting point temperature. The additional energy is being used to overcome the intermolecular forces holding the water molecules in their solid pattern. This energy is moving the particles apart, breaking or weakening the forces of attraction that keep the water molecules aligned. The solid water (ice) is being converted to liquid water; a phase change is occurring. The temperature will not increase until every solid particle has melted and the entire sample is liquid.

Temperature again increases during interval C on the graph. Energy is being absorbed by the liquid water molecules. Notice that the slope of the line during this interval is different than the slope of the line during interval A. This is due to differences in the heat capacity of ice and liquid water.

The flat line during interval D indicates that a phase change is occurring. The additional energy is being used to overcome the attractive forces holding the liquid water molecules together. The water molecules increase their kinetic energies and move farther apart, changing to water vapor. This occurs at the boiling point temperature, or 100° C. The temperature stays at the boiling point temperature until all water molecules are converted to water vapor. Once this conversion occurs, the temperature increases as energy is added, according to the heat capacity of the substance as a vapor.

A **phase diagram** is a graphical way to summarize the environmental conditions under which the different states of a substance are stable. The diagram is divided into three areas representing the three possible states of the substance (gas, liquid, or solid). Temperature and pressure determine the phase of a substance and are shown on the x-axis and y-axis of the phase diagram, respectively.

The curves separating each area represent the boundaries of phase changes Below is a typical phase diagram. It consists of three curves that divide the diagram into regions labeled "solid," "liquid," and "gas."

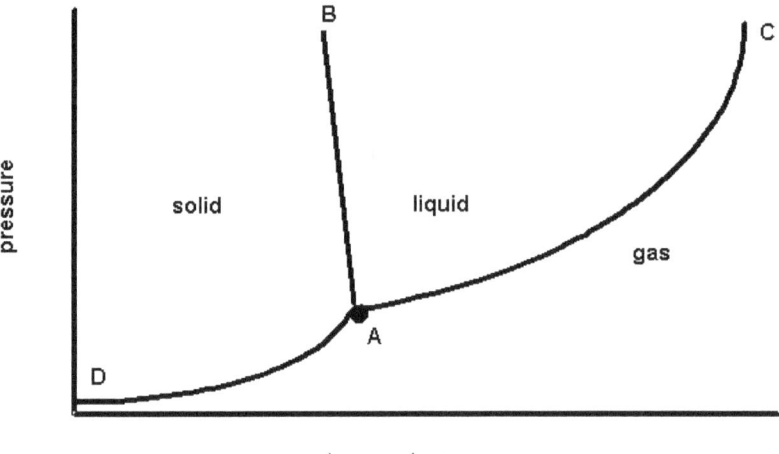

Curve **AB**, dividing the solid region from the liquid region, represents the conditions under which the solid and liquid are in equilibrium. Usually, the melting point is only slightly affected by pressure. For this reason, the melting point curve, AB, is nearly vertical.

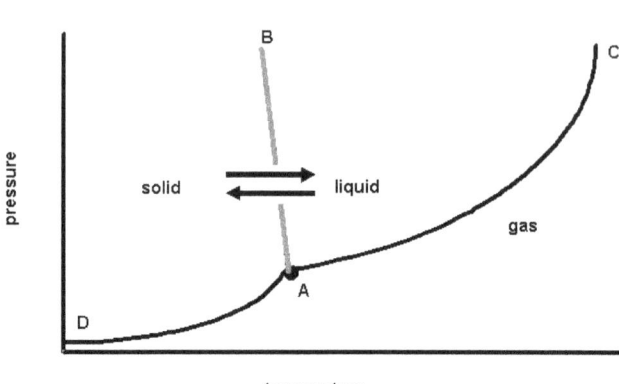

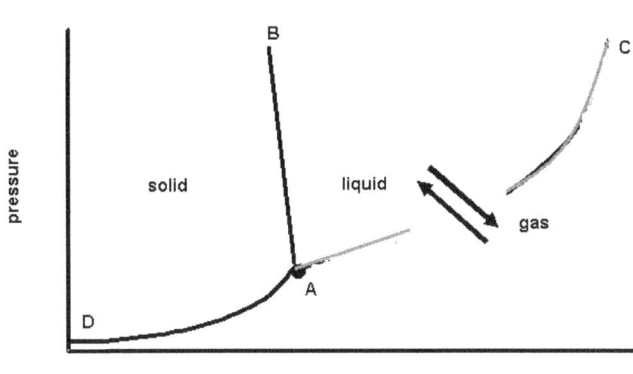

Curve **AC**, which divides the liquid region from the gaseous region, represents the boiling point of the liquid at various pressures. This temperature is much more dependent on atmospheric pressure because of the effect of pressure on gases.

Curve **AD**, which divides the solid region from the gaseous region, represents the vapor pressure of the solid at various temperatures.

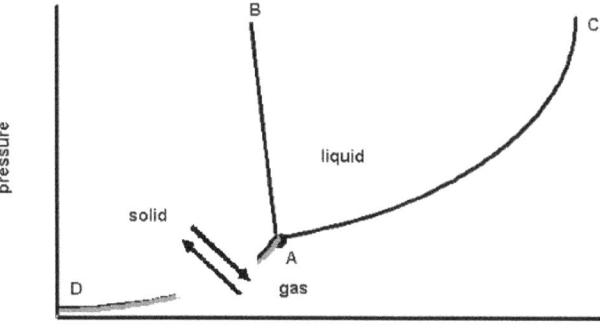

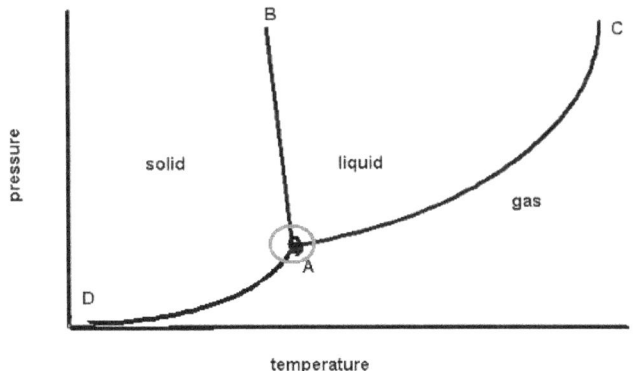

The curves intersect at **A**, the **triple point**, which is the temperature and pressure at which all three phases of a substance exist in equilibrium.

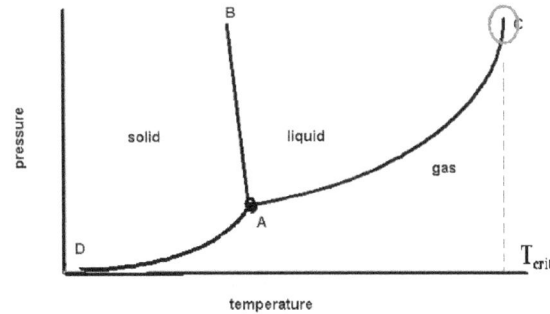

The temperature above which the liquid state of a substance no longer exists regardless of pressure is called the **critical temperature**.

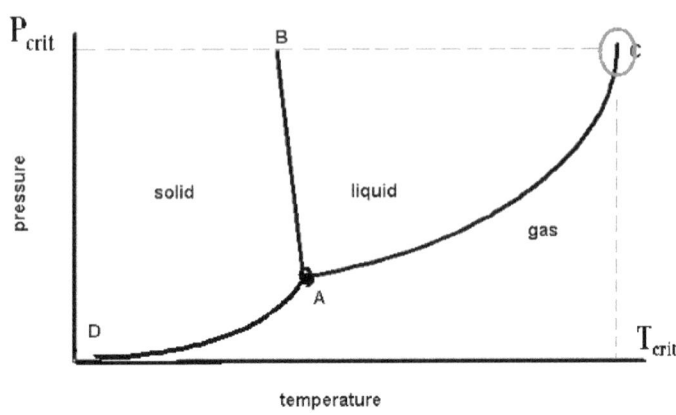

The vapor pressure at the critical temperature is called the **critical pressure**. Note that curve AC ends at the **critical point, C.**

The phase diagram for water is unusual. The solid/liquid phase boundary slopes to the left with increasing pressure because the melting point of water decreases with increasing pressure. Note that the normal melting point of water is lower than its triple point. The diagram is not drawn to a uniform scale.

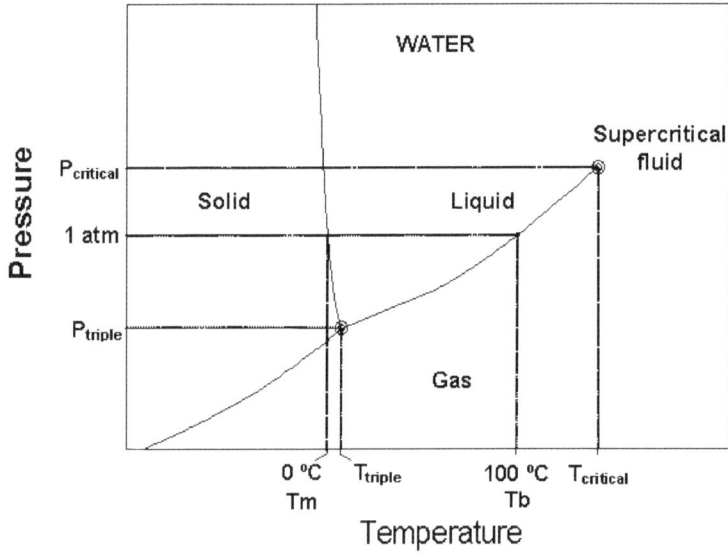

Many anomalous properties of water are discussed here:
http://www.lsbu.ac.uk/water/anmlies.html.

The **normal melting point** (T_m) and **normal boiling point** (T_b) of a substance are defined at 1 atm. Note that freezing point and melting point refer to the same temperature approached from different directions, but they represent the same concept.

This is the phase diagram for carbon dioxide, CO_2. It shows the same features as that of water, only at different temperatures and pressures.

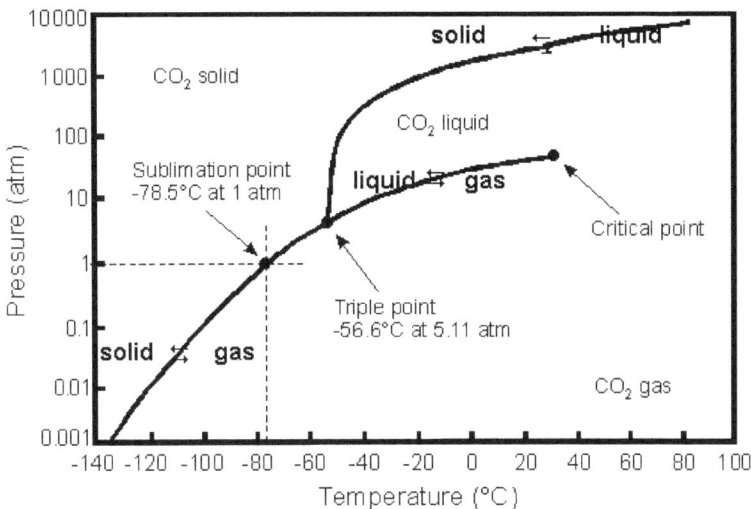

Skill 5.3 Identifies and analyzes properties of substances (i.e., elements and compounds) and mixtures

The word "matter" describes everything that has physical existence, defined as anything that has mass and takes up space. However, matter is often separated into categories. Matter can be described as either a **pure substance or a mixture.** Each of these classes can also be divided into smaller categories such as element, compound, homogeneous mixture or heterogeneous mixture based on composition.

PURE SUBSTANCES

A pure substance is a form of matter with a definite composition and distinct properties. This type of matter cannot be separated by physical processes such as filtering, centrifugation, or distillation.

Pure substances are divided into elements and compounds:

- **Elements.** A single type of matter, called an atom or element, is present. Elements can not be broken down any farther by ordinary chemical processes. They are the smallest whole part of a substance that still represents that substance.

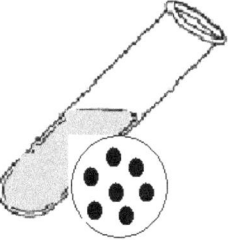

- **Compounds.** A single molecule is present, composed of two or more elements. A compound may be broken down into its elements through chemical reactions. Compounds have a uniform composition regardless of the sample size or source of the sample.

MIXTURES

Mixtures are composed of two or more pure substances that are not chemically combined. Mixtures may be of any proportion and can be physically separated by processes such as filtering, centrifuging, or distillation.

Mixtures can be classified according to particle size.

- **Homogeneous Mixtures.** Homogeneous mixtures have the same composition and properties throughout the mixture and are also known as solutions. They have a uniform color and distribution of solute and solvent particles throughout the mixture.

- **Heterogeneous Mixtures.** Heterogeneous mixtures do not have a uniform distribution of particles throughout the mixture. The different components of the mixture can be identified and separated through physical processes.

Skill 5.4   Identifies elements and isotopes by atomic number and mass number

The identity of an **element** depends on the **number of protons** in the nucleus of the atom. This value is called the **atomic number** and it is sometimes written as a subscript before the symbol for the corresponding element. Atoms and ions of a given element that differ in number of neutrons have a different mass and are called **isotopes**. A nucleus with a specified number of protons and neutrons is called a **nuclide**, and a nuclear particle, either a proton or neutron, may be called a **nucleon**. The total number of nucleons is called the **mass number** and may be written as a superscript before the atomic symbol.

$^{14}_{6}C$ represents an atom of carbon with 6 protons and 8 neutrons.

The **number of neutrons** may be found by **subtracting the atomic number from the mass number**. For example, uranium-235 has 235 – 92 = 143 neutrons because it has 235 nucleons and 92 protons.

Different isotopes have different natural abundances and nuclear properties, but an atom's chemical properties are almost entirely due to the electrons that surround the nucleus.

Some nuclei are unstable and emit particles and electromagnetic radiation. These emissions from the nucleus are known as **radioactivity**, the unstable isotopes are known as **radioisotopes**, and the nuclear reactions that spontaneously alter them are known as **radioactive decay**.

Skill 5.5 Understands the structure, significance, and history of the periodic table

The first periodic table was developed in 1869 by Dmitri Mendeleev. Mendeleev arranged the elements in order of increasing atomic mass into **columns of similar physical and chemical properties**. He then predicted the existence and the properties of undiscovered elements to fill the gaps in his table. These interpolations were treated with skepticism until three of Mendeleev's theoretical elements were discovered and were found to have the properties he predicted.

In the modern periodic table shown just after the Table of Contents, **elements are arranged in numerical order by atomic number**. The elements in a **column are known as a group**, and groups are numbered from 1 to 18. Older numbering styles used roman numerals and letters. **Elements with similar properties are called a family** or a **chemical series**. The modern table, like Mendeleev's, places elements with similar properties into columns. Families are called **group names** when they correspond to a single column. **A row of the periodic table is known as a period**. Periods of the known elements are numbered from 1 to 7.

The periodic table is also organized to correspond to electron configurations within the atom. The table may be divided into blocks corresponding to the subshell of the orbital filled most recently by an electron. Elements in the same column have similar properties because they have the same valence (outermost) electron configurations. These are the electrons that are most important in determining chemical properties (see Skill 6.1). Additional information on the organization of the periodic table and how it affects physical and chemical properties of the elements is provided in Skill 6.4.

COMPETENCY 006 THE TEACHER UNDERSTANDS THE STRUCTURE AND CHARACTERISTICS OF ATOMS

Skill 6.1 Models the atom in terms of protons, neutrons, and electron clouds

Protons have a positive charge, **neutrons** have no charge, and **electrons** have a negative charge. Atoms have no net charge and thus have an equal number of protons and electrons. **Anions** are negative ions and contain more electrons than protons. **Cations** are positive ions and contain more protons than electrons. Protons and neutrons are contained in a small volume at the center of the atom called the **nucleus**. Electrons move in the remaining space of the atom and have very little mass—about 1/1800 of the mass of a proton or neutron. Electrons are prevented from flying away from the nucleus by the attraction that exists between opposite electrical charges. This force is known as **electrostatic** or **coulombic** attraction.

Protons and neutrons each contain three **quarks**. A neutron consists of one *up* quark and two *down* quarks. A proton consists of two *up* quarks and one *down* quark. Quarks are a fundamental constituent of matter according to the current standard model of particle physics, but individual quarks are not seen. Instead they are always confined within other subatomic particles. There is no need to consider quarks when describing chemical interactions. **Only electrons are involved in chemical reactions**. The position and sizes of these particles in a helium atom is indicated in the diagram at right. A diagram like this one could never be drawn to scale. If a proton were drawn 1 cm in diameter, the atom's diameter would require a page about 1 km long.

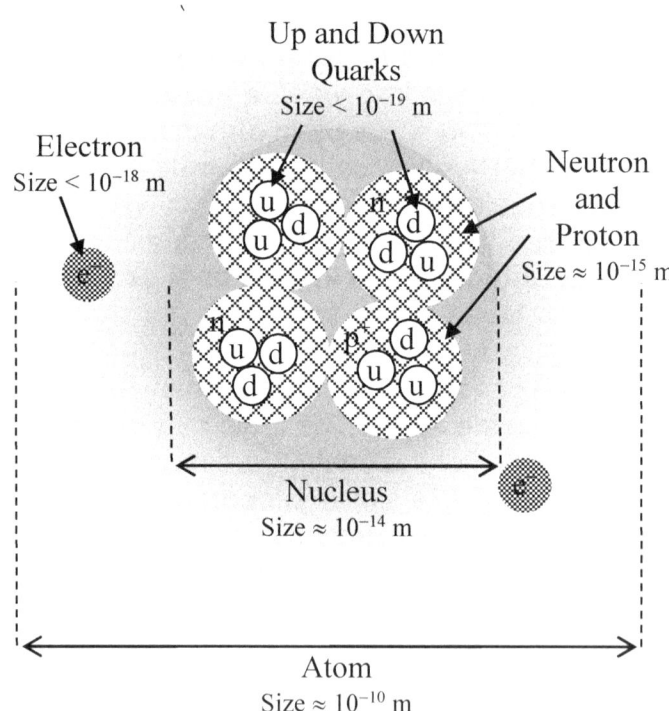

Electrons are found outside the nucleus in a fuzzy area called the electron cloud. It is not possible to know exactly where any electron is but we do know the most probable place to find an electron with a certain energy. This is an orbital or an energy level.

When an electron is in its unexcited or ground state, there are seven energy levels. These seven energy levels match the seven periods (rows) of the Periodic Table. The valence, or outermost, electrons are found in the energy level that corresponds to the period number. Each energy level varies in the number of electrons it can hold.

Within each energy level, the electrons are arranged into various sublevels called orbitals. The orbitals of the unexcited state atom include s, p, d, and f orbitals. Electrons fill these orbitals in a pre-determined pattern, starting with the lowest energy orbitals first. s orbitals are the lowest energy so they are filled first with a maximum of two electrons, followed by the p orbitals. There are three different p orbitals, each holding up to two electrons on each energy level. There are five different d orbitals followed by seven different f orbitals.

Energy level	Maximum Number of Electrons
1	2
2	8
3	18
4	32
5	50, theoretical, not filled
6	72, theoretical, not filled
7	98, theoretical, not filled

Examples of the s, p, and d orbitals are shown below:

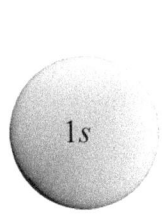
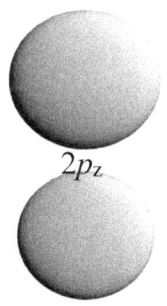
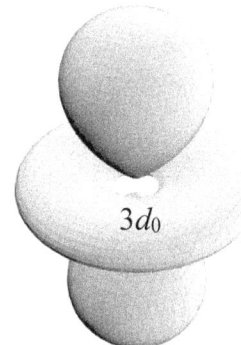

Skill 6.2   Understands atomic orbitals and electron configurations and describes the relationship between electron energy levels and atomic structure

The position of an element in the periodic table may be related to its electron configuration, and this configuration in turn results from the quantum theory describing the filling of a shell of electrons.

QUANTUM NUMBERS

The quantum-mechanical solutions from the Schrödinger Equation (described in Skills 4.1 and 6.5) utilize three quantum numbers (n, l, and m_l) to describe an orbital and a fourth (m_s) to describe an electron in an orbital. This model is useful for understanding the frequencies of radiation emitted and absorbed by atoms and chemical properties of atoms.

The **principal quantum number n** may have positive integer values (1, 2, 3, …). n is a measure of the **distance** of an orbital from the nucleus, and orbitals with the same value of n are said to be in the same **shell**. Each shell may contain up to $2n^2$ electrons. The highest quantum number n that any shell of an element has is the same as the number of the row of the periodic table in which the element is found.

The **azimuthal quantum number l** may have integer values from 0 to n-1. l describes the angular momentum of an orbital. This determines the orbital's **shape**. Orbitals with the same value of n and l are in the same **subshell**, and each subshell may contain up to $4l + 2$ electrons. Subshells are usually referred to by the principle quantum number followed by a letter corresponding to l as shown in the following table:

Azimuthal quantum number l	0	1	2	3	4
Subshell designation	s	p	d	f	g

Therefore, s subshells may have $4 \times 0 + 2 = 2$ electrons, and p subshells may have $4 \times 1 + 2 = 6$ electrons. Helium is in the first row of the periodic table, and has only a single s subshell with two electrons. This subshell would be notated as 1s.

The **magnetic quantum number** m_l or m may have integer values from $-l$ to l. This means that in any given shell, there is only one s orbital with an m value of 0. If p orbitals are present in a shell there will always be 3 p orbitals with values of -1, 0, and 1 (usually referred to as x, y, and z to denote 3-dimensional orientation). A subscript—either the value of m_l or a function of the x-, y-, and z-axes—is used to designate a specific orbital within a subshell. For example, $n=3$, $l=2$, and $m_l=0$ would be indicated as the $3d_0$ orbital. Each orbital may hold up to two electrons.

The **spin quantum number** m_s or s has one of two possible values: $-1/2$ or $+1/2$. m_s differentiates between the two possible electrons occupying an orbital.

Electrons moving through a magnet behave as if they were tiny magnets themselves spinning on their axis in either a clockwise or counterclockwise direction. These two spins may be described as $m_s = -1/2$ and $+1/2$ or as down and up.

The **Pauli exclusion principle** states that **no two electrons in an atom may have the same set of four quantum numbers**.

The following table summarizes the relationship among n, l, and m_l through $n=3$:

n	l	Subshell	m_l	Orbitals in subshell	Maximum number of electrons in subshell
1	0	1s	0	1	2
2	0	2s	0	1	2
	1	2p	−1, 0, 1	3	6
3	0	3s	0	1	2
	1	3p	−1, 0, 1	3	6
	2	3d	−2, −1, 0, 1, 2	5	10

SUBSHELL ENERGY LEVELS

In single-electron atoms (H, He$^+$, and Li^{2+}), subshells within a shell are all at the same energy level, and an orbital's energy level is only determined by n. However, in all other atoms, multiple electrons repel each other. Electrons in orbitals closer to the nucleus create a screening or **shielding effect** on electrons further away from the nucleus, preventing them from receiving the full attractive force of the nucleus. **In multi-electron atoms, both n and l determine the energy level of an orbital**. In the absence of a magnetic field, **orbitals in the same subshell with different m_l all have the same energy** and are said to be **degenerate orbitals**.

The following list orders subshells by increasing energy level:
1s < 2s < 2p < 3s < 3p < 4s < 3d < 4p < 5s < 4d < 5p < 6s < 4f < 5d < 6p < 7s < 5f < ...

This list may be constructed by arranging the subshells according to n and l and drawing diagonal arrows as shown below

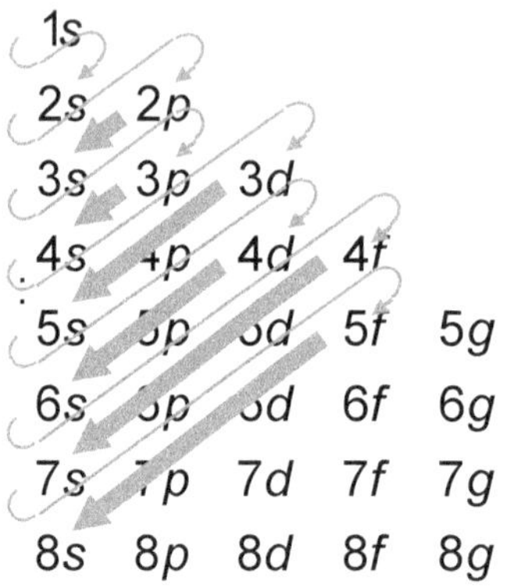

```
1s
2s  2p
3s  3p  3d
4s  4p  4d  4f
5s  5p  5d  5f  5g
6s  6p  6d  6f  6g
7s  7p  7d  7f  7g
8s  8p  8d  8f  8g
```

ELECTRON SHELL STRUCTURES

Electron shell structures (also called electron arrangements) in an atom may be represented using three methods: an **electron configuration**, an **orbital diagram**, or an **energy level diagram**.

All three methods require knowledge of the subshells occupied by electrons in an atom. The **Aufbau principle** or **building-up rule** states that **electrons at ground state fill orbitals starting at the lowest available energy levels**.

An **electron configuration** is a **list of subshells** with superscripts representing the **number of electrons** in each subshell. For example, an atom of boron has 5 electrons. According to the Aufbau principle, two will fill the 1s subshell, two will fill the next-highest energy 2s subshell, and one will occupy the 2p subshell which has an even higher energy. The electron configuration of boron is $1s^2 2s^2 2p^1$. Similarly, the electron configuration of a vanadium atom with 23 electrons is

$$1s^2 2s^2 2p^6 3s^2 3p^6 4s^2 3d^3$$

Configurations are also written with their principle quantum numbers together:

$$1s^2 2s^2 2p^6 3s^2 3p^6 3d^3 4s^2$$

Electron configurations are often written to emphasize the outermost electrons, rather than writing the entire configuration. This is done by writing the symbol in brackets for the element with a full *p* subshell from the previous shell and adding the **outer electron configuration** onto that configuration. The element with the last full *p* subshell will always be a noble gas from the right-most column of the periodic table. For the vanadium example, the element with the last full *p* subshell has the configuration $1s^2 2s^2 2p^6 3s^2 3p^6$. This is $_{18}$Ar. The configuration of vanadium may then be written as $[Ar]4s^2 3d^3$ where $4s^2 3d^3$ is the outer electron configuration.

Electron shell structures may also be written by noting the number of electrons in each shell. For vanadium, this would be 2, 8, 11, 2.

Orbital diagrams assign electrons to individual orbitals so the energy state of individual electrons may be found. This requires knowledge of how electrons occupy orbitals within a subshell. **Hund's rule** states that **before any two electrons occupy the same orbital, each other orbitals in that subshell must first contain one electron, all with parallel spins**. Electrons with up and down spins are shown by half-arrows, and these are placed in rows of orbitals (represented as boxes or dashes) according to Hund's rule, the Aufbau principle, and the Pauli exclusion principle. Below is the orbital diagram for vanadium:

  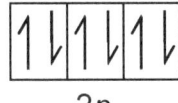  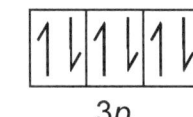  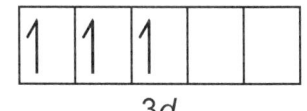

1s   2s   2p   3s   3p   4s   3d

An **energy level diagram** is an orbital diagram that shows subshells with higher energy levels higher up on the page. The energy level diagram of vanadium is:

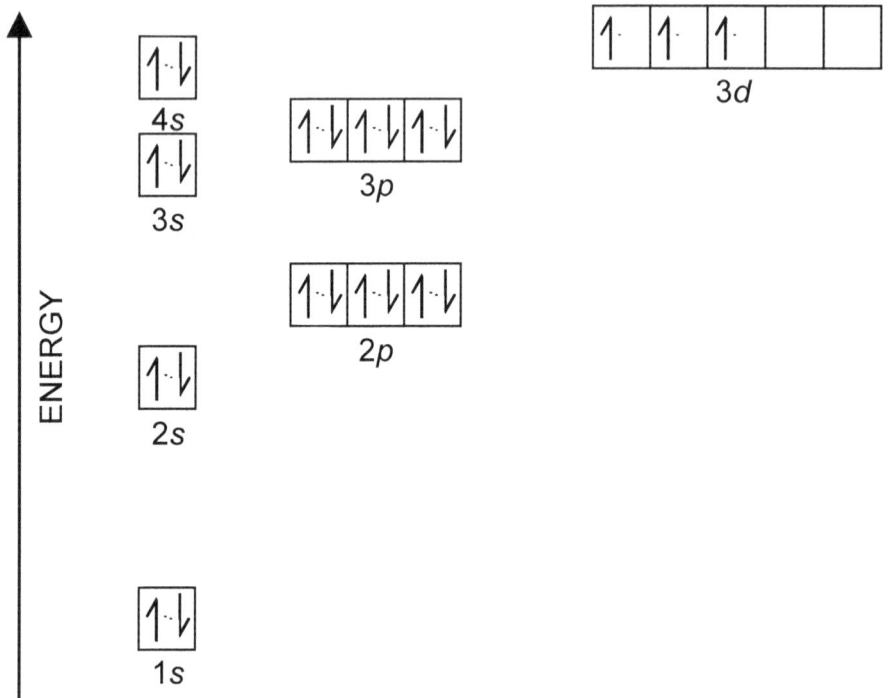

VALENCE SHELL ELECTRONS AND THE PERIODIC TABLE

Electrons in the **outermost shell** are called **valence shell electrons**. For example, the electron configuration of Se is $[Ar]4s^2 3d^{10} 4p^4$, and its valence shell electron configuration is $4s^2 4p^4$.

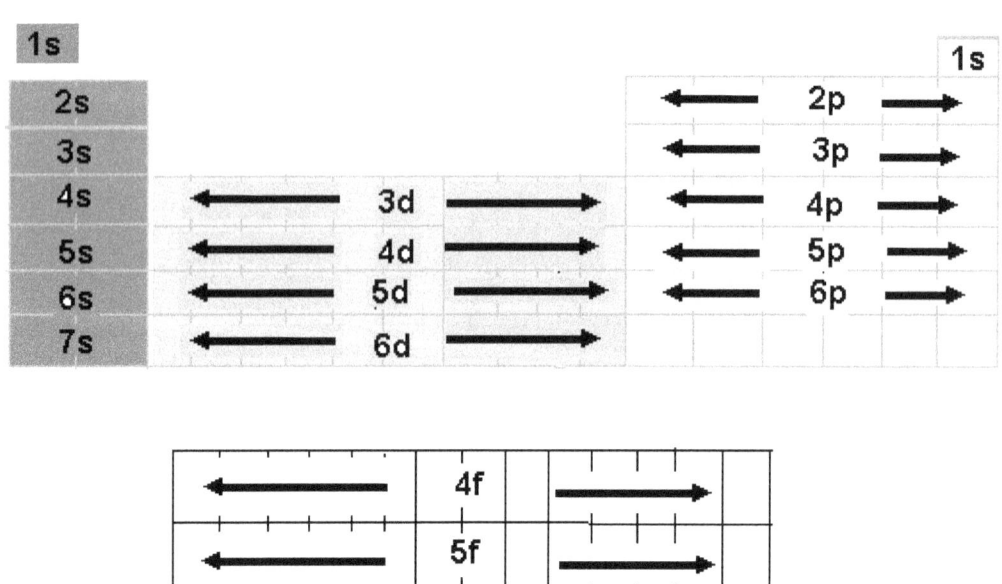

The **periodic table** may be related to the electron shell structure of any element. The table is divided up into **blocks corresponding to the subshell** designation of the most recent orbital to be filled by the building-up rule.

Elements in the s- and p-blocks are known as **main-group elements**. The d-block elements are called **transition metals**. The f-block elements are called **inner transition metals**.

The maximum number of electrons in each subshell (2, 6, 10, or 14) determines the number of elements in each block, and the order of energy levels for subshells create the pattern of blocks. These blocks also usually correspond to the value of *l* for the **outermost electron** of the atom. This has important consequences for the physical and chemical properties of the elements. The outermost shell or valence shell principle quantum number (for example, 4 for Se) is also the period number for the element in the table.

Atoms in the d- and f-blocks often have unexpected electron shell structures that cannot be explained using simple rules. Some heavy atoms have unknown electron configurations because the number of different frequencies of radiation emitted and absorbed by these atoms is very large.

http://thenewboston.org/watch.php?cat=18&number=12 contains a brief tutorial on energy level diagrams.
http://www.colorado.edu/physics/2000/applets/a2.html contains (among other things) energy level diagrams and animations of electron shells and nuclei.
http://science.howstuffworks.com/engineering/structural/roller-coaster3.htm animates the building up of energy level diagrams.

Skill 6.3 Analyzes relationships among electron energy levels, photons, and atomic spectra

The quantum structure of the atom describes electrons in discrete energy levels surrounding the nucleus. When an electron moves from a high energy orbital to a lower energy orbital, a quantum of electromagnetic radiation is emitted, and for an electron to move from a low energy to a higher energy level, a quantum of radiation must be absorbed. The particle that carries this electromagnetic force is called a **photon**. The quantum structure of the atom predicts that only photons corresponding to certain wavelengths of light will be emitted or absorbed by each atom. These distinct wavelengths are measured by **atomic spectroscopy**.

In **atomic absorption spectroscopy**, a continuous spectrum (light consisting of all wavelengths) is passed through the element. The frequencies of absorbed photons are then determined as the electrons increase in energy. An **absorption spectrum** in the visible region usually appears as a rainbow of color stretching from red to violet interrupted by a few black lines corresponding to distinct wavelengths of absorption.

In **atomic emission spectroscopy**, the electrons of an element are excited by heating or by an electric discharge. The frequencies of emitted photons are then determined as the electrons release energy. Emission spectroscopy uses the energy given off *after* absorption to establish molecular structure.

An **emission spectrum** in the visible region typically consists of lines of light at certain colors corresponding to distinct wavelengths of emission. The bands of emitted or absorbed light at these wavelengths are called **spectral lines**. **Each element has a unique line spectrum**. Light from a star (including the sun) may be analyzed to determine what elements are present.

A simple optical spectroscope separates visible light into distinct wavelengths by passing the light through a prism or diffraction grating. When electrons in hydrogen gas are excited inside a discharge tube, the emission spectroscope shown on the next page detects photons at four visible wavelengths.

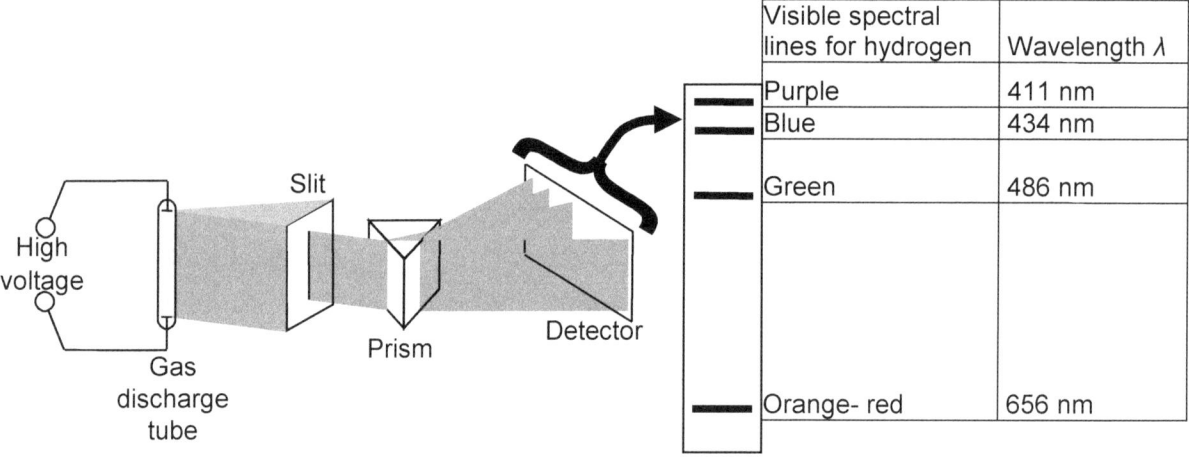

Visible spectral lines for hydrogen	Wavelength λ
Purple	411 nm
Blue	434 nm
Green	486 nm
Orange-red	656 nm

Quantum #	Radius
$n \to \infty$	$r_\infty \to \infty$
⋮	⋮
$n = 5$	$r_5 = 25a_0$
$n = 4$	$r_4 = 16a_0$
$n = 3$	$r_3 = 9a_0$
$n = 2$	$r_2 = 4a_0$
$n = 1$ ⊕	$r_1 = a_0$
(H nucleus)	

An electron may exist at distinct radial distances (r_n) from the nucleus. These distances are proportional to the square of the **principal quantum number**, n. For a hydrogen atom (shown at left), the proportionality constant is called the **Bohr radius** ($a_0 = 5.29 \times 10^{-11}$ m). This value is the mean distance of an electron from the nucleus at the ground state of $n = 1$. The distances of other electron shells are found by the formula:

$$r_n = a_0 n^2$$

As $n \to \infty$, the electron is no longer part of the hydrogen atom. Ionization occurs and the atom becomes an H^+ ion.

Photon wavelength (λ) in meters and frequency (v) in reciprocal seconds are inversely proportional to each other. The proportionality constant between them is the **speed of light** ($c = 3.00 \times 10^8$ m/s):

$$\lambda = \frac{c}{v} \quad \text{and} \quad v = \frac{c}{\lambda}$$

A quantum of energy (ΔE) emitted from or absorbed by an electron transition is directly proportional to the frequency of radiation. The proportionality constant between them is **Planck's constant** ($h = 6.63 \times 10^{-34}$ J·s):

$$\Delta E = hv \quad \text{and} \quad \Delta E = \frac{hc}{\lambda}$$

Visible wavelengths stretch from about 400 to 700 nm, and occupy only a small portion of the **electromagnetic spectrum** describing all possible types of electromagnetic radiation.

The energy of an electron (E_n) is inversely proportional to its radius from the nucleus. For a hydrogen atom, the principle quantum number determines the energy of an electron using the **Rydberg constant** ($R_H = 2.18 \times 10^{-18}$ J):

$$E_n = -\frac{R_H}{n^2}$$

The Rydberg constant is used to determine the energy of a photon emitted or absorbed by an electron transition from one shell to another in the H atom:

$$\Delta E = R_H \left(\frac{1}{n_{initial}^2} - \frac{1}{n_{final}^2} \right)$$

When a photon is absorbed, n_{final} is greater than $n_{initial}$, resulting in positive values corresponding to an endothermic process. Ionization occurs when sufficient energy is added for the atom to lose its electron from the ground state. This corresponds to an electron transition from $n_{initial} = 1$ to $n_{final} \to \infty$. The Rydberg constant is the energy required to ionize one atom of hydrogen. Photon emission causes negative values corresponding to an exothermic process because $n_{initial}$ is greater than n_{final}.

Planck's constant and the speed of light are often used to express the Rydberg constant in units of s^{-1} or length. The formulas below determine the photon frequency or wavelength corresponding to a given electron transition:

$$\nu_{photon} = \left(\frac{R_H}{h} \right) \left| \frac{1}{n_{initial}^2} - \frac{1}{n_{final}^2} \right| \quad \text{and} \quad \lambda_{photon} = \frac{1}{\left(\frac{R_H}{hc} \right) \left| \frac{1}{n_{initial}^2} - \frac{1}{n_{final}^2} \right|}$$

These formulas **relate observed lines in the hydrogen spectrum to individual transitions** from one quantum state to another.

Every line in the hydrogen spectrum corresponds to a transition between electron energy levels. Spectral lines from hydrogen emission spectroscopy are shown at right and in the table below.

Most lines in the hydrogen spectrum are not at visible wavelengths. Larger energy transitions produce ultraviolet radiation and smaller energy transitions produce infrared or longer wavelengths of radiation. Transitions between the first three and the first six energy levels of the hydrogen atom are shown in the diagram to the right. The energy transitions producing the four visible spectral lines are colored grey.

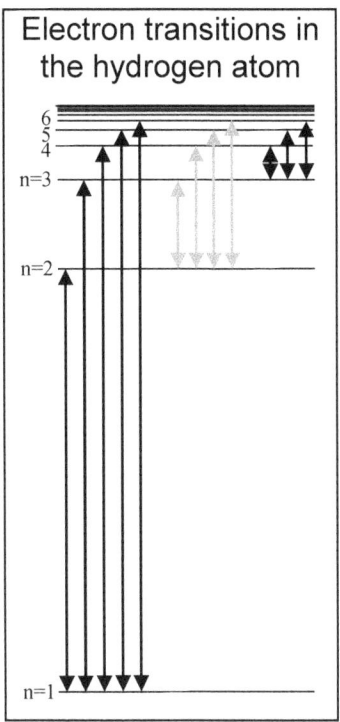

Electron transitions in the hydrogen atom

Radiation type	Wavelength λ (nm)	Frequency v (s^{-1})	Energy change ΔE (J)	Electron transition $n_{initial} \rightarrow n_{final}$
Ultraviolet	≤ 397	$\geq 7.55 \times 10^{14}$	$\leq -5.00 \times 10^{-19}$	$\infty \rightarrow 1, \ldots 2 \rightarrow 1$ $\infty \rightarrow 2, \ldots 7 \rightarrow 2$
Purple	411	7.31×10^{14}	-4.84×10^{-19}	$6 \rightarrow 2$
Blue	434	6.90×10^{14}	-4.58×10^{-19}	$5 \rightarrow 2$
Green	486	6.17×10^{14}	-4.09×10^{-19}	$4 \rightarrow 2$
Orange-red	656	4.57×10^{14}	-3.03×10^{-19}	$3 \rightarrow 2$
Infrared and beyond	≥ 821	$\leq 3.65 \times 10^{14}$	$\geq -2.42 \times 10^{-19}$	$\infty \rightarrow 3, \ldots 4 \rightarrow 3$ $\infty \rightarrow 4, \ldots 5 \rightarrow 4$

The **photoelectric effect** occurs when **light shining on a clean metal surface causes the surface to emit electrons** towards a region of the metal kept in the dark. The energy of each absorbed photon is transferred to an electron as shown to the right. If this energy is greater than the binding energy holding the electron close to nearby nuclei then the electron will move. A high energy (high frequency, low wavelength) photon will not only dislodge an electron from the "electron sea" of a metal, but it will also impart kinetic energy to the electron, making it move rapidly. These electrons in motion will produce an electric current if a circuit is present. **Solar cells** use this effect to produce electricity from sunlight. For every metal there is a minimum frequency required for the photoelectric effect to occur.

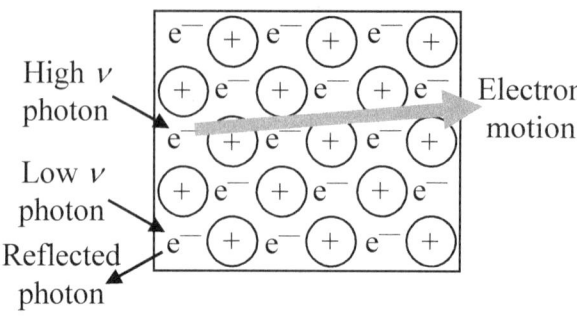

A large number of low-energy photons will not cause the photoelectric effect because each photon does not impart sufficient energy to overcome binding energy. Instead of setting the electron in motion, the electron simply emits another photon. Non-quantum **classical theories predicted that an electron could slowly build up energy** from low-energy photon absorptions and eventually accumulate enough energy to free itself from nearby nuclei, but this is not observed. The quantum structure of the atom predicts that the energy from a photon absorption event will not be stored by the electron in an intermediate energy state. **Quantum events are "all or nothing,"** and this is what is observed by photoelectric effect experiments.

Skill 6.4 Applies the concept of periodicity to predict the physical and chemical properties of an element

See Skill 5.5 for an introduction to the periodic table. A modern periodic table is provided for reference just after the Table of Contents.

The elements in a column of a periodic table are known as a group, and groups are numbered from 1 to 18. Older numbering styles used Roman numerals and letters (such as IA or VIIIA). **A row of the periodic table is known as a period**, and periods of the known elements are numbered from 1 to 7. The lanthanoids are included in period 6, and the actinoids are included in period 7.

METALS, NONMETALS, AND ATOMIC RADIUS

Elements in the periodic table are divided into the two broad categories of **metals** and **nonmetals** with a jagged line separating the two as shown in the figure.

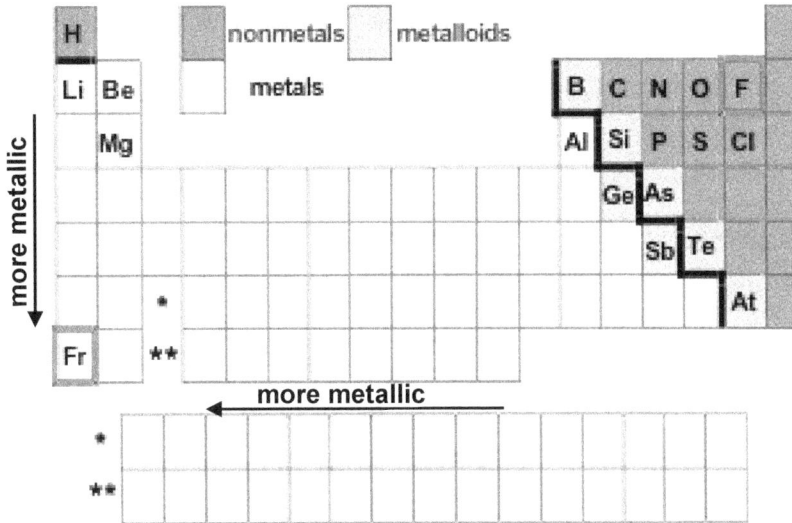

Seven elements near the line dividing metals from nonmetals exhibit some properties of each and are called **metalloids** or **semimetals**. These elements are boron, silicon, germanium, arsenic, antimony, tellurium and astatine.

The most metallic element is francium at the bottom left of the table. The most nonmetallic element is fluorine. The metallic character of elements within a group increases with period number. This means that **within a column, the more metallic elements are at the bottom**. The metallic character of elements within a period decreases with group number. This means that **within a row, the more metallic elements are on the left**. Among the main group atoms, **elements diagonal to each other have similar properties** because they have a similar metallic character. The noble gases are nonmetals, but they are an exception to the diagonal rule.

Physical properties relating to metallic character are summarized in the following table:

Element	Electrical/thermal conductivity	Malleable/ ductile as solids?	Lustrous ?	Melting point of oxides, hydrides, and halides
Metals	High	Yes	Yes	High
Metalloids	Intermediate Altered by dopants (semiconductors)	No (brittle)	Varies	Varies (oxides) Low (hydrides, halides)
Nonmetals	Low (insulators)	No	No	Low

Malleable materials can **be beaten into sheets**. **Ductile** materials can **be pulled into wires**. **Lustrous** materials **have a shine**. Oxides, hydrides, and halides are compounds with O, H, and halogens respectively. Measures of intermolecular attractions other than melting point are also higher for metal oxides, hydrides, and halides than for the nonmetal compounds. A dopant is a small quantity of an intentionally added impurity. The controlled movement of electrons in doped silicon semiconductors carries digital information in computer circuitry.

The **size of an atom** is not an exact radius due to the probabilistic nature of electron density, but we may compare radii among different atoms using a standard. As seen to the right, the sizes of neutral atoms increase with period number and decrease with group number. This trend is similar to the trend described above for metallic character. The smallest atom is helium.

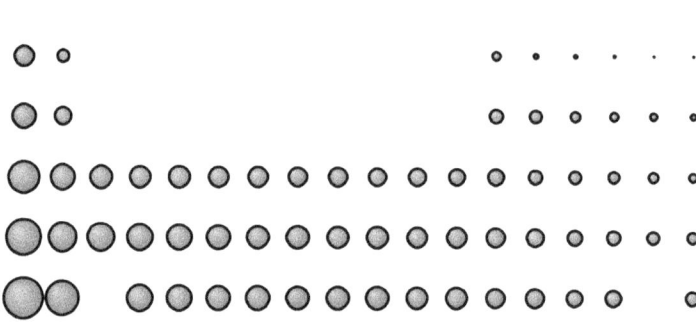

Atomic radius decreases left to right due to the electrons being pulled in tighter to the nucleus with the addition of each electron and proton. The atomic radius increases going down the periodic table due to the addition of another level of electrons with each row.

GROUP NAMES, MELTING POINT, DENSITY, AND PROPERTIES OF COMPOUNDS

Groups 1, 2, 17, and 18 are often identified with a **group name**. These names are shown in the diagram below. Several elements are generally found in nature as **diatomic molecules: (H_2, N_2, O_2, and the halogens F_2, Cl_2, Br_2, and I_2)**. Mnemonic devices to remember the diatomic elements are: "$Br_2I_2N_2Cl_2H_2O_2F_2$" (pronounced "Brinklehof" and "**H**ave **N**o **F**ear **O**f **I**ce **C**old **B**eer." Another way to remember them is by using the Rule of Sevens: the 7 of them form a number 7 on the Periodic Table and 4 of the 7 are from Group 7. These molecules are attracted to one another using **weak London dispersion forces**.

Note that **hydrogen** is <u>not</u> an alkali metal. Hydrogen is a colorless gas and is the most abundant element in the universe, but H_2 is very rare in the atmosphere because it is light enough to escape gravity and reach outer space. Hydrogen atoms form more compounds than any other element.

Alkali metals are shiny, soft, metallic solids. They have **low melting points and low densities** compared with other metals because they have a weaker metallic bond. Measures of intermolecular attractions, including **melting points, decrease further down the periodic table due to weaker metallic bonds** as atomic sizes increase.

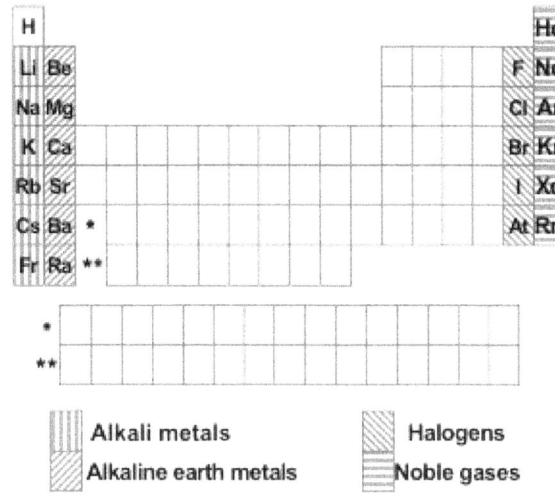

Alkaline earth metals (group 2 elements) are grey, metallic solids. They are harder, denser, and have a higher melting point than the alkali metals, but values for these properties are still low compared to most of the transition metals. Measures of bond strength such as melting points for alkaline earths do not follow a simple trend down the periodic table.

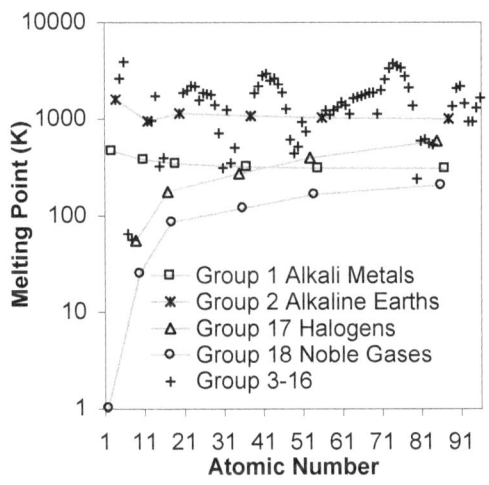

Halogens (group 17 elements) have an irritating odor. Unlike the metallic bonds between alkali metals, **London forces between halogen molecules increase in strength further down the periodic table**. Their melting points increase as shown by the triangles to the left. London forces make Br_2 a liquid and I_2 a solid at 25 °C. The lighter halogens are gases.

Noble gases (group 18 elements) have no color or odor and exist as **individual gas atoms** that experience London forces. These attractions also increase with period number as shown by the circles in the figure.

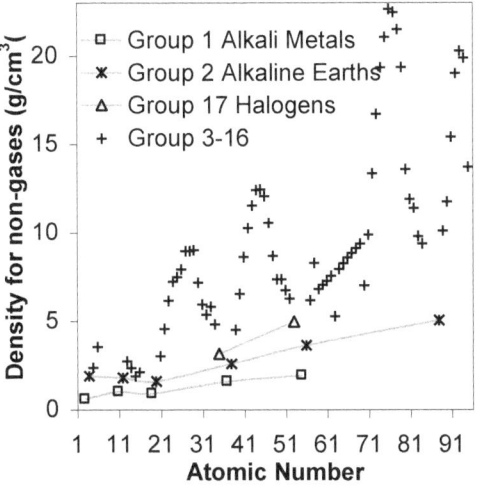

The known **densities** of liquid and solid elements at room temperature are shown below. **Intermolecular forces contribute to density** by bringing nuclei closer to each other, so the periodicity is similar to trends for melting point. These group-to-group differences are superimposed on a general trend in which **density increases with period number** because heavier nuclei make the material denser.

Trends among properties of **compounds** may often be deduced from **trends among their atoms**, but caution must be used. For example, the densities of three potassium halides are 2.0 g/cm^3 for KCl, 2.7 g/cm^3 for KBr, and 3.1 g/cm^3 for KI.

We would expect this trend for increasing atomic mass within a group. We might also expect the density of KF to be less than 2.0 g/cm^3, but it is actually 2.5 g/cm^3 due to a change in crystal lattice structure.

Much of chemistry consists of atoms **bonding** to achieve stable valence electron configurations. **Nonmetals gain electrons or share electrons** to achieve these configurations and **metals lose electrons** to achieve them.

QUALITATIVE GROUP TRENDS

When cut by a knife, the exposed surface of an **alkali metal or alkaline earth metal** quickly turns into an oxide. These elements **do not occur in nature as free metals**. Instead, they react with many other elements to form white or grey water-soluble salts. With some exceptions, the oxides of group 1 elements have the formula M_2O, their hydrides are MH, and their halides are MX (for example, NaCl). The oxides of group 2 elements have the formula MO, their hydrides are MH_2, and their halides are MX_2, for example, $CaCl_2$.

Halogens form a wide variety of oxides and also combine with other halogens. They combine with hydrogen to form HX gases, and these compounds are also commonly used as acids (hydrofluoric, hydrochloric, etc.) in aqueous solution. Halogens form salts with metals by gaining electrons to become X^- ions. Astatine is an exception to many of these properties because it is an artificial metalloid.

Noble gases are **nearly chemically inert**. The heavier noble gases form a number of compounds with oxygen and fluorine such as KrF_2 and XeO_4

ELECTRONEGATIVITY AND REACTIVITY SERIES

Electronegativity measures the ability of an atom to attract electrons in a chemical bond. The most metallic elements have the lowest electronegativity and give up their electrons easily. The most nonmetallic have the highest electronegativity, thereby attracting electrons easily.

The most powerful chemical reactions between elements occur between metals and non-metals. This also corresponds to reactions between the most and least electronegative elements. In a reaction with a metal, the most reactive chemicals are the **most electronegative elements** or compounds containing those elements. In a reaction with a nonmetal, the most reactive chemicals are the **least electronegative elements** or compounds containing them. The reactivity of elements may be described by a **reactivity series**: an ordered list with chemicals that react strongly at one end and nonreactive chemicals at the other. The following reactivity series is for metals reacting with oxygen:

Metal	K	Na	Ca	Mg	Al	Zn	Fe	Pb	Cu	Hg	Ag	Au
Reaction with O_2	Burns violently		Burns rapidly						Oxidizes slowly		No reaction	

Copper, silver, and gold (group 11) are known as the **noble metals** or **coinage metals** because they rarely react.

Fluorine is the most electronegative element in the periodic table, so the elements decrease in electronegativity going right to left and from top to bottom with the halogens being the most reactive (electronegative) group.

VALENCE AND OXIDATION NUMBERS

The term **valence** is often used to describe the number of atoms that may react to form a compound with a given atom by sharing, removing, or losing **valence electrons**. A more useful term is **oxidation number**. The **oxidation number of an ion is its charge**. The oxidation number of an atom sharing its electrons is **the charge it would have if the bonding were ionic**.

There are four rules for determining oxidation number:

1) The oxidation number of atoms in a molecule made up of a single element (i.e., a Cl atom in Cl_2) is zero because the electrons in the bond are shared equally.

2) In a compound, the more electronegative atoms are assigned negative oxidation numbers and the less electronegative atoms are assigned positive oxidation numbers equal to the number of shared electron-pair bonds. For example, hydrogen may have an oxidation number of -1 when bonded to a less electronegative element or +1 when bonded to a more electronegative element. Oxygen almost always has an oxidation number of -2. Fluorine always has an oxidation number of -1 (except in F_2).

3) The oxidation numbers in a compound must add up to zero, and the sum of oxidation numbers in a polyatomic ion must equal the overall charge of the ion.

4) The charge on a polyatomic ion is equal to the sum of the oxidation numbers for the species present in the ion. For example, the sulfate ion SO_4^{2-} has a total charge of -2. This comes from adding the -2 oxidation numbers for 4 oxygen atoms (total -8) and the +6 oxidation number for sulfur.

Example: What is the oxidation number of nitrogen in the nitrate ion NO_3^-?

Solution: Oxygen has an oxidation number of -2 (rule 2), and the sum of the oxidation numbers must be -1 (rule 3). The oxidation number for N may be found by solving for x in the equation $x + 3 \times (-2) = -1$. The oxidation number of N in NO_3^- is +5.

There is a **periodicity in oxidation numbers** as shown in the table below for oxides with the maximum oxidation number. Remember that some elements may occur in different compounds in several different oxidation states.

Group	1	2	13	14	15	16	17	18
Oxide with maximum oxidation number	Li_2O	BeO	B_2O_3	CO_2	N_2O_5		Cl_2O_7	XeO_4
	Na_2O	MgO	Al_2O_3	SiO_2	P_2O_5	SO_3	Br_2O_7	
Oxidation number	+1	+2	+3	+4	+5	+6	+7	+8

They are called "oxidation numbers" because oxygen was the element of choice for reacting with materials when modern chemistry began, and as a result, Mendeleev arranged his first periodic table similarly to this one.

ACIDITY/ALKALINITY OF OXIDES

Metal oxides form basic solutions in water because the ionic bonds break apart and the O^{2-} ion reacts to form hydroxide ions:

metal oxide $\rightarrow$ metal cation(aq) $+ O^{2-}(aq)$ and $O^{2-}(aq) + H_2O(l) \rightarrow 2\ OH^-(aq)$

Ionic oxides containing a large cation with a low charge (Rb_2O, for example) are most soluble and form the strongest bases.

Covalent oxides form acidic solutions in water by reacting with water. For example:

$$SO_3(l) + H_2O(l) \rightarrow H_2SO_4(aq) \rightarrow H^+(aq) + HSO_4^-(aq)$$

$$Cl_2O_7(l) + H_2O(l) \rightarrow 2HClO_4(aq) \rightarrow 2H^+(aq) + 2ClO_4^-(aq)$$

Covalent oxides at high oxidation states and high electronegativities form the strongest acids. Note that the periodic trends for acid and base strength of the oxide of an element follows the same pattern we've seen before.

PHYSICS OF ELECTRONS AND STABILITY OF ELECTRON CONFIGURATIONS

For an isolated atom, the **most stable system of valence electrons is a filled set of orbitals**. For the main group elements, this corresponds to group 18 (ns^2np^6 and $1s^2$ for helium), and, to a lesser extent, group 2 (ns^2).

The next most stable state is a set of degenerate half-filled orbitals. These occur in group 15 (ns^2np^3). The least stable valence electron configuration is a single electron with no other electrons in similar orbitals. This occurs in group 1 (ns^1) and to a lesser extent in group 13 (ns^2np^1).

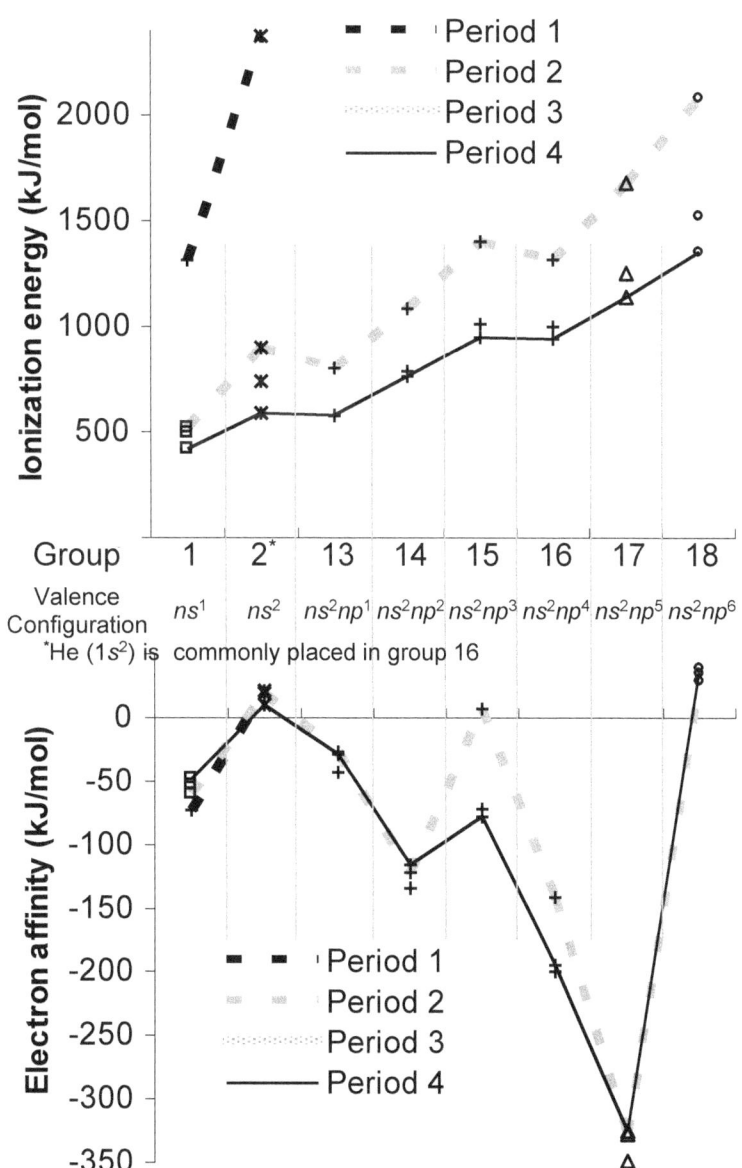

An atom's first **ionization energy** is the energy required to remove one electron according to the reaction $M(g) \rightarrow M^+(g) + e^-$.

Periodicity of ionization energy is in the opposite direction from the trend for atomic radius. The most metallic atoms have electrons further from the nucleus, and these are easier to remove.

An atom's **electron affinity** is the energy released when one electron is added according to the reaction $M(g) + e^- \rightarrow M^-(g)$. A large negative number for the exothermic reaction indicates a high electron affinity. Halogens have the highest electron affinities.

Trends in **ionization energy and electron affinity** within a period reflect the **stability of valence electron configurations**. A stable system requires more energy to change and releases less energy when changed. Note the peaks in stability for groups 2, 13, and 16 above.

SUMMARY

A summary of periodic trends is shown to the right. The properties tend to decrease or increase as shown depending on a given element's proximity to fluorine in the table.

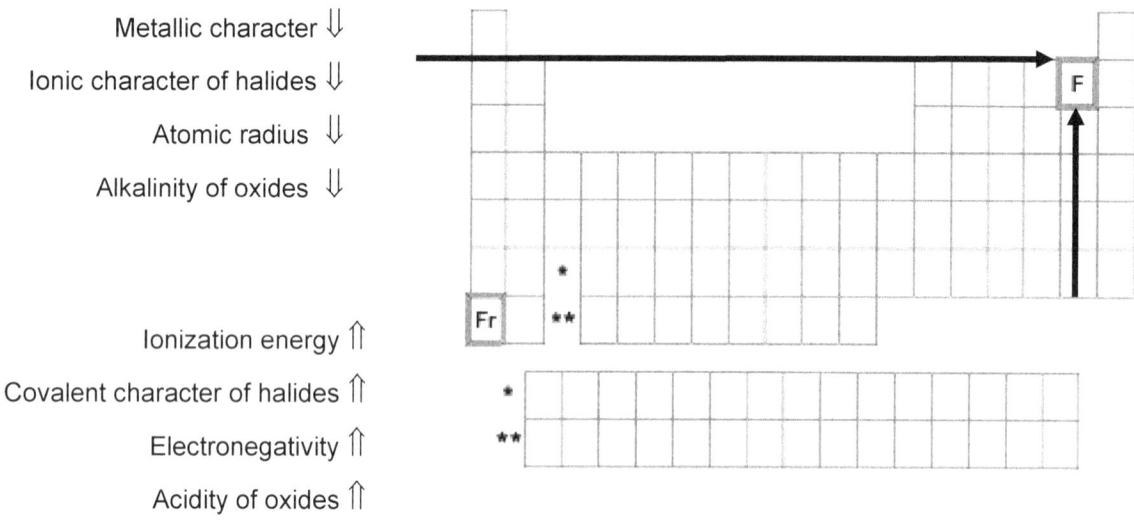

Metallic character ⇓
Ionic character of halides ⇓
Atomic radius ⇓
Alkalinity of oxides ⇓

Ionization energy ⇑
Covalent character of halides ⇑
Electronegativity ⇑
Acidity of oxides ⇑

*Note: Memorize the ones in italics; everything else increases top→bottom, left→right

Group Trends (top to bottom):
> Increases: atomic radius, nuclear charge, ionic size, shielding effect, atomic number (number of protons, number of electrons), covalent character of halides, acidity of oxides
>
> *Decreases: ionization energy, electron affinity, electronegativity, metallic character, ionic character of halides, alkalinity of oxides*

Period Trends (left to right):
> Increases: electronegativity, nuclear charge, ionization energy, electron affinity, atomic number (number of protons, number of electrons), acidity of oxides
>
> *Decreases all the way across: atomic radius, metallic character, ionic character of halides, alkalinity of oxides*
>
> *Decreases through cations (positive) and again through anions: ionic size*
>
> *Stays the same left to right: shielding effect*

http://jcrystal.com/steffenweber/JAVA/jpt/jpt.html contains an applet of the periodic table and trends.

http://www.webelements.com is an on-line reference for information on the elements.

http://www.uky.edu/Projects/Chemcomics/ has comic book pages for each element.

Skill 6.5   Understands the historical development of atomic theory

Fundamental units of matter called atoms and atoms of different types called elements were proposed by ancient philosophers without any evidence to support the belief. Modern atomic theory is credited to the work of **John Dalton** published in 1803-1807. Observations made by him and others about the composition, properties, and reactions of many compounds led him to develop the following postulates:

- Each element is composed of small particles called atoms.
- All atoms of a given element are identical in mass and other properties.
- Atoms of different elements have different masses and differ in other properties.
- Atoms of an element are not created, destroyed, or changed into a different type of atom by chemical reactions.
- Compounds form when atoms of more than one element combine.
- In a given compound, the relative number and kinds of atoms are constant.

Dalton determined and published the known relative masses of a number of different atoms. He also formulated the law of partial pressures. Dalton's work focused on the ability of atoms to arrange themselves into molecules and to rearrange themselves via chemical reactions, but he did not investigate the composition of atoms themselves. **Dalton's model of the atom** was a tiny, indivisible, indestructible **particle** of a certain mass, size, and chemical behavior, but Dalton did not deny the possibility that atoms might have a substructure.

Joseph John Thomson, often known as **J. J. Thomson**, was the first to examine this substructure. In the mid-1800s, scientists had studied a form of radiation called "cathode rays" or "electrons" that originated from the negative electrode (cathode) when electrical current was forced through an evacuated tube. Thomson determined in 1897 that **electrons have mass**, and because many different cathode materials release electrons, Thomson proposed that the **electron is a subatomic particle**. **Thomson's model of the atom** was a uniformly positive particle with electrons contained in the interior. This has been called the "plum-pudding" model of the atom where the pudding represents the uniform sphere of positive electricity and the bits of plum represent electrons. For more on Thomson, see http://www.aip.org/history/electron/jjhome.htm.

Max Planck determined in 1900 that **energy is transferred by radiation in exact multiples of a discrete unit of energy called a quantum**. Quanta of energy are extremely small, and may be found from the frequency of the radiation v, using the equation:

$$\Delta E = hv$$

where h is Planck's constant and hv is a quantum of energy.

Ernest Rutherford studied atomic structure in 1910-1911 by firing a beam of alpha particles at thin layers of gold leaf. According to Thomson's model, the path of an alpha particle should be deflected only slightly if it struck an atom, but Rutherford observed some alpha particles bouncing almost backwards, suggesting that **nearly all the mass of an atom is contained in a small positively charged nucleus**. **Rutherford's model of the atom** was an analogy to the sun and the planets - a small positively charged nucleus surrounded by circling electrons and empty space. Rutherford's experiment is explained in greater detail in this flash animation:
http://www.mhhe.com/physsci/chemistry/essentialchemistry/flash/ruther14.swf.

Niels Bohr incorporated Planck's quantum concept into Rutherford's model of the atom in 1913 to explain the **discrete frequencies of radiation emitted and absorbed by atoms with one electron** (H, He$^+$, and Li^{2+}). This electron is attracted to the positive nucleus and is closest to the nucleus at the **ground state** of the atom. When the electron absorbs energy, it moves into an orbit further from the nucleus and the atom is said to be in an electronically **excited state**. If sufficient energy is absorbed, the electron separates from the nucleus entirely, and the atom is ionized:

$$H \rightarrow H^+ + e^-$$

The energy required for ionization from the ground state is called the atom's **ionization energy**. The discrete frequencies of radiation emitted and absorbed by the atom correspond (using Planck's constant) to discrete energies and in turn to discrete distances from the nucleus. **Bohr's model of the atom** was a small positively charged nucleus surrounded mostly by empty space and by electrons orbiting at certain discrete distances ("shells") corresponding to discrete energy levels. Animations utilizing the Bohr model may be found at the following two URLs:

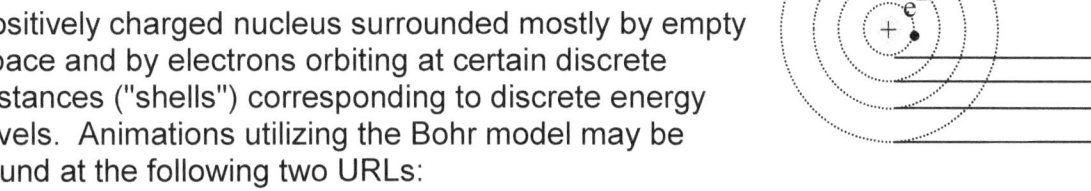

http://highered.mcgraw-hill.com/olcweb/cgi/pluginpop.cgi?it=swf::800::600::/sites/dl/free/007299181x/59229/Bohr_Nav.swf::The%20Bohr%20Atom
and http://www.learnerstv.com/animation/animation.php?ani=110&cat=physics.

Depending on the experiment, radiation appears to have wave-like or particle-like traits. In 1923-1924, **Louis de Broglie** applied this **wave/particle duality to all matter with momentum**. The discrete distances from the nucleus described by Bohr corresponded to permissible distances where standing waves could exist. **De Broglie's model of the atom** described electrons as **matter waves in standing wave orbits** around the nucleus. The first three standing waves corresponding to the first three discrete distances are shown in the figure to the above. De Broglie's model may be found at the following two URLs:
http://www.physicsland.net/physlets/mp1a5.htm and
http://ne.phys.kyushu-u.ac.jp/seminar/MicroWorld2_E/2Part1_E/2P11_E/deBroglie_wave_E.htm

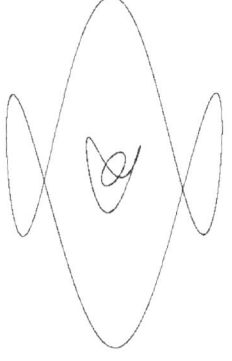

The realization that both matter and radiation interact as waves led **Werner Heisenberg** to the conclusion in 1927 that the act of observation and measurement requires the interaction of one wave with another. This interaction results in an **inherent uncertainty** in the location and momentum of the particles observed. This limitation in the measurement of phenomena at the subatomic level is known as the **Heisenberg uncertainty principle**, and it applies to the location and momentum of electrons in an atom. A discussion of this principle and Heisenberg's other contributions to quantum theory is located here: http://www.aip.org/history/heisenberg/.

When **Erwin Schrödinger** studied the atom in 1925, he replaced the idea of precise orbits with regions in space called **orbitals** where electrons were likely to be found. **The Schrödinger equation** describes the **probability** that an electron will be in a given region of space, a quantity known as **electron density** or Ψ^2. The diagrams below are surfaces of constant Ψ^2 found by solving the Schrödinger equation for the hydrogen atom $1s$, $2p_z$ and $3d_0$ orbitals. Additional representations of solutions may be found here: http://library.wolfram.com/webMathematica/Physics/Hydrogen.jsp.

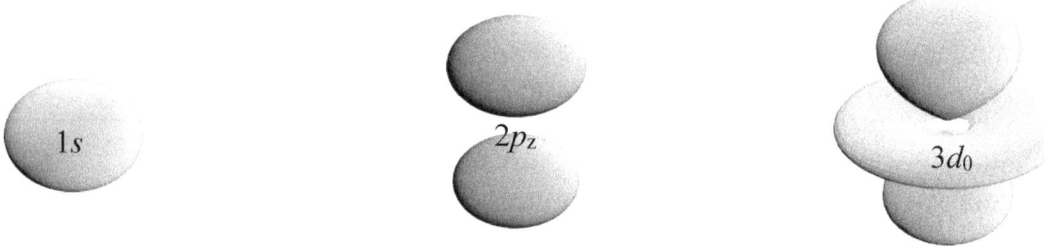

Schrödinger's model of the atom is a mathematical formulation of quantum mechanics that describes the electron density of orbitals. It is the atomic model that has been in use from shortly after it was introduced up until the present.

Wolfgang Pauli helped develop quantum mechanics in the 1920s by developing the concept of spin and the **Pauli exclusion principle**, which states that if two electrons occupy the same orbital, they must have different spin (intrinsic angular momentum). This principle has been generalized to other quantum particles.

Friedrich Hund determined a set of **rules to determine the ground state** of a multi-electron atom in the 1920s. One of these rules is called **Hund's Rule** in introductory chemistry courses, and describes the order in which electrons fill orbitals and their spin.

TEACHER CERTIFICATION STUDY GUIDE

COMPETENCY 007   THE TEACHER UNDERSTANDS THE PROPERTIES OF GASES

Skill 7.1   Understands interrelationships among temperature, moles, pressure, and volume of gases contained within a closed system

The relationships among temperature, pressure, volume and moles of gases were found by experimental observation and may now be explained by the kinetic molecular theory.

Boyle's law states that the volume of a fixed amount of gas at constant temperature is inversely proportional to the gas pressure. In other words, increasing the pressure causes a gas to contract, in a mathematically proportional manner:

$$V \propto \frac{1}{P}$$

Problem: A 1.5 L gas has a pressure of 0.56 atm. What will be the volume of the gas if the pressure doubles to 1.12 atm at constant temperature?

Solution: This is a pressure-volume relationship at constant temperature, so using Boyle's law:

$P_1 = 0.56$ atm
$V_1 = 1.5$ L
$P_2 = 1.12$ atm
$V_2 = ?$

Use the equation $P_1V_1 = P_2V_2$, rearrange to solve for $V_2 = \frac{P_1 V_1}{P_2}$.

Substitute and solve. $V_2 = 0.75$ L

Pressure can be in atmospheres, Pascals, or mm Hg as long as it is the same units for P_1 and P_2.

Charles' law states that the volume of a fixed amount of gas at constant pressure is directly proportional to absolute temperature. In other words, increasing the temperature causes a gas to expand, in a mathematically proportional manner:

$$V \propto T$$

Or $V = kT$ where k is a constant. This gives a mathematical equation $\frac{V_1}{T_1} = \frac{V_2}{T_2}$.

Changes in temperature or volume can be found using Charles' law.

Problem: What is the new volume of a gas if 0.50 L of that gas at 25°C is heated to 35°C at constant pressure?

Solution: This is a volume-temperature change so use Charles' law. Temperature must be on the Kelvin scale. K = °C + 273.

T_1 = 25°C + 273 = 298K
V_1 = 0.50 L
T_2 = 308K
V_2 = ?

Use the equation: $\frac{V_1}{T_1} = \frac{V_2}{T_2}$ and rearrange for $V_2 = \frac{T_2 V_1}{T_1}$.

Substitute and solve

V_2 = 0.52L.

Gay-Lussac's law states that the pressure of a fixed amount of gas in a fixed volume is proportional to absolute temperature, or:

$$P \propto T$$

Or $P = kT$ where k is a constant. This gives the mathematical equation $\frac{P_1}{T_1} = \frac{P_2}{T_2}$.

Changes in temperature or pressure (with a constant volume) can be found using Gay-Lussac's law.

Problem: A 2.25 L container of gas at 25°C and 1.0 atm pressure is cooled to 15°C. How does the pressure change if the volume of gas remains constant?

Solution: This is a pressure-volume change so use Gay-Lussac's law. Change the temperatures to the Kelvin scale. K = °C + 273.

P_1 = 1.0 atm
T_1 = 25 °C + 273 = 298
T_2 = 15 °C + 273 = 288

Use the equation $\dfrac{P_1}{T_1} = \dfrac{P_2}{T_2}$ to solve.

Rearrange the equation to solve for P_2, substitute and solve.

$P_2 = \dfrac{P_1 T_2}{T_1} = 0.97$ atm

The **combined gas law** uses the above laws to determine a proportionality expression that is used for a constant quantity of gas:

$$V \propto \dfrac{T}{P}$$

The combined gas law is often expressed as an equality between identical amounts of an ideal gas in two different states ($n_1 = n_2$):

$$\dfrac{P_1 V_1}{T_1} = \dfrac{P_2 V_2}{T_2}$$

Problem: 1.5 L of a gas at STP is allowed to expand to 2.0 L at a pressure of 2.5 atm. What is the temperature of the expanded gas?

Solution: Since pressure, temperature and volume are all changing, use the combined gas law to determine the new temperature of the gas. STP means "Standard Temperature and Pressure." Standard temperature is 273 K and standard pressure is 1.0 atm.

P_1 = 1.0 atm
T_1 = 273K
V_1 = 1.5 L
V_2 = 2.0L
P_2 = 2.5 atm
T_2 = ?

Using this equation, $\frac{P_1V_1}{T_1} = \frac{P_2V_2}{T_2}$, rearrange to solve for T_2.

$$T_2 = \frac{P_2V_2T_1}{P_1V_1}$$

Substitute and solve:

$T_2 = 910$ K or 637 °C (after subtracting 273)

Avogadro's hypothesis states that equal volumes of different gases at the same temperature and pressure contain equal numbers of molecules. **Avogadro's law** states that the volume of a gas at constant temperature and pressure is directly proportional to the quantity of gas, or:

$$V \propto n$$

where n is the number of moles of gas.

Together, Avogadro's law and the combined gas law yield:

$$V \propto \frac{nT}{P}$$

The proportionality constant R – the **ideal gas constant** – is used to express this proportionality as the **ideal gas law**:

$$PV = nRT$$

The ideal gas law is useful because it contains all the information of Charles', Avogadro's, Boyle's, and the combined gas laws in a single expression.

If pressure is given in atmospheres and volume is given in liters, a value for R of **0.08206 L-atm/(mol-K)** is used. If pressure is given in Pascal (newtons/m²) and volume in cubic meters, then the SI value for R of **8.314 J/(mol-K)** may be used. This is because a joule is defined as a Newton-meter. A value for R of **8.314 m³-Pa/(mol-K)** is identical to the ideal gas constant using joules.

Problem: What volume will 0.50 mole of an ideal gas occupy at 20.0 °C and 1.5 atm?

Solution: Since the problem deals with moles of gas as well as temperature and pressure, use the ideal gas law to find volume.

R = 0.0821 atm L/mol K. The SI value for R of **8.314 J/(mol-K)** may be used because a joule is defined as a Newton-meter. A value for R of **8.314 m³-Pa/(mol-K)** is identical to the ideal gas constant using joules.

$$PV = nRT \qquad V = nRT/P$$

$$V = nRT / P = 0.50 \text{ mol } (0.0821 \text{ atm L/mol K}) \, 293 \text{ K} / 1.5 \text{ atm}$$
$$V = 8.0 \text{ L}$$

Problem: At STP, 0.250 L of an unknown gas has a mass of 0.429 g. Is the gas SO_2, NO_2, C_3H_8, or Ar? Support your answer.

Solution: Identify what is given and what is asked.

Given: $T_1 = 273K$
$P_1 = 1.0$ atm
$V_1 = 0.250$ L
Mass = 0.429 g

Determine: Identity of the gas. In order to do this, you must find the molar mass (MM) of the gas. $n = \dfrac{mass}{MM}$. Find the number of moles of gas present using PV = nRT and then determine the MM to compare to choices given in the problem.

Solve for n = $\dfrac{PV}{RT}$ = (1.0 atm)(0.250 L) / (0.0821 atm L/mol Kl)(273 K)
n = 0.011 moles

$$MM = \dfrac{mass}{n} = 0.429 \text{ g}/0.011 \text{ mol} = 39.0 \text{ g/mol}$$

Compare to MM of SO_2 (96 g/mol), NO_2 (46 g/mol), C_3H_8 (44 g/mol) and Ar (39.9 g/mol). It is closest to Ar, so the gas is probably Argon.

Many problems are given at "**standard temperature and pressure**" or "**STP**." Standard conditions are *exactly* **1 atm (101.325 kPa)** and **0° C (273.15 K)**. At STP, one mole of an ideal gas has a volume of:

$$V = \frac{nRT}{P}$$

$$= \frac{(1\text{ mole})\left(0.08206\ \frac{\text{L-atm}}{\text{mol-K}}\right)(273\text{ K})}{1\text{ atm}} = 22.4\text{ L}.$$

This value of 22.4 L is known as the **standard molar volume** of any gas at STP.

Tutorials for gas laws may be found online at: www.chemistrycoach.com/tutorials-6.htm .

Skill 7.2   Analyzes data obtained from investigations with gases in a closed system and determines whether the data are consistent with the ideal gas law

The basic equation above expresses the ideal gas law and can be used to evaluate the results of laboratory experiments. To test whether gases in an experiment behave according to the ideal gas law, two approaches may be used:

- All of the variables in the equation may be measured for a known quantity of gas and the data entered into the equation to see if the equality holds true. If it does, the data are consistent with the ideal gas law. Care must be taken to avoid experimental and units errors as discussed in Skill 7.3.

- An equality may be set up between two different experimental states as described in Skill 7.1. The two experimental states may be created in the laboratory for a known quantity of gas by first creating an initial state with a known temperature, pressure, and volume. Then, one or two of the parameters can be varied (i.e., temperature, volume, and/or pressure) and the effect on the dependent variable(s) measured. The data can then be entered into the equality to determine if the results for the dependent variable(s) are the same as would be predicted by solving the equation.

Skill 7.3   Applies the gas laws (e.g., Charles' law, Boyle's law, combined gas law, Avogadro's law) to predict gas behavior in a variety of systems

Solving ideal gas law problems is a straightforward process of algebraic manipulation. **Errors commonly arise from using improper units**, particularly for the ideal gas constant R. An absolute temperature scale must be used, usually the Kelvin scale (Celsius cannot be used). Volume and pressure units often vary from problem to problem.

If pressure is given in atmospheres and volume is given in liters, a value for R of **0.08206 L-atm/(mol-K)** is used. If pressure is given in pascal (newtons/m²) and volume in m³, then the SI value for R of **8.314 J/(mol-K)** may be used because a joule is defined as a newton-meter or a pascal-m³. A value for R of **8.314 Pa-m³/(mol-K)** is identical to the ideal gas constant using joules.

For examples of problems using Charles' law, Boyle's law, Gay-Lussac's law, Avogadro's law and the combined gas law, see Skill 7.1.

The ideal gas law (PV = nRT) may also be rearranged to determine gas molar density in moles per unit volume (molarity):

$$\frac{n}{V} = \frac{P}{RT}$$

Gas density d in grams per unit volume is found through multiplication by the molecular weight M (g/mol):

$$d = \frac{nM}{V} = \frac{PM}{RT}$$

Molecular weight may also be determined from the density of an ideal gas by rearranging the equation above:

$$M = \frac{dV}{n} = \frac{dRT}{P}$$

Example: Determine the molecular weight of an ideal gas that has a density of 3.24 g/L at 800 K and 3.00 atm.

Solution: $M = \dfrac{dRT}{P} = \dfrac{\left(3.24 \frac{g}{L}\right)\left(0.08206 \frac{L\text{-atm}}{mol\text{-K}}\right)(800 \text{ K})}{3.00 \text{ atm}} = 70.9 \dfrac{g}{mol}$

A flash animation tutorial for problems involving a piston may be found at
http://www.mhhe.com/physsci/chemistry/essentialchemistry/flash/gasesv6.swf.

Skill 7.4 Applies Dalton's law of partial pressure in various systems, as in collecting a gas over water

For mixtures of gases in a container, each gas exerts a **partial pressure** that is the same as it would have if it were present in the container alone. **Dalton's law** of partial pressures states that the total pressure of a gas mixture is simply the sum of the partial pressures:

$$P_{total} = P_1 + P_2 + P_3 + \ldots$$

Dalton's law may be applied to the ideal gas law:

$$P_{total}V = (P_1 + P_2 + P_3 + \ldots)$$

Skill 7.5 Understands the relationship between Kinetic Molecular Theory and the ideal gas law

The relationship between **kinetic energy** and **intermolecular forces** determines whether a collection of molecules will be a gas, liquid, or solid. In a gas, the energy of intermolecular forces is much weaker than the kinetic energy of the molecules. Therefore, Kinetic Molecular Theory is usually applied to gases.

Gas **pressure** results from molecular collisions with container walls. The **number of molecules** striking an **area** on the walls and the **average kinetic energy** per molecule are the only factors that contribute to pressure. A higher **temperature** increases speed and kinetic energy. There are more collisions at higher temperatures, but the average distance between molecules does not change, and thus density does not change in a sealed container.

Kinetic molecular theory explains why the pressure and temperature of gases behave the way they do, using the following assumptions:

1. The energies of intermolecular attractive and repulsive forces may be neglected.
2. Average kinetic energy of the molecules is proportional to absolute temperature.
3. Energy can be transferred between molecules during collisions and the collisions are elastic, so the average kinetic energy of the molecules doesn't change due to collisions.
4. The volume of all molecules in a gas is negligible compared to the total volume of the container.

Strictly speaking, molecules also contain some kinetic energy associated with rotation or other motions. The movement of a molecule from one place to another is called **translation**. Translational kinetic energy is the form that is transferred by collisions, and kinetic molecular theory ignores other forms of kinetic energy because they are relatively small and not proportional to temperature.

The following table summarizes the application of kinetic molecular theory to an increase in container volume, number of molecules, and temperature:

Effect of an **increase** in one variable holding the other two constant	Effect: − = decrease, 0 = no change, + = increase						
	Average distance between molecules	Density in a sealed container	Average speed of molecules	Average translational kinetic energy of molecules	Collisions with container walls per second	Collisions per unit area of wall per second	Pressure (P)
Volume of container (V)	+	−	0	0	−	−	−
Number of molecules	−	+	0	0	+	+	+
Temperature (T)	0	0	+	+	+	+	+

Additional details on the kinetic molecular theory may be found at http://hyperphysics.phy-astr.gsu.edu/hbase/kinetic/ktcon.html. An animation of gas particles colliding is located at http://comp.uark.edu/~jgeabana/mol_dyn/.

Skill 7.6 Knows how to apply the ideal gas law to analyze mass relationships between reactants and products in chemical reactions involving gases

The ideal gas law allows us to not only characterize gases at certain conditions, but to investigate reactions between gases. In problems such as these, **knowledge of both stoichiometry and the gas laws is needed**. This is most clearly demonstrated with the following example.

Example: Calculate the volume of gaseous NO_2 generated from the combustion of 100 grams of NH_3 when the following reaction occurs at STP:

$$4NH_3 (g) + 7O_2 (g) \rightarrow 4NO_2 (g) + 6H_2O (l)$$

Solution: First we must calculate how many moles of NH_3 are present in 100 g, knowing that the molecular weight is 17.034 g/mol:

$$100 \text{ g } NH_3 / (17.034 \text{ g/mol}) = 5.87 \text{ mol } NH_3$$

The molar ratio between NH_3 and NO_2 is 1:1. Therefore, 5.87 mol of NO_2 will be formed in this reaction. STP (standard temperature and pressure) occurs at 273.15 K and 1 atm. Rearranging the ideal gas law and using the appropriate units of R = 0.08206 L-atm/K-mol:

$$V = nRT/P$$

V = (5.87 mol NO_2 × 0.08206 L-atm/K-mol × 273.15 K)/1 atm = 132 L NO_3

The example above is a typical example of a gas stoichiometry problem. In other problems, the density of the gas will be included and a different version of the ideal gas law will be more helpful, as discussed in Skill 7.3:

$$d = \frac{nM}{V} = \frac{PM}{RT}$$

COMPETENCY 008 THE TEACHER UNDERSTANDS PROPERTIES AND CHARACTERISTICS OF IONIC AND COVALENT BONDS

Skill 8.1 Relates the electron configuration of an atom to its chemical reactivity

Nonmetals gain electrons or share electrons to achieve stable configurations and **metals lose electrons** to achieve them. Elements of similar types may share electrons to reach a stable configuration.

Valence electrons are the outermost electrons and are therefore the electrons primarily involved in chemical reactions. The **Octet Rule** states that when forming chemical bonds, atoms tend to gain or lose electrons so that their outermost shell has eight electrons. When there are less than four valence electrons, the atom tends to lose electrons to get back to the previous energy level that was full. However, when the outer shell is more than half full (has more than four valence electrons) the atom tends to gain electrons to complete the valence energy level.

For example, aluminum has 13 electrons with a configuration of $1s^2 2s^2 2p^6 3s^2 3p^1$. There are only three electrons in the 3rd energy level and ideally there would be eight. This can be accomplished by filling the $3p$ orbital with five electrons or by losing the $3s^2$ and $3p^1$ electrons. It takes less energy to lose three electrons than to gain five electrons, so that is typically what happens when aluminum forms compounds. When these electrons are lost, an Al^{3+} ion forms with an electron configuration of $1s^2 2s^2 2p^6$, which now has a complete octet in the outer shell.

Families with valence configurations s^1, s^2, or $s^2 p^1$ tend to lose electrons to form ionic compounds. Note that atoms with electrons in the d or f orbitals have s^1 or s^2 as their valence configuration of electrons. Families with valence configurations $s^2 p^2$, $s^2 p^3$, $s^2 p^4$, and $s^2 p^5$ tend to gain electrons to form ionic compounds or share electrons to form covalent bonds. The noble gas family with an $s^2 p^6$ configuration has a complete octet in its valence shell, and this configuration tends to be inert. However, the heavier noble gases form a number of compounds with oxygen and fluorine such as KrF_2 and XeO_4.

As discussed in Skill 6.4, elements with completely full outermost shells (e.g., noble gases) are the most stable, and elements with half-full outermost shells (with four valence electrons, one in each orbital) are also relatively stable. The most reactive elements are those that are closest to the stable configurations and only have one or two electrons to gain or lose to reach them.

This information helps us to understand some other characteristics. For example, the elements in the alkali metal family are not found as free elements in nature. This is due to their high chemical activity. The one valence electron in the outermost energy level is highly unstable and tends to be easily lost, forming many different ionic compounds in the process. On the other end of the periodic table, the halogen family consists of covalent molecules instead of free elements. The valence energy level is missing only one electron, and is easily completed by two halogen atoms sharing electrons to form a covalent molecule.

Skill 8.2   Compares and contrasts characteristics of ionic and covalent bonds

Ionic Bonds

An **ionic bond** describes the electrostatic forces that exist between **particles of opposite charge.** An ionic bond is the result of one atom losing electrons to another atom. The atom that loses electrons becomes positively

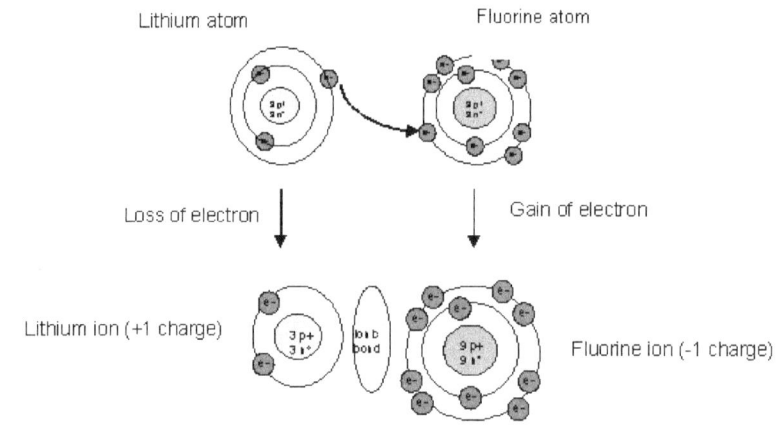

charged and the atom that gains electrons becomes negatively charged. The bond is formed through the attraction between the positive and negative ions.

Due to low ionization energies, metals have a tendency to lose valence electrons relatively easily, whereas non-metals, which have high ionization energies and high electronegativities, gain electrons easily. Therefore, metals and non-metals form ionic bonds with each other.

SINGLE AND MULTIPLE COVALENT BONDS

A **covalent bond** forms when at least one pair of electrons is shared by two atoms. The shared electrons are found in the outermost valence energy level and lead to a lower energy if they are shared in a way that creates a noble gas configuration (a full octet). Covalent, or molecular, bonds occur when a non-metal is bonding to a non-metal. This is due primarily to the fact that non-metals have high ionization energies and high electronegativities. Neither atom wants to give up electrons; both want to gain them. In order to fill both octets, the electrons can be shared between the two atoms.

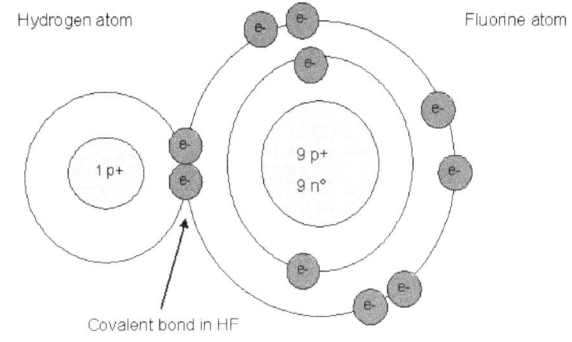

Covalent bond in HF

Sharing of electrons can be equal or unequal, resulting in a separation of charge (polar) or an even distribution of charge (non-polar). The polarity of a bond can be determined through an examination of the electronegativities of the atoms involved in the bond. The more electronegative atom will have a stronger attraction to the electrons, thus possessing the electrons more of the time. This results in a partial negative charge (δ^-) on the more electronegative atom and a partial positive charge (δ^+) on the less electronegative atom.

The simplest covalent bond is between the two single electrons of hydrogen atoms. Covalent bonds may be represented by an electron pair (a pair of dots) or a line as shown below. The shared pair of electrons provides each H atom with two electrons in its valence shell (the 1s orbital), so both have the stable electron configuration of helium.

$$H\cdot \; + \; \cdot H \longrightarrow \begin{array}{c} H\!:\!H \\ H\!-\!H \end{array}$$

Chlorine molecules have 7 electrons in their valence shell and share a pair of electrons so both have the stable electron configuration of argon.

$$:\!\ddot{\underset{..}{Cl}}\!\cdot \; + \; \cdot\!\ddot{\underset{..}{Cl}}\!: \longrightarrow \; :\!\ddot{\underset{..}{Cl}}\!:\!\ddot{\underset{..}{Cl}}\!:$$

$$:\!\ddot{\underset{..}{Cl}}\!-\!\ddot{\underset{..}{Cl}}\!:$$

In the previous two examples, a single pair of electrons was shared, and the resulting bond is referred to as a **single bond**. When two electron pairs are shared, two lines are drawn, representing a **double bond**, and three shared pairs of electrons represents a **triple bond** as shown below for CO_2 and N_2. The remaining electrons are in **unshared pairs**.

$$\ddot{\ddot{O}}::C::\ddot{\ddot{O}}$$

$$\ddot{\ddot{O}}=C=\ddot{\ddot{O}}$$

$$:N::N:$$

$$:N\equiv N:$$

POLAR/NONPOLAR COVALENT BONDS

Electron pairs shared between **two atoms of the same element are shared equally (a non-polar bond)**. At the other extreme, **in ionic bonding there is no electron sharing** because the electron is transferred completely from one atom to the other. Most bonds fall somewhere between these two extremes, and the electrons are **shared unequally (a polar bond)**.

The polarity of a bond can be determined through an examination of the electronegativities of the atoms involved in the bond. The more electronegative atom will have a stronger attraction to the electrons, thus possessing the electrons more of the time. This results in a partial negative charge (δ^-) on the more electronegative atom as shown below on the hydrogen atom and a partial positive charge (δ^+) on the less electronegative atom as shown below on the chlorine atom. Such bonds are referred to as polar bonds. A molecule with a positive region and a negative region is called a dipole.

$$\overset{\delta+ \quad \delta-}{H-Cl} \quad \overset{\longrightarrow}{H-Cl}$$

Skill 8.3   Applies the "octet" rule to construct Lewis structures

Lewis dot structures are a method for keeping track of each atom's valence electrons in a molecule. Drawing Lewis structures is a three-step process:

1) Add up the number of valence shell electrons for each atom. If the compound is an anion, add the charge of the ion to the total electron count because anions have "extra" electrons. If the compound is a cation, subtract the charge of the ion.

2) Write the symbols for each atom in a spatial arrangement showing how the atoms connect to each other.

3) Draw a single bond (one pair of electron dots or a line) between each pair of connected atoms. Place the remaining electrons around the atoms as unshared pairs. If every atom has an octet of electrons (except H atoms, which have only two electrons), the Lewis structure is complete. Shared electrons count towards both atoms. If there are too few electron pairs to complete the octets with single bonds, draw multiple bonds (two or three pairs of electron dots between the atoms) until an octet is formed around each atom. If there are too many electron pairs to complete the octets with single bonds then the octet rule is broken for this compound.

Example: Draw a Lewis dot structure for HCN.

Solution:

1) From their locations in the main group of the periodic table, we know that each atom contributes the following number of electrons: H – 1, C – 4, and N – 5. Because it is a neutral compound, the molecule will have a total of 10 valence electrons.

2) The atoms are connected with C at the center and are therefore drawn as:

$$H \ C \ N$$

It is not possible for H to be the central atom because H has only one valence electron. Therefore, it will always have only a single bond to one other atom. If N were the central atom then the formula would probably be written as HNC.

3) First, try connecting the atoms with single bonds. This gives the structure to the right. H has two electrons to fill its valence subshells, but C and N only have six each. A triple bond between these atoms fulfills the octet rule for C and N and is the correct Lewis structure.

$$H : C ::: N :$$

To select the most probable Lewis dot structure for a compound or molecule that follows the octet rule, review the structures and compare to the method for constructing Lewis dot structures from the previous page.

Example: Which of the electron-dot structures given below for nitrous oxide (laughing gas), N_2O, is/are acceptable?

A) :N::N:O:

B) :N:N::O:

C) :N:::N::O:

Solution: Both nitrogen and oxygen follow the octet rule so the Lewis structure should show each atom in the molecule with 8 electrons, either shared or unshared. Upon examination, only choice A) provides each atom in the molecule with 8 electrons. Choice B) has only 6 electrons around each of the nitrogen atoms and choice C) has 10 electrons around the center nitrogen atom.

Skill 8.4   Identifies and describes the arrangement of atoms in molecules, ionic crystals, polymers, and metallic substances

MOLECULES

Atoms in molecules are held together by covalent bonds, which may be polar or non-polar, depending on the relative electronegativities of the individual atoms in the molecule and how the charge is distributed. Certain valence electrons are shared between the atoms in single, double, or triple bonds. Electron pairs in other orbitals are unshared. The geometry of atoms within a molecule is largely determined by electron-electron repulsion and the shape of the orbitals within which the electrons are located. See Skill 8.10 for a detailed discussion of molecular geometry.

IONIC CRYSTALS

Chemical compounds form when two or more atoms join together. A stable compound occurs when the total energy of the combination of the atoms together is lower than the atoms separately. The combined state suggests an attractive force exists between the atoms. This attractive force is called a chemical bond. This *electrostatic interaction* between an anion and a cation results in an ionic bond. Elements that form an ionic bond with each other have a large difference in their electronegativity. When these ionic bonds occur in a solid, anions and cations pack together into a **crystal lattice** as shown to the right for NaCl. Ionic compounds are also known as **salts**.

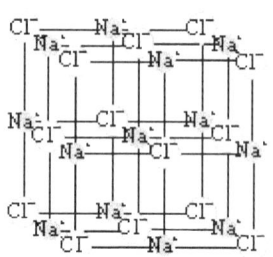

POLYMERS

Polymers are long-chain organic molecules made up of many repeating units. Polymers may be natural compounds such as cellulose or rubber, or they may be manufactured compounds such as polyvinylchloride (PVC) or polyethylene. Polymers consist of a long central chain of carbon atoms, which may have various repeating side branches. Because these molecules are so long and have a repetitive structure, the attractive forces between molecules are much stronger than between most molecules. Polymeric chains may be attracted to each other through ionic bonds or hydrogen bonds. This frequently gives polymers both strength and flexibility, properties for which they are highly prized.

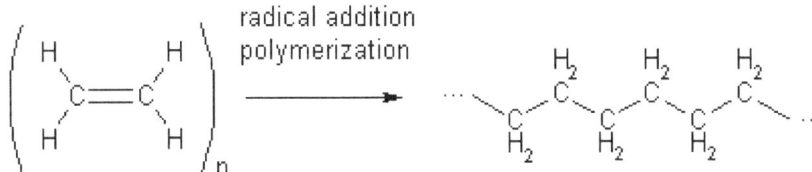

Metallic substances

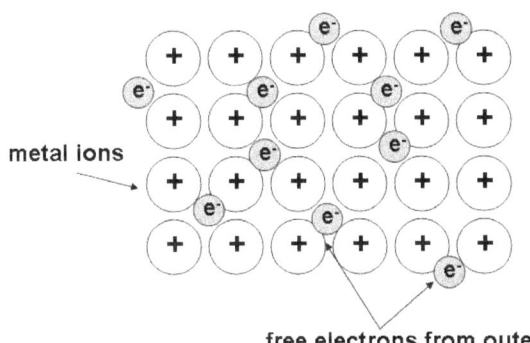

Metallic bonds occur when bonds are formed between two or more metal atoms. Metallic properties such as low ionization energy, conductivity, and malleability suggest that metals possess strong forces of attraction between atoms but still have electrons that are able to move freely in all directions throughout the metal. This "sea of electrons" model describes a structure where electrons are quickly and easily transferred among metal atoms. The metallic bond results from the force of attraction between the moving electrons and the positive nuclei left behind. The strength of metallic bonds usually results in regular structures and high melting and boiling points.

Skill 8.5 Understands the influence of bonding forces on the physical and chemical properties of ionic and covalent substances

Electronegativity is a measure of **the ability of an atom to attract electrons** in a chemical bond. Metallic elements have low electronegativities and nonmetallic elements have high electronegativities. Examples of electronegativities for the first few rows of the periodic table are shown in the figure below.

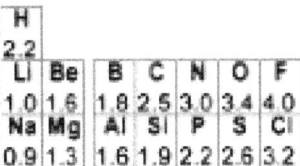

Linus Pauling developed the concept of electronegativity and its relationship to different types of bonds in the 1930s.

A **large electronegativity difference** (greater than 1.7) results in an **ionic bond**. Any bond composed of two different atoms will be slightly polar, but for a **small electronegativity difference** (less than 0.4), the distribution of charge in the bond is so nearly equal that the result is called a **nonpolar covalent bond**. An **intermediate electronegativity difference** (from 0.4 to 1.7) results in a **polar covalent bond**.

Example: HCl is polar covalent because Cl has a very high electronegativity (it is near F in the periodic table) and H is a nonmetal (and so it will form a covalent bond with Cl), but H is near the dividing line between metals and nonmetals, so there is still a significant electronegativity difference between H and Cl. Using the numbers in the table above, the electronegativity for Cl is 3.2 and it is 2.2 for H. The difference of $3.2 - 2.2 = 1.0$ places this bond in the middle of the range for polar covalent bonds.

COVALENT BONDS IN A NETWORK SOLID

A covalent network solid may be considered **one large molecule connected by covalent bonds**. These materials are **very hard, strong, and have a high melting point**. Diamond, C_n or C_∞, and quartz, $(SiO_2)_n$ or $(SiO_2)_\infty$, are two examples.

IONIC BONDS

All common salts (compounds with **ionic bonds**) are solids at room temperature. **Salts are brittle, have a high melting point**, and do not conduct electricity because their ions are not free to move in the crystal lattice. Salts do conduct electricity in molten form. The formation of a salt is a highly exothermic reaction between a metal and a nonmetal.

Salts in solid form are generally stable compounds, but in molten form or in solution, their component ions often react to form a more stable salt. Some salts decompose to form more stable salts, as in the decomposition of molten potassium chlorate to form potassium chloride and oxygen:

$$2KClO_3(l) \rightarrow 2KCl(s) + 3O_2(g)$$

METALLIC BONDS

The physical properties of metals are attributed to the **electron sea model of metallic bonds** shown to the right. Metals **conduct heat and electricity** because electrons are not associated with specific atoms and they are able to flow throughout the material. They are called **delocalized** electrons. Metals are **lustrous** because electrons at their surface reflect light at many different wavelengths.

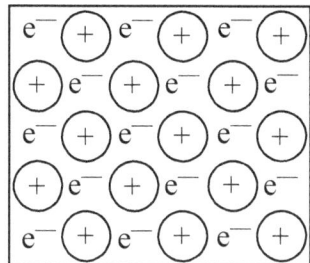

Metals are **malleable** and **ductile** because the electrons are able to rearrange their positions to maintain the integrity of the solid when the metallic lattice is deformed, acting like glue between the cations. The strengths of different metallic bonds can be related to the relative amounts and positions of electrons present.

Alkali metals contain only one valence electron, and that electron is a considerable distance away from the nucleus because it is shielded from nuclear attraction by the noble gas configuration of the remaining electrons. The result is a weak metallic bond and a low melting point. Heavier alkali metals contain a valence electron even further from the nucleus, resulting in a very weak metallic bond and a further lowering of the melting point. With two valence electrons and smaller atoms, alkaline earth metals have stronger metallic bonds than the alkali metals.

The metal with the weakest metallic bonds is mercury. Hg is a liquid at room temperature because Hg atoms hold on tightly to a stable valence configuration of full s, f, and d subshells. Fewer electrons are shared to create bonds than in other metals.

The reactivity of metals increases with lower electronegativity in reactions with nonmetals to form ionic bonds.

Bond type is actually a continuum as shown in the following chart for common bonds. Note that the **C-H bond** is considered **nonpolar**.

Type of bonding	Electronegativity difference	Bond
		Fr^+—F^-
Very ionic		Na^+—F^-
	3.0	
	⋮	⋮
Ionic		Na^+—Cl^-
	2.0	Na^+—Br^-
Mostly ionic		Na^+—I^-
Mostly polar covalent	1.5	C^+—$F^{\delta-}$
		H^+—$O^{\delta-}$
Polar covalent	1.0	H^+—$Cl^{\delta-}$
		$C^{\delta+}$=$O^{\delta-}$
		H^+—$N^{\delta-}$
		C^+—$Cl^{\delta-}$
	0.5	$C^{\delta+}$≡$N^{\delta-}$
Mostly nonpolar covalent		C—H
Fully nonpolar covalent	0	H_2, N_2, O_2, F_2, Cl_2, Br_2, I_2, C—C, S—S

Increasing ionic character ⇑

Skill 8.6 **Identifies and describes intermolecular and intramolecular forces**

Intramolecular forces include ionic, covalent, and metallic bonds described in Skills 8.2, 8.4, and 8.5, and exist **within molecules**. These are the forces that hold molecules and solid structures together, and are generally much stronger than intermolecular forces.

Intermolecular forces are described in Skill 8.7 below, and include various types of attraction **between molecules**. While these forces are generally much weaker than intramolecular forces, they are still very important in explaining the properties of liquids and even some solids such as polymers.

Skill 8.7 **Uses intermolecular forces to explain the physical properties of a given substance**

ION-DIPOLE INTERACTIONS

Salts tend to dissolve in polar solvents such as water. An ion with a full charge in a polar solvent will **orient nearby solvent molecules** so that their opposite partial charges are pointing towards the ion. In aqueous solution, certain salts react to form solid **precipitates** if a combination of their ions is insoluble.

For example, table salt is NaCl. In water, it ionizes to Na^+ and Cl^-. The Na^+ ions will tend to be attracted to the O end of the H_2O molecule, while the Cl^- ions will tend to orient toward the H atoms in the H_2O molecule. The polarity of the water molecule makes it easier for the ionic compound to dissolve, as it helps pull the ions apart.

DIPOLE-DIPOLE INTERACTIONS

The intermolecular forces between polar molecules are known as dipole-dipole interactions. The partial positive charge of one molecule is attracted to the partial negative charge of its neighbor.

HYDROGEN BONDS

Hydrogen bonds are particularly **strong dipole-dipole interactions** that form between the **H atom** of one molecule and an **F, O**, or **N atom** of an adjacent molecule. The partial positive charge on the hydrogen atom is attracted to the partial negative charge on the electron pair of the other atom. The hydrogen bond between two water molecules is shown as the dashed line below:

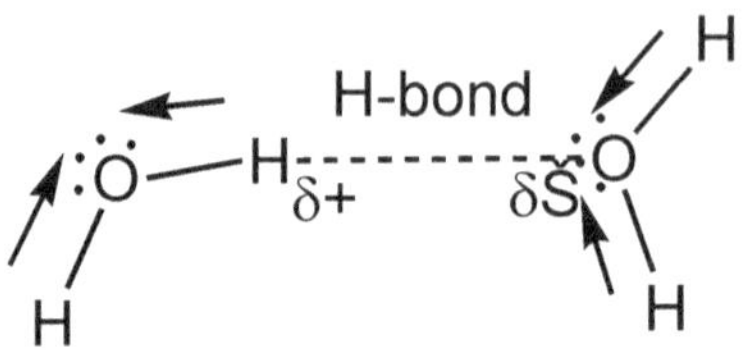

Except in larger molecules, hydrogen bonds are usually an intermolecular force, not a bonding mechanism within a single molecule. Intermolecular forces are also sometimes described as "secondary molecular bonds".

ION-INDUCED DIPOLE

When a nonpolar molecule (or a noble gas atom) encounters an ion, its **electron density is temporarily distorted** resulting in an **induced dipole** that will be attracted to the ion. Intermolecular attractions due to induced dipoles in a nonpolar molecule are known as **London forces** or **Van der Waals interactions**. These are very weak intermolecular forces.

For example, carbon tetrachloride, CCl_4, has polar bonds but is a nonpolar molecule due to the tetrahedral symmetry of those bonds. An aluminum cation will draw the non-bonded electrons of the chlorine atom towards it, distorting the molecule (this distortion has been exaggerated in the figure) and creating an attractive force as shown by the dashed line below.

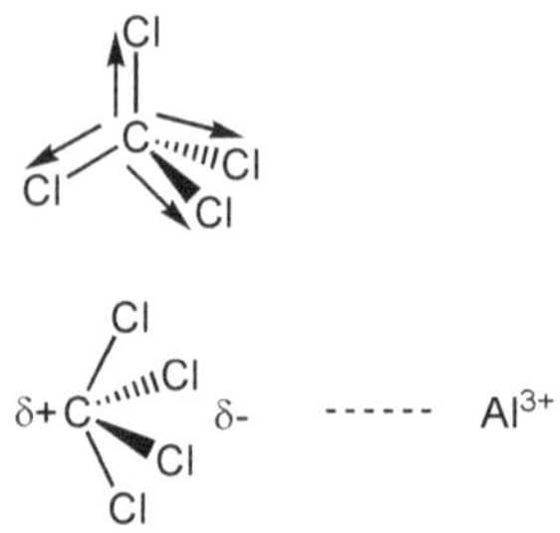

DIPOLE-INDUCED DIPOLE

The partial charge of **a permanent dipole may also induce a dipole in a nonpolar molecule** resulting in an attraction similar to but weaker than that created by an ion.

LONDON DISPERSION FORCE: INDUCED DIPOLE – INDUCED DIPOLE

The above two examples required a permanent charge to induce a dipole in a nonpolar molecule. A nonpolar molecule may also induce a temporary dipole on its identical neighbor in a pure substance. These forces occur because at any given moment, electrons are located within a certain region of the molecule, and **the instantaneous location of electrons will induce a temporary dipole** on neighboring molecules. For example, an isolated helium atom consists of a nucleus with a 2+ charge and two electrons in a spherical electron density cloud. An attraction between He atoms due to London dispersion forces (shown below by the dashed line) occurs when the electrons happen to be distributed unevenly on one atom, inducing a dipole on its neighbor. This dipole is due to intermolecular repulsion of electrons and the attraction of electrons to neighboring nuclei.

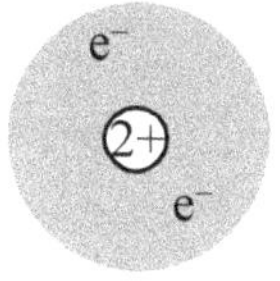

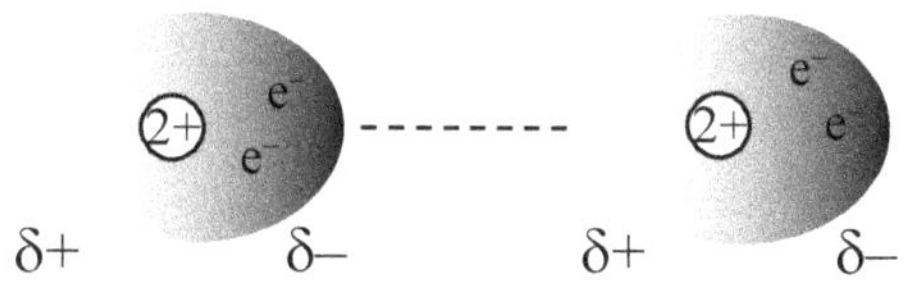

The strength of London dispersion forces **increases for larger molecules** because a larger electron cloud is more easily polarized. The strength of London dispersion forces also **increases for molecules with a larger surface area** because there is greater opportunity for electrons to influence neighboring molecules if there is more potential contact between the molecules. Paraffin in candles is an example of a solid held together by weak London forces between large molecules. These materials are soft.

IMPACT ON PHYSICAL PROPERTIES

If two substances are being compared, the material with the **greater intermolecular attractive forces** (i.e. the stronger intermolecular bond) will require more energy to pull apart the molecules. Substances with greater intermolecular forces will have the following properties:

FOR SOLIDS:
Higher melting point
Higher enthalpy of fusion
Greater hardness
Lower vapor pressure

FOR LIQUIDS:
Higher boiling point
Higher critical temperature
Higher critical pressure
Higher enthalpy of vaporization
Higher viscosity
Higher surface tension
Lower vapor pressure

FOR GASES:
Intermolecular attractive forces are neglected for ideal gases, as they seldom have observable effects.

For example, H_2O and NH_3 are liquids at room temperature because they contain hydrogen bonds. These bonds are of intermediate strength, so the melting point of these compounds is lower than room temperature and their boiling point is higher than room temperature. H_2S contains weaker dipole-dipole interactions than H_2O because the sulfur atoms do not form hydrogen bonds. Therefore, H_2S is a gas at room temperature due to its low boiling point. Small non-polar molecules such as CO_2, N_2, or atoms such as He are gases at room temperature due to very weak London forces, but larger non-polar molecules such as octane or CCl_4 may be liquids, and very large non-polar molecules such as paraffin will be soft solids.

Skill 8.8   Applies the concepts of electronegativity, electron affinity, and oxidation state to analyze chemical bonds

See Skills 6.4, 8.1, 8.2, and 8.5 for discussions of these relationships.

Skill 8.9   Evaluates energy changes in the formation and dissociation of chemical bonds

Chemical energy is the **energy stored in substances due to the arrangement of atoms** within the substance. When atoms are rearranged during chemical reactions, energy is either released or consumed. It is the energy released from chemical reactions that fuels our economy and powers our bodies. Most of the electricity produced on the planet comes from chemical energy released by the burning of petroleum, coal, and natural gas. ATP is the molecule used by our bodies to carry chemical energy form cell to cell.

The energy in molecules is located in the **bonds between the atoms**. To break these bonds requires energy. Once broken apart, the atoms, ions, or molecules rearrange themselves to form new substances, making new bonds. Making new bonds releases energy.

If during a chemical reaction, **more energy is needed to break the reactant bonds than is released when the products form new bonds,** the reaction is **endothermic** and heat is absorbed. The environment becomes colder.

On the other hand, if **more energy is released when the products form new bonds than is needed to break the reactant bonds,** the reaction is **exothermic** and the excess energy is released to the environment as heat. The temperature of the environment goes up.

BOND ENERGIES

The total energy absorbed or released in the reaction can be determined by using **heats of formation** or **bond energies**. The total energy change of the reaction is equal to the total energy of all of the bonds of the products minus the total energy of all of the bonds of the reactants.

Propane (C_3H_8) is a common fuel used in heating homes and backyard grills. When burned, the combustion reaction shown below takes place and excess energy is released and used for heating or cooking:

$$C_3H_8\,(g) + 5O_2\,(g) \rightarrow 3CO_2\,(g) + 4H_2O\,(l)$$

The total energy of the products is found from the bonds in the carbon dioxide molecules and the water molecules:

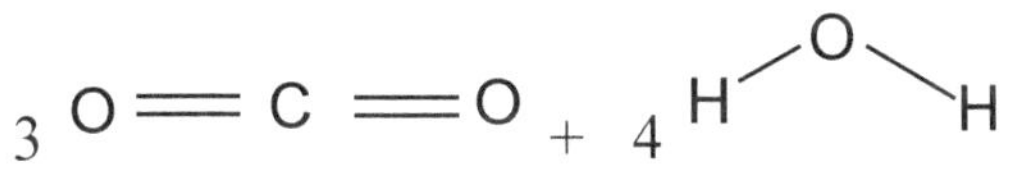

$$3\;O=C=O \;+\; 4\;H\!-\!O\!-\!H$$

or 6 C=O bonds and 8 H–O bonds.

A table of bond energies gives the following information:

C=O   743 kJ/mol
H–O   463 kJ/mol

For these molecules there would be:

$$(6 \times -743 \text{ kJ/mol}) + (8 \times -463 \text{ kJ/mol}) = -8162 \text{ kJ}$$

energy released when these molecules form. Negative values are used to indicate energy released for this exothermic process of bond formation.

The reactants are these:

$$\begin{array}{c} H\quad H\quad H \\ |\quad\;\; |\quad\;\; | \\ H-C-C-C-H \\ |\quad\;\; |\quad\;\; | \\ H\quad H\quad H \end{array} \quad + 5\; O=O$$

or 2 C–C bonds, 8 C–H bonds, and 5 O=O bonds.

These bonds require the following energy to break:

C–C   348 kJ/mol
C–H   412 kJ/mol
O=O   498 kJ/mol

The total energy required for the reactants would be:

(2 x 348 kJ) + (8 x 412 kJ) + (5 x 498 kJ) = 6482 kJ

energy required. Positive values are used to indicate energy required for the endothermic process of bond destruction.

The total energy change that occurs during the combustion of propane is found from the sum of the energy released by the formation of the product bonds and the energy required to break the reactant bonds:

-8162 kJ + 6482 kJ = -1680 kJ

energy released for every mole of propane that burns.

HEAT OF REACTION

The **enthalpy** (H) of a material is the **sum of its internal energy and the mechanical work** it can do by driving a piston. The differences between internal energy and enthalpy are not important. The key concept is that a change in the **enthalpy** of a substance is the total **energy** change caused by **adding and/or removing heat** at constant pressure.

When a material is heated, **thermal energy is used to break the intermolecular bonds** holding the material together. Similarly, bonds are formed with the release of thermal energy when a material cools. Therefore, **the energy of a material increases during a phase change that requires heat and decreases during a phase change that releases heat**. For example, the energy of H_2O increases when ice melts and decreases when water freezes.

When a chemical reaction takes place, the enthalpies of the products will differ from the enthalpies of the reactants. There is an energy change for the reaction ΔH_{rxn}, determined by **the sum of the products minus the sum of the reactants**:

$$\Delta H_{rxn} = H_{product\ 1} + H_{product\ 2} + \ldots - H_{reactant\ 1} - H_{reactant\ 2} \ldots$$

The enthalpy change for a reaction is commonly called the **heat of reaction**.

If the enthalpies of the products are greater than the enthalpies of the reactants then ΔH_{rxn} **is positive** and the reaction is **endothermic**. Endothermic reactions **absorb heat** from their surroundings. The simplest endothermic reactions break chemical bonds.

If the enthalpies of the products are less than the enthalpies of the reactants then ΔH_{rxn} **is negative** and the reaction is **exothermic**. Exothermic reactions **release heat** into their surroundings. The simplest exothermic reactions form new chemical bonds.

The heat absorbed or released by a chemical reaction often has the impact of changing the temperature of the reaction vessel and of the chemicals themselves. The measurement of these heat effects is known as **calorimetry**.

The enthalpy change of a reaction ΔH_{rxn} **is equal in magnitude but has the opposite sign to the enthalpy change for the reverse reaction**. If a series of reactions lead back to the initial reactants then the net energy change for the entire process is zero.

When a reaction is composed of sub-steps, the **total enthalpy change will be the sum of the changes for each step**. Even if a reaction in reality contains no steps, we may still write any number of reactions in series that lead from the reactants to the products and their sum will be the heat of the overall reaction of interest. The ability to add together these enthalpies to form ultimate products from initial reactants is known as **Hess' Law**. It is used to determine one heat of reaction from others:

$$\Delta H_{net\ rxn} = H_{rxn\ 1} + H_{rxn\ 2} + \ldots$$

Exothermic reactions are more likely to occur spontaneously than endothermic reactions. Molecules usually seek the lowest possible energy state. However, entropy also plays a critical role in determining whether a reaction occurs.

A **standard** thermodynamic value occurs with all components at 25° C and 100 kPa. This *thermodynamic standard state* is slightly different from the *standard temperature and pressure* (STP) often used for gas law problems (0° C and 1 atm = 101.325 kPa). Standard thermodynamic values of common chemicals are listed in tables.

The **heat of formation** ΔH_f of a chemical is the heat taken up (positive) or emitted (negative) when elements react to form the chemical. It is also called the enthalpy of formation. The **standard heat of formation** $\Delta H_f°$ is the heat of formation with all reactants and products at 25° C and 100 kPa.

Elements in their **most stable form** are assigned a value of $\Delta H_f° = 0$ kJ/mol. Different forms of an element in the same phase of matter are known as **allotropes**.

Example: The heat of formation for carbon as a gas is:

$$\Delta H_f° \text{ for } C(g) = 718.4 \ \frac{kJ}{mol}$$

C in the solid phase exists in three allotropes. A C_{60} *buckyball* (above right) contains C atoms linked with aromatic bonds and arranged in the shape of a soccer ball. C_{60} was discovered in 1985. *Diamond* (middle right) contains single C–C bonds in a three-dimensional network. The most stable form at 25° C is *graphite* (below right). Graphite is composed of C atoms with aromatic bonds in sheets.

$$\Delta H_f° \text{ for } C_{60} (buckminsterfullerene \text{ or } buckyball) = 38.0 \ \frac{kJ}{mol}$$

$$\Delta H_f° \text{ for } C_\infty (diamond) = 1.88 \ \frac{kJ}{mol}$$

$$\Delta H_f° \text{ for } C_\infty (graphite) = 0 \ \frac{kJ}{mol}$$

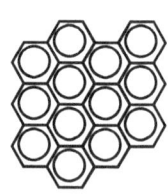

Heat of combustion ΔH_c (also called enthalpy of combustion) is the heat of reaction when a chemical **burns in O_2** to form completely oxidized products such as **CO_2 and H_2O**. It is also the heat of reaction for **nutritional molecules that are metabolized** in the body. The standard heat of combustion $\Delta H_c°$ takes place at 25° C and 100 kPa. **Combustion is always exothermic**, so the negative sign for values of ΔH_c is often omitted. If a combustion reaction is used in Hess' Law, the value must be negative.

Example: Determine the standard heat of formation $\Delta H_f°$ for ethylene:

$$2C(graphite) + 2H_2(g) \rightarrow C_2H_4(g)$$

Solution: Use the heat of combustion for ethylene:

$$\Delta H_c° = 1411.2 \frac{kJ}{mol\ C_2H_4} \quad \text{for} \quad C_2H_4(g) + 3O_2(g) \rightarrow 2CO_2(g) + 2H_2O(l)$$

and the following two heats of formation for CO_2 and H_2O:

$$\Delta H_f° = -393.5 \frac{kJ}{mol\ C} \quad \text{for} \quad C(graphite) + O_2(g) \rightarrow CO_2(g)$$

$$\Delta H_f° = -285.9 \frac{kJ}{mol\ H_2} \quad \text{for} \quad H_2(g) + \frac{1}{2}O_2(g) \rightarrow H_2O(l)$$

Use Hess' Law after rearranging the given reactions so they cancel to yield the reaction of interest. Combustion is exothermic, so ΔH for this reaction is negative. We are interested in C_2H_4 as a product, so we take the opposite (endothermic) reaction. The given ΔHs are multiplied by stoichiometric coefficients to give the reaction of interest as the sum of the three:

$$2CO_2(g) + 2H_2O(l) \rightarrow C_2H_4(g) + 3O_2(g) \quad \Delta H = 1411.2 \frac{kJ}{mol\ reaction}$$

$$2C(graphite) + 2O_2(g) \rightarrow 2CO_2(g) \quad \Delta H = -787.0 \frac{kJ}{mol\ reaction}$$

$$2H_2(g) + O_2(g) \rightarrow 2H_2O(l) \quad \Delta H = -571.8 \frac{kJ}{mol\ reaction}$$

$$2C(graphite) + 2H_2(g) \rightarrow C_2H_4(g) \quad \Delta H_f° = 52.4 \frac{kJ}{mol}$$

Skill 8.10   Understands the relationship between covalent bonding, hybridization, and molecular geometry

RESONANCE

O_2 contains a total of 12 valence electrons and the following Lewis structure:

$$\ddot{\underset{..}{O}}=\ddot{\underset{..}{O}}$$

Ozone (O_3) has a total of 18 valence electrons, and two Lewis structures are equally possible for this molecule:

Equivalent Lewis structures are called **resonance forms**. A double-headed arrow is used to indicate resonance. The actual molecule does not have a double bond on one side and a single bond on the other. The **molecular structure is in an average state between the resonance forms**.

HYBRIDIZED ATOMIC ORBITALS

Electron shell structures are built up by considering different energy levels for different subshells to explain spectroscopic data about individual atoms. However, when Lewis dot structures are drawn (see Skill 8.3) or molecular geometries are determined, all valence electrons are treated identically to explain the bonding between atoms regardless of whether the electrons once belonged to the *s* or the *p* subshell of their atom. Reconciling these views of the individual and the bonded atom requires a theory known as hybridization.

Hybridization describes the pre-bonding **promotion of one or more electrons** from a lower energy subshell to a higher energy subshell followed by a **combination** of the orbitals into degenerate **hybrid orbitals**.

Example: A boron atom has the valence electron configuration $2s^2 2p^1$ as shown to the right. Before bonding to three other atoms, the capability to form three equivalent bonds is achieved by hybridization. First a 2*s* electron is promoted to an empty *p* orbital. Next the occupied orbitals combine into three hybrid $2sp^2$ orbitals. Now three electrons in degenerate orbitals are available to create covalent bonds with three atoms.

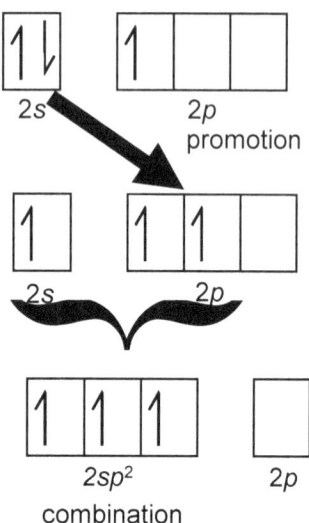

Hybridization occurs for atoms with a valence electron configuration of ns^2, ns^2np^1, or ns^2p^2. For period 2, this corresponds with Be, B, C, and N in the NH_3^+ ion.

An atom joined to its neighbor by **multiple covalent bonds** is prepared for bonding by hybridization with incomplete combination. Electrons that remain in p orbitals can contribute additional bonds between the same two atoms.

Example: An isolated carbon atom has the initial valence electron configuration $2s^22p^2$, shown at right. Hybridization to four $2sp^3$ orbitals occurs before bonding to four atoms (see next page). Three hybrid sp^2 orbitals form if there is one double bond and the C atom is bonded to three atoms. One electron remains in the p orbital. Two hybrid sp orbitals occur if there is a triple bond or two double bonds. In this case, C is bonded to two atoms with two electrons remaining in p orbitals.

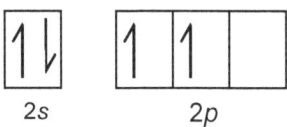

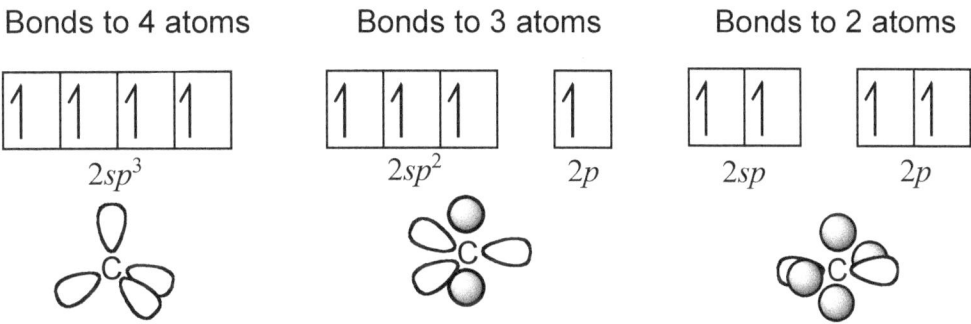

Note: p orbitals are shaded in the diagrams. These models are meant to illustrate the **locations** and **angles** of hybrid and p orbitals relative to the central atom. A mathematical solution would also show that each type of hybrid orbital (sp^3, sp^2, and sp) has a slightly different shape compared to the other two.

See
http://www.mhhe.com/physsci/chemistry/essentialchemistry/flash/hybrv18.swf
for a flash animation tutorial of hybridization.

MOLECULAR ORBITAL THEORY

The electron configurations of isolated atoms are found in atomic orbitals, the configurations of atoms about to bond are represented by atomic and hybridized orbitals, and **the electron configurations of molecules are represented by molecular orbitals**. Molecular orbital theory is an advanced topic, but it may be simplified to representing the **bonds between atoms as overlapping electron density shapes from atomic orbitals**. There are two typical locations for molecular orbitals.

The **bonding sigma orbital** (σ) surrounds a **line drawn between the two atoms** in a bond. At least one electron pair in every bond is in a bonding σ orbital. Sigma bonds get their name from *s* orbitals because the spherical electron density shapes of two *s* orbitals overlap to form a σ orbital. A drawing of this overlap and the resulting molecular orbital is shown to the right for H_2. Hybrid or *p* atomic orbitals also form σ orbitals when they overlap such that the axis between the bonded atoms runs through the center of the combined electron density.

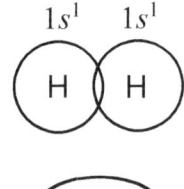
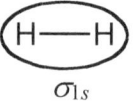

The **bonding pi orbital** (π) follows regions **separate from a line drawn between the two atoms** in a bond. Two overlapping *p* orbitals will form π bonds to contain the additional shared electrons in molecules with double or triple bonds. π bonds prevent atoms from rotating about the central axis between them.

In CH_4, the electron densities of the four sp^3 orbitals of C each overlap with an *s* orbital of H to form four σ bonds. In C_2H_4 (an alkene), two sp^2 orbitals on each C overlap with H *s* orbitals, the remaining sp^2 orbitals overlap with each other in a σ bond, and the *p* orbitals (drawn as shaded shapes) overlap with each other above and below the C atoms in a π bond (also drawn as shaded shapes). In CO_2, the C atom has two *sp* hybrid orbitals and two *p* orbitals. These form one σ bond and one π bond with the two unfilled *p* orbitals on each O atom. In C_2H_2 (an alkyne), a triple bond forms with one σ and two π bonds.

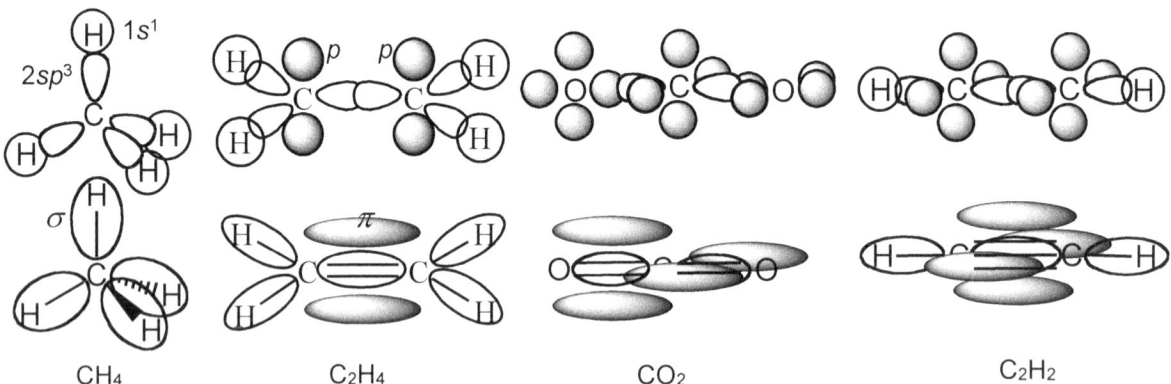

Molecules with double bonds next to each other and aromatic molecules based on benzene contain **more than two π orbitals on adjacent atoms**. The bonds, as well as the entire molecules, are described as being **conjugated**. Electrons in these molecules are free to move from one bond to the next **on the same molecule** and so are **delocalized**. Delocalized electrons are found throughout the entire substance in materials with metallic bonds.

Benzene (C_6H_6) has the following resonance forms:

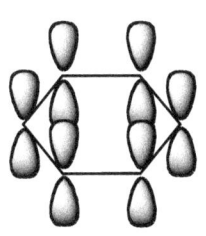 ⟷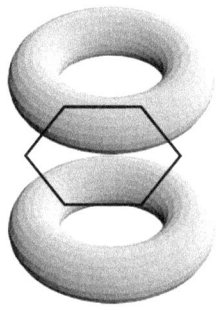

Each carbon atom in benzene bonds to three atoms, so their electrons are in three sp^2 orbitals and one p orbital as we've seen for C_2H_4. The p orbitals are shown as the shaded shapes below on the left (only the C–C bonds are shown). The p atomic orbitals combine to form molecular orbitals with delocalized electrons as shown in the bonding π molecular orbital below to the right.

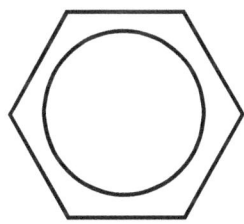 Aromatic molecules are often drawn with a circle in the center of their benzene rings (shown to the left) to show delocalized π electrons. The atoms of a benzene molecule are all located in the same plane. This is in contrast to molecules that contain only σ bonds as shown to the right for cyclohexane, C_6H_{12}.

Molecular orbital theory also predicts **antibonding orbitals** that **prevent bonding** because they are at a higher energy level than the electrons on individual atoms. Antibonding electrons play a role in explaining why molecules like H_2 form while molecules like He_2 do not, but they are not required to predict molecular structures. For more on this aspect of molecular orbital theory, see http://www.chm.davidson.edu/vce/molecularorbitals/.

ELECTRON PAIRS

Molecular geometry is predicted using the valence-shell electron-pair repulsion or **VSEPR** model. VSEPR uses the fact that **electron pairs around the central atom of a molecule repel each other**. Imagine you are one of two pairs of electrons in bonds around a central atom (like a bonds in BeH₂ in the table below). You want to be as far away from the other electron pair as possible, so you will be on one side of the atom and the other pair will be on the other side. There is a straight line (or a 180° angle) between you to the other electron pair on the other side of the nucleus. In general, electron pairs lie at the **largest possible angles** from each other.

Electron pairs	Geometrical arrangement		Predicted bond angles	Example
2	:—X—:	Linear	180°	H—Be—H
3	(trigonal planar diagram)	Trigonal planar	120°	F—B(—F)—F (BF₃)
4	(tetrahedral diagram)	Tetrahedral	109.5°	CH₄
5	(trigonal bipyramidal diagram)	Trigonal bipyramidal	120° and 90°	PF₅
6	(octahedral diagram)	Octahedral	90°	SF₆

X represents a generic central atom. Lone pair electrons on F are not shown in the example molecules.

UNSHARED ELECTRON PAIRS

The **shape of a molecule is given by the locations of its atoms**. Outer atoms are connected to central atoms by shared electrons, but unshared electrons also have an important impact on molecular shape. Unshared electrons may determine the angles between atoms. Molecular shapes in the following table take into account total and unshared electron pairs.

Electron pairs	Molecular shape				
	All shared pairs	1 unshared pair	2 unshared pairs	3 unshared pairs	4 unshared pairs
2	A—X—A Linear				
3	Trigonal planar	Bent			
4	Tetrahedral	Trigonal pyramidal	Bent		
5	Trigonal bipyramidal	Seesaw or sawhorse	T-shaped	Linear	
6	Octahedral	Square pyramidal	Square planar	T-shaped	Linear

X represents a generic central atom bonded to atoms labeled A.

ALTERED BOND ANGLES

Unpaired electrons also have a stronger impact on molecular shape. The shared electron pairs are each attracted partially to the central atom and partially to the other atom in the bond, but the unpaired electrons are different. They are attracted to the central atom, but there is nothing on their other side, so they are free to expand toward the central atom. That expansion means that they take up more room than the other electron pairs, and the others are all squeezed a little closer together. Multiple bonds have a similar effect because more space is required for more electrons. In general, **unshared electron pairs and multiple bonds decrease the angles between the remaining bonds**. A few examples are shown in the following tables.

Compound	CH_4	NH_3	H_2O
Unshared electrons	0	1	2
Shape	Tetrahedral	Trigonal pyramidal	Bent

Compound	BF_3	C_2H_4 (ethylene)
Multiple bonds	0	1
Shape	Trigonal planar	Trigonal planar

SUMMARY

To use VSEPR to predict molecular geometry, perform the following steps:

1) Write out Lewis dot structures.

2) Use the Lewis structure to determine the number of unshared electron pairs and bonds around each central atom, counting multiple bonds as one.

3) The second table of this skill gives the arrangement of total and unshared electron pairs to account for electron repulsions around each central atom.

4) For multiple bonds or unshared electron pairs, decrease the angles slightly between the remaining bonds around the central atom.

5) Combine the results from the previous two steps to determine the shape of the entire molecule.

http://www.shef.ac.uk/chemistry/vsepr/ provides good explanations and diagrams of molecular geometries using VSEPR.

http://cowtownproductions.com/cowtown/genchem/09_16T.htm provides some practice for determining molecular shape.

COMPETENCY 009   THE TEACHER UNDERSTANDS AND INTERPRETS CHEMICAL NOTATION AND CHEMICAL EQUATIONS

Skill 9.1   Identifies elements, ions, and compounds using scientific nomenclature

Basic notation for elements, ions, and compounds is described in Skills 5.4 (elements and isomers), 6.4 (ions), 6.2 (orbital notation), and 9.3-9.4 (compounds and stoichiometric equations). The following sections include additional information on nomenclature for organic chemistry.

Organic compounds that **contain only carbon and hydrogen** are called **hydrocarbons**. The 1979 IUPAC organic nomenclature is used and taught most often today, and it is the nomenclature described here. Hydrocarbon molecules may be divided into the classes of **cyclic** and **open-chain** depending on whether they contain a ring of carbon atoms. Open-chain molecules may be divided into **branched** or **straight-chain** categories.

Hydrocarbons are also divided into classes called **aliphatic** and **aromatic**. Aromatic hydrocarbons are related to benzene and are always cyclic. Aliphatic hydrocarbons may be open-chain or cyclic. Aliphatic cyclic hydrocarbons are called **alicyclic**. Aliphatic hydrocarbons are one of three types: alkanes, alkenes, and alkynes.

ALKANES

Alkanes contain only single bonds. Alkanes have the maximum number of hydrogen atoms possible for their carbon backbone, so they are called **saturated**. Alkenes, alkynes, and aromatics are **unsaturated** because they have fewer hydrogen atoms.

Straight-chain alkanes are also called **normal alkanes**. These are the simplest hydrocarbons. They consist of a linear chain of carbon atoms. The names of these molecules contain the suffix -*ane* and a **root based on the number of carbons in the chain** according to the table on the following page. The first four roots, *meth-*, *eth-*, *prop-*, and *but-* have historical origins in chemistry, and the remaining alkanes contain common Greek number prefixes. Alkanes have the general formula C_nH_{2n+2}.

A single molecule may be represented in multiple ways. Methane and ethane in the table are shown as three-dimensional structures with dashed wedge shapes attaching atoms behind the page and thick wedge shapes attaching atoms in front of the page.

Number of carbons	Name	Formula	Structure
1	Methane	CH_4	(tetrahedral structure of methane)
2	Ethane	C_2H_6	(structure of ethane)
3	Propane	C_3H_8	$H_3C-CH_2-CH_3$
4	Butane	C_4H_{10}	$H_3C-CH_2-CH_2-CH_3$
5	Pentane	C_5H_{12}	$H_3C-CH_2-CH_2-CH_2-CH_3$
6	Hexane	C_6H_{14}	$H_3C-CH_2-CH_2-CH_2-CH_2-CH_3$
7	Heptane	C_7H_{16}	$H_3C-CH_2-CH_2-CH_2-CH_2-CH_2-CH_3$
8	Octane	C_8H_{18}	$H_3C-CH_2-CH_2-CH_2-CH_2-CH_2-CH_2-CH_3$

Additional ways that pentane might be represented are:

n- pentane (the n represents a *normal* alkane)
$CH_3CH_2CH_2CH_2CH_3$
$CH_3(CH_2)_3CH_3$

If one hydrogen is removed from an alkane, the residue is called an **alkyl** group. The -ane suffix is replaced by an –yl- infix when this residue is used as a **functional group**. Functional groups are used to systematically build up the names of organic molecules.

Branched alkanes are named using a four-step process:

1) Find the longest continuous carbon chain. This is the parent hydrocarbon.
2) Number the atoms on this chain beginning at the end near the first branch point. Number functional groups from the attachment point.
3) Determine the numbered locations and names of the substituted alkyl groups. Use *di-*, *tri-*, and similar prefixes for alkyl groups represented more than once. Separate numbers by commas and groups by dashes.
4) List the locations and names of alkyl groups in alphabetical order by their name (ignoring the *di-*, *tri-* prefixes) and end the name with the parent hydrocarbon.

Example: Name the following hydrocarbon:

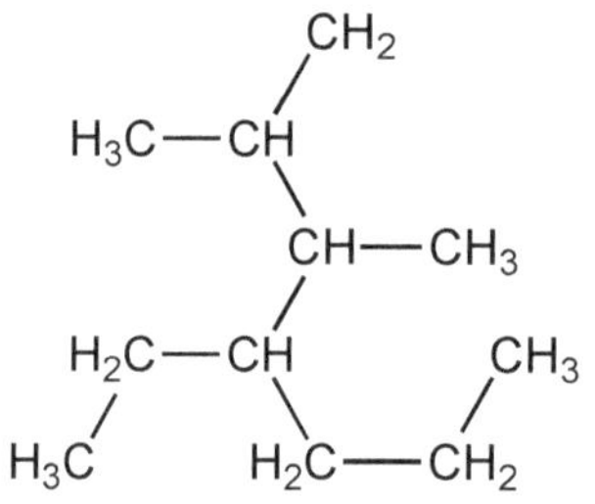

$$\begin{array}{c}
CH_2 \\
H_3C-CH \\
CH-CH_3 \\
H_2C-CH \quad CH_3 \\
H_3C \quad H_2C-CH_2
\end{array}$$

Solution:

1) The longest chain is seven carbons in length, as shown by the bold lines below. This molecule is a heptane.

2) The atoms are numbered from the end nearest the first branch as shown:

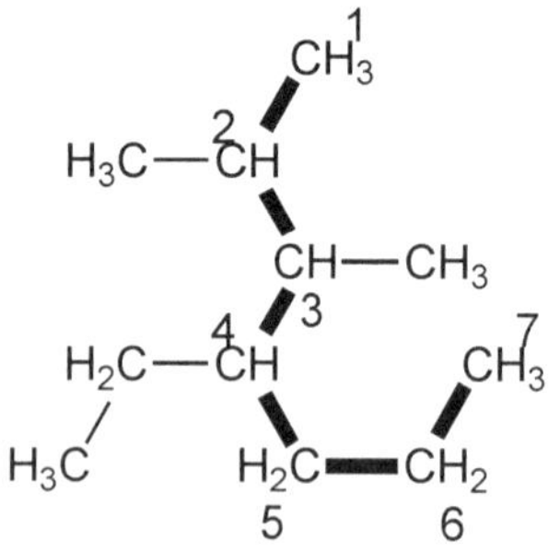

$$\begin{array}{c}
\overset{1}{CH_3} \\
H_3C-\overset{2}{CH} \\
CH-CH_3 \\
\overset{4}{H_2C}-\overset{3}{CH} \quad \overset{7}{CH_3} \\
H_3C \quad \underset{5}{H_2C}-\underset{6}{CH_2}
\end{array}$$

3) Methyl groups are located at carbons 2 and 3 (2,3-dimethyl), and an ethyl group is located at carbon 4.

4) "Ethyl" precedes "methyl" alphabetically. The hydrocarbon name is: 4-ethyl-2,3-dimethylheptane.

The following branched alkanes have accepted common names:

Structure	Systematic name	Common name
(H₃C)₂CH—CH₃	2-methylpropane	isobutane
H₃C—CH₂—CH(CH₃)—CH₃	2-methylbutane	isopentane
C(CH₃)₄	2,2-dimethylpropane	neopentane

The following alkyl groups have accepted common names. The systematic names assign a number of 1 to the attachment point:

Structure	Systematic name	Common name
(H₃C)₂CH—	1-methylethyl	isopropyl
(H₃C)₂CH—CH₂—	2-methylpropyl	isobutyl
H₃C—CH₂—CH(CH₃)—	1-methylpropyl	sec-butyl
(H₃C)₃C—	1,1-dimethylethyl	tert-butyl

ALKENES

Alkenes contain one or more double bonds. Alkenes are also called olefins. The suffix used in the naming of alkenes is *-ene*, and the number roots are those used for alkanes of the same length.

A number preceding the name shows the location of the double bond for alkenes of length four and above. Alkenes with one double bond have the general formula C_nH_{2n}. Multiple double bonds are named using *-diene*, *-triene*, etc. The infix *–enyl-* is used for functional groups after a hydrogen is removed from an alkene. Ethene and propene have the common names **ethylene** and **propylene**. The ethenyl group has the common name **vinyl** and the 2-propenyl group has the common name **allyl**.

Examples:

$H_2C=CH_2$ ethylene or ethene

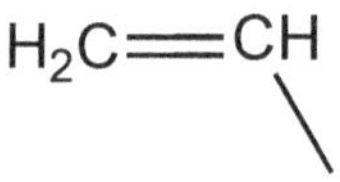

$H_2C=CH\diagdown$ vinyl or ethenyl group

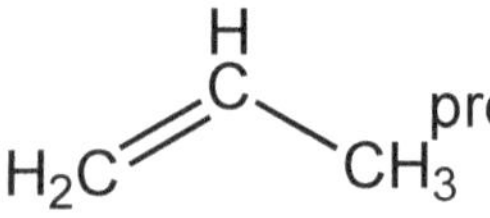

propylene or propene

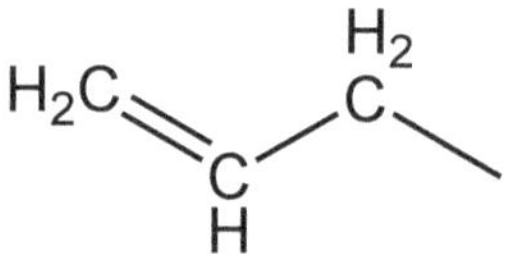

allyl or 2-propenyl group

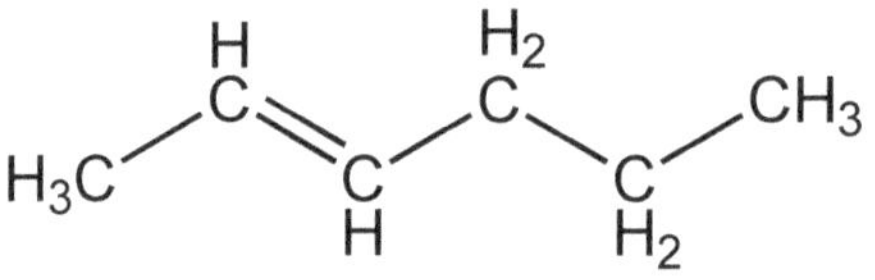

2-hexene

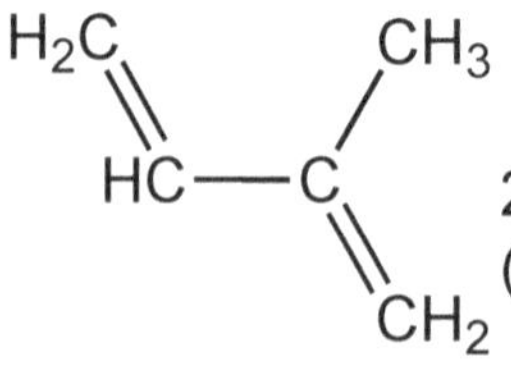

2-methyl-1,3-butadiene (common name: isoprene)

Cis-trans isomerism is often part of the complete name for an alkene. Note that isoprene contains two adjacent double bonds, so it is a **conjugated** molecule.

Note that isoprene contains two adjacent double bonds, so it is a **conjugated** molecule.

ALKYNES AND ALKENYNES

Alkynes contain one or more triple bonds. They are named in a similar way to alkenes. The suffix used for alkynes is *-yne*. Ethyne is often called **acetylene**. Alkynes with one triple bond have the general formula C_nH_{2n-2}. Multiple triple bonds are named using *-diyne*, *-triyne*, etc. The infix *–ynyl-* is used for functional groups composed of alkynes after the removal of a hydrogen atom.

Hydrocarbons with **both double and triple bonds are known as alkenynes**. The locant number for the double bond precedes the name, and the locant for the triple bond follows the infix *–en-* and precedes the suffix *-yne*.

Examples:

HC≡CH   acetylene or ethyne

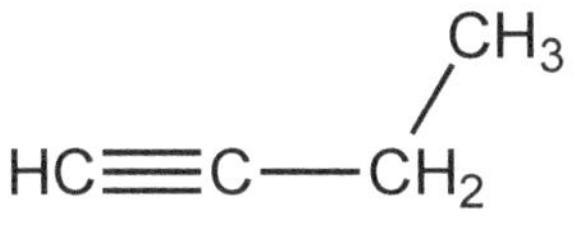

HC≡C—CH₂—CH₃ (with CH₃ branch)   1-butyne

HC≡C—C≡C—CH₃   1,3-pentadiyne

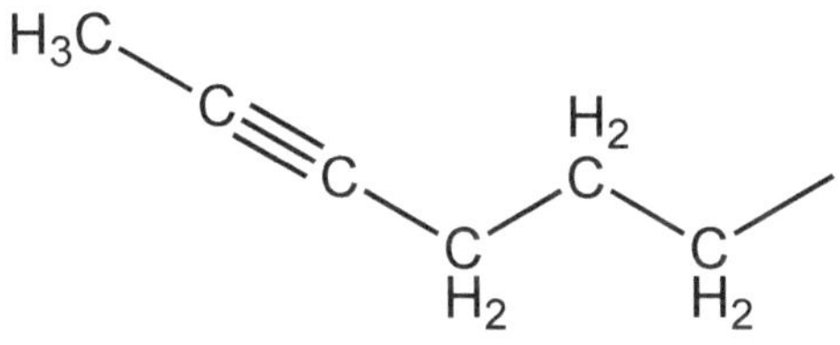

(structure)   4-hexynyl group

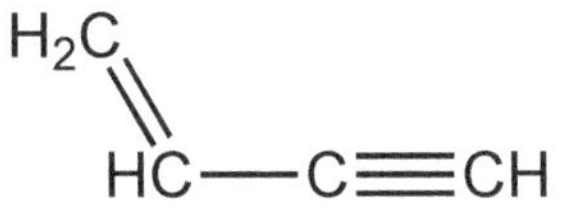

H₂C=CH—C≡CH   1-buten-3-yne (common name vinylacetylene)

CYCLOALKANES, -ENES, AND -YNES

Alicyclic hydrocarbons use the prefix *cyclo-* before the number root for the molecule. The structures for these molecules are often written as if the molecule lay entirely within the plane of the paper even though in reality, these rings dip above and below a single plane. When there is more than one substitution on the ring, numbering begins with the first substitution listed in alphabetical order.

Cis-trans isomerism is often part of the complete name for a cycloalkane.

Examples:

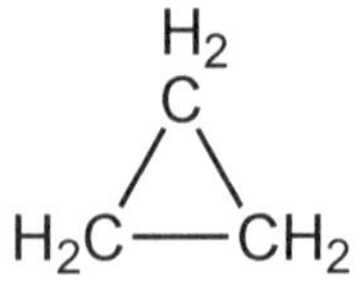

cyclopropane

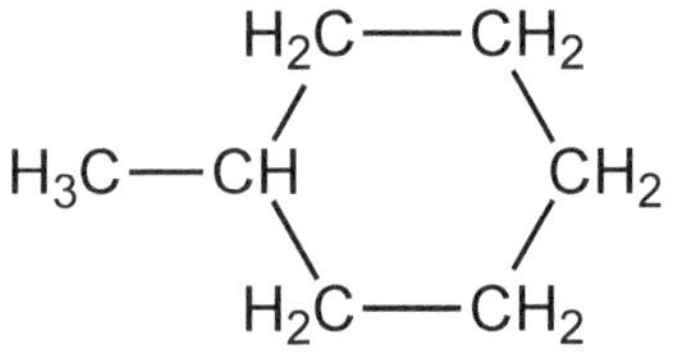

methylcyclohexane   or

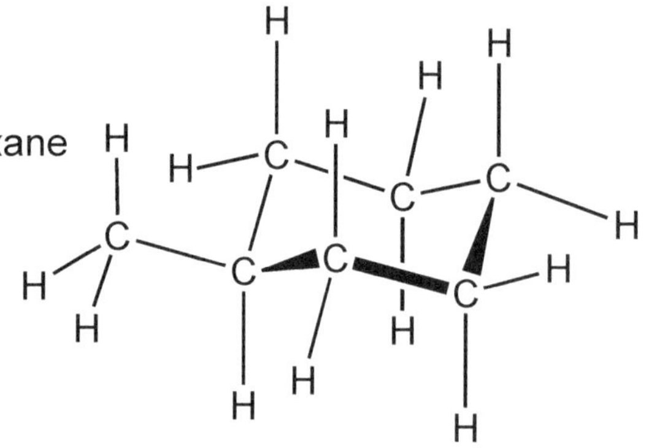

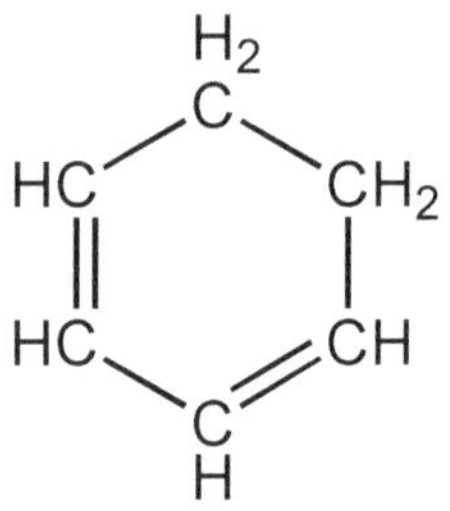

1,3-cyclohexadiene   or

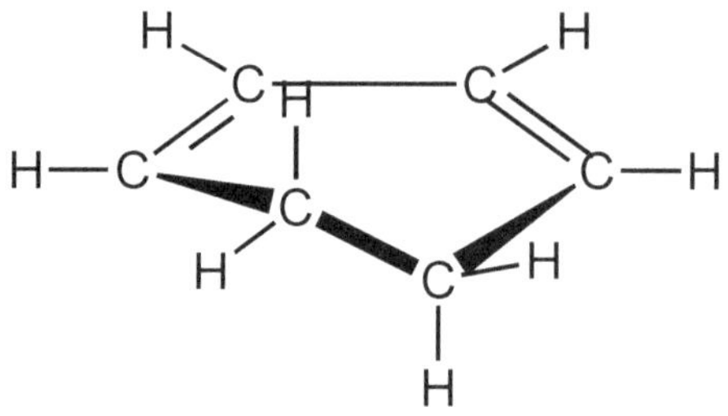

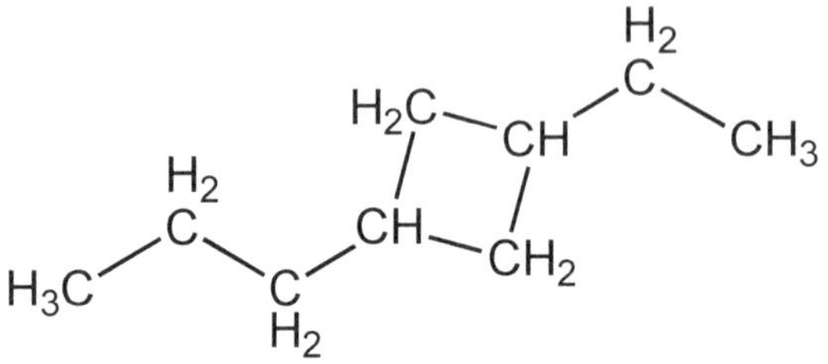

1-ethyl-3-propylcyclobutane

AROMATIC HYDROCARBONS

Aromatic hydrocarbons are structurally related to benzene or made up of benzene molecules fused together. These molecules are called **arenes** to distinguish them from alkanes, alkenes, and alkynes. All atoms in arenes lie in the same plane. In other words, aromatic hydrocarbons are flat. Aromatic molecules have electrons in delocalized π orbitals that are free to migrate throughout the molecule.

Substitutions onto the benzene ring are named in alphabetical order using the lowest possible locant numbers. The prefix *phenyl-* may be used for C_6H_5- (benzene less a hydrogen) attached as a functional group to a larger hydrocarbon residue. Arenes in general form aryl functional groups. A phenyl group may be represented in a structure by the symbol Ø. The prefix *benzyl-* may used for $C_6H_5CH_2-$ (methylbenzene with a hydrogen removed from the methyl group) attached as a functional group.

Examples: benzene

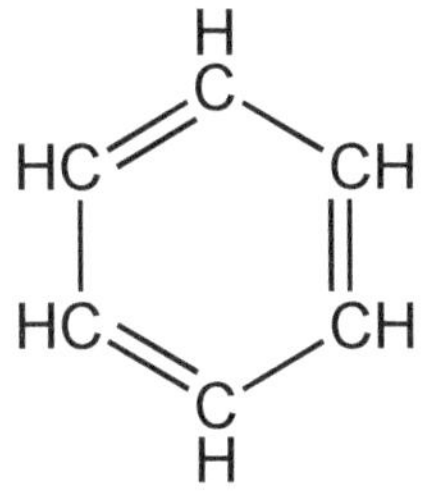

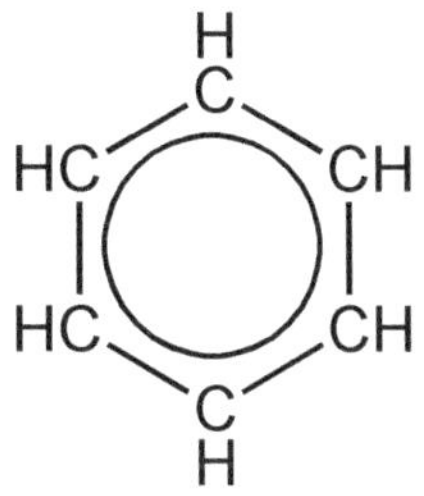

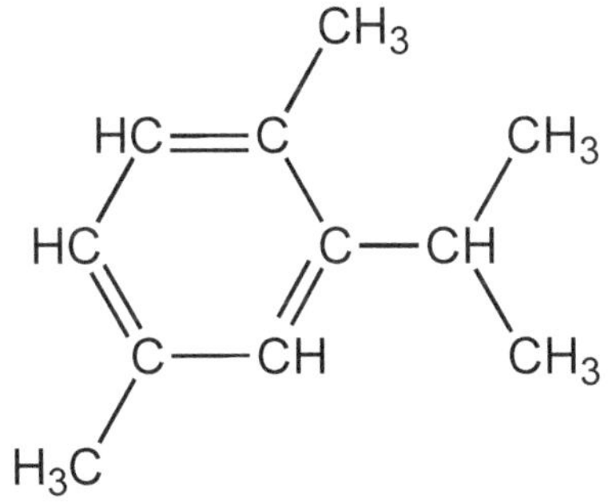

2-isopropyl-1,4-dimethylbenzene

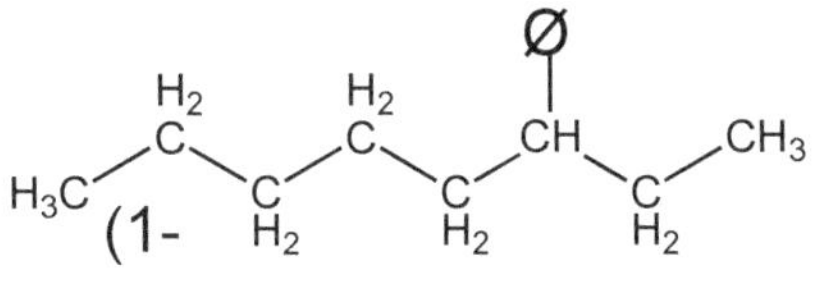

3-phenyloctane or (1- benzene

The most often used common names for aromatic hydrocarbons are listed in the table below. Naphthalene is the simplest molecule formed by fused benzene rings.

Structure	Systematic name	Common name
(benzene ring with one CH₃)	methylbenzene	toluene
(benzene ring with two adjacent CH₃)	1,2-dimethylbenzene	*ortho*-xylene or *o*-xylene
(benzene ring with two meta CH₃)	1,3-dimethylbenzene	*meta*-xylene or *m*-xylene
(benzene ring with two para CH₃)	1,4-dimethylbenzene	*para*-xylene or *p*-xylene
(benzene ring with CH=CH₂)	ethenylbenzene	styrene
(fused double benzene rings)		naphthalene

Many organic molecules contain **functional groups**, which are groups of atoms of a particular arrangement that give the entire molecule certain characteristics. Functional groups are named according to the composition of the group. For example, the carboxyl group shown at right is the arrangement of –COOH atoms that gives a molecule acidic properties.

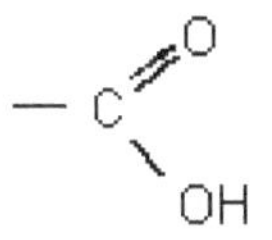

Some functional groups are polar and can ionize. For example, the hydrogen atom in the –COOH group can be removed (providing H⁺ ions in solution). When this occurs, the oxygen atom retains both the electrons it shared with the hydrogen atom and this gives the molecule a negative charge:

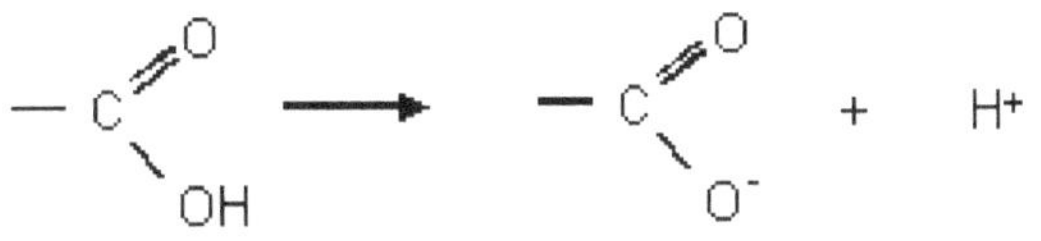

If polar or ionizing functional groups are attached to hydrophobic molecules, the molecule may become hydrophilic due to the functional group. Some ionizing functional groups are: –COOH, –OH, –CO, and –NH$_2$

Some common functional groups are described below.

HYDROXYL GROUP

The hydroxyl group, –OH, is the functional group identifying alcohols. The hydroxyl group makes the molecule polar, which increases the solubility of the compound.

CARBONYL GROUP

The carbonyl group is a –C=O attached to either a carbon chain or a hydrogen atom. It is found in aldehydes and ketones.

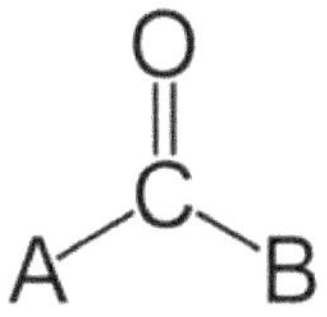

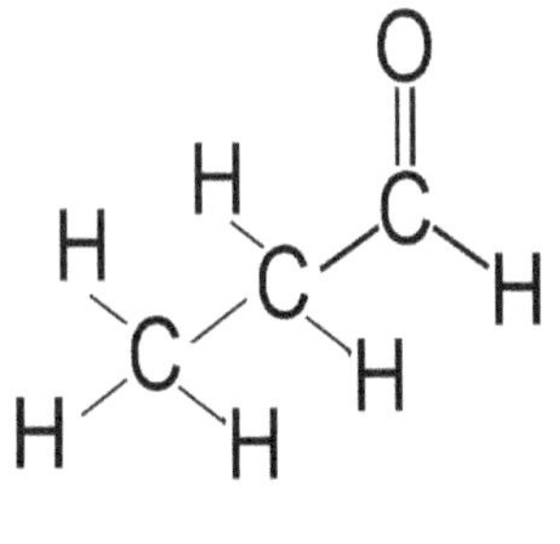

Aldehyde

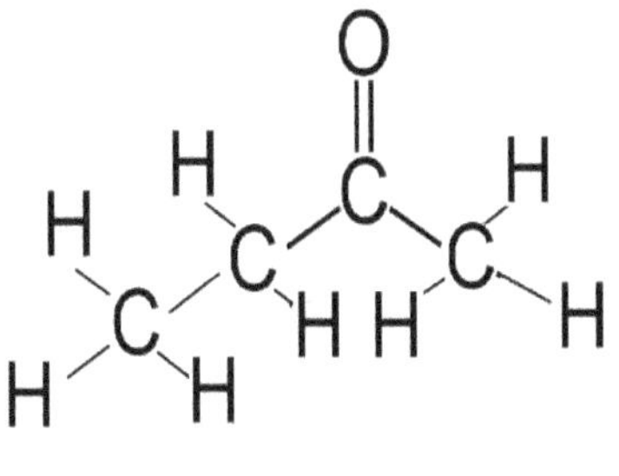

Ketone

If the carbon atom is bonded to a hydrogen atom, the molecule is an aldehyde. If the carbon is attached to two carbon chains, the molecule is a ketone. The double-bonded oxygen atom is highly electronegative, so it creates a molecule that will exhibit polar properties.

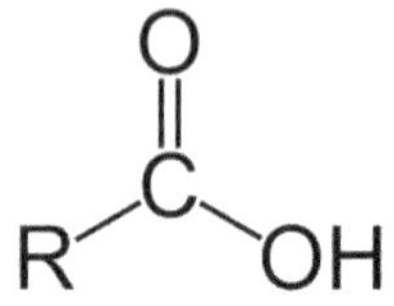

Carboxyl group

The –COOH group has the ability to donate a proton (H^+ ion), giving the molecule acidic properties.

AMINO GROUP

An amino group contains an ammonia-like functional group composed of a nitrogen atom and two hydrogen atoms covalently bonded. The nitrogen atom has unshared electrons and can accept protons. This gives the molecule basic properties. An organic compound that contains an amino group is called an amine. The amines are weak bases because the unshared electron pair of the nitrogen atom can form a covalent bond with a proton. Another molecule that contains an amino group is an amino acid. It consists of the $-NH_2$ group of an amine and the –COOH group of an acid. The amino acid glycine is shown below.

$$H-\underset{\underset{NH_2}{|}}{CH}-COOH$$

SULFHYDRYL GROUP

A **thiol** is a compound that contains the functional group composed of a sulfur atom and a hydrogen atom (–SH). This functional group is referred to either as a *thiol group* or a *sulfhydryl group*. More traditionally, thiols have been referred to as *mercaptans*.

The small difference in electronegativity between the sulfur atom and the hydrogen atom produces a non-polar covalent bond. This does not allow hydrogen bonding, giving thiols lower boiling points and less solubility in water than alcohols of a similar molecular mass.

PHOSPHATE GROUP

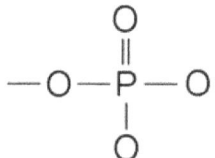

The phosphate ion is contained in a hydrocarbon chain within the molecule. This molecule is ideal for energy transfer reactions (ATP) because of its symmetry and rotating double bond.

In biological systems, phosphates are most commonly found in the form of adenosine phosphates (AMP, ADP and ATP) and in DNA and RNA and can be released by the hydrolysis of ATP or ADP.

The **acyl group** is

There are non-systematic number roots for hydrocarbon derivatives containing acyl groups or derived from acyl groups. These are the ketones, carboxylic acids, esters, nitriles, and amides:

Number of carbons (including the acyl carbon)	Systematic prefix	Accepted prefix for acyl and nitrile functional groups
1	meth–	form–
2	eth–	acet–
3	prop–	propion–
4	but–	butyr–
5	pent–	pent–
6 and above	same for larger numbers	

Several functional groups utilize oxygen.

Class of molecule	Functional group	Structure	Affix	Example
Alcohol	Hydroxyl —OH	primary, secondary, tertiary	–ol	ethanol
Ether	Oxy	R₁–O–R₂	–oxy–	methoxyethane or ethyl methyl ether

Class of molecule	Functional group	Structure	Affix	Example
Aldehyde	Carbonyl $\overset{O}{\underset{}{\overset{\|}{C}}}$	$\overset{:O:}{\underset{R\quad H}{\overset{\|}{C}}}$	–al	$\overset{H_2}{\underset{}{}}$ propionaldehyde or propanal
Ketone		$\overset{:O:}{\underset{R_1\quad R_2}{\overset{\|}{C}}}$	–one	$H_3C-\overset{O}{\underset{}{\overset{\|}{C}}}-CH_3$ acetone
Carboxylic acid	Carboxyl $\overset{O}{\underset{OH}{\overset{\|}{C}}}$	$\overset{:O:}{\underset{R\quad \ddot{O}H}{\overset{\|}{C}}}$	–oic acid	$HC\overset{O}{\underset{OH}{\overset{\|}{}}}$ formic acid or methanoic acid
Ester	Oxycarbonyl $\overset{O}{\underset{O}{\overset{\|}{C}}}$	$\overset{:O:}{\underset{R_2\quad \ddot{O}\quad R_1}{\overset{\|}{C}}}$	–yl –oate	methyl butyrate or methyl butanoate
Acid anhydride	Carbonyloxycarbonyl $\overset{O}{\underset{}{\overset{\|}{C}}}-O-\overset{O}{\underset{}{\overset{\|}{C}}}$	$\overset{:O:}{\underset{R_1}{\overset{\|}{C}}}-\ddot{O}-\overset{:O:}{\underset{R_2}{\overset{\|}{C}}}$	–oic anhydride	$H_3C-\overset{O}{\underset{}{\overset{\|}{C}}}-O-\overset{O}{\underset{}{\overset{\|}{C}}}-CH_3$ acetic anhydride or ethanoic anhydride

Derivatives utilizing other atoms are also common, as shown in this table:

Class of molecule	Functional group	Structure	Affix	Example
Nitrile	Cyanide —C≡N	R—C≡N:	–nitrile	H₃C—C≡N acetonitrile or ethanonitrile
Amine	Amino —N—	primary R—NH₂; secondary R₁—NH—R₂; tertiary R₁—N(R₂)—R₃	–amine	H₃C—CH₂—NH₂ ethanamine
Amide	Aminocarbonyl (C(=O)–N)	primary R—C(=O)—NH₂; secondary R₂—C(=O)—NH—R₁; tertiary R₃—C(=O)—N(R₂)—R₁	–amide	H₃C—CH₂—C(=O)—NH₂ propionamide or propanamide
Alkyl halide	Halide —X (where X is F, Cl, Br, or I)	R—X:	fluoro– chloro– bromo– iodo–	H₃C—CH(Br)—CH₂—CH₃ 2-bromobutane

Hydrocarbon derivatives and functional groups may be identified using the tables found in the previous section. One way to memorize the derivatives utilizing oxygen is to divide them into pairs with a hydrogen atom in the first element of the pair replaced by a hydrocarbon in the second element. These pairs are:

1) alcohol/ether
2) aldehyde/ketone
3) carboxylic acid/ester

A FINAL WORD ABOUT IUPAC ORGANIC NOMENCLATURE

"IUPAC nomenclature" has become a synonym for "correct nomenclature," but the most recent IUPAC recommendations for organic nomenclature are ignored in most textbooks and curricula in the United States. This situation is similar to the nomenclature for inorganic chemistry in that the older nomenclature is "systematic enough" to be taught and to avoid most errors, but is a poor choice to name new compounds in an unambiguous way.

Two important differences between the 1979 and more recent nomenclature involve the use of locant numbers:

1) The 1979 nomenclature usually places locant numbers before the name of the entire compound, but the 1993 recommendations suggest placing locant numbers immediately before the affixes that they represent.
2) The 1979 nomenclature always assigns a locant number of 1 to the attachment point of groups, but the 1993 nomenclature recommends stating the attachment point explicitly before "–yl–." This decreases the complexity of hydrocarbon residues.

The 1993 nomenclature permits the 1979 nomenclature as "naming method a" and presents the newer method as a "method b." In provisional 2004 recommendations, the newer "method b" names are usually explicitly preferred. The newer method is more commonly used in Europe and elsewhere. These differences are shown on the following page for some of the hydrocarbons.

Skill 9.2   Uses and interprets symbols, formulas, and equations in describing interactions of matter and energy in chemical reactions

As noted above, basic notation for elements, ions, and compounds is described in Skills 5.4 (elements and isomers), 6.4 (ions), 6.2 (orbital notation), and 9.3-9.4 (compounds and stoichiometric equations). See also Skill 8.9 for a discussion of equations and symbols related to energy in chemical reactions.

The IUPAC is the **International Union of Pure and Applied Chemistry**, an organization that formulates naming rules for chemical elements and compounds. **Organic compounds contain carbon**, and they have a separate system of nomenclature, but some of the simplest molecules containing carbon also fall within the scope of inorganic chemistry.

The symbols of the chemical elements are a single capital letter or a capital letter with a lowercase letter. In most cases, the capital letter is the letter starting the name of the element; however, the names used for some chemicals were their old Latin names. If another element already has the symbol an element would have, a new two-letter symbol is devised. All the symbols can be seen on the periodic table.

Naming rules depend on whether the chemical is an ionic compound or a molecular compound containing only covalent bonds. There are special rules for naming acids. The rules below describe a group of traditional "semi-systematic" names accepted by IUPAC.

IONIC COMPOUNDS: CATION

Ionic compounds are named with the **cation (positive ion) first**. Nearly all cations in inorganic chemistry are **monatomic**, meaning they just consist of one atom (like Ca^{2+}, the calcium ion.) This atom will usually be a **metal ion**. For common ionic compounds, the **alkali metals always have a 1+ charge** and the **alkali earth metals always have a 2+ charge**. See **0009** for a review of these elements.

Many metals (usually transition metals) may form cations of more than one charge. In this case, a Roman numeral in parenthesis after the name of the element is used to indicate the ion's charge in a particular compound. This Roman numeral method is known as the **Stock system**. An older nomenclature used the suffix *–ous* for the lower charge and *–ic* for the higher charge and is still used occasionally.

Example: Fe^{2+} is the iron(II) ion and Fe^{3+} is the iron(III) ion.

The only common inorganic **polyatomic cation** is ammonium: NH_4^+.

IONIC COMPOUNDS: ANION

The **anion** (negative ion) is named and written last. Monatomic anions are formed from nonmetallic elements and are named by **replacing the end of the element's name with the suffix *–ide.***

Examples: Cl^- is the chloride ion, S^{2-} is the sulfide ion, and N^{3-} is the nitride ion.

These anions also end with –*ide*:

C_2^{2-}	N_3^-	O_2^{2-}	O_3^-	S_2^{2-}	CN^-	OH^-
carbide or acetylide	azide	peroxide	ozonide	disulfide	cyanide	hydroxide

Oxoanions (also called oxyanions) **contain one element in combination with oxygen**. Many common polyatomic anions are oxoanions that **end with the suffix –*ate*.** If you memorize the "-*ate*" ions, you can quickly determine the corresponding "-*ite*" ions. If an element has two possible oxoanions, the one with the element at a lower oxidation state **ends with –*ite*.** This anion will also usually have **one less oxygen per atom.** See **0009** for a discussion of oxidation numbers. Additional oxoanions are named with the prefix *hypo-* if they have a lower oxidation number (and one less oxygen) than the –*ite* form and the prefix *per–* if they have a higher oxidation number (and one more oxygen) than the –*ate* form. Note the chlorate series of hypochlorite (ClO^-), chlorite (ClO_2^-), chlorate (ClO_3^-), and perchlorate (ClO_4^-).

Common examples:

					CO_3^{2-}	carbonate		
		SO_3^{2-}	sulfite		SO_4^{2-}	sulfate		
		PO_3^{3-}	phosphite		PO_4^{3-}	phosphate		
$N_2O_2^{2-}$	hyponitrite	NO_2^-	nitrite		NO_3^-	nitrate		
ClO^-	hypochlorite	ClO_2^-	chlorite		ClO_3^-	chlorate	ClO_4^-	perchlorate
BrO^-	hypobromite	BrO_2^-	bromite		BrO_3^-	bromate	BrO_4^-	perbromate
					MnO_4^{2-}	manganate	MnO_4^-	permanganate
					CrO_4^{2-}	chromate	CrO_8^{3-}	perchromate

Note that manganate/permanganate and chromate/perchromate are exceptions to the general rules because there are –*ate* ions but no –*ite* ions and because the charge changes.

Other polyatomic anions that end with –*ate* are:

$(COO)_2^{2-}$	$Cr_2O_7^{2-}$	SCN^-	HCO_2^-	$CH_3CO_2^-$
oxalate	dichromate	thiocyanate	formate	acetate

HCO_2^- and $CH_3CO_2^-$ are condensed **structural formulas** because they show how the atoms are linked together. Their molecular formulas would be CHO_2^- and $C_2H_3O_2^-$

If an H atom is added to a polyatomic anion with a negative charge greater than one, the word *hydrogen* or the prefix *bi-* are used for the resulting anion. If two H atoms are added, *dihydrogen* is used.

Examples: bicarbonate or hydrogen carbonate ion: HCO_3^-
dihydrogen phosphate ion: $H_2PO_4^-$

IONIC COMPOUNDS: HYDRATES

Water molecules often occupy positions within the lattice of an ionic crystal. These compounds are called **hydrates**, and the water molecules are known as **water of hydration**. The water of hydration is added after a centered dot in a formula. In a name, a number-prefix (listed below for molecular compounds) indicating the number of water molecules is followed by the root *–hydrate*.

IONIC COMPOUNDS: PUTTING IT ALL TOGETHER

We now have the tools to name most common salts given a formula and to write a formula for them given a name. To determine a formula given a name, the number of anions and cations that are needed to achieve a neutral charge must be found.

Example: Determine the formula of cobalt(II) phosphite octahydrate.

Solution: For the cation, find the symbol for cobalt (Co) and recognize that it is the Co^{2+} ion from the Roman numerals. For the anion, remember the phosphite ion is PO_3^{3-}. A neutral charge is achieved with 3 Co^{2+} ions (3 x +2 = +6) for every 2 PO_3^{3-} ions (2 x -3 = -6 which cancels the +6). Add eight (octa- means 8) H_2O for water of hydration for the answer:

$$Co_3(PO_3)_2 \cdot 8H_2O.$$

MOLECULAR COMPOUNDS

Molecular compounds (compounds making up molecules with a neutral charge) are usually composed entirely of nonmetals and are named by placing the **less electronegative atom first**. See **0009** for the relationship between electronegativity and the periodic table. The suffix *–ide* is added to the second, more electronegative atom, and prefixes indicating numbers are added to one or both names if needed.

Prefix	mono-	di-	tri-	tetra-	penta-	hexa-	hepta-	octa-	nona-	deca-
Meaning	1	2	3	4	5	6	7	8	9	10

The final "o" or "a" may be left off these prefixes for oxides.

The electronegativity requirement is the reason the compound with two oxygen atoms and one nitrogen atom is called nitrogen dioxide, NO_2 and not dioxygen nitride O_2N. The hydride of sodium is NaH, sodium hydride, but the hydride of bromine is HBr, hydrogen bromide (or hydrobromic acid if it's in aqueous solution). Oxygen is only named first in compounds with fluorine such as oxygen difluoride, OF_2, and fluorine is never placed first because it is the most electronegative element.

Examples: N_2O_4, dinitrogen tetroxide (or tetraoxide)
Cl_2O_7, dichlorine heptoxide (or heptaoxide)
ClF_5 chlorine pentafluoride

ACIDS

There are special naming rules for acids that correspond with the **suffix of their corresponding anion** if hydrogen were removed from the acid. Anions ending with *–ide* correspond to acids with the prefix *hydro–* and the suffix *–ic*. Anions ending with *–ate* correspond to acids with no prefix that end with *–ic*. Oxoanions ending with *–ite* have associated acids with no prefix and the suffix *–ous*. The *hypo–* and *per–* prefixes are maintained. Some examples are shown in the following table:

anion	anion name	acid	acid name
Cl^-	chloride	$HCl(aq)$	hydrochloric acid
CN^-	cyanide	$HCN(aq)$	hydrocyanic acid
CO_3^{2-}	carbonate	$H_2CO_3(aq)$	carbonic acid
SO_3^{2-}	sulfite	$H_2SO_3(aq)$	sulfurous acid
SO_4^{2-}	sulfate	$H_2SO_4(aq)$	sulfuric acid
ClO^-	hypochlorite	$HClO(aq)$	hypochlorous acid
ClO_2^-	chlorite	$HClO_2(aq)$	chlorous acid
ClO_3^-	chlorate	$HClO_3(aq)$	chloric acid
ClO_4^-	perchlorate	$HClO_4(aq)$	perchloric acid

Example: What is the molecular formula of phosphorous acid?

Solution: If we remember that the *–ous* acid corresponds to the *–ite* anion, and that the *–ite* anion has one less oxygen than (or has an oxidation number 2 less than) the *–ate* form, we only need to remember that phosphate is PO_4^{3-}. Then we know that phosphite is PO_3^{3-} and phosphorous acid is H_3PO_3.

TEACHER CERTIFICATION STUDY GUIDE

For additional resources, see:
http://www.wbu.edu/academics/schools/math_and_science/chemistry/resources/inonomen/quiz.htm sample questions.

http://quizlet.com/1395973/chemistry-exam-3-review-naming-inorganic-compounds-practice-flash-cards/

http://www.iupac.org/nc/home/publications/technical-reports/guidelines-for-drafting-reports/4-nomencl.html?sword_list%5B%5D=inorganic - IUPAC's report on inorganic nomenclature

PROPERLY WRITTEN AND NAMED FORMULAS

Here are some ways to identify improper formulas that are emphasized below by underlining them.

In all common names for **ionic compounds, number prefixes are not used** to describe the number of anions and cations.

Examples: $CaBr_2$ is calcium bromide, not calcium dibromide.
$Ba(OH)_2$ is barium hydroxide, not barium dihydroxide.
Cu_2SO_4 is copper(I) sulfate, not dicopper sulfate or copper(II) sulfate or dicopper sulfur tetroxide.

All ionic compounds must have a **neutral charge in their formula** representations.

Example: MgBr is an improperly written formula because Mg ion always exists as 2+ and Br ion is always a 1– ion. $MgBr_2$, magnesium bromide, is correct.

Proper oxoanions and acids use the correct prefixes and suffixes.

Example: HNO_3 is nitric acid because NO_3^- is the nitrate ion.

In both ionic and molecular compounds, the **less electronegative element comes first**.

Example: CSi is an improperly written formula because Si is below C on the periodic table and therefore less electronegative. SiC, silicon carbide, is correct.

PROPERLY WRITTEN CHEMICAL EQUATIONS

A properly written chemical equation must contain properly written formulas and must be **balanced**. Chemical equations are written to describe a certain number of moles of specific reactants becoming a certain number of moles of specific reaction products. Chemical equations obey the law of conservation of mass in that no atoms are created or destroyed, so each element has the same number of total atoms on the left of the arrow as it has on the right of the arrow when the equation is balanced. The number of moles of each compound is indicated by its **stoichiometric coefficient**. The number of atoms of an element is determined by multiplying the coefficient by the subscript, with subscripts outside of parentheses being multiplied by subscripts inside the parenthesis. This is done for each element in each compound. Then all the atoms of that element on that side of the arrow are added together.

Example: In the reaction

$$2H_2(g) + O_2(g) \rightarrow 2H_2O(l),$$

Hydrogen has a stoichiometric coefficient of two, oxygen has a coefficient of one, and water has a coefficient of two because 2 moles of hydrogen react with 1 mole of oxygen to form two moles of water.

The number of atoms of hydrogen on the left is 4 which is found by multiplying the coefficient of 2 by the subscript of 2. The number of atoms of hydrogen on the right is found in the same way to be 4. The number of atoms of oxygen on the left is 2 since the coefficient of 1 is multiplied by the subscript of 2. Using the same method on the right, the coefficient of 2 is multiplied by the subscript of 1 (no subscript means there is one) to obtain a total of 2 atoms of oxygen. Therefore, this reaction is balanced.

In a balanced equation, the stoichiometric coefficients are chosen such that the equation contains an **equal number of each type of atom on each side**. In our example, there are four H atoms and two O atoms on each side. Therefore, the equation is balanced with respect to atoms.

Reactions among ions in aqueous solution may often be represented in three ways. When solutions of hydrochloric acid and sodium hydroxide are mixed, a reaction occurs and heat is produced. The **molecular equation** for this reaction is:

$$HCl(aq) + NaOH(aq) \rightarrow H_2O(l) + NaCl(aq)$$

It is called a molecular equation because the **complete chemical formulas** of reactants and products are shown. But in reality, both HCl and NaOH are strong electrolytes and exist in solution as ions. This is represented by a **complete ionic equation** that shows all the dissolved ions:

$$H^+(aq) + Cl^-(aq) + Na^+(aq) + OH^-(aq) \rightarrow H_2O(l) + Na^+(aq) + Cl^-(aq).$$

Because Na$^+$(aq) and Cl$^-$(aq) appear as both reactants and products, they play no role in the reaction. Ions that appear in identical chemical forms on both sides of an ionic equation are called **spectator ions**. When spectator ions are removed from a complete ionic equation, the result is a **net ionic equation**:
$$H^+(aq) + OH^-(aq) \rightarrow H_2O(l)$$
These **redox** reactions must have equal charges on both sides as well as equal numbers of each ion.

PREDICT PRODUCTS OF CHEMICAL EQUATIONS

Once we have an idea of the **reaction type**, we can make a fairly accurate prediction about the products of chemical equations, and also balance the reactions. **General reaction types** are listed in the following table. Some reaction types have multiple names.

Reaction type	General equation	Example
Combination	$A + B \rightarrow C$	$2H_2 + O_2 \rightarrow 2H_2O$
Synthesis		
Decomposition	$A \rightarrow B + C$	$2KClO_3 \rightarrow 2KCl + 3O_2$
Single substitution		
Single displacement	$A + BC \rightarrow AB + B$	$Mg + 2HCl \rightarrow MgCl_2 + H_2$
Single replacement		
Double substitution		
Double displacement		
Double replacement	$AC + BD \rightarrow AD + BC$	$HCl + NaOH \rightarrow NaCl + H_2O$
Ion exchange		
Metathesis		
Isomerization	$A \rightarrow A'$	cyclopropane C_3H_6 $\rightarrow$ propene C_3H_6

Example: Determine the products of a reaction between Cl₂ and a solution of NaBr.

Solution: The first step is to write "$Cl_2 + NaBr(aq) \rightarrow ?$"

> Now examine the possible choices from the table. Decomposition and isomerization reactions require only one reactant. Since this reaction has two reactants and one of them is an element, it is not a decomposition or isomerization reaction. It also can't be a double substitution reaction because one of the reactants is an element. A synthesis reaction to form some NaBrCl compound would require very unusual valences! The most likely reaction is a single displacement reaction: Cl replaces Br in aqueous solution with Na:
> $$Cl_2 + NaBr(aq) \rightarrow NaCl(aq) + Br_2.$$
> After balancing, the equation is:
> $$Cl_2 + 2NaBr(aq) \rightarrow 2NaCl(aq) + Br_2.$$

Many **specific reaction types** also exist. Always determine the complete ionic equation for reactions in solution. This will help you determine the reaction type. The most common specific reaction types are summarized in the following table:

Reaction type	General equation	Example
Precipitation (0025)	Molecular: $AC(aq) + BD(aq) \rightarrow AD(s \text{ or } g) + BC(aq)$	Molecular: $NiCl_2(aq) + Na_2S(aq) \rightarrow NiS(s) + 2NaCl(aq)$
	Net ionic: $A^+(aq) + D^-(aq) \rightarrow AD(s \text{ or } g)$	Net ionic: $Ni^{2+}(aq) + S^{2-}(aq) \rightarrow NiS(s)$
Acid-base neutralization (0019)	Arrhenius: $H^+ + OH^- \rightarrow H_2O$	Arrhenius: $HNO_3 + NaOH \rightarrow NaNO_3 + H_2O$ $H^+ + OH^- \rightarrow H_2O$ (net ionic)
	Brønsted-Lowry: $HA + B \rightarrow HB + A$	Brønsted-Lowry: $HNO_3 + KCN \rightarrow HCN + KNO_3$ $H^+ + CN^- \rightarrow HCN$ (net ionic)
	Lewis: $A + :B \rightarrow A:B$	Lewis: $BF_3 + :NH_3 \rightarrow F_3B-NH_3$
Redox (0020)	Full reaction: $A + B \rightarrow C + D$	$Ni + CuSO_4 \rightarrow NiSO_4 + Cu$ $Ni + Cu^{2+} \rightarrow Ni^{2+} + Cu$ (net ionic)

	Half reactions:	$Ni \rightarrow Ni^{2+} + 2e^-$
	$A \rightarrow C + e^-$ and $e^- + B \rightarrow D$	$2e^- + Cu^{2+} \rightarrow Cu$
Combustion	organic molecule $+ O_2 \rightarrow CO_2 + H_2O +$ heat	$2C_2H_6 + 7O_2 \rightarrow 4CO_2 + 6H_2O$

Whether precipitation occurs among a group of ions—and which compound will form the precipitate—may be determined by the solubility rules. The possibility that oxidation numbers may change among the reactants indicates an electron transfer and a redox reaction. Combustion reactants consist of an organic molecule and oxygen.

If protons are available for combination or substitution then it's likely they are being transferred from an acid to a base. An unshared electron pair on one of the reactants may form a bond in a Lewis acid-base reaction.

The possibility that oxidation numbers may change among the reactants indicates an electron transfer and a redox reaction.

Combustion reactants consist of an organic molecule (C-H) and oxygen.

Example: Determine the products and write a balanced equation for the reaction between sodium iodide and lead(II) nitrate in aqueous solution.

Solution: This is basically a double replacement reaction. We know that sodium iodide is NaI and lead(II) nitrate is $Pb(NO_3)_2$ from **0016**. The reactants of the complete ionic equation are:

$$Na^+(aq) + Pb^{2+}(aq) + I^-(aq) + NO_3^-(aq) \rightarrow ?$$

The solubility rules indicate that lead iodide is insoluble and will form as a precipitate. The unbalanced net ionic equation is then:

$$Pb^{2+}(aq) + I^-(aq) \rightarrow PbI_2(s)$$

and the unbalanced molecular equation is:

$$NaI(aq) + Pb(NO_3)_2(aq) \rightarrow PbI_2(s) + NaNO_3(aq).$$

Balancing yields:

$$2NaI(aq) + Pb(NO_3)_2(aq) \rightarrow PbI_2(s) + 2NaNO_3(aq).$$

TEACHER CERTIFICATION STUDY GUIDE

Skill 9.3 **Understands mass relationships involving percent composition, empirical formulas, and molecular formulas**

The **percent composition** of a substance is the **percentage by mass of each element**. Chemical composition is used to verify the purity of a compound in the lab. An impurity will make the actual composition vary from the expected one.

To determine percent composition from a formula, follow these steps:

1) Write down the **number of atoms each element contributes** to the formula.
2) Multiply these values by the molecular weight of the corresponding element to determine the **grams of each element in one mole** of the formula.
3) Add the values from step 2 to obtain the **formula mass**.
4) Divide each value from step 2 by the formula mass from step 3 and multiply by 100% to obtain the **percent composition of each element**.

Example: What is the chemical composition of ammonium carbonate $(NH_4)_2CO_3$?

Solution:

1) $(NH_4)_2CO_3$ contains 2 N, 8 H, 1 C, and 3 O atoms.

2) $$\frac{2 \text{ mol N}}{\text{mol }(NH_4)CO_3} \times \frac{14.0 \text{ g N}}{\text{mol N}} = 28.0 \text{ g N/mol }(NH_4)CO_3$$

$$8(1.0) = 8.0 \text{ g H/mol }(NH_4)CO_3$$
$$1(12.0) = 12.0 \text{ g C/mol }(NH_4)CO_3$$
$$3(16.0) = 48.0 \text{ g O/mol }(NH_4)CO_3$$

3) Sum is $\overline{96.0 \text{ g }(NH_4)CO_3/\text{mol }(NH_4)CO_3}$

4) $\%N = \dfrac{28.0 \text{ g N/mol }(NH_4)_2CO_3}{96.0 \text{ g }(NH_4)_2CO_3/\text{mol }(NH_4)_2CO_3} = 0.292 \text{ g N/g }(NH_4)_2CO_3 \times 100\% = 29.2\%$

$\%H = \dfrac{8.0}{96.0} \times 100\% = 8.3\%$ $\%C = \dfrac{12.0}{96.0} \times 100\% = 12.5\%$ $\%O = \dfrac{48.0}{96.0} \times 100\% = 50.0\%$

If we know the chemical composition of a compound, we can calculate an **empirical formula** for it. An empirical formula is the **simplest formula** using the smallest set of integers to express the **ratio of atoms** present in a molecule.

To determine an empirical formula from a percent composition, following these steps:

1) Change the "%" sign to grams for a basis of 100 g of the compound.
2) Determine the moles of each element in 100 g of the compound.
3) Divide the values from step 1 by the smallest value to obtain ratios.
4) Multiply by an integer if necessary to get a whole-number ratio.

Example: What is the empirical formula of a compound with a composition of 63.9% Cl, 32.5% C, and 3.6% H?

Solution:

1) We will use a basis of 100 g of the compound containing 63.9 g Cl, 32.5 g C, and 3.6 g H.

2) In 100 g, there are: $63.9 \text{ g Cl} \times \dfrac{\text{mol Cl}}{35.45 \text{ g Cl}} = 1.802 \text{ mol Cl}$

$$32.5/12.01 = 2.706 \text{ mol C}$$
$$3.6/1.01 = 3.56 \text{ mol H}$$

3) Dividing these values by the smallest yields:

$$\dfrac{2.706 \text{ mol C}}{1.802 \text{ mol Cl}} = 1.502 \text{ mol C/mol Cl}$$

$$\dfrac{3.56 \text{ mol H}}{1.802 \text{ mol Cl}} = 1.97 \text{ mol H/mol Cl}$$

Therefore, the elements are present in a ratio of C:H:Cl=1.5:2:1

4) Multiply the entire ratio by 2 because you cannot have a fraction of an atom. This corresponds to a ratio of 3:4:2 for an empirical formula of $C_3H_4Cl_2$.

The **molecular formula** describing the **actual number of atoms in the molecule** might actually be $C_3H_4Cl_2$ or it might be $C_6H_8Cl_4$ or some other multiple that maintains a 3:4:2 ratio.

TEACHER CERTIFICATION STUDY GUIDE

Skill 9.4   **Interprets and balances chemical equations using conservation of atoms, mass, and charge**

A properly written chemical equation must contain properly written formulas and must be **balanced**. Chemical equations are written to describe a certain number of moles of reactants becoming a certain number of moles of products. The number of moles of each compound is indicated by its **stoichiometric coefficient**.

Example: In the reaction:
$$2H_2(g) + O_2(g) \rightarrow 2H_2O(l)$$

hydrogen has a stoichiometric coefficient of two, oxygen has a coefficient of one, and water has a coefficient of two because 2 moles of hydrogen react with 1 mole of oxygen to form two moles of water.

In a balanced equation, the stoichiometric coefficients are chosen so that the equation contains an **equal number of each type of atom on each side**. In our example, there are four H atoms and two O atoms on both sides. Therefore, the equation is balanced with respect to atoms.

Balancing equations is a four-step process.

1) Write an **unbalanced equation**.
2) Determine the **number of each type of atom on each side** of the equation to find out if the equation is already balanced. If not, continue with Step 3.
3) Assume that **the molecule with the most atoms** has a stoichiometric coefficient of one, and determine the other stoichiometric coefficients required to create the **same number of atoms on each side** of the equation.
4) Multiply all the stoichiometric coefficients by a whole number if necessary to eliminate fractional coefficients.

Example: Balance the chemical equation describing the combustion of methanol in oxygen to produce only carbon dioxide and water.

Solution:

1) The structural formula of methanol is CH₃OH, so its molecular formula is CH₄O. The formula for carbon dioxide is CO₂. Therefore the unbalanced equation is:

$$CH_4O + O_2 \rightarrow CO_2 + H_2O$$

2) On the left there are 1 C, 4 H, and 3 O atoms. On the right, there are 1 C, 2 H, and 3 O atoms. The equation is close to being balanced but there is still work to do.

3) Assuming that CH₄O has a stoichiometric coefficient of one means that the left side has 1 C and 4 H that are currently missing on the right. Therefore the stoichiometric coefficient of CO₂ will be 1 to balance C and the stoichiometric coefficient of H₂O will be 2 to balance H. Now we have:

$$CH_4O + ?O_2 \rightarrow CO_2 + 2H_2O$$

and only oxygen remains unbalanced. There are 4 O on the right, and one of these is accounted for by methanol, leaving 3 O to be accounted for by O₂. This gives a stoichiometric coefficient of 3/2 and a balanced equation:

$$CH_4O + \frac{3}{2}O_2 \rightarrow CO_2 + 2H_2O$$

4) Whole-number coefficients are achieved by multiplying by two:

$$2CH_4O + 3O_2 \rightarrow 2CO_2 + 4H_2O$$

Reactions among ions in aqueous solution may be represented in three ways. When solutions of hydrochloric acid and sodium hydroxide are mixed, a reaction occurs and heat is produced. The **molecular equation** for this reaction is:

$$HCl(aq) + NaOH(aq) \rightarrow H_2O(l) + NaCl(aq)$$

It is called a molecular equation because the **complete chemical formulas** of reactants and products are shown. But in reality, both HCl and NaOH are strong electrolytes and exist in solution as ions. This is represented by a **complete ionic equation** that shows all the dissolved ions:

$$H^+(aq) + Cl^-(aq) + Na^+(aq) + OH^-(aq) \rightarrow H_2O(l) + Na^+(aq) + Cl^-(aq)$$

Because Na$^+$(aq) and Cl$^-$(aq) appear as both reactants and products, they play no role in the reaction. Ions that appear in identical chemical forms on both sides of an ionic equation are called **spectator ions** because they aren't part of the action. When spectator ions are removed from a complete ionic equation, the result is a **net ionic equation** that shows the actual changes that occur to the chemicals when these two solutions are mixed together:

$$H^+(aq) + OH^-(aq) \rightarrow H_2O(l)$$

An additional requirement for **redox** reaction is that the equation contains an **equal charge on each side**. In the example above, the positive charge on the H$^+$ ion cancels out the negative charge on the OH$^-$ ion giving an overall neutral charge for both sides of the equation. Redox reactions may be divided into half-reactions which either gain or lose electrons.

Skill 9.5   Understands mass and mole relationships in chemical equations

To convert mass to moles:

1. First determine the molar mass (molecular weight) of the substance by adding the masses for each element in the substance and multiplying by the number of atoms present:

    Example: Determine the molar mass of CuSO$_4$.

    Solution: 1 mole of Cu = 63.5 g + 1 mol of S = 32 g + 4 mol O = 4 x 16 or 48 g = 143.5 g/mol

2. Determine the number of moles present using the molar mass conversion: 1 mol = molar mass of substance.

    Example: If you have 315 g of CuSO$_4$, how many moles is that?

    Solution: 315 g x 1 mol/143.5 g = 2.20 mol CuSO$_4$

Moles to grams conversions are just the reverse of the process above.

To convert the mass of a reactant to the mass of a product or vice versa, use a three-step process:

1) Convert grams of the given compound (known mass) to moles (known moles) using molecular weight.
2) The moles of the given compound (known moles) are related to the number of moles of the second compound (unknown moles) using their stoichiometric coefficients from the balanced reaction equation.
3) Convert moles of the second compound (unknown moles) to grams (unknown mass) using molecular weight of the second compound.

These steps are often combined in one series of multiplications, which may be described as **"grams to moles to moles to grams."** Another way to look at them is **"grams of known to moles of known to moles of unknown to grams of unknown**.

Example: What mass of oxygen is required to consume 95.0 g of ethane in the following reaction?

$$2C_2H_6 + 7O_2 \rightarrow 4CO_2 + 6H_2O$$

Solution:

$$95.0 \text{ g } C_2H_6 \times \underbrace{\frac{1 \text{ mol } C_2H_6}{30.1 \text{ g } C_2H_6}}_{\text{step 1}} \times \underbrace{\frac{7 \text{ mol } O_2}{2 \text{ mol } C_2H_6}}_{\text{step 2}} \times \underbrace{\frac{32.0 \text{ g } O_2}{1 \text{ mol } O_2}}_{\text{step 3}} = 359 \text{ g } O_2$$

By expressing the molecular mass of the first or given compound as moles per gram, the grams of the known cancel. By putting the moles of the known compound on the bottom with the molecular coefficient of the unknown compound on top in the second conversion the moles of the known are canceled and converted to moles of unknown. And finally, by expressing the molecular mass of the second compound as grams per mole, its moles are converted to grams for the final answer and the units (by canceling) end up as grams of the unknown.

Skill 9.6 Solves stoichiometric problems including limiting reagents, reaction yield, and percent yield

GASES

The progress of reactions that produce or consume a gas may be described by measuring gas volume instead of mass. The best way to solve these problems is to use the ideal gas equation to interconvert volume and number of moles:

$$n = \frac{PV}{RT} \quad \text{and} \quad V = \frac{RT}{nP}.$$

If a volume is given, the steps are "**volume to moles to moles to grams**." If a mass is given, the steps will be "**grams to moles to moles to volume**."

Example: What volume of oxygen in liters is generated at 40° C and 1 atm by the decomposition of 280 g of potassium chlorate in the following reaction?

$$2KClO_3 \rightarrow 2KCl + 3O_2(g)$$

Solution: We are given a mass and asked for a volume, so the steps in the solution will be "grams to moles to moles to volume." Solving first for moles:

$$280 \text{ g } KClO_3 \times \frac{1 \text{ mol } KClO_3}{122.548 \text{ g } KClO_3} \times \frac{3 \text{ mol } O_2}{2 \text{ mol } KClO_3} = 3.427 \text{ mol } O_2$$

then for volume:

$$V = \frac{RT}{nP} = \frac{\left(0.08206 \frac{\text{L-atm}}{\text{mol-K}}\right)(273.15 + 40)\text{K}}{(3.427 \text{ mol } O_2)(1 \text{ atm})} = 7.50 \text{ L } O_2$$

Solutions In solution stoichiometry problems, the moles of solute for each solution must first be determined. This is done using the molarity definition. Once the moles of solute are determined, the problem becomes a mole-mole stoichiometry problem or a limiting reactant problem.

Example: How much of a 0.50 M $Pb(NO_3)_2$ solution is required to completely react with 25 g of KI?

$$Pb(NO_3)_2 \text{ (aq)} + 2 \text{ KI (s)} \rightarrow PbI_2 \text{ (s)} + 2 \text{ KNO}_3 \text{ (aq)}$$

Solution:

1. Find the moles of KI reacting:
   25 g KI x 1 mol KI/166 g/mol = 0.15 mol

2. Use the mole ratio from the balanced equation:
   0.15 mol KI x 1 mol $Pb(NO_3)_2$/2 mol KI = 0.075 mol $Pb(NO_3)_2$ needed to react.

3. Use molarity to determine the volume of $Pb(NO_3)_2$ required.
   M = mol solute/L solution, or L solution = mol solute/M
   0.075 mol/0.50 M = 0.15 L or 150 mL

The **limiting reagent** of a reaction is the **reactant that runs out first**. This reactant **determines the amount of products formed**, and any **other reactants remain unconverted** to product and are called **excess reagents**.

Example: Consider the reaction $3H_2 + N_2 \rightarrow 2NH_3$ and suppose that 3 mol H_2 and 3 mol N_2 are available for this reaction. What is the limiting reagent?

Solution: The equation tells us that 3 mol H_2 will react with one mol N_2 to produce 2 mol NH_3. This means that H_2 is the limiting reagent because when it is completely used up 2 mol N_2 will still remain.

The limiting reagent may be determined by **dividing the number of moles of each reactant by its stoichiometric coefficient.** This determines the moles of reactant if each reactant were limiting. The **lowest result** will indicate the actual limiting reagent. Remember to use moles and not grams for these calculations.

Example: 50.0 g Al and 400 g Br₂ react according the following equation:

$$2Al + 3Br_2 \rightarrow 2AlBr_3$$

until the limiting reagent is completely consumed. Find the limiting reagent, the mass of AlBr₃ formed, and the excess reagent remaining after the limiting reagent is consumed.

Solution: First convert both reactants to moles:

$$50.0 \text{ g Al} \times \frac{1 \text{ mol Al}}{26.982 \text{ g Al}} = 1.853 \text{ mol Al}$$

$$\text{and } 400. \text{ g Br}_2 \times \frac{1 \text{ mol Br}_2}{159.808 \text{ g Br}_2} = 2.503 \text{ mol Br}_2.$$

The final digits in the intermediate results above are italicized because they are insignificant. Dividing by stoichiometric coefficients gives:

$$1.853 \text{ mol Al} \times \frac{\text{mol reaction}}{2 \text{ mol Al}} = 0.9265 \text{ mol reaction if Al is limiting}$$

$$2.503 \text{ mol Br}_2 \times \frac{\text{mol reaction}}{3 \text{ mol Br}_2} = 0.8343 \text{ mol reaction if Br}_2 \text{ is limiting.}$$

Br₂ is the lower value and is the limiting reagent.

The reaction is expected to produce:

$$2.503 \text{ mol Br}_2 \times \frac{2 \text{ mol AlBr}_3}{3 \text{ mol Br}_2} \times \frac{266.694 \text{ g AlBr}_3}{\text{mol AlBr}_3} = 445 \text{ g AlBr}_3$$

The reaction is expected to consume:

$$2.503 \text{ mol Br}_2 \times \frac{2 \text{ mol Al}}{3 \text{ mol Br}_2} \times \frac{26.982 \text{ g Al}}{\text{mol Al}} = 45.0 \text{ g Al}$$

50.0 g Al − 45.0 g Al = 5.0 g Al which will remain.

CALCULATE PERCENT YIELD

The **yield of a reaction is the amount of product** obtained. This value is nearly always less than what would be predicted from a stoichiometric calculation because side-reactions may produce different products, the reverse reaction may occur, and some material may be lost during the procedure. The yield from a stoichiometric calculation on the limiting reagent is called the theoretical yield. **Percent yield is the actual yield divided by the theoretical yield times 100%:**

$$\text{Percent yield} = \frac{\text{Actual yield}}{\text{Theoretical yield}} \times 100\%.$$

Example: 387 g AlBr₃ are produced by the reaction described in the previous example. What is the percent yield?

Solution: $\dfrac{387 \text{ g AlBr}_3}{445 \text{ g AlBr}_3} \times 100\% = 87.0\%$ yield.

COMPETENCY 010   THE TEACHER UNDERSTANDS TYPES AND PROPERTIES OF SOLUTIONS

Skill 10.1   Analyzes factors that affect solubility (e.g., temperature, pressure, polarity of solvents and solutes)

GAS SOLUBILITY

Pressure does not dramatically alter the solubility of solids or liquids, but kinetic molecular theory predicts that **increasing the partial pressure of a gas will increase the solubility of the gas** in a liquid. If a substance is distributed between gas and solution phases and pressure is exerted, more gas molecules will impact the gas/liquid interface per second, so more will dissolve until a new equilibrium is reached at a higher solubility. **Henry's law** describes this relationship as a direct proportionality:

$$\text{Solubility of gas in liquid (in } \frac{\text{mol solute}}{\text{L solution}}) \propto P_{gas}$$

For example, **carbonated drinks** contain CO_2 bottled under high pressure, permitting the gas to dissolve into aqueous solution. When the bottle is opened, the partial pressure of CO_2 in the gas phase rapidly decreases to the value in the atmosphere and the gas bubbles out of solution. When the bottle is closed again, CO_2 gas pressure builds up in the bottle until a saturated solution at equilibrium is again obtained. Nitrogen also increases in the bloodstream of deep-sea divers when they experience high pressures. If they return to atmospheric pressure too rapidly, large bubbles of nitrogen gas will form in their blood and cause a potentially lethal condition known as **the bends** or **decompression sickness**. The diver must enter a hyperbaric (high pressure) chambers to redissolve the nitrogen back into the blood and lower the pressure slowly to atmospheric conditions.

Increasing the temperature decreases the solubility of a gas in a liquid because kinetic energy opposes intermolecular attractions and permits more molecules to escape from the liquid phase. The vapor pressure of a pure liquid increases with temperature for the same reason. Greater kinetic energy favors material in the gas phase.

LIQUID AND SOLID SOLUBILITY

For solid and liquid solutes, temperature effects depend on whether the solute absorbs or releases heat as it goes into solution. If a compound is dissolved in water and the solution becomes hot, the solution process is exothermic. If the solution becomes cold, the solution process is endothermic. The graphs below show how the temperature of water may change upon addition of an inorganic compound.

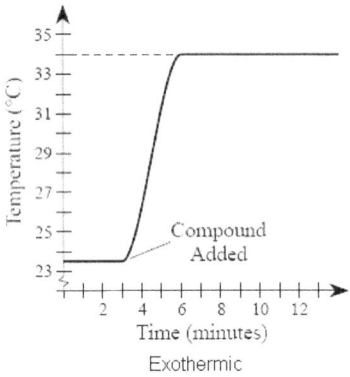
Exothermic

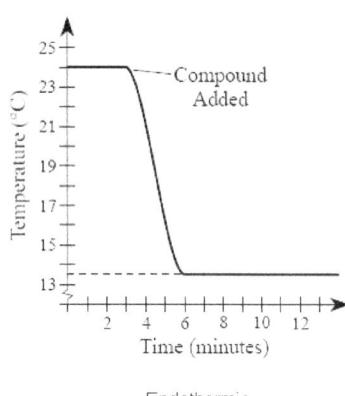
Endothermic

The energy change associated with the process in which a solute dissolves in a solvent is called the **heat of solution**. This energy change is the net result of two processes: 1) the energy required to break the solute-solute bonds, called the **crystal lattice energy**, and 2) the energy released when the solute particles bond with the solvent molecules, called the **heat of hydration**.

Example: What is the heat of solution for KCl in water?

Solution: The crystal lattice energy of KCl, the energy necessary to break apart the KCl crystal lattice and form free ions, is represented by:

$$KCl\ (s) \rightarrow K^+\ (g) + Cl^-\ (g) \qquad \Delta H = +167.6\ \text{kcal}$$

The heat of hydration of KCl, the energy released when the free ions are hydrated, is represented by:

$$K^+\ (g) + Cl^-\ (g) \rightarrow K^+\ (aq) + Cl^-\ (aq) \qquad \Delta H = -163.5\ \text{kcal}$$

The overall reaction is endothermic, and the heat of solution is positive since more energy is required in the first step than is released by the second step.

$$KCl\ (s) \rightarrow K^+\ (aq) + Cl^-\ (aq) \qquad \Delta H = +4.1\ \text{kcal}$$

Three processes occur when a solution is formed:

1) Solute particles are separated from each other, and heat is required to break these bonds.
2) Solvent particles are separated from each other to create space for solute particles, and heat is required to break these bonds also.
3) Solute and solvent particles interact with each other forming new bonds and releasing heat.

If the heat required for the first two processes is greater than the heat released by the third, then the entire reaction may be written as an endothermic process:

$$\text{Solute} + \text{Solvent} + \text{Heat} \rightarrow \text{Solution}$$

According to Le Chatelier's principle, **solubility will increase with increasing temperature for an endothermic reaction**. This occurs for most salts in water, including NaCl and KNO_3.

However, heat is released when many solutes enter solution, and the entire reaction is exothermic:

$$\text{Solute} + \text{Solvent} \rightarrow \text{Solution} + \text{Heat}$$

Solubility will decrease with increasing temperature for an exothermic reaction. For example, this is the case for cerium(III) sulfate, $Ce_2(SO_4)_3$, dissolving in water.

The following table summarizes the impact of temperature and pressure on solubility:

Effect on solution of an **increase** in one variable with the other constant	− = decrease, **0** = no/small change, **+** = increase, **++** = strong increase				
	Gas solute in liquid solvent			Solid and liquid solutes	
	Average kinetic energy of molecules	Collisions of gas with liquid interface	Solubility	Solubility for an endothermic heat of solution	Solubility for an exothermic heat of solution
Pressure	0	++	+	0	0
Temperature	+	+	−	+	−

Intermolecular forces in the solution process

Solutions tend to form when the intermolecular attractive forces between solute and solvent molecules are about as strong as those that exist in the solute alone or in solvent alone. For example, NaCl dissolves in water because:

1) The water molecules interact with the Na^+ and Cl^- ions with sufficient strength to overcome the attraction between them in the salt crystal.

2) Na^+ and Cl^- ions interact with the water molecules with sufficient strength to overcome the attraction water molecules have for each other in the liquid.

The intermolecular attraction between solute and solvent molecules is known as **solvation**. When the solvent is water, it is known as **hydration**. The figure to the right shows a hydrated Na⁺ ion.

POLAR AND NONPOLAR SOLUTES AND SOLVENTS

A nonpolar liquid like heptane (C_7H_{16}) has intermolecular bonds with relatively weak London dispersion forces. Heptane is immiscible in water because the attraction that water molecules have for each other via hydrogen bonding is strong in comparison. Unlike Na^+ and Cl^- ions, heptane molecules cannot break these bonds. Because bonds of similar strength must be broken and formed for solvation to occur, nonpolar substances tend to be soluble in nonpolar solvents, and ionic and polar substances are soluble in polar solvents like water. Polar molecules are often called **hydrophilic** and non-polar molecules are called **hydrophobic**. This observation is often stated as "**like dissolves like**." Network solids (e.g., diamond) are soluble in neither polar nor nonpolar solvents because the covalent bonds within the solid are too strong for these solvents to break.

ELECTROLYTES

Compounds that are completely ionized in water are called **strong electrolytes** because these solutions easily conduct electricity. Most salts are strong electrolytes. For example, all NaCl is present in solution as ions. Other compounds (including many acids and bases) may dissolve in water without completely ionizing. These compounds are referred to as **weak electrolytes** and their ions are at equilibrium with the larger molecule. Those compounds that dissolve with no ionization (e.g., glucose, $C_6H_{12}O_6$) are called **nonelectrolytes**.

Skill 10.2 Identifies characteristics of saturated, unsaturated, and supersaturated solutions

When two or more pure materials mix in a homogeneous way (with their molecules intermixing on a molecular level), the mixture is called a **solution**. Dispersions of small particles that are larger than molecules are called **colloids**. Liquid solutions are the most common, but any two phases may form a solution. When a pure liquid and a gas or solid form a liquid solution, the pure liquid is called the **solvent** and the non-liquids are called **solutes**. When all components in the solution were originally liquids, then the one present in the greatest amount is called the solvent and the others are called solutes. Solutions with water as the solvent are called **aqueous** solutions. The amount of solute in relation to the amount of solvent is called its **concentration**. A solution with a small concentration of solute is called **dilute**, and a solution with a large concentration of solute is called **concentrated**.

As solid solute particles (circles in the figure to the right) dissolve in a liquid solvent (grey background), the concentration of the solute increases, and the chance that dissolved solute (grey circles) will collide with the remaining non-dissolved solid (white circles) also increases. A collision may result in the solute particle reattaching to the solid. This process is called **crystallization**, and is the opposite of the solution

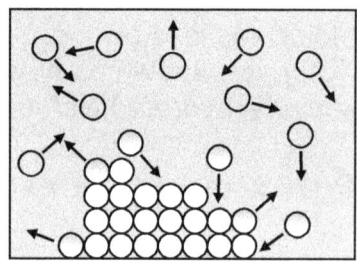

process. Particles in the act of dissolving or crystallizing are half-shaded in the figure. An animation of the solution process may be found here: http://www.mhhe.com/physsci/chemistry/essentialchemistry/flash/molvie1.swf.

Equilibrium occurs when no additional solute will dissolve because the rates of crystallization and solution are equal.

$$\textbf{Solute + Solvent} \underset{\text{Crystallize}}{\overset{\text{Dissolve}}{\longleftrightarrow}} \textbf{Solution}$$

A solution at equilibrium with non-dissolved solute is a **saturated** solution. The amount of solute required to form a saturated solution in a given amount of solvent is called the **solubility** of that solute. If less solute is present, the solution is called **unsaturated**. It is also possible under certain special conditions to have more solute than the equilibrium amount, resulting in a solution that is termed **supersaturated**.

Pairs of liquids that mix in all proportions are called **miscible**. Liquids that don't mix are called **immiscible**.

Skill 10.3   Determines the molarity, molality, and percent composition of aqueous solutions

In a solution, the amount of solute that is dissolved in a given amount of solvent is called concentration. Solutions with a lot of solute dissolved for the amount of solvent present are referred to as concentrated solutions while solutions with little solute dissolved for the amount of solvent present are referred to as dilute. However, these expressions give very little information about the actual quantities present in the solution. Expressions of percent by mass or volume, molarity, molality, or parts per million give more information about the quantity of solute and solvent present in a solution.

PERCENT COMPOSITION

Percent by mass or volume expresses the amount of solute present as a percentage of the total solution present:

$$\% \text{ by mass} = \frac{\text{mass of solute}}{\text{mass of solute + mass of solvent}} \times 100\%$$

$$\% \text{ by volume} = \frac{\text{volume of solute}}{\text{volume of solute + volume of solvent}} \times 100\%$$
$$\text{(or total volume of solution)}$$

Example: What is the percent by mass of a solution prepared by dissolving 4.0 g of CH_3COOH in 35.0 g of water?

Solution:

$$\% \text{ by mass} = \frac{\text{mass of solute}}{\text{mass of solute + mass of solvent}} \times 100\%$$

$$= 4 \text{ g} / (4 \text{ g} + 35 \text{ g}) = 10\%$$

Example: The label on a 500 mL bottle of hydrogen peroxide, H_2O_2, says 3% by volume. How much hydrogen peroxide does it contain?

Solution: Rearranging the volume equation above:

Volume of solute = volume of solution x % by volume / 100%

Volume of H_2O_2 = 3% x 500 mL / 100% = 15 mL

Molarity

Molarity (M) is a concentration expressed as the moles of solute present in a given volume (L) of the solution:

$$M = \frac{\text{mol solute}}{\text{L solution}}$$

Example: What is the molarity of 3.50 L of solution that contains 90.0 g of sodium chloride?

Solution: Grams must be converted to moles within the molarity equation:

M = 90.0 g NaCl x (1 mol / 58.5 g) / 3.50 L = 0.440 M

Example: What is the molarity of a 5.00 liter solution that was made with 10.0 moles of $CuCl_2$?

Solution: We can use the original formula. Note that in this particular example, where the number of moles of solute is given, the identity of the solute ($CaCl_2$) has nothing to do with solving the problem.

$$\text{Molarity} = \frac{\text{\# of moles of solute}}{\text{Liters of solution}}$$

Given: # of moles of solute = 10.0 moles
Liters of solution = 5.00 liters

$$\text{Molarity} = \frac{10.0 \text{ moles of } CaCl_2}{5.00 \text{ Liters of solution}} = 2.00 \text{ M}$$

Answer = 2.00 M

Example: A 250 ml solution is made with 0.50 moles of NaCl. What is the molarity of the solution?

Solution: In this case we are given ml, while the formula calls for L. We must change the ml to Liters as shown below:

$$250 \text{ ml} \times \frac{1 \text{ liter}}{1000 \text{ ml}} = 0.25 \text{ liters}$$

Now, solve the problem using the equation:

$$\text{Molarity} = \frac{\text{\# of moles of solute}}{\text{Liters of solution}}$$

Given: Number of moles of solute = 0.50 moles of NaCl
Liters of solution = 0.25 L of solution

$$\text{Molarity} = \frac{0.50 \text{ moles of NaCl}}{0.25 \text{ L}} = 2.0 \text{ M solution}$$

Answer = 2.0 M solution of NaCl

Rarely do we see or use concentrated solutions. The majority of solutions that we come across in our daily lives are dilute solutions. Molarity is useful for dilutions because the moles of solute remain unchanged if more solvent is added to the solution:

$$(\text{Initial molarity})(\text{Initial volume}) = (\text{molarity after dilution})(\text{final volume})$$

or

$$M_{initial} V_{initial} = M_{final} V_{final}$$

Example: How much water and how much 12 M HCl must be used to prepare 500 mL of a 1 M HCl solution?

Solution: $M_i V_i = M_f V_f$
$V_i = M_f V_f / M_i = 41.66$ mL

Thus, 41.66 mL of 12 M HCl is added to enough water to make 500 mL of solution. (about 458 mL of water)

MOLALITY

Molality (m) is a concentration expressed as the moles of solute present in a given mass (kg) of the solvent:

$$\text{Molality} = \frac{\text{moles solute}}{\text{mass of solvent in kilograms}}$$

Molality is a useful measure of concentration in situations where solution density (and thus, volume) is changing and the impact of this change is not important. The molarity of a solution will change with temperature because the liquid will expand or contract. Molality will remain constant. Because water typically has a density of one kilogram per liter, the molality and molarity of aqueous solutions at room temperature have roughly the same numerical value. Molality is used in calculating freezing point depressions and boiling point elevations.

Example: Calculate the molality when 75.0 grams of $MgCl_2$ is dissolved in 500.0 g of solvent.

Solution: Since m = # mol solute / Kg solvent

First we need the number mol solute ($MgCl_2$)

mol = 75.0 g $MgCl_2$ / 95.3 g/mol = 0.787 mol

We also need kg of solvent so 500.0 g of solvent needs to be converted to kg.

Kg = 500.0 g x 1 kg/1000 g = 0.5000 kg

Now it is just a matter of substituting into the molality formula:

molality = 0.787 mol/0.5000 kg =1.57 m

Example: What is the molality of a solution composed of 2.55 g of acetone, $(CH_3)_2CO$, dissolved in 200 g of water?

Solution: First, convert the units: 2.55 g x 1 mol / 58 g = 0.044 mol acetone, and 200 g water = 0.200 kg water.

m = 0.044 mol / 0.200 kg water = 0.22 m

PARTS PER MILLION

Parts per million (ppm) is frequently used when very small amounts of solute are present, such as contaminants in water. When dealing with very small amounts of solute, it is more convenient to use the expression parts per million (ppm) or even parts per billion (ppb). In comparison, a 1% saline (NaCl) solution means that there is 1 part NaCl per one hundred parts water.

Example: What is the concentration of a solution in percent, ppm, and ppb that contains 10 g of NaCl dissolved in 90 grams of H_2O?

Solution: The total mass of the solution is 10 g + 90 g = 100 g. Therefore:

Percent by weight=10 g NaCl / 100 g Solution = 0.1 x 100% = 10%
ppm=10 g NaCl / 100 g Solution=0.1 x 1,000,000 = 100,000 ppm
ppb=10 g NaCl / 100 g Solution=0.1 x 1,000,000,000 =100,000,000 ppb

NORMALITY

The **normality** (N) of a solution is defined as the number of **equivalents** of a solute per liter of solution:

$$\text{Normality} = \frac{\text{equivalents solute}}{\text{volume of solution in liters}}$$

An equivalent is defined according to the type of reaction being examined, but the number of equivalents of solute is always a whole number multiple of the number of moles of solute, and so the normality of a solute is always a whole-number multiple of its molarity. An equivalent is defined so that one equivalent of one reagent will react with one equivalent of another reagent.

For acid-base reactions (see Competency 013), an equivalent for an acid is the quantity that supplies one mol of H^+ and an equivalent for a base is the quantity reacting with one mol of H^+. For example, one mole of H_2SO_4 in an acid-base reaction supplies two moles of H+. The mass of one equivalent of H_2SO_4 is half of the mass of one mole of H_2SO_4, and its normality is twice its molarity. In a redox reaction (see Competency 014), an equivalent is the quantity of a substance that gains or loses one mol of electrons.

MOLE FRACTION

Mole fraction expresses the proportion of a component in a solution relative to the entire number of moles present. If you were able to pick out a molecule at random from a solution, the mole fraction of a component represents the probability that the molecule you picked would be from that particular component. Mole fractions for all components must add up to one and are unitless.

$$\text{Mole fraction of a component} = \frac{\text{moles of component}}{\text{total moles of all components}}$$

Skill 10.4   Analyzes precipitation reactions and derives net ionic equations

IONIC EQUATIONS

When two or more pure materials mix in a homogeneous way (with their molecules intermixing on a molecular level), the mixture is called a **solution**. Particles in solution are free to move about and collide with each other, vastly increasing the likelihood that a reaction will occur compared with particles in a solid phase. Reactions among ions in aqueous solution are often represented in three ways. When solutions of hydrochloric acid and sodium hydroxide are mixed, a reaction occurs and heat is produced. The **molecular equation** for this reaction is:

$$HCl(aq) + NaOH(aq) \rightarrow H_2O(l) + NaCl(aq)$$

It is called a molecular equation because the **complete chemical formulas** of reactants and products are shown. But in reality, both HCl and NaOH are strong electrolytes and exist in solution as ions. This is represented by a **complete ionic equation** that shows all the dissolved ions:

$$H^+(aq) + Cl^-(aq) + Na^+(aq) + OH^-(aq) \rightarrow H_2O(l) + Na^+(aq) + Cl^-(aq)$$

Because $Na^+(aq)$ and $Cl^-(aq)$ appear as both reactants and products, they play no role in the reaction. Ions that appear in identical chemical forms on both sides of an ionic equation are called **spectator ions** because they aren't part of the action.

When spectator ions are removed from a complete ionic equation, the result is a **net ionic equation** that shows the actual changes that occur to the chemicals when these two solutions are mixed together:

$$H^+(aq) + OH^-(aq) \rightarrow H_2O(l)$$

PRECIPITATION REACTIONS

Aqueous solutions may react to produce an insoluble substance that will fall out of solution as a **precipitate** in a **precipitation reaction**. Aqueous solution may also react to form **additional water** or a different chemical in aqueous solution.

Given a cation and anion in aqueous solution, we can determine if a precipitate will form according to some common **solubility rules**:

1) Salts with NH_4^+ or with a cation from group 1 of the periodic table are soluble in water.

2) Nitrates (NO_3^-), acetates ($C_2H_3O_2^-$), chlorates (ClO_3^-), and perchlorates (ClO_4^-) are soluble.

3) Cl^-, Br^-, and I^- salts are soluble except in the presence of Ag^+, Hg_2^{2+}, or Pb^{2+}, with which they will form precipitates.

4) Sulfates (SO_4^{2-}) are soluble except in the presence of Ca^{2+}, Ba^{2+}, Ag^+, Hg_2^{2+}, or Pb^{2+}.

5) Hydroxides (OH^-) are insoluble except with cations from rule 1 or in the presence of Ca^{2+}, Sr^{2+}, or Ba^{2+}.

6) Sulfides (S^{2-}), sulfites (SO_3^{2-}), phosphates (PO_4^{3-}), and carbonates (CO_3^{2-}) are insoluble except with cations from rule 1.

Skill 10.5   Analyzes the colligative properties of solutions (e.g., vapor-pressure lowering, osmotic pressure changes, boiling-point elevation, freezing-point depression)

A **colligative** property is a physical property of a solution that **depends on the number of solute particles present in solution** and usually not on the identity of the solutes involved.

VAPOR PRESSURE LOWERING, BOILING POINT ELEVATION, FREEZING POINT LOWERING

After a nonvolatile solute is added to a liquid solvent, a smaller fraction of the molecules at the liquid-gas interface are now volatile and capable of escaping into the gas phase. On the other hand, the vapor consists of essentially pure solvent that is able to condense freely.

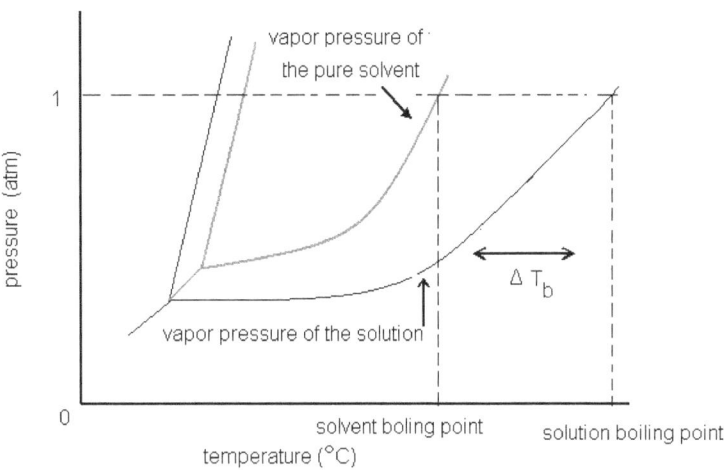

This imbalance drives equilibrium away from the vapor phase and into the liquid phase and **lowers the vapor pressure** by an amount proportional to the number of solute particles present. It follows from a lowered vapor pressure that a higher temperature is required to achieve a vapor pressure equal to the external pressure over the liquid. Thus **the boiling point is raised** by an amount proportional to the number of solute particles present.

Solute particles in a liquid solvent are not normally soluble in the solid phase of that solvent. When solvent crystals freeze, they typically align themselves with each other at first and keep the solute out. This means that only a fraction of the molecules in the liquid at the liquid-solid interface are capable of freezing while the solid phase consists of essentially pure solvent that is able to melt freely. This imbalance drives equilibrium away from the solid phase and into the liquid phase and **lowers the freezing point** by an amount proportional to the number of solute particles present.

Boiling point elevation and freezing point depression are both caused by a lower fraction of solvent molecules in the liquid phase than in the other phase. For pure water at 1 atm there is equilibrium at the normal boiling and freezing points. For water with a high solute concentration, equilibrium is not present under these conditions.

OSMOTIC PRESSURE

A **semipermeable membrane** is a material that permits some particles to pass through it but not others. The diagram below shows a membrane that permits solvent but not solute to pass through it. When a semipermeable membrane separates a dilute solution from a concentrated solution, the solvent flows from the dilute to the concentrated solution (i.e., from higher solvent to lower solvent concentration) in a process called **osmosis** until equilibrium is achieved. Notice that there is now more solvent on the side that originally had the higher concentration of solute.

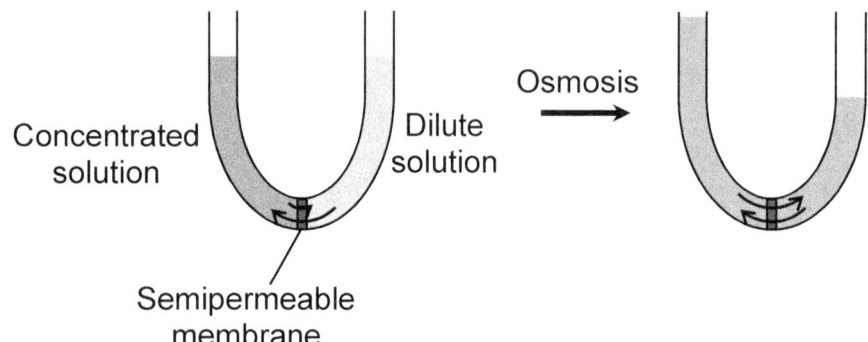

The pressure required to prevent osmosis from a pure solvent into a solution is called **osmotic pressure**. Osmotic pressure is proportional to the molarity of the solution and thus it is a colligative property of solutions. The osmotic pressure of a pure solvent is zero.

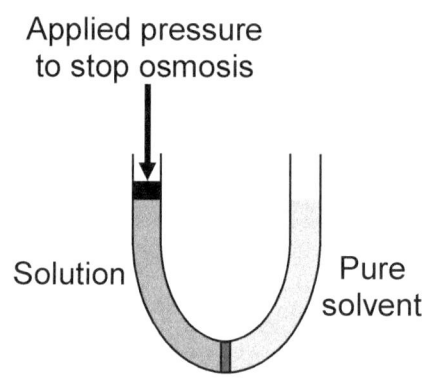

A simulation of solutes and solvent molecules interacting and an animation of osmotic flow between two flexible compartments can be found here:
http://cr.middlebury.edu/biology/labbook/diffusion/OsmPages4a.htm.
A simulation of the osmotic pressure experiment above for NaCl, sucrose, and albumin (a protein) is found here:
http://arbl.cvmbs.colostate.edu/hbooks/cmb/cells/pmemb/hydrosim.html.
Typical changes in a pressure/temperature phase diagram after adding a non-volatile solute are shown here:
http://chemmovies.unl.edu/ChemAnime/SOLND/SOLND.html.

Quantitative colligative property problems typically involve a change in a property related to a solute concentration using a direct proportionality.

Raoult's law states that the vapor pressure of a solution with nonvolatile solutes is the mole fraction of the solvent multiplied by the pure solvent vapor pressure:

$$P^{vapor}_{solution} = P^{vapor}_{pure\ solvent} (\text{mole fraction})_{solvent}$$

Raoult's law is often used to describe the vapor pressure change from a pure solvent to a solution using the solute concentration:

$$\Delta P^{vapor} = P^{vapor}_{solution} - P^{vapor}_{pure\ solvent} = P^{vapor}_{pure\ solvent}(\text{mole fraction})_{solvent} - P^{vapor}_{pure\ solvent}$$

$$= -P^{vapor}_{pure\ solvent}(1 - (\text{mole fraction})_{solvent})$$

$$= -P^{vapor}_{pure\ solvent}(\text{mole fraction})_{solute}$$

Different concentration units are used for other colligative properties to express a **change from pure solvent**. The following table summarizes these expressions for nonelectrolytes:

Colligative property	Equation for property X $\Delta X = X_{solution} - X_{pure\ solvent}$	Proportionality constant
Vapor pressure lowering	$\Delta P^{vapor} = -P^{vapor}_{pure\ solvent}(\text{mole fraction})_{solute}$	Pure solvent vapor pressure
Boiling point elevation	$\Delta T_b = K_b(\text{molality})$	Solvent-dependant constant K_b
Freezing point lowering	$\Delta T_f = -K_f(\text{molality})$	Solvent-dependant constant K_f
Osmotic pressure	$P_{osmotic} = RT(\text{molarity})$	(Gas constant) x (Temperature)

For solutions that contain electrolytes, the change from the pure solvent to a solution is different from what is predicted by the above equations. Due to their ionic nature, these substances will dissociate to put many more ions in solution than their molal concentration would predict. The total number of ions affects the colligative properties just as the number of molecules would for a nonpolar solute.

The **van 't Hoff factor** (i) is an important factor in predicting the change in boiling point or freezing point of a solution after a solute has been added. The van 't Hoff factor is symbolized by the lower-case letter i. It is a unitless constant directly associated with the degree of dissociation of the solute in the solvent:

- Substances which do not ionize in solution, like sugar, have $i = 1$.
- Substances which ionize into two ions, like NaCl, have $i = 2$.
- Substances which ionize into three ions, like $MgCl_2$, have $i = 3$.

This pattern continues for any number of particles into which a solute dissociates.

Many colligative property problems compare one solution to another and may be solved without the use of the previous expressions. All that is required for these comparison problems is knowledge of what the colligative properties are, how they are altered, and which solution contains the greater concentration of dissolved particles.

Example: One mole of each of the following compounds is added to water in separate flasks to make 1.0 L of solution:

> Potassium phosphate
> Silver chloride
> Sodium chloride
> Sugar (sucrose)

- A. Which solution will exhibit the greatest change in the freezing point temperature?

- B. Which solution will exhibit the least change in the boiling point temperature? Be sure to explain your choices.

Solution: Determine the molecular formulas and analyze the choices for solubility and dissociation:

Potassium phosphate	KH_2PO_4	soluble in water → 4 ions
Silver chloride	$AgCl$	soluble in water → 2 ions
Sodium chloride	$NaCl$	soluble in water → 2 ions
Sugar (sucrose)	$C_{12}H_{22}O_{11}$	soluble in water → 1 molecule

- A. Of the choices, potassium phosphate forms the most ions so given that the molar concentration of all of the choices is the same, K_3PO_4 will affect the boiling point temperature and the freezing point temperature the most. For every 1 mole of K_3PO_4 that dissolves, 4 moles of ions will be present in solution.

- B. Sucrose, a nonelectrolyte, will have the least effect on the freezing point and boiling point temperatures because it is a molecular substance and does not dissociate into ions. For every 1 mole of sugar in solution, only 1 mole of molecules will be present.

Changes to boiling point temperature and freezing point temperature may be determined by looking at the molal concentration of the solute, according to the equations in the table above.

For **boiling point temperature changes**:

$$\Delta T_b = mk_b i$$

where m is the molal concentration of the solute, K_b is a constant specific to each solvent, and i is the number of particles or ions in solution. For water, $K_b = 0.52°$ C/m.

For **freezing point temperature changes**:

$$\Delta T_f = mk_f i$$

where m is the molal concentration of the solute, K_f is a constant specific to each solvent, and i is the number of particles or ions in solution. For water, $K_f = -1.86°$ C/m.

Example: How much will the boiling point temperature change if 31.5 grams of potassium chloride is added to 225 g of water?

Solution: First convert the units and identify the constants. KCl is an electrolyte that dissociates into two ions, so $i = 2$.

Mass of water = 225 g = 0.225 kg
Concentration of KCl = 31.5 g / 74.5 g/mol = 0.423 mole
m = 0.423 mol / 0.225 kg = 1.88 m
K_b = 0.52° C/m
$i = 2$
$\Delta T_b = mk_b i$ = 1.88 m (0.56° C/m) 2 = 1.96° C

Example: How many grams of benzoic acid ($C_7H_6O_2$, a nonelectrolyte) must be added to 178 g of water to increase the boiling point temperature by 4° C?

Solution: First convert the units and identify the constants. Benzoic acid is a nonelectrolyte so $i = 1$.

Mass of water = 178 g = 0.178 kg
Molecular weight of benzoic acid = 122 g/mol
$\Delta T = 4°$ C
$K_b = 0.52°$ C/m

Rearranging the equation above and first solving for molality of benzoic acid:

$$m = \Delta T_b / K_b i = 4 / 0.52° \text{ C/m} \times 1 = 7.69 \text{ m}$$

Next, solve for grams of benzoic acid:

$$7.69 \text{ m} \times 0.178 \text{ kg water} = 1.37 \text{ mol}$$
$$1.37 \text{ mol} \times 122 \text{ g/mol} = 167 \text{ g benzoic acid}$$

Example: The mixture used to make ice cream does not freeze until the temperature reaches -15 to -18° C. Using ice alone, the temperature will only go down to 0° C. To reach the lower temperature needed to freeze the ice cream, salt (NaCl) is added to several 2.3 kg bags of ice. How much salt is needed to freeze the ice cream?

Solution: Each sodium chloride particle dissociates into a Na^+ ion and a Cl^- ion. Therefore, NaCl has an *i* value of 2. The temperature change needed is -15° C and the K_f value for water is -1.86° C/*m*.

Rearranging the freezing point depression expression we can determine the *molality* of the salt-ice solution that will reach -15° C.

$$m = \frac{\Delta T}{K_f \, i} = \frac{-15° \text{ C}}{-1.86° \text{ C}/m \times 2} = 4.0 \, m$$

m = moles/kg, so the moles of NaCl needed can be determined from the kilograms of ice used:

$$4.0 \text{ mol/kg} \times 2.3 \text{ kg} = 9.3 \text{ mol NaCl}$$

Now, the mass of NaCl needed can be found by using the relationship between moles and molecular weight:

$$9.3 \text{ mol} \times 58.5 \text{ g/mol} = 540 \text{ g of NaCl needed for every bag of ice used.}$$

The most common errors in solving all types of colligative property problems arise from considering some value other than **the number of particles in solution**. Remember that one mole of glucose (*aq*) forms one mole of hydrated particles, but one mole of NaCl (*aq*) forms two moles of hydrated particles, and one mole of $Al_2(SO_4)_3$ (*aq*) forms five moles of hydrated particles.

We would expect a 0.5 M solution of glucose to have roughly the same colligative properties as a 0.25 M solution of sodium hydroxide and a 0.1 M solution of aluminum sulfate. Also remember that non-dissolved solids do not contribute anything to colligative properties.

Skill 10.6 Understands the properties of electrolytes and explains the relationship between concentration and electrical conductivity

Any compound that dissolves in water will cause an increase in the electrical conductivity of the water. However, depending on the compound, the increase in conductivity will vary. Compounds that do not increase the electrical conductivity of water are referred to as **nonelectrolytes**. Conversely, those that do increase conductivity are called **electrolytes**. Among electrolytes, there are **weak electrolytes** and **strong electrolytes**. Most salts are strong electrolytes, meaning that they completely dissociate in water. Other compounds (including many acids and bases) may dissolve in water without completely ionizing and are **weak electrolytes.** Compounds that dissolve with no ionization (e.g., glucose, $C_6H_{12}O_6$) are **nonelectrolytes.** The ability of a solution to conduct electricity depends not only the inherent electrolytic strength of the dissolved compound, but on the concentration of that compound, as will be shown below.

To understand conductivity, we must first review some basic electrical theory. If electrical current flows through a wire, the amount of current that flows depends upon the resistance in the wire according to **Ohm's Law**:

$$V = IR$$

where V is the voltage, I the current, and R the resistance. In a wire, the resistance depends upon the geometry of the wire and the material from which it is made. To obtain a measure of resistance independent of geometry, we often calculate the resistivity, r as:

$$r = RA/L$$

where A is the cross sectional area of the wire and L is the length of the wire. An electrolytic solution conducts electricity similarly to a wire. **The conductance of ionic solutions is the result of the movement of ions through the solution to the electrodes.** However, for a solution it is more common to refer to conductivity k, which is the inverse of resistivity:

$$k = 1/r$$

For a given chemical compound it is even more convenient to determine its equivalent conductance, L:

$$L = kv$$

where v is the volume of solution containing one gram equivalent of solute. Equivalent conductance allows us to measure conductance on a "per ion basis." We can determine the increase in solution conductivity by multiplying the equivalent conductance by the solute concentration, as described below.

Experiments to measure the conductivity of a solution may be performed with a conductivity meter. Electrodes are immersed in the solution, and the conductivity measured depends on the type and concentration of ions present, the solvent, the area of the electrode, and the distance between the electrodes.

Imagine the solvent is pure water and the solute is NaCl. In the water alone, there are very few charged species (ions) present and the conductivity measured will be low. The addition of ions such as those in a 0.10 N solution of NaCl (L = 106.8 W^{-1}cm^{2}mol^{-1}) will increase the conductivity of the solution as follows:

$$k = L/v = 106.8 \text{ W}^{-1}\text{cm}^2\text{mol}^{-1} \times 0.01 \text{ mol}/1000 \text{ cm}^3 = 10.68 \times 10^{-6} \text{ W}^{-1}\text{cm}^{-1}$$

Notice that this means that a **greater increase in conductivity will be achieved with either a higher concentration or a compound with larger equivalent conductance.** However, it must also be noted that at a certain solute concentration, solution conductivity begins to decline again because the mobility of individual ions is limited by high concentration of other ions.

ELECTROLYTIC AND ELECTROCHEMICAL SYSTEMS

See Skill 14.3 for electrolytic cells, electrodes, and half-reactions.

See Skill 14.2 for information on half reactions and solving the resultant redox equations.

Skill 10.7 Analyzes models to explain the structural properties of water and evaluates the significance of water as a solvent in living organisms and the environment

Many of the unique qualities of water stem from the hydrogen bonds that form between the molecules. **Hydrogen bonds** are particularly **strong dipole-dipole interactions** that form between a **H atom** of one molecule and a **F, O, or N atom** of an adjacent molecule. The partial positive charge on the hydrogen atom is attracted to the partial negative charge on the electron pair of the other atom. The hydrogen bond between two water molecules is shown as the dashed line below:

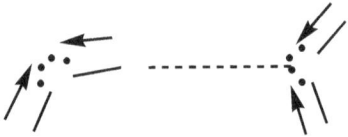

This intermolecular force translate into unique properties that impact biological systems. First, the hydrogen bonds govern the shape of the crystals that form when water freezes. Thus, relatively large spaces of air are present between the frozen water molecules. Because these spaces do not exist when the water is in liquid form, ice is less dense and will float on liquid water. This means that water freezes from the top and provides an insulating layer of ice on the surface of bodies of water, thus allowing organisms in the water to continue living.

Second, while water is a small molecule, the hydrogen bonds allow it to act like a larger one. Specifically, the extra energy required to break the hydrogen bonds means that water has a much higher boiling point than other molecules of similar size. If this were not the case, water on Earth would be a gas all of the time and life would not be possible.

Finally, water is considered a universal solvent, in that it dissolves more substances than any other liquid. When a crystal of salt is dropped into water, the water surrounds the atoms in the salt, forming a hydration sphere. The water molecules continue interacting with the atoms on the surface of the crystal until the entire crystal is dissolved. This both dissolves the salt crystal and disrupts the organization of the water molecules. This disruption prevents the formation of ice crystals and this explains both why oceans resist freezing and why salting roads prevents the formation of ice.

COMPETENCY 011 THE TEACHER UNDERSTANDS ENERGY TRANSFORMATIONS THAT OCCUR IN PHYSICAL AND CHEMICAL PROCESSES

Skill 11.1 Analyzes the energy transformations that occur in phase transitions

See Skill 5.2 for a discussion of energy absorbed and released during phase changes, and Skill 11.4 below for further discussion of thermodynamic concepts related to phase changes.

Skill 11.2 Solves problems in calorimetry (e.g., determining the specific heat of a substance, finding the standard enthalpy of formation and reaction of substances)

See Skill 8.9 for information on solving these problems and Skill 11.4 below for general thermodynamic concepts and a detailed example..

Skill 11.3 Applies the law of conservation of energy to analyze and evaluate energy exchanges that occur in exothermic and endothermic processes

See Skill 8.9 for information on solving these problems and Skill 11.4 below for general thermodynamic concepts and a detailed example.

Skill 11.4 Understands thermodynamic relationships among spontaneous reactions, entropy, enthalpy, temperature, and Gibbs free energy

See Skill 8.9 for a full discussion of bond dissociation energies, heats of formation and enthalpy.

ENERGY

Energy is the **driving force for change**. Energy has units of joules (J). Temperature remains constant during phase changes, so the **speed** of molecules and their **translational kinetic energy do not change** during a change in phase.

The **internal energy** of a material is the **sum of the total kinetic energy** of its molecules and the **potential energy** of interactions between those molecules. Total kinetic energy includes the contributions from translational motion and other components of motion such as rotation. The potential energy includes **energy stored in the form of resisting intermolecular attractions** between molecules.

ENTHALPY

The **enthalpy** (*H*) of a material is the **sum of its internal energy and the mechanical work** it can do by driving a piston. We usually don't deal with mechanical work in high school chemistry, so the differences between internal energy and enthalpy are not important. The key concept is that a change in the **enthalpy** of a substance is the total **energy** change caused by **adding or removing heat** at constant pressure.

When a material is heated and experiences a phase change, **thermal energy is used to break the intermolecular bonds** holding the material together. Similarly, bonds are formed with the release of thermal energy when a material changes its phase during cooling. Therefore, **the energy of a material increases during a phase change that requires heat and decreases during a phase change that releases heat**. For example, the energy of H_2O increases when ice melts and decreases when water freezes.

Hess' law states that energy changes are state functions. The amount of energy depends only on the states of the reactants and the state of the products, but not on the intermediate steps. Energy (enthalpy) changes in chemical reactions are the same, regardless whether the reactions occur in one or several steps. The total energy change in a chemical reaction is the sum of the energy changes in its many steps leading to the overall reaction.

ENTROPY

Entropy (S) may be thought of as **the disorder in a system** or as a measure of the **number of states a system may occupy**. Changes due to entropy occur in one direction with no driving force. For example, a small volume of gas released into a large container will expand to fill it, but the gas in a large container never spontaneously collects itself into a small volume. This occurs because a large volume of gas has more disorder and has more places for gas molecules to be. This change occurs because **processes increase in entropy** when given the opportunity to do so. Entropy has units of J/K.

If two different chemicals are at the same temperature, in the same state of matter, and they have the same number of molecules, their entropy difference will depend mostly on the number of ways the atoms within the two chemicals can rotate, vibrate, and flex. Most of the time, **the more complex molecule will have the greater entropy** because there are more energetic and spatial states in which it may exist.

In the solid phase, each molecule may vibrate a little, but it is otherwise locked into place in an ordered position and may only be in a relatively small number of locations. In the gas phase, however, each molecule could be almost anywhere and there is greater disorder. Therefore, **the entropy of a material increases during a phase change that raises the freedom of molecular motion and**

decreases during a phase change that prevents molecular motion. Entropy also increases with temperature because molecules experience more disorder when they have a wider range of energy states to occupy.

Based on this principle, gases have greater entropy than liquids, liquids have greater entropy than solids, and matter in the same state increases in entropy with temperature. Entropy is also an extensive property of matter. **A greater number of moles will have a larger entropy.**

If two different chemicals are at the same temperature, in the same state of matter, and they have the same number of molecules, their entropy difference will depend mostly on the number of ways the atoms within the two chemicals can rotate, vibrate, and flex. Most of the time, **the more complex molecule will have the greater entropy** because there are more energetic and spatial states in which it may exist.

At zero Kelvin (0 K), there is no energy available for a chemical to sample different states. The **absolute entropy**, S, of a pure crystalline solid at 0 K is zero. Absolute entropy may be measured and calculated for different substances at different temperatures.

The **entropy change of a reaction**, ΔS, is given by the sum of the absolute entropies of all the products multiplied by their stoichiometric coefficients minus the sum of all the reactants multiplied by their stoichiometric coefficients:

For the reaction: $aA + bB \leftrightarrow pP + qQ$

$$\Delta S = pS(P) + qS(Q) - aS(A) - bS(B)$$

SPONTANEITY AND GIBBS FREE ENERGY

A reaction with a **negative ΔH (enthalpy) and a positive ΔS (entropy)** causes a decrease in energy and an increase in entropy. **These reactions will always occur spontaneously.** A reaction with a positive ΔH and a negative ΔS causes an increase in energy and a decrease in entropy. These reactions never occur to an appreciable extent because the reverse reaction takes place spontaneously.

Whether reactions with the remaining two possible combinations (i.e., both ΔH and ΔS positive or negative) occur depends on the temperature. If $\Delta H - T\Delta S$ (known as the **Gibbs Free Energy, ΔG**) is negative, the reaction will take place. If it is positive, the reaction will not occur to an appreciable extent. If $\Delta H - T\Delta S = 0$ exactly, then at equilibrium there will be 50% reactants and 50% products.

A spontaneous reaction is called *exergonic*. A non-spontaneous reaction is known as *endergonic*. These terms are used much less often than *exothermic* and *endothermic*.

Example (part 1): Determine the standard heat of formation $\Delta H_f°$ for ethylene:

$$2C(graphite) + 2H_2(g) \rightarrow C_2H_4(g).$$

Use the heat of combustion for ethylene:

$$\Delta H_c° = 1411.2 \frac{kJ}{mol\ C_2H_4} \quad \text{for } C_2H_4(g) + 3O_2(g) \rightarrow 2CO_2(g) + 2H_2O(l)$$

and the following two heats of formation for CO₂ and H₂O:

$$\Delta H_f° = -393.5 \frac{kJ}{mol\ C} \quad \text{for } C(graphite) + O_2(g) \rightarrow CO_2(g)$$

$$\Delta H_f° = -285.9 \frac{kJ}{mol\ H_2} \quad \text{for } H_2(g) + \frac{1}{2}O_2(g) \rightarrow H_2O(l).$$

Also find the standard change in entropy $\Delta S°$ for the formation of C₂H₄ given:

$$S°(C(graphite)) = 5.7 \frac{J}{mol\ K} \quad S°(H_2(g)) = 130.6 \frac{J}{mol\ K} \quad S°(C_2H_4(g)) = 219.4 \frac{J}{mol\ K}$$

Example (part 2): Will graphite and hydrogen gas react to form C₂H₄ at 25 °C and 100 kPa?

Solution: Use Hess's Law after rearranging the given reactions so they cancel to yield the reaction of interest. Combustion is exothermic, so ΔH for this reaction is negative. We are interested in C₂H₄ as a product, so we take the opposite (endothermic) reaction. The given ΔH are multiplied by stoichiometric coefficients to give the reaction of interest as the sum of the three:

$$2CO_2(g) + 2H_2O(l) \rightarrow C_2H_4(g) + 3O_2(g) \quad \Delta H = 1411.2 \frac{kJ}{mol\ reaction}$$

$$2C(graphite) + 2O_2(g) \rightarrow 2CO_2(g) \quad \Delta H = -787.0 \frac{kJ}{mol\ reaction}$$

$$2H_2(g) + O_2(g) \rightarrow 2H_2O(l) \quad \Delta H = -571.8 \frac{kJ}{mol\ reaction}$$

$$2C(graphite) + 2H_2(g) \rightarrow C_2H_4(g) \quad \Delta H_f^\circ = 52.4 \frac{kJ}{mol}$$

-787.0 kJ/mol is found by multiplying 2 × 393.5 kJ/mol because 2 mol react. The same is true for the -571.8 kJ/mol; 2 mol react so it becomes 2 × -285.9 kJ/mol. The value for the first equation is not multiplied by 2 because the ΔH is for the equation as it is written.

The entropy change is found from:

$$\Delta S^\circ = S^\circ(C_2H_4) - 2S^\circ(C) - 2S^\circ(H_2) = 219.4 \frac{J}{mol\ K} - 2 \times 5.7 \frac{J}{mol\ K} - 2 \times 130.6 \frac{J}{mol\ K}$$

$$= -53.2 \frac{J}{mol\ K}.$$

This reaction is endothermic with a decrease in entropy, so it is endergonic. Graphite and hydrogen gas will not react to form C₂H₄.

In the diagram that follows, we look at the oxidation of carbon into CO and CO₂. The direct oxidation of carbon (graphite) into CO₂ yields an enthalpy of

393 kJ/mol. When carbon is oxidized into CO and then CO is oxidized to CO_2, the enthalpies are -110 and -283 kJ/mol respectively.

The sum of enthalpy in the two steps is exactly -393 kJ/mol, same as the one-step reaction.

The two reaction steps are:

$C + \frac{1}{2} O_2 \rightarrow CO$, $\Delta H° = -110$ kJ/mol
$CO + \frac{1}{2} O_2 \rightarrow CO_2$, $\Delta H° = -283$ kJ/mol.

Adding the two equations together and canceling out the intermediate, CO, on both sides leads to

$C + O_2 \rightarrow CO_2$, $\Delta H° = (-110) + (-283) = -393$ kJ/mol.

Application of Hess's law enables us to calculate ΔH, $\Delta H°$, and ΔH_f for chemical reactions that are impossible to measure, providing that we have all the data of related reactions.

The enthalpy of combustion for H_2, C(graphite) and CH_4 are -285.8, -393.5, and -890.4 kJ/mol respectively. Calculate the standard enthalpy of formation ΔH_f for CH_4.

Using the equations and their ΔH values

(1) $H_2(g) + 0.5\ O_2(g) \rightarrow H_2O(l)$ $\Delta H = -285.8$ kJ/mol
(2) $C(graphite) + O_2(g) \rightarrow CO_2(g)$ $\Delta H = -393.5$ kJ/mol
(3) $CH_4(g) + 2O_2(g) \rightarrow CO_2(g) + 2H_2O(l)$ $\Delta H = -890.4$ kJ/mol

Find: $C + 2H_2 \rightarrow CH_4$

2 $(H_2(g) + 0.5\ O_2(g) \rightarrow H_2O(l))$ $\Delta H = -285.8$ kJ/mol)

or $2H_2(g) + O_2(g) \rightarrow 2H_2O(l)$ $\Delta H = -571.6$ kJ

+ $C(graphite) + O_2(g) \rightarrow CO_2(g)$ $\Delta H = -393.5$ kJ

+ $CO_2(g) + 2H_2O(l) \rightarrow CH_4(g) + 2O_2(g)$ $\Delta H = +890.4$ kJ

―――――――――――――――――――――――――――

$C(graphite) + 2H_2(g) \rightarrow CH_4(g)$ $\Delta H = -74.7$ kJ

From these data, we can construct an energy level diagram for these chemical combinations as follows:

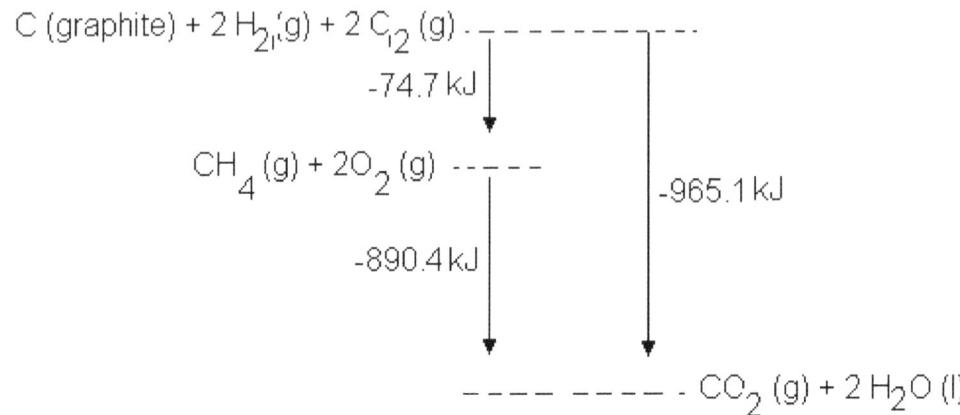

TEACHER CERTIFICATION STUDY GUIDE

DOMAIN III.	CHEMICAL REACTIONS

COMPETENCY 012   **THE TEACHER UNDERSTANDS CHEMICAL KINETICS AND EQUILIBRIUM**

Skill 12.1   **Analyzes factors (e.g., temperature, pressure, concentration, catalysts) that influence the rate of a chemical reaction**

In order for one species to be converted to another during a chemical reaction, the reactants must collide. The collisions between the reactants determine how fast the reaction takes place. However, during a chemical reaction, only a fraction of the collisions between the appropriate reactant molecules convert them into product molecules. This occurs for two reasons:

1) Not all collisions occur with a **sufficiently high energy** for the reaction to occur.
2) Not all collisions **orient the molecules properly** for the reaction to occur.

The **activation energy** (E_a) of a reaction is the **minimum energy needed to overcome the barrier to the formation of products** and allow the reaction to occur.

At the scale of individual molecules, a reaction typically involves a very small period of time when old bonds are broken and new bonds are formed. During this time, the molecules involved are in a **transition state** between reactants and products. A threshold of maximum energy is crossed when the arrangement of molecules is in an unfavorable intermediate state between reactants and products known as the **activated complex**. Formulas and diagrams of activated complexes are often written within brackets to indicate they are transition states that are present for extremely small periods of time.

The activation energy (E_a) is the difference between the energy of the reactants and the energy of the activated complex. The energy change during the reaction (ΔE) is the difference between the energy of the products and the energy of the reactants. The activation energy of the reverse reaction is $E_a - \Delta E$. These energy levels are represented in an **energy diagram** such as the one shown on the following page for $NO_2 + CO \rightarrow NO + CO_2$. This is an exothermic reaction because the products are lower in energy than the reactants.

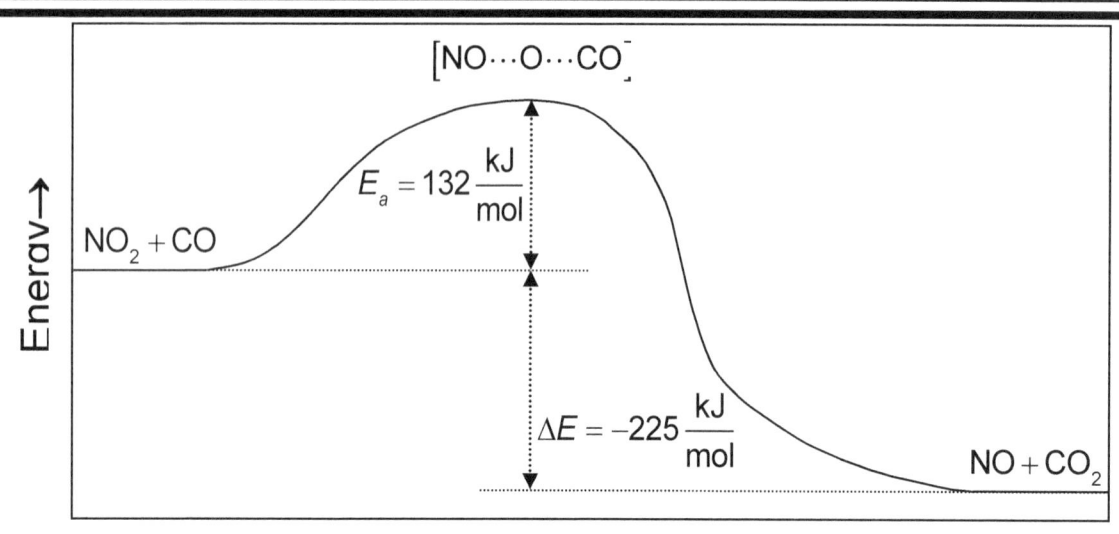

An energy diagram is a conceptual tool, so there is some variability in how its axes are labeled. The y-axis of the diagram is usually labeled energy (E), but it is sometimes labeled "enthalpy (H)" or (rarely) "free energy (G)." There is an even greater variability in how the x-axis is labeled. The terms "reaction pathway," "reaction coordinate," "course of reaction," or "reaction progress" may be used on the x-axis, or the x-axis may remain without a label.

The energy diagrams of an endothermic and exothermic reaction are compared below.

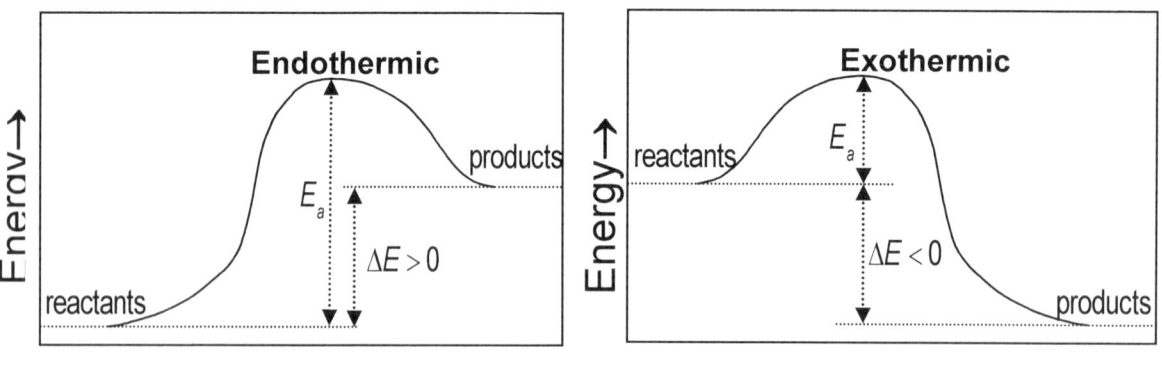

The rate of most simple reactions **increases with temperature** because a **greater fraction of molecules have the kinetic energy** required to overcome the reaction's activation energy. The chart below shows the effect of temperature on the distribution of kinetic energies in a sample of molecules. These curves are called **Maxwell-Boltzmann distributions**. The shaded areas represent the fraction of molecules containing sufficient kinetic energy for a reaction to occur. This area is larger at a higher temperature; so more molecules are above the activation energy and more molecules react per second.

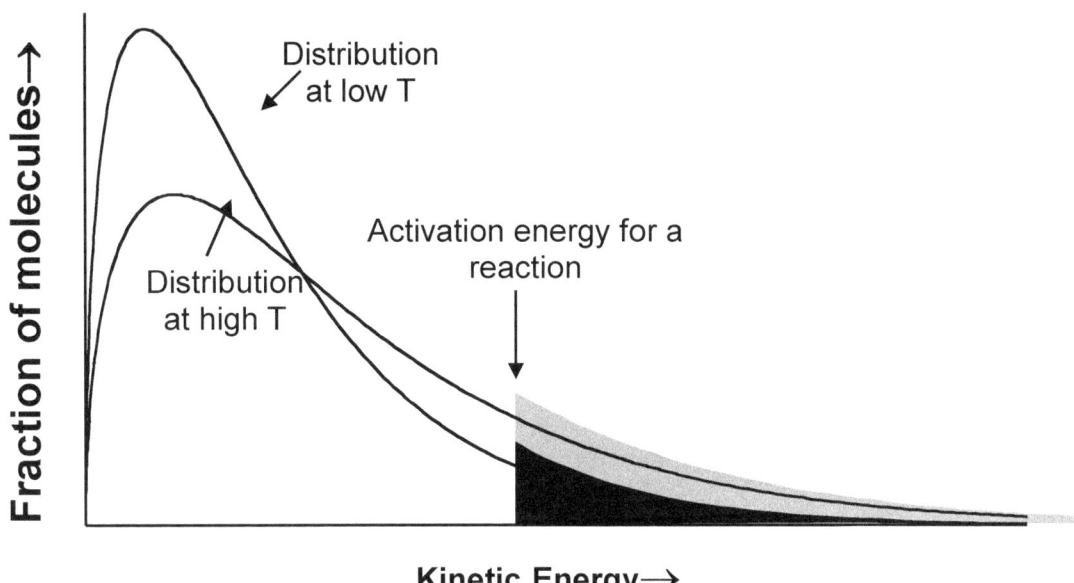

http://www.mhhe.com/physsci/chemistry/essentialchemistry/flash/activa2.swf provides an animated audio tutorial on energy diagrams.

Kinetic molecular theory may be applied to reaction rates in addition to physical constants like pressure. **Reaction rates increase with reactant concentration** because more reactant molecules are present and more are likely to collide with one another in a certain volume at higher concentrations. The nature of these relationships determines the rate law for the reaction. For ideal gases, the concentration of a reactant is its molar density, and this varies with pressure and temperature as discussed in Skill 7.1.

Kinetic molecular theory also predicts that **reaction rate constants (values for *k*) increase with temperature** for two reasons:

1) More reactant molecules will collide with each other per second.
2) These collisions will each occur at a higher energy that is more likely to overcome the activation energy of the reaction.

A **catalyst** is a material that increases the rate of a chemical reaction without changing itself permanently in the process. Catalysts provide an alternate reaction mechanism for the reaction to proceed in the forward and in the reverse direction. Therefore, **catalysts have no impact on the chemical equilibrium** of a reaction. They will not make a less favorable reaction more favorable.

Catalysts reduce the activation energy of a reaction. This is the amount of energy needed for the reaction to begin. Molecules with such low energies that they would have taken a long time to react will react more rapidly if a catalyst is present.

The impact of a catalyst may also be represented on an energy diagram. **A catalyst increases the rate of both the forward and reverse reactions by lowering the activation energy** for the reaction. Catalysts provide a different activated complex for the reaction at a lower energy state.

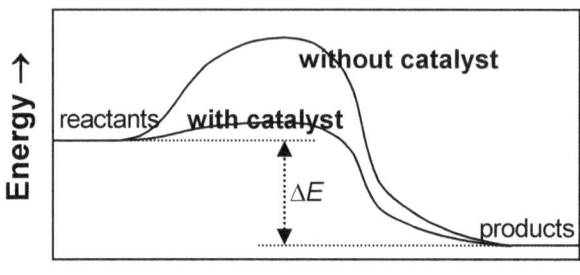

Reaction pathway →

There are two types of catalysts: **Homogeneous catalysts** are in the same physical phase as the reactants. Biological catalysts are called **enzymes**, and most are homogeneous catalysts. A typical homogeneous catalytic reaction mechanism involves an initial reaction with one reactant followed by a reaction with a second reactant and release of the catalyst:

$$A + C \rightarrow AC$$
$$B + AC \rightarrow AB + C$$

Net reaction: $A + B \xrightarrow{\text{catalyst C}} AB$

Heterogeneous catalysts are present in a different physical state from the reactants. A typical heterogeneous catalytic reaction involves a solid surface onto which molecules in a fluid phase temporarily attach themselves in a way that favors a rapid reaction. Catalytic converters in cars utilize heterogeneous catalysis to break down harmful chemicals in exhaust.

A system at equilibrium is in a state of balance because forward and reverse processes are taking place at equal rates. If equilibrium is disturbed by changing concentration, pressure, or temperature, the state of balance is upset for a period of time before the equilibrium shifts to achieve a new state of balance. **Le Chatelier's principle states that equilibrium will shift to partially offset the impact of an altered condition**.

CHANGE IN REACTANT AND PRODUCT CONCENTRATIONS

If a chemical reaction is at equilibrium, Le Chatelier's principle predicts that **adding a substance**—either a reactant or a product—will shift the reaction so **a new equilibrium is established by consuming some of the added substance**. Removing a substance will cause the reaction to move in the direction that forms more of that substance.

Example: The reaction $CO + 2H_2 \leftrightarrow CH_3OH$ is used to synthesize methanol. Equilibrium is established, and then additional CO is added to the reaction vessel. Predict the impact on each reaction component after CO is added.

Solution: Le Chatelier's principle states that the reaction will shift to partially offset the impact of the added CO. Therefore, the concentration of CO will decrease, and the reaction will "shift to the right." The concentration of H_2 will also decrease and the concentration of CH_3OH will increase.

CHANGE IN PRESSURE FOR GASES

If a chemical reaction is at equilibrium in the gas phase, Le Chatelier's principle predicts that **an increase in pressure** will shift the reaction so **a new equilibrium is established by decreasing the number of moles of gas present**. A decrease in the number of moles partially offsets this rise in pressure. Decreasing pressure will cause the reaction to move in the direction that forms more moles of gas. These changes in pressure might result from altering the volume of the reaction vessel at constant temperature.

Example: The reaction $N_2 + 3H_2 \leftrightarrow 2NH_3$ is used to synthesize ammonia. Equilibrium is established. Next the reaction vessel is expanded at constant temperature. Predict the impact on each reaction component after this expansion occurs.

Solution: The expansion will result in a decrease in pressure. Le Chatelier's principle states that the reaction will shift to partially offset this decrease by increasing the number of moles present. There are 4 moles of gas on the left side of the equation and 2 moles of gas on the right, so the reaction will shift to the left. N_2 and H_2 concentration will increase. NH_3 concentration will decrease.

CHANGE IN TEMPERATURE

Le Chatelier's principle predicts that **when heat is added** at constant pressure to a system at equilibrium, **the reaction will shift in the direction that absorbs heat** until a new equilibrium is established. For an endothermic process, the reaction will shift to the right towards product formation. For an exothermic process, the reaction will shift to the left towards reactant formation. If you understand the application of Le Chatelier's principle to concentration changes, then writing "heat" on the appropriate side of the equation will help you understand its application to changes in temperature.

Example: $N_2 + 3H_2 \leftrightarrow 2NH_3$ is an exothermic reaction. First equilibrium is established and then the temperature is decreased. Predict the impact of the lower temperature on each reaction component.

Solution: Since the reaction is exothermic, we may write it as:

$$N_2 + 3H_2 \leftrightarrow 2NH_3 + \text{heat}$$

To find the impact of temperature on equilibrium processes, we may consider heat as if it were a reaction component. Le Chatelier's principle states that after a temperature decrease, the reaction will shift to partially offset the impact of a loss of heat. Therefore more heat will be produced, and the reaction will shift to the right. N_2 and H_2 concentration will decrease. NH_3 concentration will increase.

A flash animation with audio that demonstrates Le Chatelier's principle can be found at:
http://www.mhhe.com/physsci/chemistry/essentialchemistry/flash/lechv17.swf.

Skill 12.2   Solves problems involving rate laws and determines the rate law of a reaction from experimental data

OBTAINING REACTION RATES FROM CONCENTRATION DATA

The rate of any process is measured by its change per unit time. The speed of a car is measured by its change in position with time using units of miles per hour. The speed of a chemical reaction is usually measured by a change in the concentration of a reactant or product with time using units of **molarity per second** (M/s). The molarity of a chemical is represented in mathematical equations using brackets.

The **average reaction rate** is the change in concentration of either reactant or product per unit time during a time interval:

$$\text{Average reaction rate} = \frac{\text{Change in concentration}}{\text{Change in time}}$$

Reaction rates are positive quantities. Product concentrations increase and reactant concentrations decrease with time, so a different formula is required depending on the identity of the component of interest:

$$\text{Average reaction rate} = \frac{[\text{product}]_{final} - [\text{product}]_{initial}}{\text{time}_{final} - \text{time}_{iniial}}$$

$$= \frac{[\text{reactant}]_{initial} - [\text{reactant}]_{final}}{\text{time}_{final} - \text{time}_{iniial}}$$

The **reaction rate** at a given time refers to the **instantaneous reaction rate**. This is found from the absolute value of the **slope of a curve of concentration vs. time**. An estimate of the reaction rate at time t may be found from the average reaction rate over a small time interval surrounding t. For those familiar with calculus notation, the following equations define reaction rate, but calculus is not needed for this skill:

$$\text{Reaction rate at time } t = \frac{d[\text{product}]}{dt} = -\frac{d[\text{reactant}]}{dt}$$

Example: The following concentration data describe the decomposition of N_2O_5 according to the reaction $2N_2O_5 \rightarrow 4NO_2 + O_2$:

Time (sec)	[N$_2$O$_5$] (M)
0	0.0200
1000	0.0120
2000	0.0074
3000	0.0046
4000	0.0029
5000	0.0018
7500	0.0006
10000	0.0002

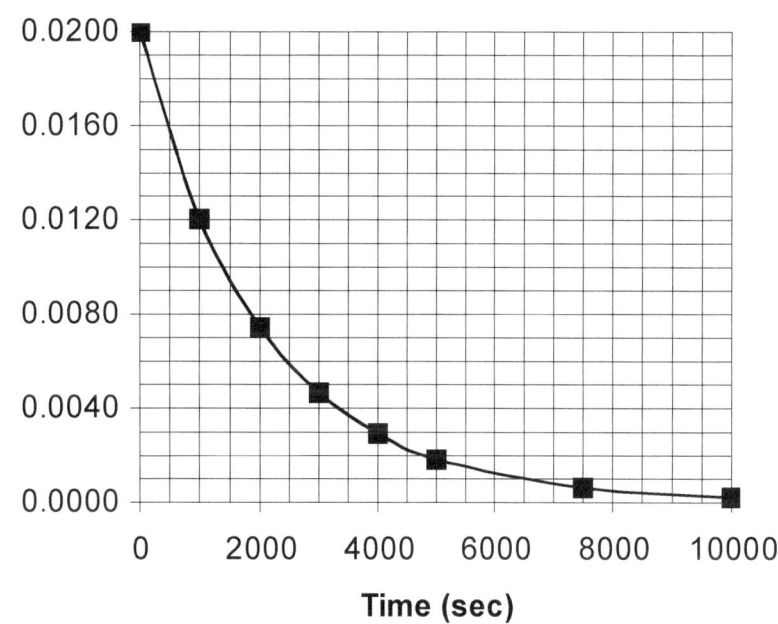

Determine the average Reaction rate from 1000 to 5000 seconds and the instantaneous reaction rate at 0 and at 4000 seconds.

Solution: The average reaction rate from 1000 to 5000 seconds is found from:

$$\frac{[\text{reactant}]_{\text{initial}} - [\text{reactant}]_{\text{final}}}{\text{time}_{\text{final}} - \text{time}_{\text{iniial}}} = \frac{0.0120 \text{ M} - 0.0018 \text{ M}}{5000 \text{ sec} - 1000 \text{ sec}} = 2.55 \times 10^{-6} \frac{M}{s}$$

Instantaneous reaction rates are found by drawing lines tangent to the curve, finding the slopes of these lines, and forcing these slopes to be positive values, as shown on the following page.

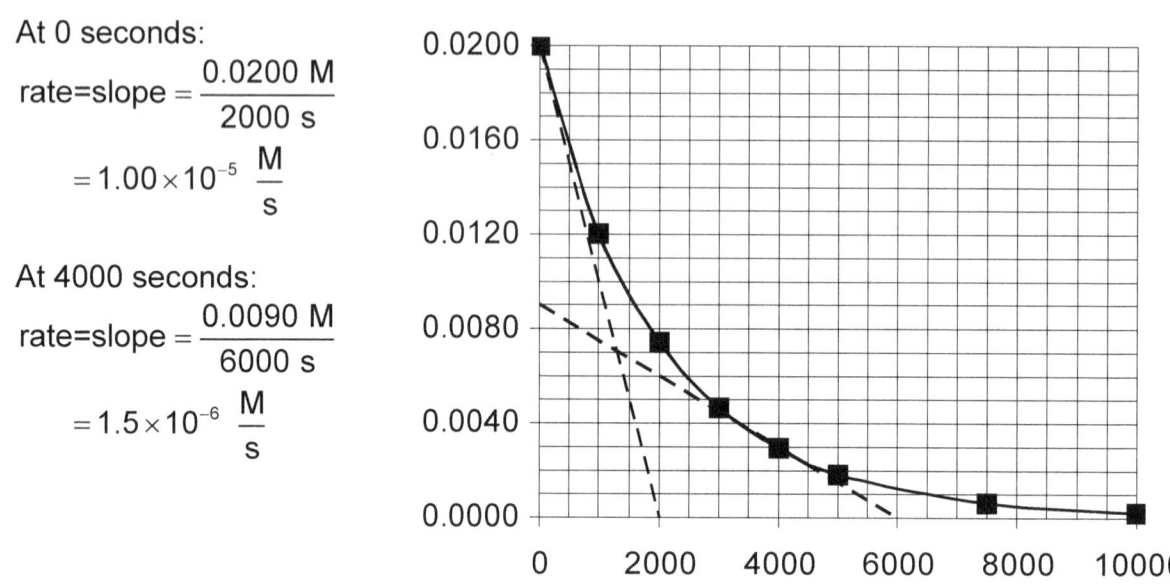

At 0 seconds:
rate = slope = $\dfrac{0.0200\ M}{2000\ s}$
$= 1.00 \times 10^{-5}\ \dfrac{M}{s}$

At 4000 seconds:
rate = slope = $\dfrac{0.0090\ M}{6000\ s}$
$= 1.5 \times 10^{-6}\ \dfrac{M}{s}$

Time (sec)

DERIVING RATE LAWS FROM REACTION RATES

A **rate law** is an **equation relating a reaction rate to concentrations of the reactants**. The rate laws for most reactions discussed in high-school level chemistry are of the form:

$$\text{Rate} = k[\text{reactant 1}]^a [\text{reactant 2}]^b \ldots$$

In the above general equation, k is called the **rate constant**. a and b are called **reaction orders**. Most reactions considered in introductory chemistry have a reaction order of zero, one, or two. The sum of all reaction orders for a reaction is called the **overall reaction order**. Rate laws cannot be predicted from the stoichiometry of a reaction. They must be determined by experiment or derived from knowledge of reaction mechanisms.

If a reaction is zero order for a reactant, the concentration of that reactant has no impact on the rate as long as some reactant is present. If a reaction is first order for a reactant, the reaction rate is proportional to the reactant's concentration. For a reaction that is second order with respect to a reactant, doubling that reactant's concentration increases reaction rate by a factor of four. Rate laws are determined by finding the appropriate reaction order describing **the impact of reactant concentrations on reaction rate**.

Reaction rates typically have units of M/s (moles/liter-sec) and concentrations have units of M (moles/liter). For units to cancel properly in the expression above, the units of the rate constant k must vary with overall reaction order as shown in the following table. The value of k may be determined by finding the slope of a plot charting a function of concentration against time.

These functions may be memorized or computed using calculus.

Overall reaction order	Units of rate constant k	Method to determine k for rate laws with one reactant
0	M/sec	−(slope) of a chart of [reactant] vs. t
1	sec^{-1}	−(slope) of a chart of ln[reactant] vs. t
2	M^{-1}sec^{-1}	slope of a chart of 1/[reactant] vs. t

As an alternative to using the rate constant k, the course of **first order reactions** may be expressed in terms of a **half-life**, $t_{halflife}$. The half-life of a reaction is the time required for a reactant concentration to reach half of its initial value. First order rate constants and half-lives are inversely proportional:

$$t_{halflife} = \frac{\ln 2}{k_{first\ order}} = \frac{0.693}{k_{first\ order}}$$

Example: Derive a rate law for the reaction $2N_2O_5 \rightarrow 4NO_2 + O_2$ using data from the previous example.

Solution: Three methods will be used to solve this problem.

1) In the previous example, we found the following two **instantaneous reaction rates**:

Time (sec)	[N$_2$O$_5$] (M)	Reaction rate (M/sec)
0	0.0200	1.00X10^{-5}
4000	0.0029	1.5X10^{-6}

A decrease in reactant concentration to 0.0029/0.0200=14.5% of its initial value led to a nearly proportional decrease in reaction rate to 15% of its initial value. In other words, reaction rate remains proportional to reactant concentration. The reaction is first order:

$$\text{Rate} = k\left[N_2O_5\right].$$

We may estimate a value for the rate constant by dividing reaction rates by the concentration:

$$k_{first\ order} = \frac{\text{Rate}}{\left[N_2O_5\right]}.$$

Time (sec)	[N$_2$O$_5$] (M)	Reaction rate (M/sec)	k (sec^{-1})
0	0.0200	1.00X10^{-5}	5.00X10^{-4}
4000	0.0029	1.5X10^{-6}	5.2X10^{-4}

2) We could estimate this rate constant by finding **average reaction rates** in each small time interval and assuming this rate occurs halfway between the two concentrations:

Time (sec)	[N$_2$O$_5$] (M)	Average rate (M/sec)	Halfway [N$_2$O$_5$] (M)	k (sec^{-1})
0	0.0200	8.00X10^{-6}	0.0160	5.00X10^{-4}
1000	0.0120	4.6X10^{-6}	0.0097	4.7X10^{-4}
2000	0.0074	2.8X10^{-6}	0.0060	4.7X10^{-4}
3000	0.0046	1.7X10^{-6}	0.0038	4.5X10^{-4}
4000	0.0029	1.1X10^{-6}	0.0024	4.7X10^{-4}
5000	0.0018	4.8X10^{-7}	0.0012	4.0X10^{-4}
7500	0.0006	2X10^{-7}	0.0004	4X10^{-4}
10000	0.0002			

3) If **concentration data** are given then no rate data needs to be found to determine a rate constant. For a first order reaction, chart the natural logarithm of concentration against time and find the slope.

Time (sec)	[N$_2$O$_5$] (M)	ln[N$_2$O$_5$]
0	0.0200	-3.91
1000	0.0120	-4.41
2000	0.0074	-4.90
3000	0.0046	-5.37
4000	0.0029	-5.83
5000	0.0018	-6.30
7500	0.0006	-7.39
10000	0.0002	-8.46

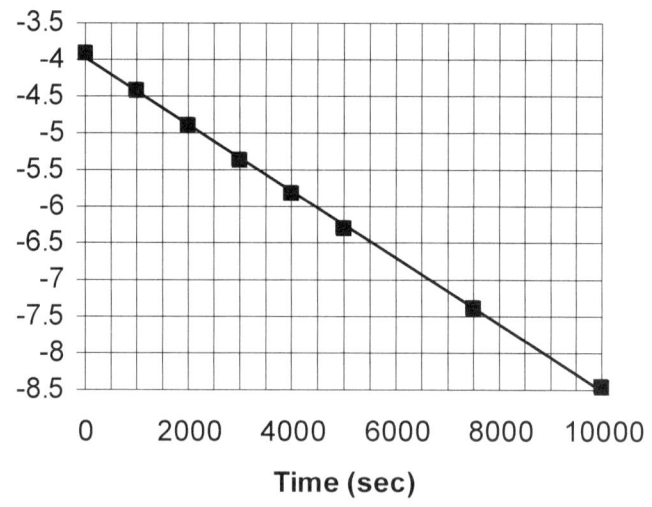

The slope may be determined from a best-fit method or it may be estimated from $\frac{-8.46-(-3.91)}{10000}=-5\times10^{-4}$.

The rate law describing this reaction is: Rate $=\left(5\times10^{-4}\frac{M}{sec}\right)[N_2O_5]$

DERIVING RATE LAWS FROM SIMPLE REACTION MECHANISMS

A **reaction mechanism** is a series of **elementary reactions** that explain how a reaction occurs. These elementary reactions are also called elementary processes or elementary steps. **A reaction mechanism cannot be determined from reaction stoichiometry**. Stoichiometry indicates the number of molecules of reactants and products in an **overall reaction**. Elementary steps represent a **single event**. This might be a collision between two molecules or a single rearrangement of electrons within a molecule.

The simplest reaction mechanisms consist of a single elementary reaction. The number of molecules required determines the rate laws for these processes.

DERIVATION OF RATE LAWS FROM SIMPLE REACTION MECHANISMS

A **reaction mechanism** is a series of **elementary reactions** that explain how a reaction occurs. These elementary reactions are also called elementary processes or elementary steps. **A reaction mechanism cannot be determined from reaction stoichiometry**. Stoichiometry indicates the number of molecules of reactants and products in an **overall reaction**. Elementary steps represent a **single event**. This might be a collision between two molecules or a single rearrangement of electrons within a molecule.

The simplest reaction mechanisms consist of a single elementary reaction. The number of molecules required determines the rate laws for these processes. For a **unimolecular process**:

$$A \rightarrow \text{products}$$

the number of molecules of A that decompose in a given time will be proportional to the number of molecules of A present. Therefore unimolecular processes are first order:

$$Rate = k[A]$$

For **bimolecular processes**, the rate law will be second order:

$$\text{For } A + A \rightarrow \text{products: } Rate = k[A]^2$$

$$\text{For } A + B \rightarrow \text{products: } Rate = k[A][B]$$

Most reaction mechanisms are multi-step processes involving **reaction intermediates**. Intermediates are chemicals that are formed during one elementary step and consumed during another, but they are not overall reactants or products. In many cases one elementary reaction in particular is the slowest and determines the overall reaction rate. This slowest reaction in the series is called the **rate-limiting step** or rate determining step.

Example: The overall reaction $NO_2\ (g) + CO\ (g) \rightarrow NO\ (g) + CO_2\ (g)$
is composed of the following elementary reactions in the gas phase:

$$NO_2 + NO_2 \rightarrow NO + NO_3$$
$$NO_3 + CO \rightarrow NO_2 + CO_2$$

The first elementary reaction is very slow compared to the second. Determine the rate law for the overall reaction if NO_2 and CO are both present in sufficient quantity for the reaction to occur. Also name all reaction intermediates.

Solution: The first step is rate limiting because it is slower. In other words, almost as soon as NO_3 is available, it reacts with CO, so the rate-limiting step is the formation of NO_3. The first step is bimolecular. Therefore, the rate law for the entire reaction is:

$$Rate = k[NO_2]^2$$

NO_3 is formed during the first step and consumed during the second. NO_3 is the only reaction intermediate because it is neither a reactant nor a product of the overall reaction.

Skill 12.3   Understands principles of chemical equilibrium

A dynamic equilibrium consists of two **opposing reversible processes** that both occur at the **same rate**. *Balance* is a synonym for equilibrium. A system at equilibrium is stable; it does not change with time. Equilibria are drawn with a double arrow.

When a process at equilibrium is observed, it often doesn't seem like anything is happening, but **at a microscopic scale, two events are taking place that balance each other**. An example is presented on the right. Arrows in this diagram represent the movement of molecules. When water is placed in a closed container, the water evaporates until the air in the container is saturated. After this occurs, the water level no longer changes, so an observer at the macroscopic scale would say that evaporation has ceased, but the reality on a microscopic scale is that 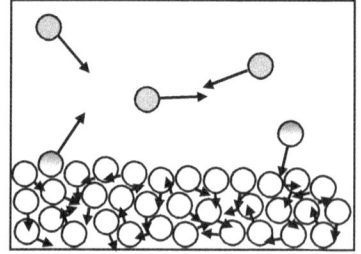 both evaporation and condensation are taking place at the same rate. All equilibria between different phases of matter have this dynamic character on a microscopic scale.

Chemical reactions often do not "go to completion." Instead, products are generated from reactants up to a certain point when the reaction no longer seems to occur, leaving some reactant unaltered. At this point, the system is in a state of **chemical equilibrium** because **the rate of the forward reaction is equal to the rate of the reverse reaction**. An example is shown to the right. Arrows in this diagram represent the chemical reactions of individual molecules. An observer at the macroscopic scale might say that no reaction is taking place at equilibrium, but at a microscopic scale, both the forward and reverse reactions are occurring at the same rate.

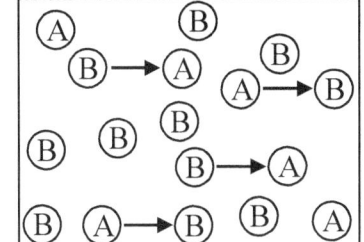

Homogeneous equilibrium refers to a chemical equilibrium among reactants and products that are all in the same phase of matter. **Heterogeneous equilibrium** takes place between two or more chemicals in different phases.

If a reaction at equilibrium is disturbed, changes occur to reestablish equilibrium. **Le Chatelier's principle** states that the equilibrium will be reestablished in a manner that counteracts the effect of the initial disturbance.

A reaction at equilibrium contains a constant ratio of chemical species. This ratio is determined by an **equilibrium constant**. The mathematical relationship between the concentrations of the reactants and products of a system is called the law of mass action. It governs equilibrium expressions.

Consider the general balanced reaction:

$$mA + nB \leftrightarrow pR + qS$$

where m, n, p, and q are stoichiometric coefficients and A, B, R, and S are chemical species.

An **equilibrium expression** relating the concentrations of chemical species at equilibrium is determined by the equation:

$$K_{eq} = \frac{[R]^p [S]^q}{[A]^m [B]^n}$$

where K_{eq} is a constant value called the **equilibrium constant**. Product concentrations raised to the power of their stoichiometric coefficients are placed in the numerator and reactant concentrations raised to the power of their coefficients are placed in the denominator.

Every reaction has a unique value of K_{eq} that varies only with temperature. Alternate subscripts are often given to the equilibrium constant. K_c or K with no subscript is often used instead of K_{eq} to represent the equilibrium constant. Other subscripts are used for specific reactions.

Example: Write the equilibrium expression for the reaction:

$$2HI\ (g) \leftrightarrow H_2\ (g) + I_2\ (g)$$

Solution: $K_{eq} = \dfrac{[H_2][I_2]}{[HI]^2}$

The units associated with equilibrium constants in the expression above are molarity raised to the power of an integer that depends on the stoichiometric coefficients of the reaction, but it is common practice to write these constants as dimensionless values. Multiplying or dividing the equilibrium expression by 1 M as needed achieves these dimensionless values. **The equilibrium expression for a reaction written in one direction is the reciprocal of the expression for the reaction in the reverse direction.**

For a heterogeneous equilibrium (a chemical equilibrium with components in different phases), reactants or products may be pure liquids or solids. The concentration of a pure liquid or solid in moles/liter cannot change. It is a constant property of the material, and these constants are incorporated into the equilibrium constant. Therefore the concentrations of pure liquids and solids are absent from equilibrium expressions for heterogeneous equilibria.

Example: Write the equilibrium expression for the redox reaction between copper and silver:
$$Cu\ (s) + 2Ag^+\ (aq) \leftrightarrow Cu^{2+}\ (aq) + 2Ag\ (s)$$

Solution: $K_{eq} = \dfrac{[Cu^{2+}]}{[Ag^+]^2}$ The solids do not appear in the equilibrium expression.

Skill 12.4 Solves problems involving principles of chemical equilibrium

CALCULATION OF UNKNOWN CONCENTRATIONS AND CONCENTRATION UNITS

Many types of K_{eq} problems require the calculation of an unknown concentration at equilibrium from known quantities. These problems require only algebra to solve. Remember that equilibrium constants are forced to be dimensionless values. If all concentrations are represented in the same units, it is OK to be a little less cautious with units than for other problems.

Example: The reaction
$$N_2\ (g) + 3H_2\ (g) \leftrightarrow 2NH_3\ (g)$$

achieves equilibrium in the presence of 0.27 M H_2 and 0.094 M N_2. What is the ammonia concentration under these conditions if the reaction at the given temperature has an equilibrium constant of K_{eq} = 0.11?

Solution: First we will solve this problem without worrying about units because all concentrations are given in M:

$$K_{eq} = \frac{\left[NH_3\right]^2}{\left[N_2\right]\left[H_2\right]^3} = \frac{\left[NH_3\right]^2}{(0.094)(0.27)^3} = 0.11$$

Solving for [NH₃] yields: $\left[NH_3\right] = \sqrt{(0.11)(0.094)(0.27)^3} = 0.014$ M.
This is the preferred method for solving these problems.

If units are to be treated rigorously then a more explicit definition of K_{eq} is written. This assures us that we achieve a dimensionless value for K_{eq} by repeatedly multiplying by 1 M:

$$K_{eq} = \frac{\left[NH_3\right]^2 (1\ M)^2}{\left[N_2\right]\left[H_2\right]^3} = \frac{\left[NH_3\right]^2 (1\ M)^2}{(0.094\ M)(0.27\ M)^3} = 0.11$$

Solving for [NH₃] yields:

$$\left[NH_3\right] = \sqrt{(0.11)\frac{(0.094\ M)(0.27\ M)^3}{(1\ M)^2}} = 0.014\ M.$$

DETERMINING THE DIRECTIONALITY OF A REACTION

Some K_{eq} problems give every concentration value for a reaction that is not at equilibrium and ask which direction the reaction will proceed for a given equilibrium constant. Solving these problems is a two step process:

1) Insert the non-equilibrium reaction concentrations into the equilibrium expression to obtain a **reaction quotient**, Q.

2) If Q < K_{eq}, there are too many reactant molecules for the products, and the reaction proceeds to the right. If Q > K_{eq}, there are too many product

molecules for the reactants, and the reaction proceeds to the left. If $Q = K_{eq}$, the reaction is at equilibrium.

Example: Predict the direction in which the reaction

$$H_2 (g) + I_2 (g) \leftrightarrow 2HI (g)$$

will proceed if initial concentrations are 0.004 mM H_2, 0.006 mM I_2, and 0.011 mM HI, given $K_{eq} = 48$.

Solution:

1) The reactant quotient is $Q = \dfrac{[HI]^2}{[H_2][I_2]} = \dfrac{(0.011)^2}{(0.004)(0.006)} = 5$.

2) The reactant quotient is less than K_{eq}. That is, 5 < 48. Therefore, the numerator (products) of the reaction quotient is too small for the denominator (reactants). The trend towards equilibrium with time will increase the numerator relative to the denominator until a ratio of 48 is achieved. More reactants will turn into products and the reaction will proceed to the right.

SPECIAL EQUILIBRIUM CONSTANTS

A few equilibrium constants are used often enough to have their own unique nomenclature.

The **solubility-product constant** (K_{sp}) is the equilibrium constant for an ionic solid in contact with a saturated aqueous solution. The two processes with equal rates in this case are dissolution and crystallization:

Ionic compound(s) $\leftrightarrow$ p cation$^+$ (aq) + q anion$^-$ (aq)

$$K_{sp} = [\text{cation}^+]^p [\text{anion}^-]^q$$

This is an example of a heterogeneous equilibrium, so the concentration of pure solid is not included as a variable. K_{sp} is a different quantity from solubility. K_{sp} is an equilibrium constant, and solubility is the mass of solid that is able to dissolve in a given quantity of water.

Example: Solid lead chloride ($PbCl_2$) is allowed to dissolve in pure water until equilibrium has been reached and the solution is saturated. The concentration at saturation of Pb^{2+} is 0.016 M. What is K_{sp} for $PbCl_2$?

Solution: The reaction and solubility product are shown below:

$$PbCl_2\ (s) \leftrightarrow Pb^{2+}\ (aq) + 2Cl^-\ (aq)$$

$$K_{sp} = \left[Pb^{2+}\right]\left[Cl^-\right]^2$$

The only source of both ions in solution is $PbCl_2$, so the concentration of Cl^- must be twice that for Pb^{2+}, or 0.032 M. Therefore,

$$K_{sp} = (0.016)(0.032)^2 = 1.6 \times 10^{-5}$$

The **acid-dissociation constant** (K_a) is the equilibrium constant for the ionization of a weak acid to a hydrogen ion and its conjugate base:

$$HX\ (aq) \leftrightarrow H^+\ (aq) + X^-\ (aq)$$

$$K_a = \frac{\left[H^+\right]\left[X^-\right]}{[HX]}$$

Polyprotic acids have a unique value for each dissociation: K_{a1}, K_{a2}, etc.

Example: Hydrofluoric acid is dissolved in pure water until [H$^+$] reaches 0.006 M. What is the concentration of undissociated HF? K_a for HF is 6.8×10^{-4}.

Solution: Use the reaction and equation for K_a shown above. The principle source of both ions is dissociation of HF (ionization of water is negligible). Therefore [F$^-$] = [H$^+$] = 0.006 M, and

$$[HF] = \frac{\left[H^+\right]\left[F^-\right]}{K_a} = \frac{(0.006)^2}{6.8 \times 10^{-4}} = 0.05\ M$$

The **base-dissociation constant** (K_b) is the equilibrium constant for the addition of a proton to a weak base by water to form its conjugate acid and an OH$^-$ ion. In these reactions, it is water that is dissociating as a result of reaction with the base:

Weak base (aq) + H$_2$O (l) $\leftrightarrow$ conjugate acid (aq) + OH$^-$ (aq)

$$K_b = \frac{[\text{conjugate acid}]\left[OH^-\right]}{[\text{weak base}]}$$

The concentration of water is nearly constant and is incorporated into the dissociation constant.

For ammonia (the most common weak base), the equilibrium reaction and base-dissociation constant are:

$$NH_3\ (aq) + H_2O\ (l) \leftrightarrow NH_4^+\ (aq) + OH^-\ (aq)$$

$$K_b = \frac{[NH_4^+][OH^-]}{[NH_3]}$$

Example: K_b for ammonia at 25° C is 1.8x10⁻⁵. What is the concentration of OH⁻ in an ammonia solution at equilibrium containing 0.2 M NH₃ at 25° C?

Solution: Call $x = [OH^-]$. The principle source of both ions is NH₃ (ionization of water is negligible). Therefore, $x = [OH^-] = [NH_4^+]$.

$$K_b = \frac{[NH_4^+][OH^-]}{[NH_3]} = \frac{x^2}{0.2} = 1.8 \times 10^{-5}$$

Solving for x yields: $x = \sqrt{(0.2)(1.8 \times 10^{-5})} = 0.002$ M OH⁻

The **ion-product constant for water** (K_w) is the equilibrium constant for the dissociation of H₂O. Water molecules may donate protons to other water molecules in a process known as autoionization:

$$2H_2O\ (l) \leftrightarrow H_3O\ (aq) + OH^-\ (aq)$$

A hydrated water molecule is often referred to as H⁺ (aq), so the above equation may be rewritten as the following reaction that defines K_w. As with K_b, the concentration of water is nearly constant.

$$H_2O\ (l) \leftrightarrow H^+\ (aq) + OH^-\ (aq)$$

$$K_w = [H^+][OH^-] = 1.0 \times 10^{-14}\ \text{at 25°C}$$

Example: A) What is the concentration of OH⁻ in an aqueous solution with an H⁺ concentration of 2.5x10⁻⁶ M?

B) What is the concentration of H⁺ when pure water reaches equilibrium?

Solution: A) $K_w = [H^+][OH^-] = (2.5 \times 10^{-6})[OH^-] = 1.0 \times 10^{-14}$.

Solving for $[OH^-]$ yields $[OH^-] = \dfrac{1.0 \times 10^{-14}}{2.5 \times 10^{-6}} = 4.0 \times 10^{-9}$.

B) The autoionization of pure water creates an equal concentration of the two ions [H⁺] = [OH⁻].

Therefore, $K_w = [H^+]^2 = 1.0 \times 10^{-14}$.

Solving for $[H^+]$ yields $[H^+] = 1.0 \times 10^{-7}$.

Skill 12.5 Identifies the chemical properties of a variety of common household chemicals (e.g., baking soda, bleach, ammonia) in order to predict the potential for chemical reactivity

Chemical concepts often involve events taking place on scales that are too small for us to see. But the application of those concepts is all around us when we work and play, cook and clean, and eat and drink.

Relating chemistry to everyday activities often requires other content in this text in combination with **strong common sense reasoning**. There are some things that many people believe they know about everyday activities that aren't true.

For example, many people believe that cooks add salt when they boil water to decrease the amount of time it takes for the water to boil, but this is *false*. In reality, adding salt increases the boiling point of water and so water will take *more* time to boil. However, once the water is boiling, the fact that it is at a higher temperature means food will take less time to cook. (Note: Salt added to water used to cook pasta helps the pasta keep its shape.)

Boiling point elevation is a colligative property because more salt molecules at the liquid-vapor interface means fewer water molecules there, shifting:

$$H_2O\ (l) \leftrightarrow H_2O\ (g)$$

to the left according to Le Chatelier's Principle. Therefore the vapor pressure at 100° C will decrease below 1 atm, and a higher temperature along with more time will be required for boiling. However, all of **this knowledge will go to waste if you rely on a mistaken belief** instead of reasoning through the situation.

A common example of an everyday neutralization reaction is the use of **antacids**. These chemicals are bases that neutralize excess gastric acid in the stomach and provide increased buffering capacity. Gastric acid is mostly HCl. An everyday application of the thermochemistry of reactions is in the field of **nutrition**. The energy value of food is measured in "**nutritional calories**," a unit equal to 4814 Joules. We inhale oxygen to convert organic molecules (our fuel) to carbon dioxide and water just as a flame uses oxygen to complete the same reaction, obtaining the same **heat of combustion**.

An ancient example of the human exploitation of chemical reactions is the use of yeast. Yeast is a fungus (*Saccharomyces cerevisiae* is the species used by man) that feeds on sugars. It extracts energy from the sugar and the byproducts of this "digestion" are **carbon dioxide and alcohols**. Thus, when yeast is incorporated into bread dough, the trapped carbon dioxide makes the bread rise, and alternately, when the yeast is combined with water and malted barley it makes beer.

Another commonly used leavener is **baking soda**, sodium bicarbonate. Baking soda is a **base** that is combined with acids in cooking (such as buttermilk, vinegar, sour cream, or yogurt) to create CO_2 bubbles. These bubbles cause baked goods to rise. Bleach and ammonia are other examples of household bases used for cleaning.

It is critical to take appropriate safety measures (e.g., gloves, goggles, proper disposable, avoiding mixing with other chemicals). One particularly dangerous reaction between household chemicals is that of **bleach and ammonia**. Bleach is typically a 5% solution of NaOCl in water and ammonia (NH_3) is a component of many glass cleaners:

$$HOCl + NH_3 \rightarrow NH_2Cl + H_2O$$

The products of this reaction are water and chloroamine, which is powerful respiratory irritant and can even be deadly.

Examples of electrochemistry are also present around the home. An addition to **batteries** is the prevention of **corrosion**. Corrosion is a redox reaction that oxidizes elemental metals to cations and removes their atoms from metallic bonds.

Resources at http://www.chemcases.com/ apply several chemical concepts to descriptions of consumer products.

COMPETENCY 013 THE TEACHER UNDERSTANDS ACIDS, BASES, AND THEIR REACTIONS

Skill 13.1 Identifies the general properties of and relationships among acids, bases, and salts

It was recognized centuries ago that many substances could be divided into the two general categories. **Acids** have a sour taste (as in lemon juice), dissolve many metals, and turn litmus paper red. **Bases** have a bitter taste (as in soaps), feel slippery, and turn litmus paper blue. In general, acids give up protons (H^+) while bases accept protons. See Skill 13.2 for detailed definitions of acids and bases.

The chemical reaction between an acid and a base is called **neutralization**. The products of a neutralization reaction are a **salt** and water, for example:

$$H_2SO_4 + 2NaOH \rightarrow Na_2SO_4 + 2H_2O$$

$$\text{Acid} + \text{Base} \rightarrow \text{Salt} + \text{Water}$$

Litmus paper is an example of an **acid-base indicator**, a substance that changes color when added to an acid or a base.

There are special naming rules for acids that correspond with the **suffix of their corresponding anion** if hydrogen were removed from the acid. Anions ending with *–ide* correspond to acids with the prefix *hydro–* and the suffix *–ic*. Anions ending with *–ate* correspond to acids with no prefix that end with *–ic*. Oxoanions ending with *–ite* have associated acids with no prefix and the suffix *–ous*. The *hypo–* and *per–* prefixes are maintained. Some examples are shown in the following table:

anion	anion name	acid	acid name
Cl^-	chloride	HCl (*aq*)	hydrochloric acid
CN^-	cyanide	HCN (*aq*)	hydrocyanic acid
CO_3^{2-}	carbonate	H_2CO_3 (*aq*)	carbonic acid
SO_3^{2-}	sulfite	H_2SO_3 (*aq*)	sulfurous acid
SO_4^{2-}	sulfate	H_2SO_4 (*aq*)	sulfuric acid
ClO^-	hypochlorite	HClO (*aq*)	hypochlorous acid
ClO_2^-	chlorite	$HClO_2$ (*aq*)	chlorous acid
ClO_3^-	chlorate	$HClO_3$ (*aq*)	chloric acid
ClO_4^-	perchlorate	$HClO_4$ (*aq*)	perchloric acid

Example: What is the molecular formula of phosphorous acid?

Solution: If we remember that the *–ous* acid corresponds to the *–ite* anion, and the *–ite* anion has one less oxygen than (or has an oxidation number 2 less than) the *–ate* form, we only need to remember that phosphate is PO_4^{3-}. Then we know that phosphite is PO_3^{3-} and phosphorous acid is H_3PO_3.

Skill 13.2 Identifies acids and bases using models of Arrhenius, Brønsted-Lowry, and Lewis

Arrhenius definition of acids and bases

Svante **Arrhenius** proposed in the 1880s that **acids form H^+ ions and bases form OH^- ions in water**. The net ionic reaction for neutralization between an Arrhenius acid and base always produces water as shown below for nitric acid and sodium hydroxide:

$$HNO_3(aq) + NaOH(aq) \rightarrow NaNO_3(aq) + H_2O(l)$$

$$H^+(aq) + NO_3^-(aq) + Na^+(aq) + OH^-(aq) \rightarrow NO_3^-(aq) + Na^+(aq) + H_2O(l) \text{ (complete ionic)}$$

$$H^+(aq) + OH^-(aq) \rightarrow H_2O(l) \text{ (net ionic)}$$

The H^+ (*aq*) ion

In acid-base systems, **"protonated water" or "H^+ (*aq*)" are shorthand for a mixture of water ions**. For example, HCl reacting in water may be represented as a dissociation reaction:

$$HCl\ (aq) \rightarrow H^+\ (aq) + Cl^-\ (aq)$$

The same reaction may be described as the transfer of a proton to water to form H_3O^+:

$$HCl\ (aq) + H_2O \rightarrow Cl^-\ (aq) + H_3O^+\ (aq)$$

H_3O^+ is called a **hydronium ion**. Its Lewis structure is shown below to the left. In reality, the hydrogen bonds in water are so strong that H^+ ions exist in water as a mixture of species in a hydrogen bond network. Two of them are shown below at center and to the right. Hydrogen bonds are shown as dashed lines.

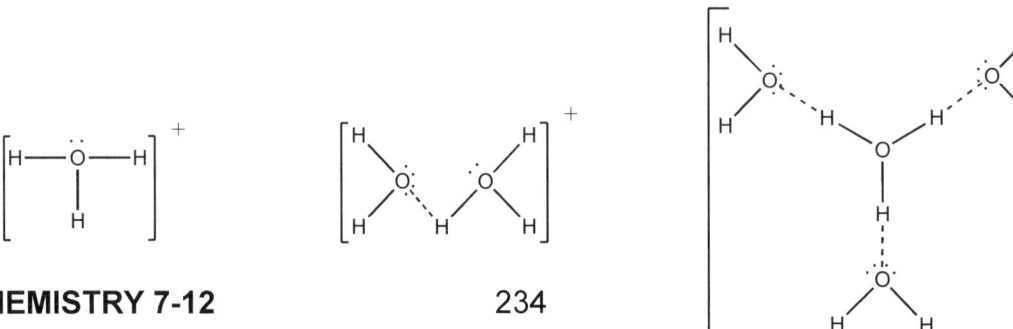

BRØNSTED-LOWRY DEFINITION OF ACIDS AND BASES

In the 1920s, Johannes **Brønsted** and Thomas **Lowry** recognized that **acids can transfer a proton to bases** regardless of whether an OH⁻ ion accepts the proton. In an equilibrium reaction, the direction of proton transfer depends on whether the reaction is read left to right or right to left, so **Brønsted acids and bases exist in conjugate pairs with and without a proton**. Acids that are able to transfer more than one proton are called **polyprotic acids**.

Examples:

1) In the reaction:
$$HF\ (aq) + H_2O\ (l) \leftrightarrow F^-\ (aq) + H_3O^+\ (aq)$$

HF transfers a proton to water. Therefore HF is the Brønsted acid and H_2O is the Brønsted base. But in the reverse direction, hydronium ions transfer a proton to fluoride ions. H_3O^+ is the conjugate acid of H_2O because it has an additional proton, and F^- is the conjugate base of HF because it lacks a proton.

2) In the reaction:
$$NH_3\ (aq) + H_2O\ (l) \leftrightarrow NH_4^+\ (aq) + OH^-\ (aq)$$

water transfers a proton to ammonia. H_2O is the Brønsted acid and OH^- is its conjugate base. NH_3 is the Brønsted base and NH_4^+ is its conjugate acid.

3) In the reaction:
$$H_3PO_4 + HS^- \leftrightarrow H_2PO_4^- + H_2S$$

$H_3PO_4/H_2PO_4^-$ is one conjugate acid-base pair and H_2S/HS^- is the other.

4) H_3PO_4 is a polyprotic acid. It may further dissociate to transfer more than one proton:
$$H_3PO_4 \leftrightarrow H_2PO_4^- + H^+$$
$$H_2PO_4^- \leftrightarrow HPO_4^{2-} + H^+$$
$$HPO_4^{2-} \leftrightarrow PO_4^{3-} + H^+$$

LEWIS DEFINITION OF ACIDS AND BASES

The transfer of a proton from a Brønsted acid to a Brønsted base requires that the base accept the proton. When Lewis diagrams are used to draw the proton donation of Brønsted acid-base reactions, it is always clear that the base must contain an unshared electron pair to form a bond with the proton. For example, ammonia contains an unshared electron pair in the following reaction:

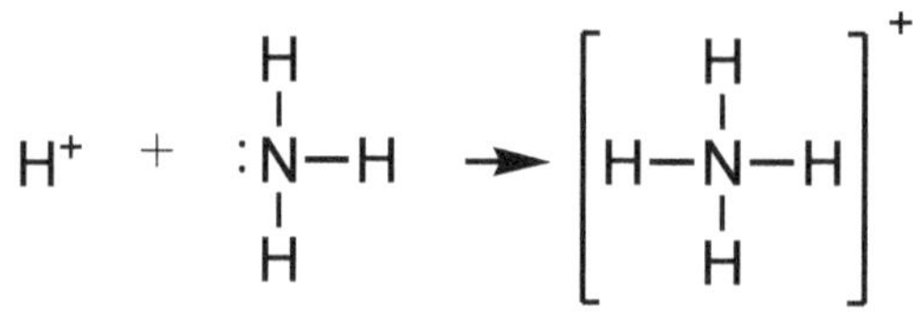

$$H^+ + :NH_3 \rightarrow [NH_4]^+$$

In the 1920s, Gilbert N. **Lewis** proposed that **bases donate unshared electron pairs to acids**, regardless of whether the donation is made to a proton or to another atom. Boron trifluoride is an example of a Lewis acid that is not a Brønsted acid because it is a chemical that accepts an electron pair without involving an H$^+$ ion:

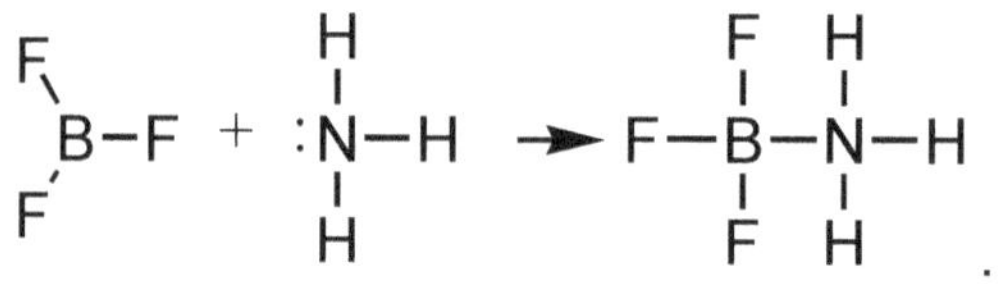

$$BF_3 + :NH_3 \rightarrow F_3B-NH_3$$

The Lewis theory of acids and bases is more general than the Brønsted-Lowry theory, but Brønsted-Lowry's definition is used more frequently. The terms "acid" and "base" most often refer to Brønsted acids and bases, and the term "Lewis acid" is usually reserved for chemicals like BF$_3$ that are not also Brønsted acids.

SUMMARY OF DEFINITIONS

A Lewis base transfers an electron pair to a Lewis acid. A Brønsted acid transfers a proton to a Brønsted base. These exist in conjugate pairs at equilibrium. In an Arrhenius base, the proton acceptor (electron pair donor) is OH$^-$. All Arrhenius acids/bases are Brønsted acids/bases and all Brønsted acids/bases are Lewis acids/bases. Each definition is a subset of the one that comes before it.

Skill 13.3   Differentiates between strong and weak acids and bases

STRONG AND WEAK ACIDS AND BASES

Strong acids and bases are strong electrolytes, and weak acids and bases are weak electrolytes, so **strong acids and bases completely dissociate in water**, but weak acids and bases do not.

Example: $HCl(aq) + H_2O(l) \rightarrow H_3O^+(aq) + Cl^-(aq)$ goes to completion because HCl is a strong acid. The acids in the examples on the previous page were all weak.

The aqueous dissociation constants K_a and K_b quantify acid and base strength, respectively. Another way of looking at acid dissociation is that strong acids transfer protons more readily than H_3O^+ transfers protons, so they protonate water, the conjugate base of H_3O^+. In general, **if two acid/base conjugate pairs are present, the stronger acid will transfer a proton to the conjugate base of the weaker acid**.

Acid and base **strength is not related to safety**. Weak acids like HF may be extremely corrosive and dangerous.

The most **common strong acids and bases** are listed in the following table:

Strong acid		Strong base	
HCl	Hydrochloric acid	LiOH	Lithium hydroxide
HBr	Hydrobromic acid	NaOH	Sodium hydroxide
HI	Hydroiodic acid	KOH	Potassium hydroxide
HNO_3	Nitric acid	$Ca(OH)_2$	Calcium hydroxide
H_2SO_4	Sulfuric acid	$Sr(OH)_2$	Strontium hydroxide
$HClO_4$	Perchloric acid	$Ba(OH)_2$	Barium hydroxide

A flash animation tutorial demonstrating the difference between strong and weak acids is located at
http://www.mhhe.com/physsci/chemistry/essentialchemistry/flash/acid13.swf.

TRENDS IN ACID AND BASE STRENGTH

The strongest acid in a polyprotic series is always **the acid with the most protons** (e.g., H_2SO_4 is a stronger acid than HSO_4^-). The strongest acid in a series with the same central atom is always **the acid with the central atom at the highest oxidation number** (e.g., $HClO_4 > HClO_3 > HClO_2 > HClO$). The strongest acid in a series with different central atoms at the same oxidation number is usually **the acid with the central atom at the highest electronegativity** (e.g., $HClO > HBrO > HIO$).

Skill 13.4 Applies the relationship between hydrogen ion concentration and pH for acids and bases

ION-PRODUCT CONSTANT (K_W)

The **ion-product constant for water** (K_w) is the equilibrium constant for the dissociation of H_2O. Water molecules may donate protons to other water molecules in a process known as autoionization:

$$2H_2O\ (l) \leftrightarrow H_3O^+\ (aq) + OH^-\ (aq)$$

The above equation may be rewritten as the following reaction that defines K_w. As with K_b, the concentration of water is nearly constant:

$$H_2O\ (l) \leftrightarrow H^+\ (aq) + OH^-\ (aq)$$

$$K_w = [H^+] + [OH^-] = 1.0 \times 10^{-14} \text{ at } 25°\text{C}$$

Pure water at equilibrium has an equal concentration of the two ions. Therefore,

$$K_w = [H^+]^2 = 1.0 \times 10^{-14}$$

Solving for $[H^+]$ yields $[H^+] = 1.0 \times 10^{-7}$ M **for pure water**.

The **product of K_a for an acid and K_b for its conjugate base will always be K_w**. This is demonstrated below for the weak acid, HF and its conjugate base, F^-:

$$HF\ (aq) \leftrightarrow H^+\ (aq) + F^-\ (aq) \qquad K_a = \frac{[H^+][F^-]}{[HF]}$$

$$F^-\ (aq) + H_2O\ (l) \leftrightarrow HF\ (aq) + OH^-\ (aq) \qquad K_b = \frac{[HF][OH^-]}{[F^-]}$$

Multiplication of K_a and K_b yields:
$$K_a \times K_b = \left(\frac{[H^+][F^-]}{[HF]}\right)\left(\frac{[HF][OH^-]}{[F^-]}\right)$$
$$= [H^+][OH^-] = K_w$$

DEFINITION OF pH AND pKa

The concentration of H^+ (aq) ions is often expressed in terms of pH. **The pH of a solution is the negative base-10 logarithm of the hydrogen-ion molarity:**

$$pH = -\log[H^+] = \log(1/[H^+])$$

A ten-fold increase in [H⁺] decreases the pH by one unit. [H⁺] may be found from pH using the expression:

$$[H^+] = 10^{-pH}$$

Because [H⁺] = 10⁻⁷ M for pure water, **the pH of a neutral solution is 7**. In an **acidic solution**, [H⁺] > 10⁻⁷ M and **pH < 7**. In a basic solution, [H⁺] < 10⁻⁷ M and **pH > 7**.

Example: An aqueous solution has an H⁺ ion concentration of 4.0x10⁻⁹. Is the solution acidic or basic? What is the pH of the solution?

Solution: The solution is basic because [H⁺] < 10⁻⁷ M.

$$pH = -\log[H^+] = -\log 4 \times 10^{-9} = 8.4$$

The negative base-10 log is a convenient way of representing other small numbers used in chemistry by placing the letter "p" before the symbol. Values of K_a are often represented as pK_a, with $pK_a = -\log K_a$.

CALCULATING pH AND H+ CONCENTRATION

The concentration of H⁺(*aq*) ions is often expressed in terms of pH. **The pH of a solution is the negative base-10 logarithm of the hydrogen-ion molarity.**

$$pH = -\log[H^+] = \log\left(\frac{1}{[H^+]}\right).$$

A ten-fold increase in [H⁺] decreases the pH by one unit. [H⁺] may be found from pH using the expression:

$$[H^+] = 10^{-pH}.$$

$[H^+] = 10^{-7}$ M for pure water with $[H^+] = [OH^-]$. Thus **the pH of a neutral solution is 7**. In an **acidic solution**, $[H^+] > 10^{-7}$ M and **pH < 7**. In a basic solution, $[H^+] < 10^{-7}$ M and **pH > 7**.

The negative base-10 log is a convenient way of representing other small numbers used in chemistry by placing the letter "p" before the symbol. Values of K_a are often represented as pK_a, with $pK_a = -\log K_a$. The concentration of OH⁻ (*aq*) ions may also be expressed in terms of pOH, with $pOH = -\log[OH^-]$.

The ion-product constant of water, $K_w = [H^+][OH^-] = 1.0 \times 10^{-14}$ at 25 °C. The value of K_w can used to determine the relationship between pH and pOH by taking the negative log of the expression:
$$-\log K_w = -\log[H^+] - \log[OH^-] = -\log(10^{-14}).$$
Therefore: $pH + pOH = 14$.

Example: An aqueous solution has an H^+ ion concentration of 4.0×10^{-9}. Is the solution acidic or basic? What is the pH of the solution? What is the pOH?

Solution: The solution is basic because $[H^+] < 10^{-7}$ M.

$$pH = -\log[H^+] = -\log 4 \times 10^{-9}$$
$$= 8.4.$$
$pH + pOH = 14$. Therefore $pOH = 14 - pH = 14 - 8.4 = 5.6$.

The pH and $[H^+]$ of a **solution containing a strong acid or strong base** may be found using stoichiometry alone for a strong acid, and stoichiometry together with K_w for a base.

Example: What is the pH of a solution of 0.020 M $Ca(OH)_2$?

Solution: $Ca(OH)_2$ is a strong base, so it completely dissociates:

$$Ca(OH)_2(aq) \rightarrow Ca^{2+}(aq) + 2OH^-(aq)$$

The stoichiometry of the dissociation may be used to determine $[OH^-]$:

$$\frac{0.020 \text{ mol } Ca(OH)_2}{L} \times \frac{2 \text{ mol } OH^-}{1 \text{ mol } Ca(OH)_2} = \frac{0.040 \text{ mol } OH^-}{L} = 0.040 \text{ M } OH^-$$

Using the ion-product constant of water, we may find $[H^+]$:

$$K_w = 1.0 \times 10^{-14} = [H^+][OH^-] = [H^+](0.040)$$

Rearranging to solve for $[H^+]$:

$$[H^+] = \frac{1.0 \times 10^{-14}}{0.040} = 2.5 \times 10^{-13} \text{ M}$$

Finally, we determine the pH of the solution from its hydrogen ion concentration:

$$pH = -\log[H^+] = -\log(2.5 \times 10^{-13}) = 12.6$$

The pH and [H⁺] of a **solution containing a weak acid or weak base** may be found using K_a or K_b (together with K_w for a base). If more than 5% of the electrolyte is ionized, the quadratic equation should be used. A review of the quadratic equation in the context of chemical equilibria may be found at
http://www.chem.tamu.edu/class/fyp/mathrev/mr-quadr.html.

Example: $K_a = 3.0 \times 10^{-8}$ for hypochlorous acid, HClO. What is the pH of a solution of 0.50 M HClO?

Solution: The dissociation HClO (aq) ↔ H⁺ (aq) + ClO⁻ (aq) has the equilibrium constant:

$$K_a = \frac{[H^+][ClO^-]}{[HClO]} = 3.0 \times 10^{-8}$$

Initially, HClO is 0.50 M. Let x = [H⁺] at equilibrium. We may then arrange the initial and equilibrium concentrations into a table based on what is consumed and produced according to reaction stoichiometry:

	HClO(aq)	↔	H⁺(aq)	+	ClO⁻(aq)
Initial:	0.50 M		0 M		0 M
Equilibrium:	(0.50 − x) M		x M		x M

Substitution using the equilibrium constant gives us:

$$K_a = \frac{[H^+][ClO^-]}{[HClO]} = \frac{(x)(x)}{0.50 - x} = 3.0 \times 10^{-8}$$

The expression $\dfrac{x^2}{0.50 - x} = 3.0 \times 10^{-8}$ may be rearranged to yield the quadratic:

$$x^2 + 3.0 \times 10^{-8} x - 1.5 \times 10^{-8} = 0$$

and we can solve for x using the quadratic formula:

$$x = \frac{-b \pm \sqrt{b^2 - 4ac}}{2a}$$ where $a = 1$, $b = 3.0 \times 10^{-8}$, and $c = -1.5 \times 10^{-8}$

However, it will usually be safe to estimate that x (the H⁺ concentration) is sufficiently small to avoid doing this. For this example, this will be true if x is less than 5% of 0.50 M (i.e., $x < 0.05 \times 0.50$ M or 2.5×10^{-2} M).

In that case $0.50 - x$ is roughly 0.50, and the expression $\dfrac{x^2}{0.50 - x} = 3.0 \times 10^{-8}$ simplifies to:

$$\frac{x^2}{0.50} = 3.0 \times 10^{-8}$$

Solving for x gives us:

$$x = \sqrt{1.5 \times 10^{-8}} = 1.2 \times 10^{-4} \text{ M H}^+$$

This value is less than 2.5×10^{-2} M, so we can verify that the quadratic equation was not needed. Finally, we determine the pH:

$$\text{pH} = -\log(1.2 \times 10^{-4}) = 3.9$$

A comprehensive set of lectures on pH calculation is presented at: http://www.chembuddy.com/?left=pH-calculation&right=toc.

Skill 13.5   Understands and analyzes acid-base equilibria and buffers

A **buffer solution** is a solution that **resists a change in pH** after addition of small amounts of an acid or a base. Buffer solutions require the presence of an acid to neutralize an added base and also the presence of a base to neutralize an added acid. These two components present in the buffer also must not neutralize each other.

A **conjugate acid-base pair is present in buffers** to fulfill these requirements. Buffers are prepared by mixing together **a weak acid or base and a salt of the acid or base** that provides the conjugate.

Consider the buffer solution prepared by mixing together acetic acid ($HC_2H_3O_2$) and sodium acetate ($C_2H_3O_2^-$) and containing Na^+ as a spectator ion. The equilibrium reaction for this acid/conjugate base pair is:

$$HC_2H_3O_2 \leftrightarrow C_2H_3O_2^- + H^+$$

If H⁺ ions from a strong acid are added to this buffer solution, Le Chatelier's principle predicts that the reaction will shift to the left and much of this H⁺ will be consumed to create more $HC_2H_3O_2$ from $C_2H_3O_2^-$. If a strong base that consumes H⁺ is added to this buffer solution, Le Chatelier's principle predicts that the reaction will shift to the right and much of the consumed H⁺ will be replaced by the dissociation of $HC_2H_3O_2$. The net effect is that **buffer solutions prevent large changes in pH that occur when an acid or base is added to pure water** or to an unbuffered solution.

The amount of acid or base that a buffer solution can neutralize before large pH changes begins to occur is called its **buffering capacity**. Blood and seawater both contain several conjugate acid-base pairs to buffer the solution's pH and decrease the impact of acids and bases on living things.

An excellent flash animation with audio to explain the action of buffering solutions is found at
http://www.mhhe.com/physsci/chemistry/essentialchemistry/flash/buffer12.swf.

pH OF BUFFER SOLUTIONS

The pH and [H⁺] of **a buffer solution may be estimated using the Henderson-Hasselbalch equation**:

$$pH = pK_a + \log\left(\frac{[\text{base}]}{[\text{acid}]}\right)$$

This is also called the **buffer equation**.

Expressed in terms of H⁺ concentration and K_a, the Henderson-Hasselbalch equation is:

$$-\log[H^+] = -\log K_a + \log\left(\frac{[\text{base}]}{[\text{acid}]}\right)$$

Many assumptions are required to use these equations, but other methods of calculating the pH of buffers are too difficult to appear on an examination and are beyond the scope of high school chemistry. Therefore, if you are asked for the pH of a buffer solution on the teacher certification exam, you can use the buffer equation with confidence.

Example: A solution contains 0.050 M acetic acid, $HC_2H_3O_2$, and 0.020 M of acetate ion supplied by sodium acetate, $NaC_2H_3O_2$. The K_a of acetic acid is 1.8×10^{-5}. What is the pH of the solution?

Solution: $HC_2H_3O_2$ is a weak acid, and its dissociation reaction is:

$$HC_2H_3O_2 \leftrightarrow C_2H_3O_2^- + H^+$$

Sodium acetate provides the conjugate base, so we know we have a buffer problem with Na^+ as a spectator ion. The pK_a may be found from:

$$pK_a = -\log K_a = -\log(1.8 \times 10^{-5}) = 4.8$$

From the Henderson-Hasselbalch equation:

$$pH = pK_a + \log\left(\frac{[\text{base}]}{[\text{acid}]}\right) = 4.8 + \log\left(\frac{0.02}{0.05}\right) = 4.8 + (-0.4)$$
$$= 4.4$$

An excellent flash animation with audio to explain the action of buffering solutions can be found at: http://www.mhhe.com/physsci/chemistry/essentialchemistry/flash/buffer12.swf.

Skill 13.6   Analyzes and applies the principles of acid-base titration

STANDARD TITRATION

In a typical acid-base **titration, an acid-base indicator** (such as *phenolphthalein*) or a **pH meter** is used to monitor the course of a **neutralization reaction**. The usual goal of titration is to **determine an unknown concentration** of an acid (or base) by neutralizing it with a known concentration of base (or acid).

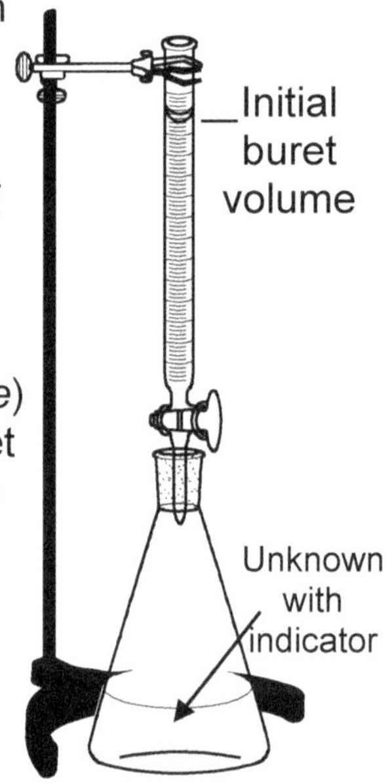

The reagent of known concentration is usually used as the **titrant**. The titrant is poured into a **buret** (also spelled *burette*) until it is nearly full, and an initial buret reading is taken. Buret numbering is close to zero when nearly full. A known volume of the solution of unknown concentration is added to a flask and placed under the buret. The indicator is added or the pH meter probe is inserted. The initial state of a titration experiment is shown to the right above.

The buret stopcock is opened and titrant is slowly added until the solution permanently changes color or the pH rapidly changes. This is the titration **endpoint**, and a final buret reading is made. The final state of a titration experiment is shown to the right below. The endpoint occurs when the **acid and base equivalents in the flask are identical**:

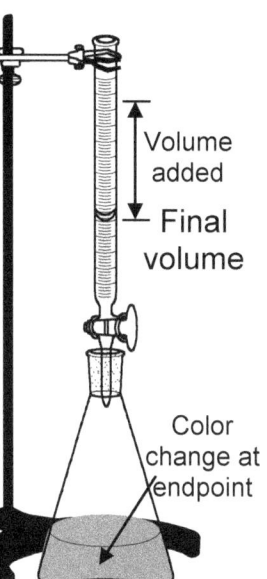

$$N_{acid} = N_{base}$$

And therefore,

$$C_{acid}V_{acid} = C_{base}V_{base}$$

The endpoint is also known as the titration **equivalence point**.

Titration data typically consist of:

$V_{initial}$ = Initial buret volume
V_{final} = Final buret volume
C_{known} = Concentration of known solution
$V_{unknown}$ = Volume of unknown solution

To determine the unknown concentration, first find the volume of titrant at the known concentration added:

$$V_{known} = V_{final} - V_{initial}$$

At the equivalence point, $N_{unknown} = N_{known}$

Therefore, $$C_{unknown} = \frac{C_{known}V_{known}}{V_{unknown}} = \frac{C_{known}(V_{final} - V_{initial})}{V_{unknown}}$$

Units of molarity may be used for concentration in the previous expressions **unless a mole of either solution yields more than one acid or base equivalent**. In that case, concentration must be expressed using **normality**.

Example: A 20.0 mL sample of an HCl solution is titrated with 0.200 M NaOH. The initial buret volume is 1.8 mL and the final buret volume at the titration endpoint is 29.1 mL. What is the molarity of the HCl sample?

Solution: Two solution methods will be used. The first method is better for those who are good at unit manipulations and less skilled at memorizing formulas. HCl contains one acid equivalent and NaOH contains one base equivalent, so we may use molarity in all our calculations.

1) Calculate the moles of the known substance added to the flask:

$$0.200 \frac{\text{mol}}{\text{L}} \times \frac{1 \text{ L}}{1000 \text{ mL}} \times (29.1 \text{ mL} - 1.8 \text{ mL}) = 0.00546 \text{ mol NaOH}$$

At the endpoint, this much of the base will neutralize 0.00546 mol HCl. Therefore, this amount of HCl must have been present in the sample before the titration:

$$\frac{0.00546 \text{ mol HCl}}{0.0200 \text{ L}} = 0.273 \text{ M HCl}$$

2) Utilize the formula: $C_{unknown} = \dfrac{C_{known}(V_{final} - V_{initial})}{V_{unknown}}$

$$C_{HCl} = \frac{C_{NaOH}(V_{final} - V_{initial})}{V_{HCl}} = \frac{0.200 \text{ M } (29.1 \text{ mL} - 1.8 \text{ mL})}{20.0 \text{ mL}} = 0.273 \text{ M HCl}$$

TITRATING WITH THE UNKNOWN

In a common variation of standard titration, the unknown is added to the buret as a titrant and the reagent of known concentration is placed in the flask. The chemistry involved is the same as in the standard case, and the mathematics is also identical except for the identity of the two volumes. For this variation, V_{known} is the volume added to the flask before titration begins and $V_{unknown} = V_{final} - V_{initial}$

Therefore:

$$C_{unknown} = \frac{C_{known} V_{known}}{V_{unknown}} = \frac{C_{known} V_{known}}{V_{final} - V_{initial}}$$

TEACHER CERTIFICATION STUDY GUIDE

Example: 30.0 mL of a 0.150 M HNO₃ solution is titrated with Ca(OH)₂. The initial buret volume is 0.6 mL and the final buret volume at the equivalent point is 22.2 mL. What is the molarity of Ca(OH)₂ used for the titration?

Solution: The same two solution methods will be used as in the previous example. 1 mol Ca(OH)₂ contains 2 base equivalents because it reacts with 2 moles of H⁺ via the reaction

$Ca(OH)_2 + 2HNO_3 \rightarrow Ca(NO_3)_2 + 2H_2O$. Therefore, normality must be used in the formula for solution method 2.

1) First calculate the moles of the substance in the flask:

$$0.150 \frac{mol}{L} \times 0.0300 \ L = 0.00450 \ mol \ HNO_3$$

This acid must be titrated with 0.00450 base equivalents for neutralization to occur at the end point. We calculate moles Ca(OH)₂ used in the titration from stoichiometry:

$$0.00450 \ \text{base equivalents} \times \frac{1 \ mol \ Ca(OH)_2}{2 \ \text{base equivalents}} = 0.00225 \ mol \ Ca(OH)_2$$

The molarity of Ca(OH)₂ is found from the volume used in the titration:

$$\frac{0.00225 \ mol \ Ca(OH)_3}{0.0222 \ L - 0.0006 \ L} = 0.104 \ M \ Ca(OH)_3$$

2) Utilize the formula:

$$C_{unknown} = \frac{C_{known} V_{known}}{V_{final} - V_{initial}}$$

Use units of normality. For HNO₃, molarity = normality because 1 mol contains 1 acid equivalent:

$$C_{Ca(OH)_2} = \frac{C_{HNO_3} V_{HNO_3}}{V_{final} - V_{initial}} = \frac{\left(0.150 \ M \times \frac{1 \ N}{1 \ M}\right)(30.0 \ mL)}{22.2 \ mL - 0.6 \ mL} = 0.208 \ N \ Ca(OH)_2$$

This value is converted to molarity. For Ca(OH)₂, normality is twice molarity because 1 mol contains 2 base equivalents:

$$0.208 \text{ N Ca(OH)}_2 \times \frac{1 \text{ M Ca(OH)}_2}{2 \text{ N Ca(OH)}_2} = 0.104 \text{ M Ca(OH)}_2$$

INTERPRETING TITRATION CURVES

A **titration curve** is a plot of a solution's **pH charted against the volume of an added acid or base**. Titration curves are obtained if a pH meter is used to monitor the titration instead of an indicator. At the equivalence point, the titration curve is nearly vertical. This is the point where the most rapid change in pH occurs. In addition to determining the equivalence point, the **shape of titration curves** may be interpreted to determine **acid/base strength and the presence of a polyprotic acid.**

The pH at the equivalence point of a titration is the **pH of the salt solution obtained when the amount of acid is equal to the amount of base**. For a strong acid and a strong base, the equivalence point occurs at the neutral pH of 7. For example, an equimolar solution of HCl and NaOH will contain NaCl (*aq*) at its equivalence point.

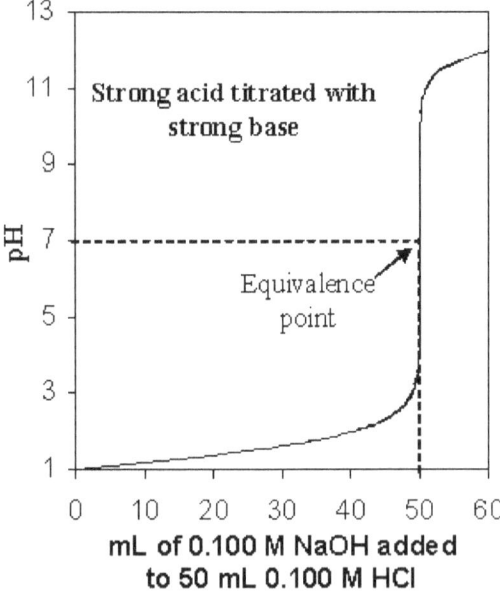
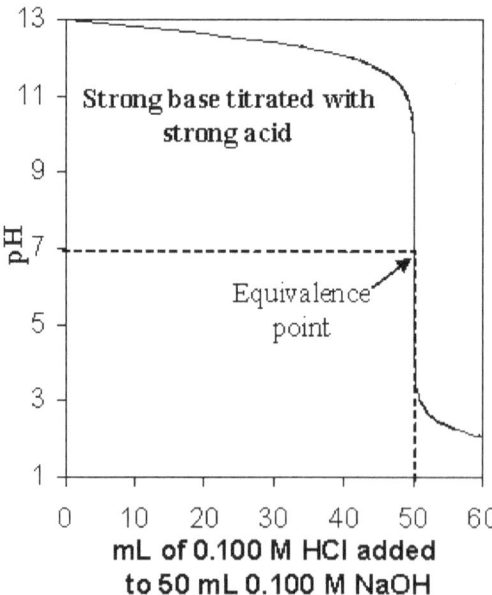

The salt solution at **the equivalence point of a titration involving a weak acid or base will not be at neutral pH**. For example, an equimolar solution of NaOH and hypochlorous acid HClO at the equivalence point of a titration will be a base because it is indistinguishable from a solution of sodium hypochlorite. A pure solution of NaClO (aq) will be a base because the ClO^- ion is the conjugate base of HClO, and it consumes $H^+(aq)$ in the reaction $ClO^- + H^+ \leftrightarrow HClO$.

In a similar fashion, an equimolar solution of HCl and NH_3 will be an acid because a solution of NH_4Cl (aq) is an acid. It generates H^+ (aq) in the reaction $NH_4^+ \leftrightarrow NH_3 + H^+$.

Contrast the following **titration curves for a weak acid and base** with those for a strong acid and strong base on the preceding page:

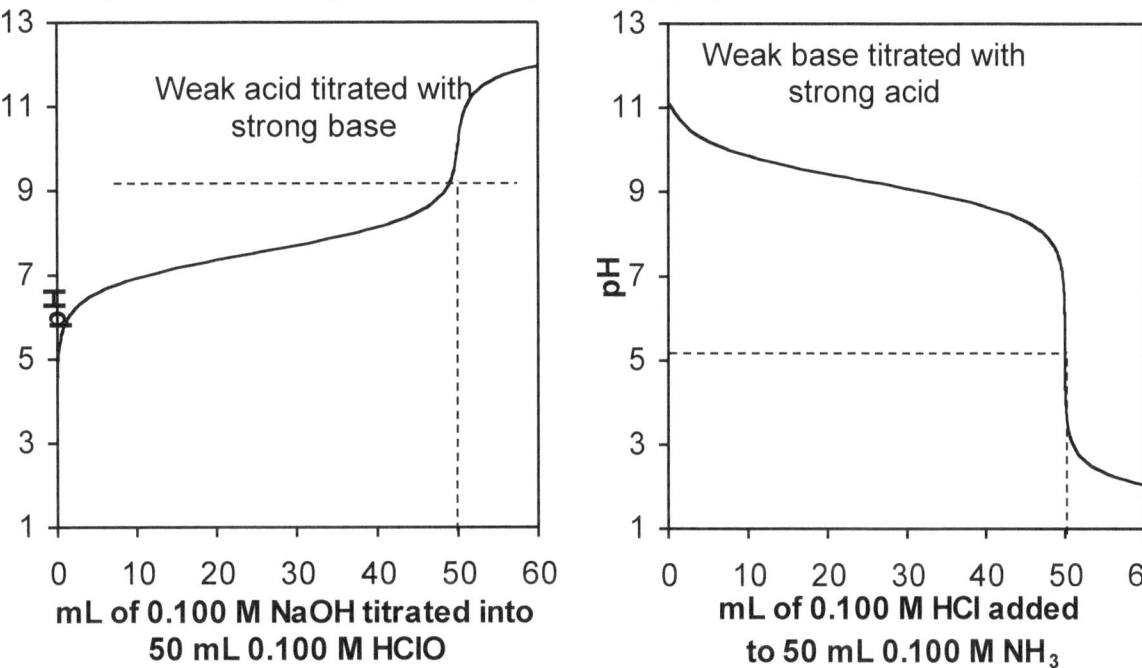

Titration of a polyprotic acid results in **multiple equivalence points** and a curve with more "bumps" as shown below for sulfurous acid and the carbonate ion.

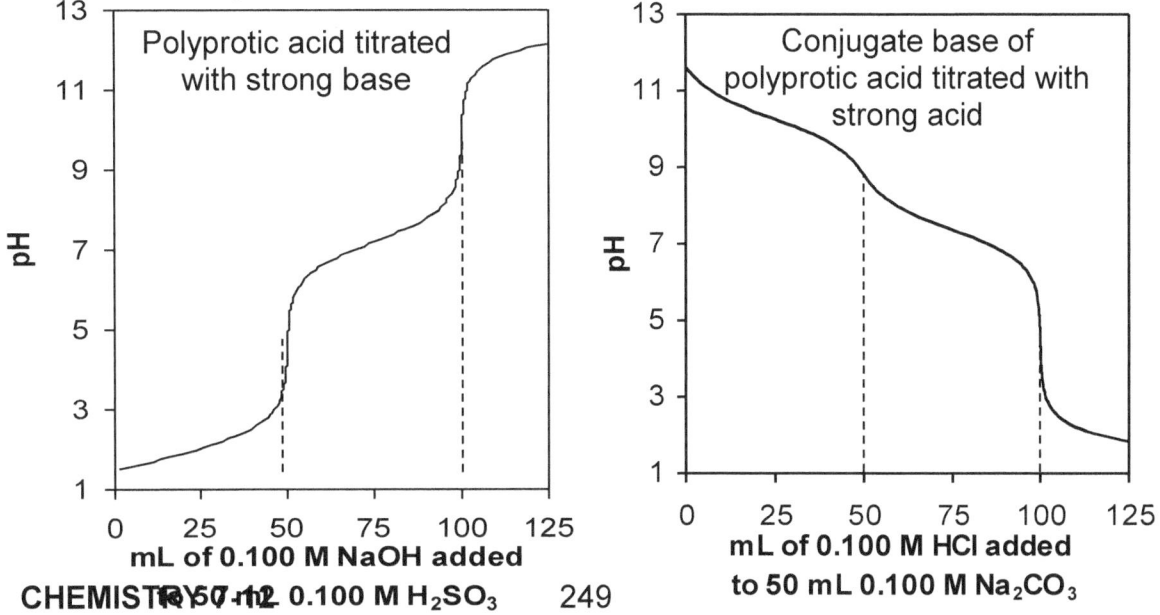

Skill 13.7 Analyzes neutralization reactions based on the principles of solution concentration and stoichiometry

The example problems in Skill 13.7 demonstrate how acid-base neutralization reactions may be analyzed using the solution method.

Skill 13.8 Describes the effects of acids and bases in the real world

Acids have a sour taste (as in lemon juice) and turn litmus paper red. Common household acids include vinegar, tomatoes, citric acids found in fruits and fruit juices, wine and beer, pickles, and on the stronger side, battery acid in the battery found in your car. Strong acids can corrode metals and burn through clothing and skin. Stomach acid is also a very strong acid that helps break down your food, and can be responsible for heartburn, acid reflux, or ulcers if the acidity gets out of balance. Many soft drinks, such as Coca-Cola®, are highly acidic (pH = 2.5), contributing to tooth decay. Certain emissions from power plants can combine with rainwater to form acid rain, which is corrosive and harmful to plants and buildings. Acids have many industrial uses, including electroplating, etching metals, cleaning metals, chemical manufacturing, iron and steel manufacturing, rubber manufacturing, oil refining, tanning, and textiles.

Bases have a bitter taste (as in soaps), feel slippery, and turn litmus paper blue. Common household bases include baking soda, bleach, ammonia, and drain cleaner. Mild bases can be used to neutralize and calm stomach upset, such as antacid or Milk of Magnesia. Strong bases can be very dangerous to clothing and skin; the slippery feeling of a weak acid is actually the fatty acids and oils in your skin dissolving. Strong bases are effective as cleaners because they dissolve organic materials without harming metal, glass, or other household surfaces. Soaps are salts that form bases when mixed with water. Bases are used in oil refining, textile manufacturing, chemical manufacturing, and as catalysts for many industrial processes.

Salts are stable forms of acids or bases or are used to buffer acid or base solutions. Blood and seawater are both slightly basic solutions that support living beings. The salts in blood and seawater buffer the solution so that the pH is not easily changed, protecting living organisms from sudden changes in their blood or in environmental conditions. The lack of salt in freshwater lakes and wetlands explains why these ecosystems are more vulnerable to the effects of acid rain than are saltwater environments.

COMPETENCY 014 **THE TEACHER UNDERSTANDS OXIDATION AND REDUCTION REACTIONS**

Skill 14.1 **Determines the oxidation state of ions and atoms in compounds**

Oxidation numbers, sometimes called oxidation states, are signed (+ or –) numbers assigned to atoms in molecules and ions. They allow us to keep track of the electrons associated with each atom. Oxidation numbers are frequently used to write chemical formulas, to help predict properties of compounds, and to help balance equations in which electrons are transferred. Knowledge of the oxidation state of an atom gives us an idea of its positive or negative character. In themselves, oxidation numbers have no physical meaning; they are used to simplify tasks that are more difficult to accomplish without them.

RULES FOR DETERMINING OXIDATION STATE

1. Free elements are assigned an oxidation state of 0.

    Example: Al, Na, Fe, H_2, O_2, N_2, and Cl_2 have zero oxidation states.

2. The oxidation state for any simple one-atom ion is equal to its charge.

    Example: The oxidation state of Na^+ is +1, Be^{2+} is +2, and F^- is -1.

3. The alkali metals (Li, Na, K, Rb, Cs and Fr) in compounds are always assigned an oxidation state of +1.

    Example: In LiOH, Li = +1; in Na_2SO_4, Na = +1.

4. Fluorine in compounds is always assigned an oxidation state of -1.

    Example: In HF_2^- and BF_2^-, F = -1.

5. The alkaline earth metals (Be, Mg, Ca, Sr, Ba, and Ra) and also Zn and Cd in compounds are always assigned an oxidation state of +2. Similarly, Al and Ga are always assigned an oxidation state of +3.

    Example: In $CaSO_4$, Ca = +2; in $AlCl_3$, Al = +3.

6. Hydrogen in compounds is assigned an oxidation state of +1, except in hydrides, where it is assigned -1.

   Example: In H_2SO_4, H = +1; in LiH, H = -1.

7. Oxygen in compounds is assigned an oxidation state of -2. One exception is peroxide (H_2O_2), where O = -1.

   Example: In H_3PO_4, O = -2.

8. The oxidation states of many other atoms may vary from compound to compound. However, their oxidation states can frequently be determined based on the following rule: the sum of the oxidation states of all the atoms in a species must be equal to the net charge on the species.

   Example: The net charge of $HClO_4$ = 0. Applying the above rules, H = +1 and 4O = -2 x 4 = -8. Therefore, the oxidation state of Cl must be +7 so that the overall charge = 1 + -8 + 7 = 0.

   Example: The net charge of CrO_4^{2-} = -2. Applying the above rules, 4O = -2 x 4 = -8. Therefore, the oxidation state of Cr must be +6 so that the overall charge = -8 + 6 = -2.

Skill 14.2 Identifies and balances oxidation and reduction reactions

Redox is shorthand for *reduction* and *oxidation*. **Reduction** is the **gain of an electron** by a molecule, atom, or ion. **Oxidation** is the **loss of an electron** by a molecule, atom, or ion. These two processes always occur together. Electrons lost by one substance are gained by another. In a redox process, the **oxidation numbers** of atoms are altered. Reduction decreases the oxidation number of an atom. Oxidation increases the oxidation number.

The easiest redox processes to identify are those involving monatomic ions with altered charges. For example, the reaction:

$$Zn(s) + Cu^{2+}(aq) \rightarrow Zn^{2+}(aq) + Cu(s)$$

is a redox process because electrons are transferred from Zn to Cu.

However, many redox reactions involve the transfer of electrons from one molecular compound to another. For example, the reaction:

$$H_2 + F_2 \rightarrow 2HF$$

is a redox process because the oxidation numbers of atoms are altered. The oxidation numbers of elements are always zero, and oxidation numbers in a compound are never zero. Fluorine is the more electronegative element, so in HF it has an oxidation number of –1 and hydrogen has an oxidation number of +1. This is a redox process where electrons are transferred from H_2 to F_2 to create HF.

In the reaction:
$$HCl + NaOH \rightarrow NaCl + H_2O$$

the H atoms on both sides of the reaction have an oxidation number of +1, the Cl atom has an oxidation number of -1, the Na atom has an oxidation number of +1, and the O atom has an oxidation number of -2. **This is not a redox process because oxidation numbers remain unchanged** by the reaction.

An **oxidizing agent** (also called an oxidant or oxidizer) has the ability to oxidize other substances by removing electrons from them. The **oxidizing agent is reduced** in the process. A **reducing agent** (also called a reductive agent, reductant or reducer) is a substance that has the ability to reduce other substances by transferring electrons to them. The **reducing agent is oxidized** in the process.

Redox reactions may also be written as **two half-reactions**, a **reduction half-reaction** with **electrons as a reactant** and an **oxidation half-reaction** with **electrons as a product**.

Example: The redox reaction:

$$Zn(s) + Cu^{2+}(aq) \rightarrow Zn^{2+}(aq) + Cu(s)$$

may be written in terms of the half-reactions:

$$2e^- + Cu^{2+}(aq) \rightarrow Cu(s)$$
$$Zn(s) \rightarrow Zn^{2+}(aq) + 2e^-$$

Determining whether a chemical equation is balanced requires an additional step for redox reactions because there must be a **charge balance**. For example, the equation:

$$Sn^{2+} + Fe^{3+} \rightarrow Sn^{4+} + Fe^{2+}$$

contains one Sn and one Fe on each side but it is not balanced because the sum of charges on the left side of the equation is +5 and the sum on the right side is +6. One electron is gained in the reduction half-reaction ($Fe^{3+} + e^- \rightarrow Fe^{2+}$), but two are lost in the oxidation half-reaction ($Sn^{2+} \rightarrow Sn^{4+} + 2e^-$).

The equation:
$$Sn^{2+} + 2Fe^{3+} \rightarrow Sn^{4+} + 2Fe^{2+}$$

is properly balanced because both sides contain the same sum of charges (+8) and the electrons cancel from the half-reactions:

$$2Fe^{3+} + 2e^- \rightarrow 2Fe^{2+}$$
$$Sn^{2+} \rightarrow Sn^{4+} + 2e^-$$

OXIDATION NUMBER METHOD

Redox reactions must be balanced to observe the Law of Conservation of Mass. This process is a little more complicated than balancing other reactions because the number of electrons lost must equal the number of electrons gained. Balancing redox reactions, then, conserves not only mass but also charge or electrons. It can be accomplished by slightly varying our balancing process.

Example: Balance the reaction:

$$Cr_2O_3 + Al \rightarrow Cr + Al_2O_3$$

Solution: Assign oxidation numbers to each atom in order to identify which atoms are losing and gaining electrons:

$$Cr_2O_3 + Al \rightarrow Cr + Al_2O_3$$
$$3+\ 2-\quad\ \ 0\quad\ \ 0\quad\ 3+\ 2-$$

Identify those atoms gaining and losing electrons:

$$Cr^{3+} \rightarrow Cr^0 \quad \text{gained 3 electrons = reduction}$$
$$Al^0 \rightarrow Al^{3+} \quad \text{lost 3 electrons = oxidation}$$

Balance the atoms and electrons:

$$Cr_2O_3 \rightarrow 2Cr + 6e^-$$
$$2Al + 6e^- \rightarrow Al_2O_3$$

Balance the half reactions by adding missing elements. Ignore elements whose
oxidation number does not change. Add H_2O to add oxygen and H^+ to add hydrogen:

$$Cr_2O_3 + \mathbf{6H^+} \rightarrow 2Cr + 6e^- + \mathbf{3H_2O}$$
$$2Al + 6e^- + \mathbf{3H_2O} \rightarrow Al_2O_3 + \mathbf{6H^+}$$

There is a need for 3 oxygen atoms on the reactant side and 6 H^+ on the product side.

Put the two half reactions together and add the species. Cancel out

the species that occur in both the reactants and products.
$Cr_2O_3(s) + 6 H^+ + 2Al (s) + 6$ electrons $+ 3 H_2O \longrightarrow 2Cr (s) + 6$ electrons $+ 3 H_2O + Al_2O_{3 (s)} + 6 H^+$

The balanced equation is: $\quad Cr_2O_3 + 2Al \rightarrow 2Cr + Al_2O_3$

Example: Balance the reaction:

$$AgNO_3 + Cu \rightarrow CuNO_3 + Ag$$

Solution: Assign oxidation numbers to identify which atoms are losing and gaining electrons:

$$AgNO_3 + Cu \rightarrow Cu(NO_3)_2 + Ag$$
$\quad\quad$ 1+5+2- $\quad$ 0 $\quad\quad$ 2+ 5+2- $\quad$ 0

Identify those atoms gaining and losing electrons:

$Ag^+ + e^- \rightarrow Ag^0$ $\quad\quad$ 1 electron gained = reduction
$Cu^0 \rightarrow Cu^{2+} + 2e^-$ $\quad\quad$ 2 electrons lost = oxidation

Balance the atoms and electrons:
$$2AgNO_3 + 2e^- \rightarrow 2Ag^0$$
$$Cu^0 \rightarrow Cu(NO_3)_2 + 2e^-$$

Balance the electrons:

$$AgNO_3 + 1 e^- \longrightarrow Ag^0$$
$$Cu^0 \longrightarrow Cu(NO_3)_2 + 2 e^-$$

1 electron gained and 2 electrons lost. Needs to be equal so 2 electrons need to be gained.

$$2 [Ag + 1 e^- \longrightarrow Ag^0] = 2 AgNO_3 + 2 e^- \longrightarrow 2 Ag^{0+}$$

Reduction: $2 AgNO_3 + 2 e^- \longrightarrow 2 Ag^0$
$\quad\quad$ Oxidation: $\quad Cu^0 \longrightarrow Cu(NO_3)_2 + 2 e^-$

Balance the half reactions by adding missing elements. Ignore elements whose oxidation number does not change. Add H_2O for oxygen and H^+ for hydrogen

$$2 AgNO_3 + 2 e^- \longrightarrow 2 Ag^0 + 2 NO_3$$
$$2NO_3 + Cu^0 \longrightarrow Cu(NO_3)_2 + 2 e^-$$

Put the two half reactions together and add the species. Cancel out the species that occur in both the reactants and products. The balanced reaction is:

$$2AgNO_3 + Cu \rightarrow Cu(NO_3)_2 + 2Ag$$

Example: Balance the reaction:

$$Ag_2S + HNO_3 \rightarrow AgNO_3 + NO + S + H_2O$$

Assign oxidation numbers:

$$Ag_2S + HNO_3 \rightarrow AgNO_3 + NO + S + H_2O$$
$$\ 1+\ 2-\ \ 1+5+2-\ \ 1+5+2-\ \ 2+2-\ \ 0\ \ 1+2-$$

Identify those atoms gaining and losing electrons:

$S^{2-} \rightarrow S^0 + 2e^-$ gained 2 electrons = oxidation
$N^{5+} + 3e^- \rightarrow N^{2+}$ lost 3 electrons = reduction

Balance the atoms:

$$2NO_3^- + Ag_2S \rightarrow S + 2e^- + 2AgNO_3$$
$$3H^+ + HNO_3 + 3e^- \rightarrow NO + 2H_2O$$

Balance electrons lost and gained:

$$6NO_3^- + 3Ag_2S \rightarrow 3S + 6e^- + 6AgNO_3$$
$$6H^+ + 2HNO_3 + 6e^- \rightarrow 2NO + 4H_2O$$

Put the two half reactions together and add the species. Cancel out the species that occur in both the reactants and products. The balanced equation is:

$$3Ag_2S + 8HNO_3 \rightarrow 6AgNO_3 + 2NO + 3S + 4H_2O$$

To balance a redox reaction which occurs in basic solution is a very similar to balancing a redox reaction which occurs in acidic conditions. First, balance the reaction as you would for an acidic solution and then adjust for the basic solution.

Example: Solid chromium(III) hydroxide, $Cr(OH)_3$, reacts with aqueous chlorate ion, ClO_3^-, in basic conditions to form chromate ions, CrO_4^{2-}, and chloride ions, Cl^-:

$$Cr(OH)_3\ (s) + ClO_3\ (aq) \rightarrow CrO_4^{2-}\ (aq) + Cl^-\ (aq)\ \ \text{(basic)}$$

Solution: Write the half-reactions:

$$Cr(OH)_3 (s) \rightarrow CrO_4^{2-} (aq)$$
$$ClO_3^- (aq) \rightarrow Cl^- (aq)$$

Balance the atoms in each half-reaction. Use H_2O to add oxygen atoms and H^+ to add hydrogen atoms:

$$H_2O (l) + Cr(OH)_3 (s) \rightarrow CrO_4^{2-} (aq) + 5H^+ (aq)$$
$$6H^+ (aq) + ClO_3^- (aq) \rightarrow Cl^- (aq) + 3H_2O (l)$$

Balance the charges of both half-reactions by adding electrons:

$$H_2O (l) + Cr(OH)_3 (s) \rightarrow CrO_4^{2-} (aq) + 5H^+ (aq) + 3e^-$$
$$6e^- + 6H^+ (aq) + ClO_3^- (aq) \rightarrow Cl^- (aq) + 3H_2O (l)$$

The number of electrons lost must equal the number of electrons gained so multiply each half-reaction by a number that will give equal numbers of electrons lost and gained:

$$2H_2O (l) + 2\,Cr(OH)_3 (s) \rightarrow 2CrO_4^{2-} (aq) + 10H^+ (aq) + 6e^-$$
$$6e^- + 6H^+ (aq) + ClO_3^- (aq) \rightarrow Cl^- (aq) + 3H_2O (l)$$

Add the two half-reactions together, canceling out species that appear on both sides of the reaction. Since the reaction occurs in basic solution and there are 4 H^+ ions on the right side, 4OH^- need to be added to both sides. Combine the H^+ and OH^- where appropriate to make water molecules to write the final balanced equation:

$$4OH^- (aq) + 2Cr(OH)_3 (s) + ClO_3^- (aq) \rightarrow 2CrO_4^{2-} (aq) + Cl^- (aq) + 5H_2O (l)$$

Skill 14.3 Uses reduction potentials to determine whether a redox reaction will occur spontaneously

A **standard cell potential**, E°_{cell}, is the voltage generated by an electrochemical cell at **100 kPa and 25° C** when all components of the reaction are pure materials or solutes at a **concentration of 1 M**. Older textbooks may use 1 atm instead of 100 kPa. Standard solute concentrations may differ from 1 M for solutions that behave in a non-ideal way, but this difference is beyond the scope of general high school chemistry.

Standard cell potentials are calculated from the **sum of the two half-reaction potentials** for the reduction and oxidation reactions occurring in the cell:

$$E^\circ_{cell} = E^\circ_{red}(cathode) + E^\circ_{ox}(anode)$$

All half-reaction potentials are relative to the reduction of H⁺ to form H_2. This potential is assigned a value of zero:

$$\text{For } 2H^+(aq \text{ at } 1\text{ M}) + 2e^- \rightarrow H_2(g \text{ at } 100\text{ kPa}), \quad E°_{red} = 0 \text{ V}.$$

The standard potential of an oxidation half-reaction $E°_{ox}$ is equal in magnitude **but has the opposite sign to the potential of the reverse reduction reaction**. Standard half-cell potentials are **tabulated as reduction potentials**. These are sometimes referred to as **standard electrode potentials $E°$**. Therefore,

$$E°_{cell} = E°(\text{cathode}) - E°(\text{anode})$$

Example: Given:

$$E° = 0.34 \text{ V} \qquad Cu^{2+}(aq) + 2e^- \rightarrow Cu(s)$$
$$E° = -0.76 \text{ V} \qquad Zn^{2+}(aq) + 2e^- \rightarrow Zn(s)$$

find the standard cell potential of the system:

$$Zn(s) + Cu^{2+}(aq) \rightarrow Zn^{2+}(aq) + Cu(s)$$

Solution: $E°_{cell} = E°(\text{cathode}) - E°(\text{anode})$

$$= E°(Cu^{2+}(aq) + 2e^- \rightarrow Cu(s)) - E°(Zn^{2+}(aq) + 2e^- \rightarrow Zn(s))$$
$$= 0.34 \text{ V} - (-0.76 \text{ V}) = 1.10 \text{ V}.$$

SPONTANEITY

When the value of E° is positive, the reaction is spontaneous. If the E° value is negative, an outside energy source is necessary for the reaction to occur. In the above example, the E° is a positive 1.10 V, therefore this reaction is spontaneous.

Skill 14.4 Explains the operating principles of electrochemical cells and the process of electroplating metals

Electrolytic cells use electricity to force nonspontaneous redox reactions to occur. **Electrochemical cells generate electricity** by permitting spontaneous redox reactions to occur. The two types of cells have some components in common.

Both systems contain two **electrodes**. An electrode is a piece of conducting metal that is used to make contact with a nonmetallic material. One electrode is an **anode**. An **oxidation reaction occurs at the anode**, so electrons are removed from a substance there. The other electrode is a **cathode**. A **reduction reaction occurs at the cathode**, so electrons are added to a substance there. Electrons flow from anode to cathode outside either device.

ELECTROLYTIC SYSTEMS

Electrolysis is a chemical process **driven by a battery** or another source of electromotive force. This source pulls electrons out of the chemical process at the anode and forces electrons in the cathode. The result is a **negatively charged cathode and a positively charged anode**.

Electrolysis of pure water forms O_2 bubbles at the anode by the oxidation half-reaction:

$$2H_2O(l) \rightarrow 4H^+(aq) + O_2(g) + 4e^-$$

and forms H_2 bubbles at the cathode by the reduction half-reaction:

$$2H_2O(l) + 2e^- \rightarrow H_2(g) + 2OH^-(aq)$$

The net redox reaction is:

$$2H_2O(l) \rightarrow 2H_2(g) + O_2(g)$$

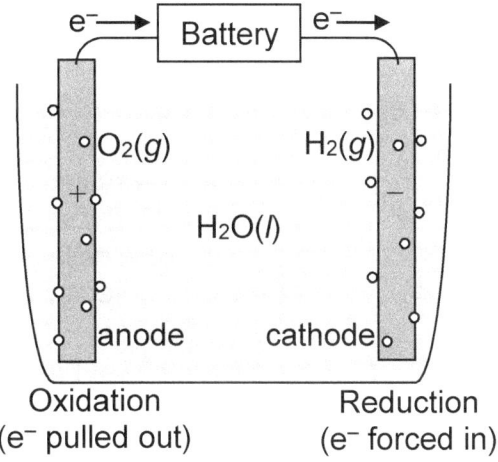

Neither electrode took part in the reaction described above. An electrode that is only used to contact the reaction and deliver or remove electrons is called an **inert electrode**. An electrode that takes part in the reaction is called an **active electrode**.

Electroplating is the process of **depositing dissolved metal cations** in a smooth even coat onto an object used as an active electrode. Electroplating is used to protect metal surfaces or for decoration. For example, to electroplate a copper surface with nickel, a nickel rod is used for the anode and the copper object is used for the cathode. $NiCl_2$ (aq) or another substance with free nickel ions is used in the electrolytic cell.

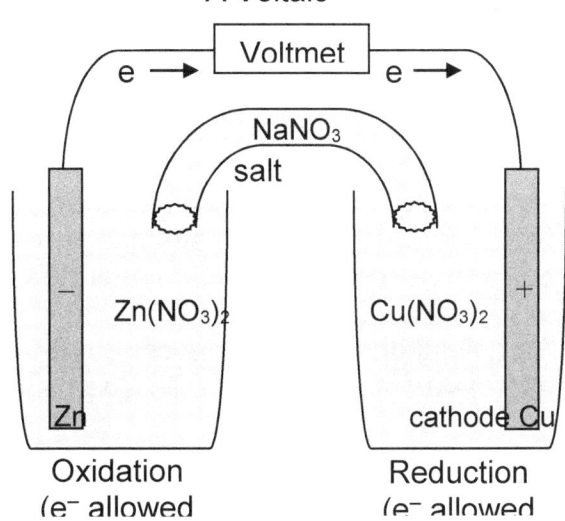

$Ni(s) \rightarrow Ni^{2+}(aq) + 2e^-$ occurs at the anode and $Ni^{2+}(aq) + 2e^- \xrightarrow{\text{onto Cu}} Ni(s)$ occurs at the cathode.

ELECTROCHEMICAL SYSTEMS

An **electrochemical cell** separates the half-reactions of a redox process into two compartments or half-cells. Electrochemical cells are also called *galvanic cells* or *voltaic cells*.

A **battery** consists of one or more electrochemical cells connected together. Electron transfer from the oxidation to the reduction reaction may only take place through an external circuit.

Electrochemical systems provide a **source of electromotive force**. This force is also called *voltage* or *cell potential* and is measured in **volts**. Electrons are allowed to leave the chemical process at the anode and permitted to enter at the cathode. The result is a **negatively charged anode and a positively charged cathode**.

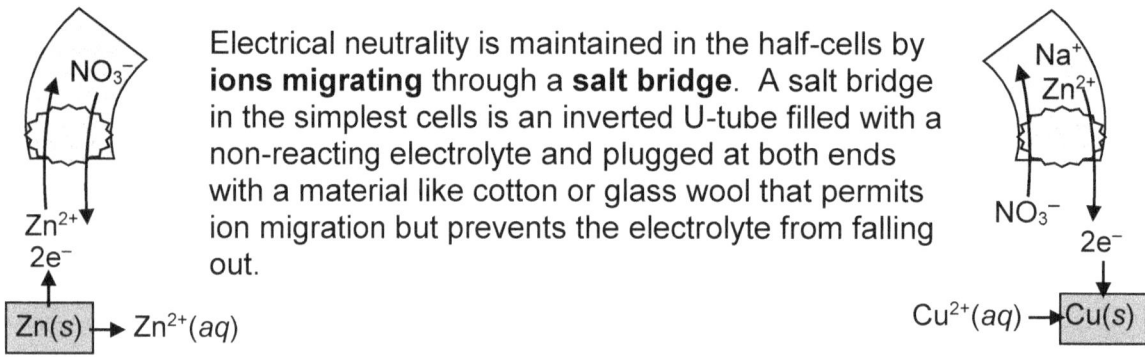

Electrical neutrality is maintained in the half-cells by **ions migrating** through a **salt bridge**. A salt bridge in the simplest cells is an inverted U-tube filled with a non-reacting electrolyte and plugged at both ends with a material like cotton or glass wool that permits ion migration but prevents the electrolyte from falling out.

The spontaneous redox reaction $Zn(s) + Cu^{2+}(aq) \rightarrow Zn^{2+}(aq) + Cu(s)$ generates a voltage in the cell above. The oxidation half-reaction $Zn(s) \rightarrow Zn^{2+}(aq) + 2e^-$ occurs at the anode. Electrons are allowed to flow through a voltmeter before they are consumed by the reduction half-reaction $Cu^{2+}(aq) + 2e^- \rightarrow Cu(s)$ at the cathode. Zinc dissolves away from the anode into solution, and copper from the solution builds up onto the cathode.

To maintain electrical neutrality in both compartments, positive ions (Zn^{2+} and Na^+) migrate through the salt bridge from the anode half-cell to the cathode half-cell and negative ions (NO_3^-) migrate in the opposite direction.

An animation of the cell described above is located at
http://www.mhhe.com/physsci/chemistry/essentialchemistry/flash/galvan5.swf.

A summary of anode and cathode properties for both cell types is contained in the table below.

		Electrolytic cell	Electrochemical cell
Anode	Half-reaction	Oxidation	Oxidation
	Electron flow	Pulled out	Allowed out
	Electrode polarity	+	−
Cathode	Half-reaction	Reduction	Reduction
	Electron flow	Forced in	Allowed in
	Electrode polarity	−	+

The reducing and oxidizing agents in a standard electrochemical cell are depleted with time. In a **rechargeable battery** (e.g., lead storage batteries in cars) the direction of the spontaneous redox reaction is reversed and **reactants are regenerated** when electrical energy is added into the system. A **fuel cell** has the same components as a standard electrochemical cell except that **reactants are continuously supplied**.

Skill 14.5   Analyzes applications of oxidation and reduction reactions from everyday life (e.g., combustion, corrosion, electroplating, batteries)

Most combustion reactions are the oxidation of a fuel material with oxygen gas. Complete burning produces carbon dioxide from all the carbon in the fuel, and water from the hydrogen in the fuel. These reactions are used mainly for the production of heat energy. The fuel value is the energy released when 1.0 gram of a material is combusted. This number is a positive number since energy is released and it is measured by calorimetry.

Biochemical combustion involves the use of enzymes to lower the activation energy so that the combustion reaction can be carried out at low temperatures, such as body temperature (37°C). In our bodies, most of the energy comes from the combustion of carbohydrates and fats. Starch, a carbohydrate, is decomposed in the intestines into glucose, $C_6H_{12}O_6$. Glucose is soluble in blood and is transported to cells where it reacts with oxygen, producing carbon dioxide and water while releasing 2803 kJ/mol of energy:

$$C_6H_{12}O_6\ (s) + 6O_2\ (g) \rightarrow 6CO_2\ (g) + 6H_2O\ (l) \qquad \Delta H = -2803\ \text{kJ}$$

Carbohydrates supply energy quickly due to their rapid breakdown. Storage of carbohydrates is limited, however.

Fats also undergo combustion in the cells to produce carbon dioxide and water:

$2C_{57}H_{110}O_6$ (s) + $163O_2$ (g) → $114CO_2$ (g) + $110H_2O$ (l)   ΔH = -75.520 kJ
(tristearin)

The fuel values of carbohydrates, fats and proteins are listed below:

	Fuel Value (kJ/g)
Carbohydrate	17
Fat	38
Protein	17

This energy is used to regulate body temperature, contract muscles, and build and repair tissues. Any excess energy is stored as fat. Fats are insoluble in water and they produce more energy per gram than carbohydrates and proteins, so they are prefect for storing excess energy.

Combustion in the body releases less energy than combustion in a calorimeter because the products are slightly different. In the body, protein, which contains nitrogen, forms urea, $(NH_2)_2CO$. However in the calorimeter, proteins form N_2 when combusted.

The combustion of fossil fuels releases energy as well. This energy is in the form of heat, and carbon dioxide and water are formed as the bonds in the fossil fuel rearrange themselves during the combustion reaction. Coal, petroleum, and natural gas are known as fossil fuels and are formed from the decay of living matter.

Natural gas is gaseous hydrocarbons, primarily methane with small amounts of ethane, propane, and butane. Natural gas has a fuel value of 49 kJ/g. Petroleum, with a fuel value around 48 kJ/g (gasoline), is a liquid that contains many small compounds, mostly hydrocarbons but also some organic compounds containing sulfur, nitrogen, and oxygen. These impurities result in air pollution when petroleum is burned. Coal is a solid that consists of large hydrocarbons as well as some impurities of sulfur, nitrogen, and oxygen. Again, it is these impurities that produce the contaminants in air pollution when coal is burned. Anthracite coal has a fuel value of 31 kJ/g, while bituminous coal has a fuel value of 32 kJ/g. The combustion of methane is shown below:

CH_4 (g) + O_2 (g) → CO_2 (g) + $2H_2O$ (g)   ΔH = -802 kJ

Electroplating and batteries are discussed in Skill 14.4.

COMPETENCY 015   THE TEACHER UNDERSTANDS NUCLEAR FISSION, NUCLEAR FUSION, AND NUCLEAR REACTIONS

Skill 15.1   Uses models to explain radioactivity and types of radioactive decay (i.e., alpha, beta, gamma)

Some nuclei are unstable and emit particles and electromagnetic radiation. These emissions from the nucleus are known as **radioactivity**; the unstable isotopes are known as **radioisotopes**; and the nuclear reactions that spontaneously alter them are known as **radioactive decay**. Particles commonly involved in nuclear reactions are listed in the following table:

Particle	Neutron	Proton	Electron	Alpha particle	Beta particle	Gamma rays
Symbol	$^1_0 n$	$^1_1 p$ or $^1_1 H$	$^{\ 0}_{-1} e$	$^4_2 \alpha$ or $^4_2 He$	$^{\ 0}_{-1} \beta$ or $^{\ 0}_{-1} e$	$^0_0 \gamma$

Nuclear equations are balanced by equating the sum of mass numbers on both sides of a reaction equation and the sum of atomic numbers on both sides of a reaction equation.

The electron is assigned an atomic number of -1 to account for the conversion during radioactive decay of a neutron to a proton and an emitted electron called a **beta particle**:

$$^1_0 n \rightarrow {}^1_1 p + {}^{\ 0}_{-1} e$$

Sulfur-35 is an isotope that decays by beta emission:

$$^{35}_{16} S \rightarrow {}^{35}_{17} Cl + {}^{\ 0}_{-1} e$$

In most cases nuclear reactions result in a **nuclear transmutation** from one element to another. Transmutation was originally connected to the mythical "philosopher's stone" of alchemy that could turn cheaper elements into gold. When Frederick Soddy and Ernest Rutherford first recognized that radioactive decay was changing one element into another, Soddy remembered saying, "Rutherford, this is transmutation!" Rutherford replied, "Soddy, don't call it transmutation. They'll have our heads off as alchemists."

Isotopes may also decay by **electron capture** from an orbital outside the nucleus:

$$^{196}_{79} Au + {}^{\ 0}_{-1} e \rightarrow {}^{196}_{78} Pt$$

A **positron** is a particle with the small mass of an electron but with a positive charge. A positron emission converts a proton into a neutron. Carbon-11 decays by positron emission:

$$^{11}_{6}C \rightarrow \,^{11}_{5}B + \,^{0}_{1}e$$

Large isotopes often decay by **alpha particle** emission:

$$^{238}_{92}U \rightarrow \,^{234}_{90}Th + \,^{4}_{2}He$$

Gamma rays are high-energy electromagnetic radiation emissions. Gamma radiation is almost always emitted when other radioactive decay occurs. Gamma rays usually aren't written into nuclear equations because neither the mass number nor the atomic number is altered. One exception is the annihilation of an electron by a positron, an event that produces only gamma radiation:

$$^{0}_{-1}e + \,^{0}_{1}e \rightarrow 2\,^{0}_{0}\gamma$$

Skill 15.2   Interprets and balances equations for nuclear reactions

Nuclear equations are balanced by equating the sum of mass numbers and the sum of atomic numbers on both sides of a reaction equation.

Example: Balance the following nuclear transmutation:

$$^{14}_{6}C \rightarrow \,^{14}_{7}N + \underline{\hspace{1cm}}$$

Solution: The sum of the mass numbers on both the left and right side of the arrow must be the same:

Left side	Right side
14	14

They are already the same so the particle emitted during decay has a mass of 0.

The sum of the charge must be the same on the left side and right side of the arrow:

Left side	Right side
6	7

The right side has one too many positive charges to balance the 6 positive charges on the left side. Adding -1 to the right side will make it balance with 6 positive charges, so the charge of the particle emitted during decay is -1.

A particle with a mass of 0 and a -1 charge is an electron, $_{-1}^{0}e$, which should be placed in the equation to complete it:

$$_{6}^{14}C \rightarrow {_{7}^{14}}N + {_{-1}^{0}}e$$

Example: Complete the following nuclear transmutation equation:

$$_{90}^{234}Th \rightarrow {_{-1}^{0}}e + \underline{\hspace{2cm}}$$

Solution: Again, the sum of the mass numbers on each side of the arrow must be the same as well as the sum of the charges on each side.

Left side	Right side
234	0

A mass of 234 is needed on the right side to equal the left side.

For the charge:

Left side	Right side
90	-1

A 91 charge is needed on the right side to equal the left side. The particle that forms from the decay of this isotope is $_{91}^{234}Pa$ and should be inserted to complete the transmutation equation:

$$_{90}^{234}Th \rightarrow {_{-1}^{0}}e + {_{91}^{234}}Pa$$

Skill 15.3 Compares and contrasts fission and fusion reactions

When two nuclei collide, they sometimes stick to each other and synthesize a new nucleus. This **nuclear fusion** was first demonstrated by the synthesis of oxygen from nitrogen and alpha particles:

$$_{7}^{14}N + {_{2}^{4}}He \rightarrow {_{8}^{17}}O + {_{1}^{1}}H$$

Fusion can also be used to create new heavy elements, causing periodic tables to become out-dated every few years. In 2004, IUPAC approved the name roentgenium (in honor of Wilhelm Roentgen, the discoverer of X-rays) for the element first synthesized in 1994 by the following reaction:

$$_{83}^{209}Bi + {_{28}^{64}}Ni \rightarrow {_{111}^{272}}Rg + {_{0}^{1}}n$$

A heavy nucleus may also split apart into smaller nuclei by **nuclear fission.**

Nuclear power currently provides 17% of the world's electricity. Heat is generated by **nuclear fission of uranium-235 or plutonium-239**. This heat is then converted to electricity by boiling water and forcing the steam through a turbine. Fission of ^{235}U and ^{239}Pu occurs when **a neutron strikes the nucleus and breaks it apart into smaller nuclei and additional neutrons**. One possible fission reaction is:

$$_{0}^{1}n + _{92}^{235}U \rightarrow _{56}^{141}Ba + _{36}^{92}Kr + 3_{0}^{1}n$$

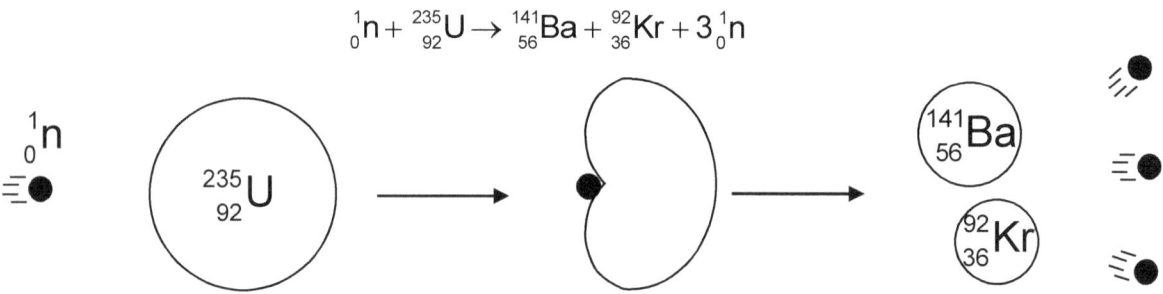

Gamma radiation, kinetic energy from the neutrons themselves, and the decay of the fission products (^{141}Ba and ^{92}Kr in the example above) all produce heat. The neutrons produced by the reaction strike other uranium atoms and produce more neutrons and more energy in a **chain reaction**. If enough neutrons are lost, the chain reaction stops and the process is called **subcritical**. If the mass of uranium is large enough that one neutron on average from each fission event triggers another fission, the reaction is said to be **critical**. If the mass is larger than this so that few neutrons escape, the reaction is called **supercritical**. The chain reaction then multiplies the number of fissions that occur and the violent explosion of an atomic bomb will take place if the process is not stopped. The concentration of **fissile material** in nuclear power plants is sufficient for a critical reaction to occur but too low for a supercritical reaction to take place.

The alpha decay of **Plutonium-238 is used as a heat source for localized power generation** in space probes and in heart pacemakers from the 1970s.

The most promising nuclear reaction for producing power by nuclear fusion is:

$$_{1}^{2}H + _{1}^{3}H \rightarrow _{2}^{4}He + _{0}^{1}n$$

Hydrogen-2 is called **deuterium** and is often represented by the symbol D. Hydrogen-3 is known as **tritium** and is often represented by the symbol T. Nuclear reactions between very light atoms similar to the reaction above are the energy source behind the sun and the hydrogen bomb.

INTERCONVERSION OF MASS AND ENERGY

With nuclear reactions, the energies involved are so great that the changes in mass become easily measurable. One can no longer assume that mass and energy are conserved separately, but must take into account their interconversion via Einstein's relationship, **E = mc²**. If mass is in grams and the velocity of light is expressed as $c = 3 \times 10^{10}$ cm sec^{-1}, then the energy is in units of g cm² sec^{-2}, or ergs. A useful conversion is from mass in amu to energy in million electron volts (MeV):

$$1 \text{ amu} = 931.4 \text{ MeV}$$

What holds a nucleus together? If we attempt to bring two protons and two neutrons together to form a helium nucleus, we might reasonably expect the positively charged protons to repel one another violently. Then what keeps them together in the nucleus?

The answer is that a helium atom is lighter than the sum of two protons, two neutrons, and two electrons. Some of the mass of the separated particles is converted into energy and dissipates when the nucleus is formed. Before the helium nucleus can be torn apart into its component particles, this dissipated energy must be restored and turned back into mass. Unless this energy is provided, the nucleus cannot be taken apart. This energy is termed the *binding energy* of the helium nucleus.

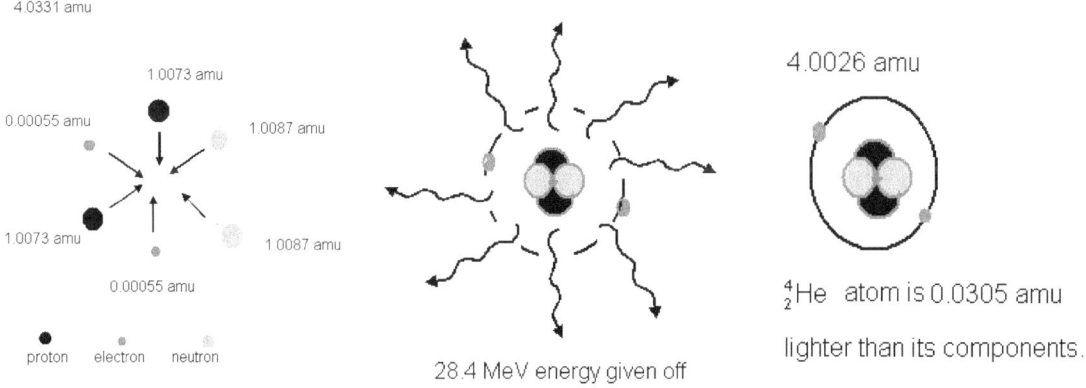

We must include electrons in this calculation because 4.0026 amu is the mass of the ⁴He atom, not the nucleus. This missing mass corresponds to 0.0305 x 931.4 MeV = 28.4 MeV of energy. If we could put a helium atom together directly from two neutrons, two protons, and two electrons, then 28.4 MeV of energy would be given off for every atom formed:

$$+2n + 2e^- \rightarrow {}^{4}_{2}He + 28.4 \text{ MeV of energy}$$

Compared to common chemical reactions, this is an enormous quantity of energy. Since 1 electron volt per atom is equivalent to 23.06 kcal per mole,

$$\text{binding energy} = 28.4 \text{ MeV atom}^{-1} \times \frac{23.06 \text{ kcal mole}^{-1}}{1 \text{ eV atom}^{-1}}$$
$$= 655{,}000{,}000 \text{ kcal mole}^{-1}$$

Compare this energy with the 83 kcal mole^{-1} required to break carbon-carbon bonds in chemical reactions.

Every atomic nucleus is lighter than the sum of the masses of the nucleons from which it is built, and this mass loss corresponds to the binding energy of the nucleus. The relative stability of two nuclei with different numbers of nucleons can be assessed by comparing their *mass loss per nucleon*.

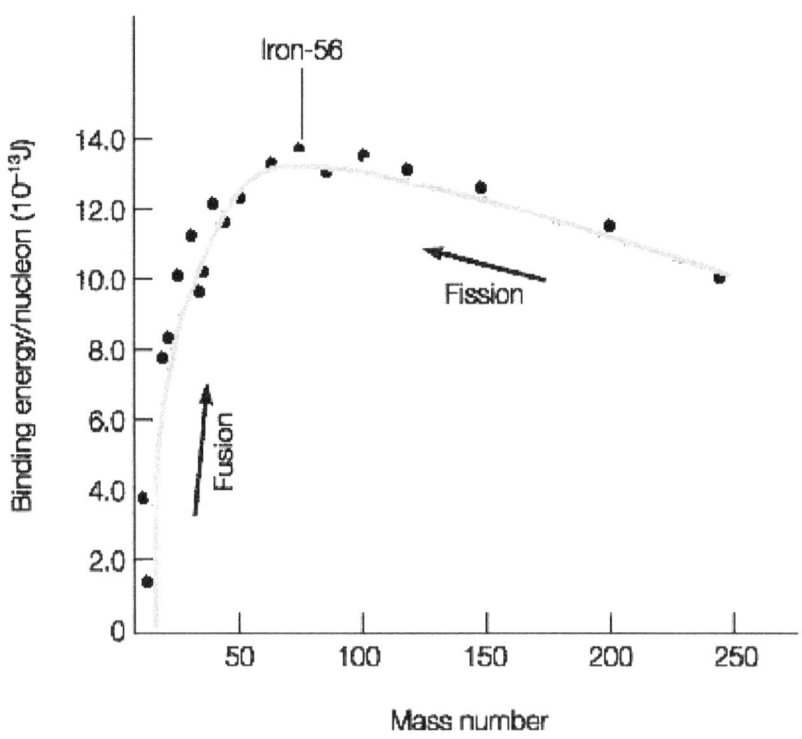

The mass loss or binding energy per nuclear particle (protons and neutrons) rises rapidly to a maximum at iron, then falls. Iron is the most stable nucleus of all. The mass losses or binding energies per nucleon are plotted above for all nuclei from helium through uranium. After some initial minor irregularities in the first- and second-row elements, the values settle down to a smooth curve, which rises to a maximum at iron, then begins a long descending slope through uranium and beyond.

For elements with smaller atomic numbers than iron, fusion of nuclei to produce heavier elements releases energy, because the products are lighter and more stable on a per-nucleon basis than the reactants. In contrast, beyond iron, fusion absorbs energy because the products are heavier on a per-nucleon basis than the reactants.

Example: What is the mass loss per nucleon for the $^{56}_{26}Fe$ atom, compared with its component protons, neutrons, and electrons?

Solution: The $^{56}_{26}Fe$ atom contains 26 protons, 26 electrons, and 30 neutrons, so the mass calculation is performed as shown below:

Mass of 26 protons:	26(1.0073) amu =	26.1898 amu
Mass of 30 neutrons:	30(1.0087) amu =	30.261 amu
Mass of 26 electrons:	26(0.00055) amu =	0.0143 amu
Total mass of components in iron-56:		56.465 amu
Mass of iron-56 atom:		55.93 amu
Total mass loss:		0.54 amu
Mass loss/nucleon:	0.54 amu/56 =	0.0096 amu

Notice that the mass loss per nucleon, and hence the binding energy per nucleon, is greater for iron (0.0096 amu) than for helium (0.0076 amu). This means that the iron nucleus is more stable relative to protons and neutrons than the helium nucleus is. If some combination of helium nuclei could be induced to produce an iron nucleus, energy would be given off, which would correspond to the increased stability of the product nucleus per nuclear particle.

Skill 15.4   Knows how to use the half-life of radioactive elements to study real-world problems (e.g., carbon dating, radioactive tracers)

The **half-life** of a reaction is the **time required to consume half the reactant**. The rate of radioactive decay for an isotope is usually also expressed as a half-life. Solving these problems is straightforward if the given amount of time is an exact multiple of the half-life. For example, the half-life of ^{233}Pa is 27.0 days. This means that of 200 grams of ^{233}Pa will decay according to the following table:

Day	Number of half-lives	^{233}Pa remaining	^{233}Pa decayed since day 0
0	0	200 g	0 g
27.0	1	100 g	100 g
54.0	2	50.0 g	150.0 g
81.0	3	25.0 g	175.0 g
108.0	4	12.5 g	187.5 g

Regardless of whether the given amount of time is an exact multiple of the half-life, the following equation may be used:

$$A_{remaining} = A_{initially} \left(\frac{1}{2}\right)^{\frac{t}{t_{halflife}}}$$

where: $A_{remaining} \Rightarrow$ amount remaining
$A_{initially} \Rightarrow$ amount initially
$t \Rightarrow$ time
$t_{halflife} \Rightarrow$ half-life

Problem: An isotope of cesium (cesium-137) has a half-life of 30 years. If 1.0 mg of cesium-137 disintegrates over a period of 90 years, how many mg of cesium-137 would remain?

Solution: Using the equation

$$A_{remaining} = A_{initially} \left(\frac{1}{2}\right)^{\frac{t}{t_{halflife}}}$$

where: $A_{remaining} \Rightarrow$ amount remaining
$A_{initially} \Rightarrow$ amount initially
$t \Rightarrow$ time
$t_{halflife} \Rightarrow$ half-life

$A_{remaining}$ = X
$A_{initially}$ = 1.0 mg
t = 90 years
$t_{1/2}$ = 30 years

then $A_{remaining}$ = 1.0 mg $(1/2)^{90/30}$ = 0.125 mg

Example: A 2.5 gram sample of an isotope of strontium-90 was formed in a 1960 explosion of an atomic bomb at Johnson Island in the Pacific Test Site. The half-life of strontium-90 is 28 years. In what year will only 0.625 grams of this strontium-90 remain?

Solution: This is a little more challenging in that substuting into the above equation gives you: 0.625 g = 2.5 $(1/2)^{x/28}$. The solution requires simplifying and then taking the natural log of both sides:

ln (0.625/2.5) = ln 0.25 = ln $(1/2^{x/28})$ x = 56 years

Add 56 years to 1960 and the year will be 2016 when only 0.625 grams of Sr-90 remain from that test.

Archeology uses nuclear chemistry for **radiometric dating**. The most commonly used nuclide for this technique is ^{14}C. ^{14}C is mostly synthesized in the upper atmosphere where extraterrestrial radiation interacts with other molecules to produce neutrons used in the reaction:

$$^{1}_{0}n + ^{14}_{7}N \rightarrow ^{14}_{6}C + ^{1}_{1}H$$

^{14}C then decays by β-emission with a half-life of 5730 years:

$$^{14}_{6}C \rightarrow ^{14}_{7}N + ^{0}_{-1}e$$

$^{14}_{6}C$ is distributed uniformly throughout the atmosphere, oceans, and living organisms because these entities all rapidly exchange carbon dioxide with one other. ^{14}C is present in these systems at a ratio of about 1 atom per trillion (10^9) atoms of non-radioactive carbon. However, after an organism dies, it no longer exchanges CO_2 with the atmosphere and its ^{14}C begins to decay with no replenishment. The time that has passed since biological material in plant fibers, wood, or bones was once alive may be estimated by comparing the fraction of $^{14}_{6}C$ present in the dead material to the fraction in living material. Natural logarithms are used:

$$t = t_{halflife} \frac{\ln\left(\frac{C_{sample}}{C_{living}}\right)}{\ln\left(\frac{1}{2}\right)}$$

where $C_{sample} \Rightarrow$ concentration in sample
$C_{initially} \Rightarrow$ concentration in living material
$t \Rightarrow$ *estimated* time before present
$t_{halflife} \Rightarrow$ half-life (5730 years for ^{14}C)

This estimate must be altered slightly by calibration curves to correct for differences in climate and cosmic background radiation over time.

The medical uses of radioactive isotopes are discussed in Skill 15.5, below.

Skill 15.5 **Identifies various issues associated with using nuclear energy (e.g., medical, commercial, environmental)**

Two important beneficial uses of radiation are in the fields of medicine and power generation. The use of fission and fusion reactions to generate power is discussed in Skill 15.3.

Medicine

Medicine uses **X-rays** as a diagnostic tool and **radioisotopes** for **diagnostic radiology** and for **radiotherapy**. In diagnostic radiology, a radioisotope is introduced into the body and its location is monitored with a **gamma camera** or other imaging equipment. **Different isotopes are localized to different tissues at specific rates**. Abnormalities in internal organs and bone structure and function are found using these techniques. The isotopes typically emit only gamma rays because alpha and beta radiation are more likely to harm the patient. **Technetium-99 is a commonly used isotope for diagnostic radiology**. Many radioisotopes are used outside the body for blood tests.

Radiotherapy uses radiation as part of **cancer treatment to destroy tumors**. Rapidly growing tumors are more vulnerable to radiation damage from β particles than non-malignant tissue. Radiotherapy works by damaging the DNA of these cells. The radioactive source may be outside the body (external radiotherapy) or introduced into the body. Isotopes used for internal radiotherapy may be injected into the body as a liquid or introduced temporarily through a catheter in a sealed container.

Cobalt-60 was a common isotope for external radiotherapy, but it has mostly been replaced by linear accelerators that provide high-energy electrons (β particles) without a dangerous isotope source. It is still used to irradiate some foods to destroy bacteria. **Iodine-131 is used to combat diseases of the thyroid** and of several types of cancer. A list of isotopes used in nuclear medicine may be found at https://www.boundless.com/chemistry/nuclear-chemistry/use-of-isotopes/isotopes-in-medicine/.

Hazards

Radioactive contamination is the uncontrolled distribution of radioactive material in an environment. The hazards of ionizing radiation were first studied in detail after the **atomic bombs dropped on Hiroshima and Nagasaki in 1945**. The worst nuclear accident in history was the **Chernobyl nuclear power plant explosion in 1986**.

Non-ionizing radiation does not carry enough energy to remove electrons from atoms, and it generally does not cause damage unless it is damage done by heating the material it contacts. Because quantum-events are all-or-nothing, a large amount of non-ionizing radiation is generally harmless, and we can safely live in a world full of lightning flashes and radio waves.

Ionizing radiation carries enough energy to remove an electron, thus turning an atom into an ion. These events can be very damaging to life because they alter the chemistry of important molecules like DNA. Very high exposure can cause radiation poisoning.

Alpha particles are high-energy helium nuclei. They **are the most destructive form of ionizing radiation.** They carry so much energy because of their charge and large mass, but **they can be stopped by a thin sheet of paper**. Alpha emitting radiation is harmful to life if it is inhaled or ingested. Most smoke detectors use alpha-emitting isotopes in a sealed container.

Beta particles are high-energy electrons. They are less harmful to matter than alpha rays because they are less energetic, but they can penetrate further into matter. A thin sheet of aluminum will stop a typical beta particle.

High energy EM radiation (e.g., some ultraviolet, all X-rays, and especially **gamma rays**) is a form of ionizing radiation. Because photons have no mass, gamma rays are less ionizing than alpha or beta particles, but gamma rays can penetrate through matter, so protection against them requires thicker shielding.

Acute exposure of large doses may cause **radiation poisoning** or **radiation burns**. Chronic exposure may result in **cancer or mutations in one's children** due damage to DNA. Organs with rapidly dividing cells such as bone marrow, intestines, and gonads are most vulnerable. Some effects do not appear until several years or decades have passed. Other organisms in the environment are just as vulnerable as humans to this danger. Because of these risks, radioactive materials are shipped in shielded containers. The risks for medical and food-processing applications that utilize radioactivity are known to be very small compared to the potential benefits, but this is considered by many to be a controversial topic.

Current opinion is that **there is a small risk to human health from even low levels of exposure** to ionizing radiation, but there is also a known quantity of **natural background radiation** that the human species has always encountered. In 1984, an employee at a nuclear power plant began to set off radiation alarms while walking *into* the plant. An investigation found that his home contained high levels of **radon gas** from natural minerals. Radon tests are now routinely performed in many homes in areas where the natural geology emits radon.

DOMAIN IV. SCIENCE LEARNING, INSTRUCTION, AND ASSESSMENT

COMPETENCY 016 THE TEACHER UNDERSTANDS RESEARCH-BASED THEORETICAL AND PRACTICAL KNOWLEDGE ABOUT TEACHING SCIENCE, HOW STUDENTS LEARN SCIENCE, AND THE ROLE OF SCIENTIFIC INQUIRY IN SCIENCE INSTRUCTION

Skill 16.1 Knows research-based theories about how students develop scientific understanding and how developmental characteristics, prior knowledge, experience, and attitudes of students influence science learning

There is a lot of debate about how students develop scientific understanding and how various factors such as developmental characteristics influence their learning of science.

In simple terms, explanations lead to understanding. The more science is explained to the students in simple, plain terms, the better they understand it. We conclude that students develop understanding of science through proper explanation. Too often it happens that an activity is done without explaining the theoretical part of it - answering the "Why" and "How" questions. When an activity is done, it has to be explained - otherwise one is simply entertaining the students.

Various factors influence understanding of science. The most important thing is that if we want good scientists or science learners, the foundation has to be laid at an early stage. Whatever they are taught has to be correct and contextualized.

Students' prior knowledge is important to their learning of science, as is their experience. Experience can be explained in different ways. The students must have good experiences in science learning. That is, they must relate learning science to positive experience.

Good attitude is important to learning anything, including science. Many students believe that science is difficult and boring. It falls upon the teacher to be creative and make science interesting.

Many schools use a discovery type of science teaching. This is good for getting the students interested in a topic or issue, but must be followed with the proper explanations. A time of de-briefing must take place to contextualize the discovery. Often students do not discover what the teacher hopes they will, but these situations can be used to understand why science is not instantaneous and why the scientific method is important.

Skill 16.2 **Understands the importance of respecting student diversity by planning activities that are inclusive by selecting and adapting science curricula, content, instructional materials, and activities to meet the interests, knowledge, understanding, abilities, and experiences of all students, including English Language Learners and students with special needs**

The term diversity is defined as the presence of a wide range of variation in the qualities or attributes under discussion. In the human context, particularly in a social context, the term diversity refers to the presence in one population of a variety of cultures, ethnic groups, languages, physical features, socio-economic backgrounds, religious faiths, sexuality, gender identity and neurology. At the international level, diversity refers to the existence of many peoples contributing their unique experiences to humanity's culture.

The teacher, as an adult, is responsible for recognizing the diversity of the students in a class, respecting their cultures and abilities and planning lessons keeping in mind that in some cases their first language is not English.

CULTURAL AND ETHNIC DIVERSITY

The teacher must be both politically correct when handling such students and compassionate and empathetic, since it is a challenge to settle in a different country and call it home. It is important to incorporate different cultural identities into lesson plans and connect them with science. For example, studying the contributions made to science by Latino scientists, African-American scientists, Native American scientists, Asian scientists, etc. In February, for instance, we may study about famous scientists of African-American origin. When this is done, the students appreciate the time and effort taken to recognize their heritage.

Decorating the classroom using ethnic material is both intellectually interesting and also creates an atmosphere of acceptance. Such efforts require a bit of time and ingenuity, but they go a long way in establishing good relationships with students and their families.

STUDENTS WITH DISABILITIES

Increasingly, educators have noticed that learning disabilities must be attended to. Such disabilities may include auditory processing disabilities, attention deficit hyperactivity disorder, visual processing disabilities (including varying degrees of blindness), autism, etc.

If a teacher notices abnormal behavioral or physical attributes of a student, it would be important to determine if this student has an IEP (Individualized Education Program) or other records that would determine whether or not this student has been evaluated. If not, the teacher might have a brief discussion with a specialist (such as the school's Special Education teacher) to determine if the noticed behavioral or physical attribute should be of concern.

Usually, at this point, if the Special Education teacher feels there is a problem, he or she will recommend the next course of action. Typically, interventions consist of instructional modifications (where the regular teacher keeps the student but modifies instruction to meet the student's needs), pull-out instruction (where a Resource Specialist, for example, may collaborate with the teacher and pull the student out to assist in certain academic areas where needed), full-day Special Education instruction (where a student is not in class with the other students, but rather in a special class designed to better assist that student), or removal from the current school (for example, students may be sent to schools that are better able to assist them with their particular needs, such as blind students).

Skill 16.3   Knows how to plan and implement strategies to encourage student self-motivation and engagement in their own learning (e.g., linking inquiry-based investigations to students' prior knowledge, focusing inquiry-based instruction on issues relevant to students, developing instructional materials using situations from students' daily lives, fostering collaboration among students)

There are two important components of teaching science. The first is theory: explaining the lesson and answering why, how, when, what, and which; out of these, why and how are the most fundamental. The second component is practical exploration, which is *doing* – gaining knowledge through experimentation. In addition to other forms of diversity, students learn material differently. Some learn better by reading, others by listening, still others by doing. Theory and practical exploration must be balanced in order for a student to understand science fully.

Students become motivated when they can contribute to their own learning. Inquiry-based instruction, in which students are encouraged to ask questions and create opportunities to find answers for those questions, is becoming popular as a means to get students more involved in science. The best way to find answers for some of their questions is to let them investigate, experiment, and find the answers themselves.

Linking of ideas is very important because the students' prior knowledge is taken into consideration. Each step of instruction is planned based on the prior knowledge of the students. When students have not got the knowledge they are expected to have for their grade level, remedial work must be done; otherwise, the students will not be able to benefit from subsequent lessons. The teacher should be aware of what has been taught in previous science courses the students are likely to have taken, as well as what is currently being taught in their other science, math, and reading courses. The more these disciplines can be linked together, the more the knowledge will be reinforced.

Another way to motivate students is to ensure that the lesson has some practical relevance to their lives. Science has to be contextualized. For example, take the question of which fertilizer is best for their lawn. This might be made into an investigation that tells them which one is best and also teaches them a bit of economics – if a fertilizer is very good and very expensive, it may not be worth it for the average person. If the fertilizer is good *and* is reasonably priced, that would be the best choice. By contrast, studying about exotic plants in a remote area in Asia probably would not generate as much interest.

Skill 16.4 Knows how to use a variety of instructional strategies to ensure all students comprehend content-related texts, including how to locate, retrieve, and retain information from a range of texts and technologies

The word 'strategy' means a careful plan or method. Instructional strategies are plans and methods used in teaching students. Success in teaching lies in using a variety of strategies to keep the students interested.

Let's examine some of the instructional strategies employed by educators:

LECTURE

This is an activity in which the teacher presents the information and knowledge orally through a series of organized and structured explanations. Student involvement is the lowest of all the strategies, and therefore, this approach should be used sparingly and in combination with other activities. Lectures can be either formal or informal. In formal lectures, the student interaction is non-existent. In informal lectures there is more interaction, and there is an increase of 20% in student retention of information.

There are ways to make the lecture method more interesting and beneficial to the students.

1. Feedback lecture – lecture lasts for only 10 minutes and then the students are divided into study groups to talk about what was discussed; students also have an opportunity to study the notes before the lecture.

2. Guided lecture – lecture lasts for 20 minutes, followed by discussion in small groups.

3. Responsive lecture – answering open-ended questions and student-generated questions.

4. Demonstration lecture – a lab/activity is demonstrated as part of the lecture.

5. Pause procedure lecture – after every 5-6 minutes of lecture, the students are given 2 minutes to compare notes with their peers and fill in any missing information.

6. Think / Write / Discuss lecture – starts with a critical thinking question; students are questioned about the topic during the lecture and at the end they are questioned again to find out how much they understood.

MNEMONIC STRATEGY

Mnemonic strategies are memory aids that provide a very systematic approach for organizing and remembering facts that have no apparent link or connection of their own. An example of a mnemonic strategy is a way of remembering the order of the planets from the sun, where the first letter of each word corresponds to the letter of a planet: My Very Excellent Mother Just Served Us Nine Pies (others can be used if you wish to leave off Pluto). These can be funny and engage the imagination of students to help them remember material that must be memorized.

RE QUEST

Re Quest is a strategy that fosters active rather than passive reading of a text. This strategy provides a structure for the students to ask questions about the learning. Both teacher and student ask each other questions about what they are doing in terms of the lesson.

RECIPROCAL TEACHING

This is an instructional activity in the form of interactive dialogue between the teacher and the students regarding the segments of the text. The dialogue involves four strategies: 1) summarizing, 2) question generating, 3) clarifying, and 4) predicting. The teacher guides the students in all of the steps.

Technology can be an important component of learning. The Internet-linked computer helps us in locating information and retrieving it. It is important for the students to be familiar with various websites which give academic information. However it is equally important for the students to locate information in books and journals. Students should be introduced to various journals in their core subjects, which provide the latest research. A school or library subscription to Science, Nature, or National Geographic would be a good place to start for finding up-to-date and accessible articles on a variety of topic areas. They can be encouraged to bring interesting articles to class that they have found on the Internet or in journals, and write or speak about them.

Skill 16.5 Understands the science teacher's role in developing the total school program by planning and implementing science instruction that incorporates schoolwide objectives and the statewide curriculum as defined in the Texas Essential Knowledge and Skills (TEKS)

Science needs to be contextualized in order for the students to relate to it. It is much easier for the students to be interested in it when it is connected to their everyday lives. The role of the science teacher is to facilitate this by planning and participating in school-wide science programs. These programs cross various disciplines and are group learning activities, though they seem simply like fun activities. Science teachers may also participate in supporting other school-wide learning goals, such as interdisciplinary reading, writing, and math competencies.

The following are some ideas which could be used as school wide science programs:

Butterfly garden: Butterflies are attractive and most of the students would be interested in them. Their beauty and movement are worth observing and their biological transformations interesting. A committee consisting of student representatives from all grade levels may be formed. Initial planning includes raising money to carry out this project; organizing a group of students across the school; preparing a small area to grow plants that would attract butterflies to lay eggs; and monitoring progress daily, observing and recording. This project lasts a few months. Another way to do this project would be to separate the students into a number of groups that could pool their observations and come up with a more complete and statistically robust set of observations.

Weather station: This is another great idea for involving the whole school. A group of students can measure and record the rainfall in a year, wind speed and direction, temperature, humidity, atmospheric pressure and any other variables of interest. Correlations can be looked for, such as a relationship between atmospheric pressure and certain weather types.

Preserving natural resources: Students are made aware of the implications of using natural resources meaningfully and economically. For instance, preserving forests starts with using paper economically, though we can afford to buy plenty of it. Awards could be instituted to reward students who come up with good ideas for school-wide conservation of resources. Another example of a way to teach students about the natural environment might be to count species diversity in a number of vacant lots or backyards, and then do the same in the same number of natural habitats.

A science teacher should also take advantage of natural phenomena such as hurricanes, volcanic eruptions, and tornadoes and teach the students about their causes. Students can track hurricane pathways and monitor volcanic eruptions.

Skill 16.6 Knows how to design and manage the learning environment (e.g., individual, small-group, whole-class settings) to focus and support student inquiries and to provide the time, space, and resources for all students to participate in field, laboratory, experimental, and nonexperimental scientific investigation

The learning environment is a very important factor in teaching any discipline. Ideally, the learning environment should be designed in such a way that the students are motivated to learn. When we talk about a learning environment, we are talking about the learning environment for the regular students. There is always a small number of students who are disruptive and interfere with the learning of other students, and these students should be handled in a different manner depending on their individual needs. It is the responsibility of the teacher to make the environment in the classroom suitable for various types of learning – individuals, pairs, small groups, or whole class setting.

The physical environment, such as the arrangement of furniture, should be modified to support the activity, e.g., if the teacher has planned collaborative pairs for learning, the tables can be moved around to achieve that. This should be done before the lesson or activity starts.

Individual teaching or independent study is a good approach for exceptional students and those who need more attention than the regular student. A few minutes of explaining the lesson or the task on hand will be very helpful. In the case of pair share or collaborative pairs, a small assignment could be given and a time frame set, at the end of which students will share as a class what they have learned. This is very good if an exceptional student and a bright student are paired. A small group is very productive as it teaches positive behaviors, including sharing information, waiting for one's turn, listening to others' ideas, views, and suggestions, and taking responsibility for doing a job in the group (writing/presenting/drawing etc.). Teaching in a whole-class setting involves traditional and modern methods such as lecture, lecture/demonstration, pause and lecture, etc. The same applies for experimental, field, and nonexperimental work, although some of these can be assigned as homework.

Today's learning, especially science, is largely inquiry-based. It is an important part of teaching to encourage the students to ask questions. Sufficient time must be given to students to ask these questions.

As a teacher, one must be a good manager, not only of the classroom but also of time, resources, and space. The teacher needs to plan how much time and energy should be given to exceptional students, bright students, regular students, and disruptive students. The exceptional and the disruptive students typically receive more of the teacher's time. Next will be the regular students, and last the bright students, since they typically need less supervision and help. If they finish work quickly, however, bright students need to be engaged, so some extra work must be available. In terms of space the same things apply. Resources must be shared equally as far as possible, since everybody has the right to have equal opportunity. However, there may be modification of resources suitable for the exceptional students, if required and available.

One thing is most important – a teacher must use logic and be able to think laterally since all the answers are not in books. The best teaching is part original thinking and part innovation and ingenuity.

Skill 16.7 Understands the rationale for using active learning and inquiry methods in science instruction and understands how to model scientific attitudes such as curiosity, openness to new ideas, and skepticism

Learning can be broadly divided into two kinds - active and passive. Active learning involves, as the name indicates, a learning atmosphere full of action whereas in passive learning students are taught in a nonstimulating and inactive atmosphere. Active learning involves and draws students into it, thereby interesting them to the point of participating and purposely engaging in learning.

It is crucial that students are actively engaged, not entertained. They should be taught the answers for "How" and "Why" questions and encouraged to be inquisitive and interested.

Active learning is conceptualized as follows:

A Model of Active Learning

Experience of	Dialogue with
Doing	Self
Observing	Others

This model suggests that all learning activities involve some kind of experience or some kind of dialogue. The two main kinds of dialogue are "dialogue with self" and "dialogue with others." The two main kinds of experience are "observing" and "doing."

Dialogue with self: Students think reflectively about a topic. They ask themselves a number of questions about the topic and try to find the answers.

Dialogue with others: When the students are listening to a book being read by another student or when the teacher is teaching, a partial dialogue takes place because the dialogue is only one-sided. When there is an exchange of ideas back and forth, either with other students or with the teacher, it becomes a dialogue with others.

Observing: This is a most important skill in science. This occurs when a learner is carefully watching or observing someone else doing an activity or experiment. This is a good experience, although it is not quite like doing the experiment personally. Observing can be made into a richer activity by enlisting the observer to record something about the experiment and using the recorded information as part of the analysis of data after the experiment.

Doing: This refers to any activity where a learner actually does something, giving the learner a firsthand experience that is very valuable.

Inquiry is invaluable to teaching in general and to teaching science, especially. The steps involved in scientific inquiry are discussed in Skill 16.8.

The scientific attitude is to be curious, open to new ideas, and skeptical. In science, there are always new research results, new discoveries, and new theories proposed. Sometimes, old theories are disproved. To view these changes rationally, one must have such openness, curiosity, and skepticism. Skepticism is a Greek word, meaning a method of obtaining knowledge through systematic doubt and continual testing. A scientific skeptic is one who refuses to accept certain types of claims without subjecting them to a systematic investigation. This should be differentiated from irrational skepticism not based on evidence.

The students may not have these attitudes inherently, but it is the responsibility of the teacher to encourage, nurture, and practice these attitudes so that students will have a good role model and gain experience applying them.

Skill 16.8 Knows principles and procedures for designing and conducting an inquiry-based scientific investigation (e.g., making observations; generating questions; researching and reviewing current knowledge in light of existing evidence; choosing tools to gather and analyze evidence; proposing answers, explanations, and predictions; communicating and defending results)

Science investigations in the classroom environment are very important because they are something a student can do by himself/herself with assistance from the teacher. Through such "active learning," the student gains experience and knowledge.

Scientific investigations are carried out by the method generally known as the Scientific Method (see Skill 2.1). The Scientific Method is composed of a series of steps to solve a problem. We use this method in order to eliminate, to the extent possible, our preconceived ideas, prejudices, and bias. When students are explained the purpose of the method, they will be able to appreciate it better.

The Scientific Method is an inquiry-based method. It consists of the following steps:

PROBLEM / QUESTION
In order to investigate, we must have a problem or question to begin with. A problem or question may come from observing, one of the most important skills in science, or from theory. The problem needs to be communicated in clear terms and in simple language, so that anybody reading it will be able to understand it.

RESEARCH / GATHERING INFORMATION
There are number of resources available to students - websites, scientific journals, magazines, books, and people who are knowledgeable and experienced, which may help them research what is already known about the topic.

FORMULATING A HYPOTHESIS
This is also known as making an educated guess. An informed guess is made regarding a possible solution to the problem, which will be tested as part of the experiment.

EXPERIMENTAL DESIGN
Conducting an experiment is very exciting and interesting, but designing the experiment well is a challenging task. It is important that students understand this. They should not rush to do an experiment, but must have a clear understanding of the different elements of an experiment: identifying the control/standard, determining the constants, and deciding on the independent and dependent variables. Involving students in the experimental design rather than having it pre-determined will greatly increase their understanding and appreciation of the experiment.

An ideal experiment at the high school level should not last more than 12-14 days.

COLLECTION OF DATA
Through conducting an experiment, we acquire data. The data should be organized and visually presented, in tabular form and/or graphically (as shown in Skill 1.5).

ANALYSIS OF THE DATA

The data should be analyzed to test the hypothesis and identify interesting patterns. Numbers are important, but they are typically not as useful or enlightening as patterns in the data.

DRAWING CONCLUSIONS

In the conclusion the investigator attempts to provide plausible answers to the initial question, determine whether the hypothesis was correct, summarize any trends or patterns observed, and make suggestions regarding subsequent research.

COMMUNICATION

Oral and written communication skills are a necessity for anybody pursuing research. Effective oral communication is needed to present the research in front of the classroom or school. Written communication is needed to present a report on the research. It should be made clear to students that, in this age of communication, those who cannot communicate effectively will be left behind. Accordingly, the evaluation system should make provision for communication skills and activities.

DEFENDING RESULTS

Defending results is as important as conducting an experiment. One can honestly defend one's own results only if the results are reliable, and experiments must be well-controlled and repeated at least twice to be considered reliable. It must be emphasized to the students that *honesty and integrity are the foundation for any type of investigation.*

Skill 16.9 Knows how to assist students with generating, refining, focusing, and testing scientific questions and hypotheses

Scientific questions are the starting point for learning. Students should be encouraged, provoked and challenged to ask good questions.

First, students need to learn to **frame** questions. The following are just a few ways in which the students can be encouraged to do this:

1. Brainstorming the topic under study
2. Discussing a topic in the class and inviting students to ask questions
3. Having students discuss the topic in small groups and come up with their own questions (this is extremely useful to students who are introverts and shy by nature).

In the case of students who are not immediately curious and inquisitive, the teacher needs to show patience in encouraging these traits, which are almost always achievable over time.

The next step is teaching students to **refine** their questions. By now the students have learned to ask questions, but the questions may not be well-designed to generate subsequent discussion. It is the responsibility of the teacher to take these questions and to convert them to "how" and "why" type, open-ended questions. For example, students may begin by asking closed-ended questions, such as, "Who landed on the moon?" This sort of question does not really generate a great amount of knowledge or provoke further thought. The teacher can modify this question to, "What did the missions to the moon accomplish?" With this type of question, a lot of subsequent discussion will be generated.

The next step is **focusing** the questions on a specific topic under discussion or investigation. Focusing is important because students are easily carried away or sidetracked. For a scientific investigation, the question also needs to focused in such a way as to generate a testable hypothesis.

The last step is **testing** scientific questions and their potential answers (hypotheses). Not all questions can be tested, but many questions can be tested and answers found by research or experimentation – for example, the question "Which fertilizer is best for rose cuttings?" Once research or experimentation has been conducted, hypotheses are either supported or disproved. If the hypothesis is disproved it must be modified.

Skill 16.10   Knows strategies for assisting students in learning to identify, refine, and focus scientific ideas and questions guiding an inquiry-based scientific investigation; to develop, analyze, and evaluate different explanations for a given scientific result; and to identify potential sources of error in an inquiry-based scientific investigation

Some strategies for assisting students in designing effective investigations and evaluating hypotheses are:

- **Brainstorming:** This is very effective when done in a relaxed atmosphere with no pressure on the students. Most students want to contribute and be recognized for their contributions.
- **Induction and deduction:** Induction is drawing conclusions based on facts or observations. Deduction is drawing conclusions based on generalizations.
- **Abstraction:** This very important strategy helps students to recognize and identify patterns and to connect them to their prior knowledge.
- **Questioning:** Allowing students to evaluate relevant questions helps them learn the technique of questioning. Focusing and refining questions are discussed in Skill 16.9. The end result of focused and refined questions is a good understanding of the problem on hand, which in turns produces an effective science investigation.

To identify errors in a science experiment, the student should be encouraged to do the following:

- Check whether all the steps of the scientific method were followed in the correct order.
- Check that the control, constants, independent variables, and dependent variable were correctly identified. Many times the variables and constants may be mixed up.
- Review other sources of error discussed in Skill 3.2 and double-checks each step, such as calibration or measurement errors, transcription errors, calculation errors, and presentation errors.

Skill 16.11 Understands how to implement inquiry strategies designed to promote the use of higher-level thinking skills, logical reasoning, and scientific problem solving in order to move students from concrete to more abstract understanding

Inquiry learning provides opportunities for students to experience and acquire thought processes through which they can gather information about the world. This requires a higher level of interaction among the learner, the teacher, the area of study, available resources, and the learning environment. Students become actively involved in the learning process as they:

1. Act upon their curiosity and interests
2. Develop questions that are relevant
3. Think their way through controversies or dilemmas
4. Analyze problems
5. Develop, clarify, and test hypotheses
6. Draw conclusions
7. Find possible solutions

The most important element in inquiry-based learning is questioning. Students must ask relevant questions and develop ways to search for answers and generate explanations. Higher-order thinking is encouraged.

Here are some **inquiry strategies**:

DEDUCTIVE INQUIRY
The main goal of this strategy is moving the student from a generalized principle to specific instances. The process of testing general assumptions, applying them, and exploring the relationships between specific elements is stressed. The teacher coordinates the information and presents important principles, themes, or hypotheses. Students are actively engaged in testing generalizations, gathering information, and applying it to specific examples.

INDUCTIVE INQUIRY

The information-seeking process of the inductive inquiry method helps students to establish facts, determine relevant questions, and develop ways to pursue these questions and build explanations. Students are encouraged to develop and support their own hypotheses. Through inductive inquiry, students experience the thought processes which require them to move from specific facts and observations to more general inferences.

INTERACTIVE INSTRUCTION

This strategy relies heavily on discussion and sharing among participants. Students develop social skills, learning from teacher and peers. They also learn organizational skills. Examples are debates, brainstorming, discussion, laboratory groups, etc.

DIRECT INSTRUCTION

This is highly teacher-oriented and is among the most commonly used strategies. It is effective for providing information or developing step-by-step skills. Examples are lectures, demonstrations, explicit teaching, etc.

INDIRECT INSTRUCTION

This is mainly student-centered. Direct and indirect instruction strategies can compliment each other. Indirect instruction seeks a high level of student involvement such as observing, investigating, drawing inferences from data, or forming hypotheses. In this strategy, the role of the teacher shifts from that of teacher/lecturer to that of facilitator, supporter, and resource person. Examples are problem solving, inquiry, concept formation, etc.

INDEPENDENT STUDY

Independent study refers to the range of instructional methods which are purposely provided to foster the development of individual student initiative, self reliance, and self improvement. Examples are independent research projects, homework, etc.

The previously mentioned strategies promote higher-level thinking skills such as problem solving, synthesizing (hypothesizing), designing (identifying the problem), analyzing data in an experiment, and connecting (logical thinking).

Skill 16.12 Knows how to guide students in making systematic observations and measurements

The starting point for any science is systematic observation. Systematic observation is observing and recording the occurrence of certain specific (naturally occurring or experimental) behaviors.

There are four descriptive observation methods:

1. Naturalistic observation: observers record occurrence of naturally occurring behavior.
2. Systematic observation: observers record the occurrence of certain specific behaviors.
3. Case study: gather detailed information about one individual.
4. Archival research: use existing information to establish occurrence of behavior.

With each type of approach, there are potential problems and limitations. We discuss here systematic observation.

Systematic observation emphasizes gathering quantitative data on certain specific behaviors. The researcher is interested in a limited set of behaviors. This allows them to study and test specific hypotheses.

The first step is to develop a coding system. The coding system is a description of behaviors and how they will be recorded. The key idea is to delimit the range of behaviors that are observed. The operational definitions of each behavior that will be recorded are defined, and occurrence of each behavior and its duration is recorded.

For example, consider the recording of animal behavior and its comparison to laboratory experiments in chemistry. Potential problems that can occur during the observation include:

1. Remaining vigilant: Following an animal in its natural habitat is difficult, especially when human presence is required. Recording devices (audio, video) are used to deal with this problem. In a laboratory experiment such as titration, a similar difficulty can arise – the titration point can be missed if the observer is not vigilant or uses too large a volume of titrant for each change.

2. Reactivity: Humans and animals often change their behavior when they are being observed. The observer must take steps to remain unobtrusive or become a participant observer. This problem should not be an issue in high school chemistry labs, but is a fundamental feature of the behavior of quantum particles.

3. Reliability: Ensuring that the coding of behavior is accurate (two or more observers are used consistently and their results compared). This is known as inter-rater or inter-observer reliability. In the laboratory, students should be sure of what variables they are measuring, what instruments they should use to perform the measures, and what units will be used to record the data.

4. Sampling: Setting up a schedule of observation intervals, using multiple observations over a range of time. This measures the behavior of an animal over a period of time and is considered to be reliable. Similarly, in physical/chemical systems, random error can be reduced by conducting measurements multiple times and taking the average of the measurements.

It is the responsibility of the teacher to introduce the process of systematic observation to students in a meaningful way. It is also the responsibility of the teacher to instruct students on how to take correct scientific measurements.

Skill 16.13 Knows how to plan learning activities in a way that uncovers common misconceptions, allows students to build upon their prior knowledge, and challenges them to expand their understanding of science

There are many common misconceptions about science. The following are a few scientific misconceptions that are or have been common in the past:

- The Earth is the center of the solar system.
- The Earth is the largest object in the solar system
- Rain comes from the holes in the clouds
- Acquired characteristics of species can be inherited
- The eye receives upright images
- Heat is not energy

Some strategies to uncover and dispel misconceptions include:

1. Planning appropriate activities, so the students can see for themselves where there are misconceptions.

2. Web search is a very useful tool to dispel (or reinforce) misconceptions. Students should be guided in how to look for answers on the Internet and learn to differentiate between "junk" science and useful information. If necessary the teacher should explain scientific literature to help the students understand it.

3. Science journals are a great source of information. Recent research is highly beneficial for the senior science students.

4. Critical thinking and reasoning are two important skills that the students should be encouraged to use to discover facts – for example, that heat is a form of energy. Here, the students have to be challenged to use their critical thinking skills to reason that heat can cause change – for example, causing water to boil – and so it is not a thing but a form of energy, since only energy can cause change.

COMPETENCY 017 **THE TEACHER KNOWS HOW TO MONITOR AND ASSESS SCIENCE LEARNING IN LABORATORY, FIELD, AND CLASSROOM SETTINGS**

Skill 17.1 **Knows how to use formal and informal assessments (e.g., projects, laboratory reports and field journals, rubrics, portfolios, student profiles, checklists) of student performance and products to evaluate student participation in and understanding of inquiry-based scientific investigations**

Assessment is the act of observing an event and making a judgment about its status. The purpose of assessment in teaching is to help the teacher determine how well students are learning and progressing.

There are four main kinds of assessment:

1. **Observation (subjective):** Watching someone or something and judging their actions.

2. **Informal continuous assessment** (less structured -- mostly subjective, some objective): Informal continuous assessment is informal because it is not formal like a test or exam. It is continuous because it occurs regularly, on a daily or weekly basis.

3. **Informal continuous assessment** (more structured -- mostly objective, but some subjective): More structured informal continuous assessment consists of setting up *assessment situations* periodically. An assessment situation is an activity that is organized specifically so that the learners can be assessed. It could be a quiz, for example, or a monitored group activity.

4. **Formal assessment (objective):** A structured, infrequent measure of learner achievement, the use of tests and exams to measure the learner's progress.

Informal assessment can be applied to homework assignments, field journals, or daily classwork, all of which are good indicators of student progress and comprehension.

There are four steps involved in informal continuous assessment:

1. **Observation:** Noticing whether there is a problem (as in homework).

2. **Diagnosis:** Identifying problems observed (e.g., the learner can correctly solve problems from two weeks ago but not from yesterday's homework, indicating a recent problem).

3. **Consolidation:** Helping the learner develop knowledge or skills needed to complete the task. With help from the teacher, the learner completes the task successfully.

4. **Followup assessment:** Continuing to evaluate the learner's work.

Evaluating students' understanding of inquiry-based learning is an informal assessment. This involves a high degree of organizational skills from the teacher. A notebook recording observations, problems, and progress may be maintained, student participation and understanding continuously monitored, and help given as necessary.

Formal assessment, on the other hand, is highly structured. It must be done at regular intervals and if progress is not satisfactory, parental involvement is essential. Tests, exams, and graded science projects are good examples of formal assessment.

Skill 17.2 Connects assessment to instruction in the science curriculum (e.g., designing assessments to match learning objectives, using assessment results to inform instructional practice)

Assessment and instruction are very closely connected because when educators are better informed of the learning progress of their students, they can make better decisions about what a student needs to learn next and how to teach that material in a manner that will maximize the students' learning outcomes.

Educators make three types of decisions using assessment skills:

1. **Instructional placement decisions:** What the student knows and where he or she should be in the instructional sequence, i.e., what to teach next.

2. **Formative evaluation decisions:** Information used to monitor a student's learning while an instructional program is underway, e.g., how quickly progress is being made, whether the instructional program is effective, whether a change in instructional program is needed to promote the learning of the student.

3. **Diagnostic decisions:** Finding out which specific problems are responsible for a student's inadequate progress and designing an instructional plan that is more effective in enhancing the learner's progress.

There are various methods of linking assessment to instruction, including behavioral assessment, mastery learning, and curriculum-based measurement.

BEHAVIORAL ASSESSMENT

This approach is based on observing target behaviors, using repeated observations, e.g., behavior during science activities, following laboratory rules, cooperating, social skills such as sharing equipment, working as a team, etc. This assessment contributes in part to the overall assessment. It is an excellent assessment tool for students of science, which requires many such social skills.

MASTERY LEARNING

The curriculum is broken down into a set of subskills, which are prioritized according to their importance. Each student is assessed according to how well he or she has mastered each subskill. This method has limitations and restricts instructional methods, and is often impractical for obtaining a broader understanding of science.

CURRICULUM-BASED MEASUREMENT (CBM)

This method allows students to know in advance how they will be assessed. Teachers use a variety of techniques and the assessment methods are manageable. In a science class, this approach could be implemented for daily lessons. It is especially useful for evaluating large assignments such as science projects, writing assignments, etc., where the students are given the criteria for assessment beforehand. This helps the students monitor and complete their assignments keeping in mind the assessment criteria. Though this method is traditionally intended for assessments over longer periods of time, it can be successfully applied to lengthier science projects.

PERFORMANCE ASSESSMENT

This is a relatively new but promising method. It incorporates three important elements: students construct responses, assessment allows teachers to observe student behavior on tasks, and scoring reveals patterns in students' learning and thinking.

- Students are encouraged to come up with their own responses, which gives them the freedom to think laterally and critically to analyze a problem and to present a solution.

- Teachers observe student behavior closely, which is very important in a science class, where experiments are sometimes done using chemicals, live animals, etc. In these situations, students need to behave properly since their own safety and that of others are involved. It is important that the students be observed very carefully and any unwanted and inappropriate behavior corrected immediately.

- Scoring reveals patterns in students' learning and thinking. This is similar to formal assessment, where students are tested for their comprehension of concepts and retention of knowledge.

The key element in using assessment methods is not to be restricted by a certain approach. If necessary, teachers should combine more than one method and try new methods as they become available. At the end of the day, what is important is not how students were taught but how much they understood and retained, and this can only be known through assessment.

Skill 17.3 Knows the importance of monitoring and assessing students' understanding of science concepts and skills on an ongoing basis by using a variety of appropriate assessment methods (e.g., performance assessment, self assessment, peer assessment, formal/informal assessment)

Assessment is evaluating student progress. To be fair and effective, assessment has to be continuous and the teacher needs to use a variety of assessment methods to eliminate assessment bias.

Any assessment approach should meet the following seven criteria:

1. Measure important learning outcomes.
2. Address each of the following three purposes:
    - students construct rather than select responses,
    - assessment formats allow teachers to observe student behavior on tasks that are of applied nature, and
    - scoring reveals patterns of student learning and thinking.
3. Provide clear descriptions of student performance that can be linked to instructional actions.
4. Be compatible with a variety of instructional models.
5. Be easily administered and scored by teachers.
6. Communicate the goals of learning to teachers and students.
7. Generate accurate, meaningful (reliable and valid) information.

In addition to **performance assessment** and the various methods of formal and informal assessment discussed in Skill 17.1, teachers may use self assessment and peer assessment methods.

Self and peer assessment are often combined or considered together. Peer assessment is assessment of students by other students. It includes providing feedback and summative grading. Peer assessment is one form of innovative assessment which aims to improve the quality of learning and empower learners, where traditional assessment methods can bypass learners' needs. Peer assessment can be considered part of peer tutoring.

Advantages of self and peer assessment include:

1. Giving students a sense of ownership and thereby motivation and responsibility.
2. Treating assessment as part of learning so mistakes become opportunities rather than failures.
3. Learning evaluation skills.
4. Encouraging deep learning.
5. Using external evaluation as model for internal self assessment of a student's own learning.

Self and peer evaluation provide lifelong learning by helping students evaluate their own and peers' achievements realistically.

Teachers need to be aware of various assessment instruments and use them meaningfully. They should be adventurous and experiment with assessment methods.

Skill 17.4   Understands the purposes and characteristics of and uses various types of assessment in science, including formative and summative assessments, and the importance of limiting the use of an assessment to its intended purpose

"Teaching and learning are reciprocal processes that depend on and affect one another. Thus, the assessment component deals with how well the students are learning and how well the teacher is teaching" (Kellough and Kellough 1999, p. 417)

There are seven purposes of assessment:

1. To assist student learning
2. To identify students' strengths and weaknesses
3. To assess the effectiveness of a particular instructional strategy
4. To assess and improve the effectiveness of curriculum programs
5. To assess and improve teaching effectiveness
6. To provide data that assists in decision making
7. To communicate with and involve parents

Good assessment has the following attributes:

- Good educational values
- Clear and well-defined goals
- Continuous
- Contextualized
- Makes educators responsible to stakeholders
- Involves parents, educators, administration, and students

There are 3 main types of assessment:

1. **Diagnostic assessment:** The purpose of diagnostic assessment is to find out the strengths, weaknesses, knowledge, and skills of students prior to instruction. Diagnostic tests are administered in the first week of the beginning of the academic year.

2. **Formative assessment:** Formative assessment is an approach in which the assessment is an integral part of instruction that informs and guides teachers as they make instructional decisions. Assessment is done for students to guide and enhance their learning. Formative assessment should be done on a regular basis throughout the academic year. In theory, formative tests are not graded but are used solely as an ongoing diagnostic tool; hence the results are primarily used for modifying and adjusting instruction to benefit the students. In a science class, formative assessment could be accomplished through quizzes, daily classwork, or homework.

3. **Summative assessment:** Summative assessment occurs in the form of a test usually given at the end of a semester, term, chapter, or year. High stakes tests like the ACT and SAT are also examples of summative assessments. Though they are helpful to teachers in organizing their methods of teaching and course curricula, summative assessments such as standardized tests can adversely affect students by overly formalizing and limiting the scope of curriculum. However, in the current K-12 system, summative assessment cannot be avoided. A number of suggestions are provided to maximize the effectiveness of summative assessment:

- **Authenticity:** Assessment must be based on classroom objectives and that which has real-world application. For example, the concepts of speed, instantaneous speed, velocity, and acceleration have real-world applications, such as in driving; and the concept of cause and effect relates to the influence of alcohol and drugs on the central nervous system and decision-making capacity.

- **Variety:** A variety of assessment techniques must be used. Assessment should include all three domains of learning – cognitive, affective, and psychomotor. Assessment of the cognitive domain includes Higher Order Thinking Skills (HOTS) such as synthesis, evaluation, analyzing, etc. Using a variety of assessment techniques such as portfolios, cooperative research projects (science projects), papers (research), and performance tests gives a more complete picture of students' strengths and weaknesses and also eliminates assessment bias against at-risk and language minority students.

- **Volume:** The number of assessments should be limited, since students – and teachers – lose interest and lose focus on the real learning objectives. When teachers lose interest it may result in creation of test papers for ease of grading rather than for assessment purposes.

- **Reliability:** Proper rubrics must be established. This guarantees that anyone assessing the test will get the same result.

Skill 17.5   Understands strategies for assessing students' prior knowledge and misconceptions about science and how to use these assessments to develop effective ways to address these misconceptions

Assessments are used to guide programs and to document student development. Science assessments focus on science concepts, processes, and applications. Before planning for instructional options, it is important that teachers plan pre-assessment strategies. It is essential to evaluate student interest, readiness, and learning needs. Formative assessment provides ongoing monitoring of student progress and provides information for targeting subsequent instruction.

Some strategies for pre-assessment within a science classroom include:

1. **Design your own investigation to answer a question:** Students independently plan a well-designed investigation to answer a question. Analysis of the plan will indicate the logical reasoning, critical and creative thinking, and planning ability of the student.

2. **Graphic organizer:** Students independently organize information on a graphic organizer. This strategy helps construct meaning and demonstrate their understanding of science concepts, processes, and applications.

3. **Individual KWL:** Students independently write what they Know, what they Want to know, and what they have Learned about a topic. Analysis of KWL reveals student interests, content knowledge, and misconceptions.

4. **Interview:** Students are asked to explain their understanding of a topic. Probing questions by the teacher help determine students' understanding of science concepts.

5. **Writing assignment:** Students are given a writing assignment that relates to a science topic. The independent response gives evidence of student development regarding processes, concepts, and applications, and their ability to communicate what they know.

TEACHER CERTIFICATION STUDY GUIDE

6. **Teacher observation:** Student performance is assessed through teacher observation of student problem solving, interest, questioning, and content knowledge.

There are many more pre-assessment strategies, and each is useful in its own way for determining students' prior knowledge and misconceptions. Once this information is gathered, strategies for dispelling misconceptions include planning assignments or research addressing the relevant topics.

Skill 17.6   **Understands characteristics of assessments, such as reliability, validity, and the absence of bias in order to evaluate assessment instruments and their results**

The characteristics of a good assessment are:

1. **Reliability:** The key to assessment reliability is the reproducibility of assessment results. A test can be a valid measure to assess the progress of students, but may not be reliable. However, it can be made reliable by designing a well-thought-out rubric and letting the students have copies of it in advance. In this case, even if somebody else grades the paper using the same rubric, the grading would be the same. This method applies mainly to projects and assignments where the students are notified in advance of the grading criteria.

2. **Validity:** The validity of the assessment refers to the extent to which the assessment measures performance on the aspects of the course which are important. That is, the test must clearly reflect the course's objectives. To explain this principle of assessment in the simplest terms, if a student is to be assessed in chemistry, he/she should be given a test in chemistry only.

3. **Absence of bias:** Bias is something that must be avoided by teachers at all cost. For instance, bias against a bilingual student due to his/her relative weakness in English could hamper a fair assessment of the student's content knowledge. Bias of any kind does not help the teacher or student. Assessment bias should be eliminated by using fair methods of assessment, an objective outlook, and an open mind.

4. **Variety:** Another method of ensuring quality assessment is to use a variety of assessment techniques. Traditionally, true/false and selected-response test items have been popular methods of assessing students. However, these are limited in scope and encourage rote memorization by students; in addition, there is a probability factor (i.e., guessing of the answers). Assessment should include all three domains of learning – cognitive, affective, and psychomotor. Assessment in the cognitive domain should include high-order processes such as synthesis and evaluation.

Portfolios, cooperative research projects, papers, and performance tests add to the variety of potential assessment tools.

Variety is not only conducive to fair assessment, it is also more interesting to students. Students will enjoy doing cooperative research projects, investigations, etc. Variety is also effective in reducing assessment bias against at-risk groups, because it provides a more comprehensive picture of student learning.

5. **Volume:** Teachers often require more summative assessments than are necessary. Students tend to resent such over-assessment and that may affect their performance on tests. In addition, over-assessment takes its toll on teachers. Thus assessments should be limited to the minimum required.

6. **Authenticity:** Assessment which addresses the course objectives and has real-life applications is called authentic assessment. In science, a good example of an authentic assessment would be an investigation that requires students to produce rather than select the answer.

Skill 17.7 Understands the role of assessment as a learning experience for students and strategies for engaging students in meaningful self-assessment and peer assessment

Assessment includes a number of things – collecting information, choosing the right assessment instruments, and implementing these in an effective and fair manner. Assessment can be used as a learning experience for the student as well as a tool for the teacher.

A number of strategies may be employed to assess students' progress and teach them simultaneously. These include:

- **Questioning:** Probing questions are very effective in teaching and understanding students' comprehension.
- **Interpreting a graphic:** Students are asked to interpret a graph, photograph, or diagram.
- **Multiple-choice, fill in the blanks, and matching terms with statements:** These are useful, but are very limited and hence should be sparingly used.
- **Essay questions:** These are very useful, as they are good indicators of students' comprehension.
- **Projects and written assignments:** These are very useful since they require higher-order thinking skills.

PEER ASSESSMENT

One way to help students understand their quality of work is by having them evaluate the work of their peers. If they are to offer any helpful feedback to other students, they themselves need to understand evaluation first. It falls to the teacher to explain expectations in very clear terms. The teacher can give students a practice assessment session. Rubrics and well designed checklists are very helpful.

For peer assessment to work effectively, the learning environment must be conducive for that. Students must be able to trust each other and feel comfortable. The teacher may need to coach the students on effective ways to present assessments and constructive criticism.

Any assessment method has wider effects than simple measurement. It can support the achievement of the planned learning outcomes or undermine them. Peer assessment in this sense is authentic: conducting peer assessments involves using discipline, knowledge, and skills, while accepting peer assessments engages others' knowledge and skills.

The use of peer assessment encourages students to believe they are part of a community of scholarship. In peer assessment, we encourage students to take part in a key aspect of education, making critical judgments regarding the work of others.

Students are a classroom resource that is not always fully utilized. Peer assessment offers possible gains in cost-effectiveness, since teachers can be managing peer assessment processes rather than assessing large numbers of students. This helps teachers to assess quality rather than quantity, since the bulk of assessment is entrusted to students.

One possible problem is the validity and reliability of peer assessment. In the case of formative assessment (peer review), the validity of peer assessment can be questioned. Another possible problem is the accuracy of grades given by peers. These problems can be handled by using double anonymity, wherein students feel free to express their opinions fearlessly and honestly. In addition, the teacher should provide students with clear measurement indicators and grading instructions.

SELF ASSESSMENT

There are three key elements involved in successful self assessment: goal setting, guided practice with assessment tools, and portfolios.

1) Goal setting: Goal setting is essential because students can evaluate their progress more clearly when they have targets against which to measure their performance. In addition, a student's motivation to learn increases when he or she has self-defined and relevant learning goals.

2) Guided practice with assessment tools: Students should be taught strategies for self monitoring and self assessment. Well-designed checklists and rubrics are used for the purpose of assessment, and practice should be given prior to beginning use of the tools.

3) Portfolios: These are powerful, organized, systematic collections of student work that tell the story of a student's effort. Portfolio assessment emphasizes evaluation of students' progress, processes, and performance over time. There are two types of portfolios: a **process portfolio** serves the purpose of a classroom-level assessment; a **product portfolio** is more summative in nature. Often, an oral presentation accompanies a product portfolio.

Reflection is the key word in self assessment. Students must be able to step back and reflect upon their learning and come up with strategies to learn more effectively. Such self assessment can help students become independent, motivated learners for life.

Skill 17.8 Recognizes the importance of selecting assessment instruments and methods that provide all students with adequate opportunities to demonstrate their achievements

The importance of assessment is to know how much the students have comprehended, retained, and applied the knowledge they acquired during their time in the class. In order to assess these aspects, the teacher must use appropriate and reliable assessment instruments and methods.

There are a number of **assessment instruments** available for teachers. Assessment instruments are of two main types:

1. **Content-oriented:** These are specifically oriented to the assessment of student mastery in a particular discipline such as chemistry. Concept tests, challenge problems, lab reports, and other projects such as writing assignments are found in this category.

2. **Process-oriented:** These are oriented towards assessing the process by which the students learned. These include classroom surveys, interview protocols, etc.

Assessment methods in use by the educator community include quizzes and tests, regular homework assignments, 3D models, short assignments, classwork, etc. These assessment instruments and methods provide a variety of opportunities for students to show their comprehension and mastery of a subject.

The advantage of using a variety of assessment instruments and methods is that assessment bias is minimized and all students have a fair chance of being assessed properly.

Skill 17.9 **Recognizes the importance of clarifying teacher expectations and student achievement by sharing evaluation criteria and assessment results with students and other appropriate educational stakeholders**

Evaluation is a process that must be done openly and in fair manner. Teachers should communicate their methods of evaluation at the beginning of the school year, preferably on the first day at school. The teacher needs to recognize the value and importance of communicating the evaluation criteria to the students and other stakeholders, such as parents.

Teacher expectations are to be clarified and communicated. A good way of doing this is to give out an information packet outlining all the aspects of evaluation that will be used along with the evaluation criteria.

Evaluation criteria may include:

1. **Comprehension:** Students' understanding of the material.
2. **Processing information:** How students process information by finding patterns, etc.
3. **Critical thinking and problem solving:** Students' ability to think critically, evaluate a given situation, and find ways to answer the problem at hand.
4. **Communication skills:** The ability to communication through both written and oral communication.

Effective and prompt communication of evaluation results is essential. Results should first be communicated to the students, then to parents in the form of reports and report cards, and finally to educational stakeholders such as administrators.

SAMPLE TEST

Directions: Read each item and select the best response.

1. A piston compresses a gas at constant temperature. Which gas properties increase?

   I. Average speed of molecules
   II. Pressure
   III. Molecular collisions with container walls per second

   A. I and II
   B. I and III
   C. II and III
   D. I, II, and III

2. The temperature of a liquid is raised at atmospheric pressure. Which property of liquids increases?

   A. Critical pressure
   B. Vapor pressure
   C. Surface tension
   D. Viscosity

3. Potassium crystallizes with two atoms contained in each unit cell. What is the mass of potassium found in a lattice 1.00×10^6 unit cells wide, 2.00×10^6 unit cells high, and 5.00×10^5 unit cells deep?

   A. 85.0 ng
   B. 32.5 µg
   C. 64.9 µg
   D. 130. µg

4. A gas is heated in a sealed container. Which of the following occur(s)?

   A. Gas pressure rises
   B. Gas density decreases
   C. The average distance between molecules increases
   D. All of the above

5. How many molecules are in 2.20 pg of a protein with a molecular weight of 150 kDa?

   A. 8.83×10^9
   B. 1.82×10^9
   C. 8.83×10^6
   D. 1.82×10^6

6. At STP, 20. µL of O_2 contain 5.4×10^{16} molecules. According to Avogadro's hypothesis, how many molecules are in 20 µL of Ne?

   A. 5.4×10^{15}
   B. 1.0×10^{16}
   C. 2.7×10^{16}
   D. 5.4×10^{16}

7. An ideal gas at 50.0° C and 3.00 atm is in a 300 cm³ cylinder. The cylinder volume changes by moving a piston until the gas is at 50.0° C and 1.00 atm. What is the final volume?

   A. 100. cm³
   B. 450. cm³
   C. 900. cm³
   D. 1.20 dm³

8. Which gas law may be used to solve the previous problem?

   A. Charles' law
   B. Boyle's law
   C. Graham's law
   D. Avogadro's law

9. One mole of an ideal gas at STP occupies 22.4 L. At what temperature will one mole of an ideal gas at 1 atm occupy 31.0 L?

   A. 34.6° C
   B. 105° C
   C. 378° C
   D. 442° C

10. Why does $CaCl_2$ have a higher normal melting point than NH_3?

    A. Covalent bonds are stronger than London dispersion forces.
    B. Covalent bonds are stronger than hydrogen bonds.
    C. Ionic bonds are stronger than London dispersion forces.
    D. Ionic bonds are stronger than hydrogen bonds.

11. Which intermolecular attraction explains the following trend in straight-chain alkanes?

Condensed structural formula	Boiling point (° C)
CH_4	-161.5
CH_3CH_3	-88.6
$CH_3CH_2CH_3$	-42.1
$CH_3CH_2CH_2CH_3$	-0.5
$CH_3CH_2CH_2CH_2CH_3$	36.0
$CH_3CH_2CH_2CH_2CH_2CH_3$	68.7

    A. London dispersion forces
    B. Dipole-dipole interactions
    C. Hydrogen bonding
    D. Ion-induced dipole interactions

12. List the substances NH_3, PH_3, $MgCl_2$, Ne, and N_2 in order of increasing melting point.

    A. N_2 < Ne < PH_3 < NH_3 < $MgCl_2$
    B. N_2 < NH_3 < Ne < $MgCl_2$ < PH_3
    C. Ne < N_2 < NH_3 < PH_3 < $MgCl_2$
    D. Ne < N_2 < PH_3 < NH_3 < $MgCl_2$

13. 1-butanol, ethanol, methanol, and 1-propanol are all liquids at room temperature. Rank them in order of increasing viscosity.

    A. 1-butanol < 1-propanol < ethanol < methanol
    B. methanol < ethanol < 1-propanol < 1-butanol
    C. methanol < ethanol < 1-butanol < 1-propanol
    D. 1-propanol < 1-butanol < ethanol < methanol

14. Which gas has a diffusion rate of 25% the rate for hydrogen?

    A. Helium
    B. Methane
    C. Nitrogen
    D. Oxygen

15. Which substance is most likely to be a gas at room temperature?

    A. SeO_2
    B. F_2
    C. $CaCl_2$
    D. I_2

16. What pressure is exerted by a mixture of 2.7 g of H_2 and 59 g of Xe at STP on a 50. L container?

    A. 0.69 atm
    B. 0.76 atm
    C. 0.80 atm
    D. 0.97 atm

17. A few minutes after opening a bottle of perfume, the scent is detected on the other side of the room. What law relates to this phenomenon?

    A. Graham's law
    B. Dalton's law
    C. Boyle's law
    D. Avogadro's law

18. Find the partial pressure of N_2 in a container at 150. kPa holding H_2O and N_2 at 50° C. The vapor pressure of H_2O at 50° C is 12 kPa.

    A. 12 kPa
    B. 138 kPa
    C. 162 kPa
    D. The value cannot be determined.

19. The normal boiling point of water on the Kelvin scale is closest to:

    A. 112 K
    B. 212 K
    C. 273 K
    D. 373 K

20. Which phases may be present at the triple point of a substance?

    I. Gas
    II. Liquid
    III. Solid
    IV. Supercritical fluid

    A. I, II, and III
    B. I, II, and IV
    C. II, III, and IV
    D. I, II, III, and IV

21. In the following phase diagram, _____ occurs as P is decreased from A to B at constant T and _____ occurs as T is increased from C to D at constant P.

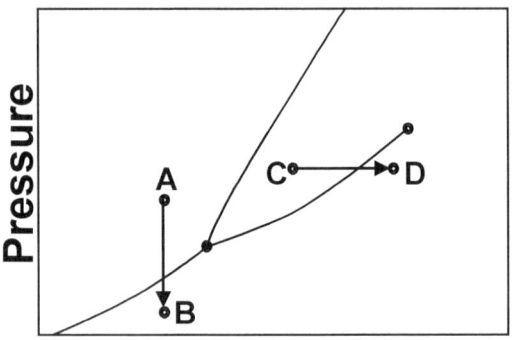

Temperature (T)

A. deposition, melting
B. sublimation, melting
C. deposition, vaporization
D. sublimation, vaporization

22. Heat is added to a pure solid at its melting point until it all becomes liquid at its freezing point. Which of the following occur(s)?

A. Intermolecular attractions are weakened.
B. The kinetic energy of the molecules does not change.
C. The freedom of the molecules to move about increases.
D. All of the above.

23. Which of the following occurs when NaCl dissolves in water?

A. Heat is required to break bonds in the NaCl crystal lattice.
B. Heat is released when hydrogen bonds in water are broken.
C. Heat is required to form bonds of hydration.
D. The oxygen end of the water molecule is attracted to the Cl⁻ ion.

24. The solubility of $CoCl_2$ is 54 g per 100 g of ethanol. Three flasks each contain 100 g of ethanol. Flask #1 also contains 40 g $CoCl_2$ in solution. Flask #2 contains 56 g $CoCl_2$ in solution. Flask #3 contains 5 g of solid $CoCl_2$ in equilibrium with 54 g $CoCl_2$ in solution. Which of the following describes the solutions present in the liquid phase of the flasks?

A. #1 - saturated, #2 - supersaturated, #3 - unsaturated.
B. #1 - unsaturated, #2 - miscible, #3 - saturated.
C. #1 - unsaturated, #2 - supersaturated, #3 - saturated.
D. #1 - unsaturated, #2 - not at equilibrium, #3 - miscible.

25. The solubility at 1.0 atm of pure CO_2 in water at 25° C is 0.034 M. According to Henry's law, what is the solubility at 4.0 atm of pure CO_2 in water at 25° C? Assume no chemical reaction occurs between CO_2 and H_2O.

   A. 0.0085 M
   B. 0.034 M
   C. 0.14 M
   D. 0.25 M

26. Carbonated water is bottled at 25° C under pure CO_2 at 4.0 atm. Later the bottle is opened at 4° C under air at 1.0 atm that has a partial pressure of 3×10^{-4} atm CO_2. Why do CO_2 bubbles form when the bottle is opened?

   A. CO_2 falls out of solution due to a drop in solubility at the lower total pressure.
   B. CO_2 falls out of solution due to a drop in solubility at the lower CO_2 pressure.
   C. CO_2 falls out of solution due to a drop in solubility at the lower temperature.
   D. CO_2 is formed by the decomposition of carbonic acid.

27. When KNO_3 dissolves in water, the water grows slightly colder. An increase in temperature will _____ the solubility of KNO_3.

   A. increase
   B. decrease
   C. have no effect on
   D. have an unknown effect with the information given on

28. An experiment requires 100. mL of a 0.500 M solution of $MgBr_2$. How many grams of $MgBr_2$ will be present in this solution?

   A. 9.21 g
   B. 11.7 g
   C. 12.4 g
   D. 15.6 g

29. 500. mg of RbOH are added to 500. g of ethanol (C_2H_6O) resulting in 395 mL of solution. Determine the molarity and molality of RbOH.

   A. 0.0124 M, 0.00488 m
   B. 0.0124 M, 0.00976 m
   C. 0.0223 M, 0.00488 m
   D. 0.0223 M, 0.00976 m

30. Which of the following would make the best solvent for Br_2?

   A. H_2O
   B. CS_2
   C. NH_3
   D. Molten NaCl

31. Which of the following is most likely to dissolve in water?

   A. H_2
   B. CCl_4
   C. SF_6
   D. CH_3OH

32. Which of the following is not a colligative property?

   A. Viscosity lowering
   B. Freezing point lowering
   C. Boiling point elevation
   D. Vapor pressure lowering

33. List the following aqueous solutions in order of increasing boiling point.

   I. 0.050 m AlCl$_3$
   II. 0.080 m Ba(NO$_3$)$_2$
   III. 0.090 m NaCl
   IV. 0.12 m ethylene glycol (C$_2$H$_6$O$_2$)

   A. I < II < III < IV
   B. I < III < IV < II
   C. IV < III < I < II
   D. IV < III < II < I

34. Osmotic pressure is the pressure required to prevent _____ from flowing from low to high _____ concentration across a semipermeable membrane.

   A. solute, solute
   B. solute, solvent
   C. solvent, solute
   D. solvent, solvent

35. A solution of NaCl in water is heated on a mountain in an open container until it boils at 100° C. The air pressure on the mountain is 0.92 atm. According to Raoult's law, what mole fraction of Na$^+$ and Cl$^-$ are present in the solution?

   A. 0.04 Na$^+$, 0.04 Cl$^-$
   B. 0.08 Na$^+$, 0.08 Cl$^-$
   C. 0.46 Na$^+$, 0.46 Cl$^-$
   D. 0.92 Na$^+$, 0.92 Cl$^-$

36. Write a balanced nuclear equation for the emission of an alpha particle by polonium-209.

   A. $^{209}_{84}Po \rightarrow {}^{205}_{81}Pb + {}^{4}_{2}He$
   B. $^{209}_{84}Po \rightarrow {}^{205}_{82}Bi + {}^{4}_{2}He$
   C. $^{209}_{84}Po \rightarrow {}^{209}_{85}At + {}^{0}_{-1}e$
   D. $^{209}_{84}Po \rightarrow {}^{205}_{82}Pb + {}^{4}_{2}He$

37. Write a balanced nuclear equation for the decay of calcium-45 to scandium-45.

   A. $^{45}_{20}Ca \rightarrow {}^{41}_{18}Sc + {}^{4}_{2}He$
   B. $^{45}_{20}Ca + {}^{0}_{1}e \rightarrow {}^{45}_{21}Sc$
   C. $^{45}_{20}Ca \rightarrow {}^{45}_{21}Sc + {}^{0}_{-1}e$
   D. $^{45}_{20}Ca + {}^{0}_{1}p \rightarrow {}^{45}_{21}Sc$

38. $^{3}_{1}H$ decays with a half-life of 12 years. 3.0 g of pure $^{3}_{1}H$ were placed in a sealed container 24 years ago. How many grams of $^{3}_{1}H$ remain?

   A. 0.38 g
   B. 0.75 g
   C. 1.5 g
   D. 3.0 g

39. Which of the following isotopes is commonly used for medical imaging in the diagnosis of diseases?

   A. cobalt-60
   B. technetium-99m
   C. tin-117m
   D. plutonium-238

40. List the following scientists in chronological order from earliest to most recent with respect to their most significant contribution to atomic theory:

   I. John Dalton
   II. Niels Bohr
   III. J. J. Thomson
   IV. Ernest Rutherford

   A. I, III, II, IV
   B. I, III, IV, II
   C. I, IV, III, II
   D. III, I, II, IV

41. Match the theory with the scientist who first proposed it:

   I. Electrons, atoms, and all objects with momentum also exist as waves.
   II. Electron density may be accurately described by a single mathematical equation.
   III. There is an inherent indeterminacy in the position and momentum of particles.
   IV. Radiant energy is transferred between particles in exact multiples of a discrete unit.

   A. I - de Broglie, II - Planck, III - Schrödinger, IV - Thomson
   B. I - Dalton, II - Bohr, III - Planck, IV - de Broglie
   C. I - Henry, II - Bohr, III - Heisenberg, IV - Schrödinger
   D. I - de Broglie, II - Schrödinger, III - Heisenberg, IV - Planck

42. How many neutrons are there in $_{27}^{60}Co$?

   A. 27
   B. 33
   C. 60
   D. 87

43. The terrestrial composition of an element is: 50.7% as a stable isotope with an atomic mass of 78.9 u and 49.3% as a stable isotope with an atomic mass of 80.9 u. Calculate the atomic mass of the element.

   A. 79.0 u
   B. 79.8 u
   C. 79.9 u
   D. 80.8 u

44. Which of the following is a correct electron arrangement for oxygen?

   A.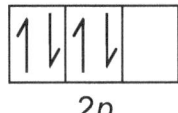
      1s   2s   2p
   B. $1s^2 1p^2 2s^2 2p^2$
   C. 2, 2, 4
   D. None of the above

45. Which of the following statements about radiant energy is **not** true?

    A. The energy change of an electron transition is directly proportional to the wavelength of the emitted or absorbed photon.
    B. The energy of an electron in a hydrogen atom depends only on the principle quantum number.
    C. The frequency of photons striking a metal determines whether the photoelectric effect will occur.
    D. The frequency of a wave of electromagnetic radiation is inversely proportional to its wavelength.

46. Match the orbital diagram for the ground state of carbon with the rule/principle it violates:

    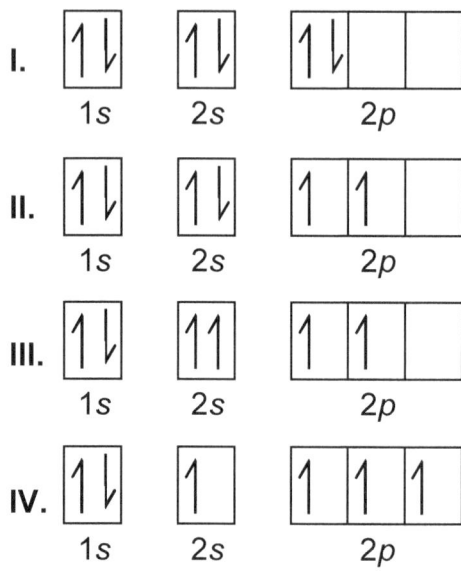

    A. I - Pauli exclusion, II - Aufbau, III - no violation, IV - Hund's
    B. I - Aufbau, II - Pauli exclusion, III - no violation, IV - Hund's
    C. I - Hund's, II - no violation, III - Pauli exclusion, IV - Aufbau
    D. I - Hund's, II - no violation, III - Aufbau, IV - Pauli exclusion

47. Select the list of atoms that is arranged in order of increasing size.

    A. Mg, Na, Si, Cl
    B. Si, Cl, Mg, Na
    C. Cl, Si, Mg, Na
    D. Na, Mg, Si, Cl

48. Based on trends in the periodic table, which of the following properties would you expect to be greater for Rb than for K?

    I. Density
    II. Melting point
    III. Ionization energy
    IV. Oxidation number in a compound with chlorine

    A. I only
    B. I, II, and III
    C. II and III
    D. I, II, III, and IV

49. Rank the following bonds from least to most polar:

    C-H, C-Cl, H-H, C-F

    A. C-H < H-H < C-F < C-Cl
    B. H-H < C-H < C-F < C-Cl
    C. C-F < C-Cl < C-H < H-H
    D. H-H < C-H < C-Cl < C-F

50. At room temperature, $CaBr_2$ is expected to be:

    A. a ductile solid
    B. a brittle solid
    C. a soft solid
    D. a gas

51. Which of the following is a proper Lewis dot structure of CHClO?

    A. [Lewis structure]
    B. [Lewis structure]
    C. [Lewis structure]
    D. [Lewis structure]

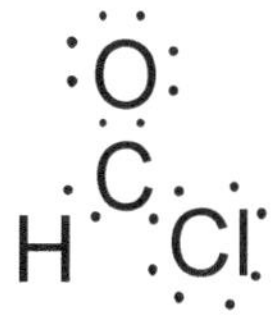

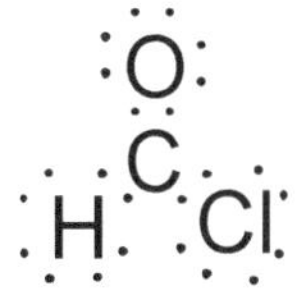

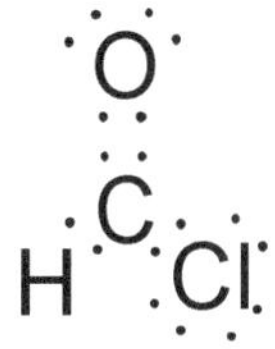

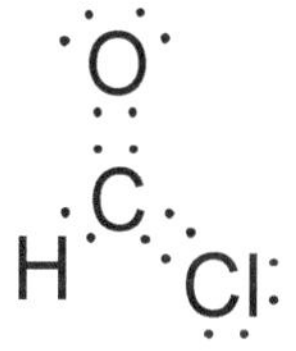

52. In C_2H_2, each carbon atom contains the following valence orbitals:

    A. p only
    B. p and sp hybrids
    C. p and sp^2 hybrids
    D. sp^3 hybrids only

53. Which statement about molecular structures is false?

A. 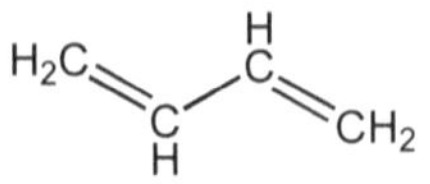 H₂C=CH−CH=CH₂ is a conjugated molecule.
B. A bonding σ orbital connects two atoms by the straight line between them.
C. A bonding π orbital connects two atoms in a separate region from the straight line between them.
D. The anion with resonance forms

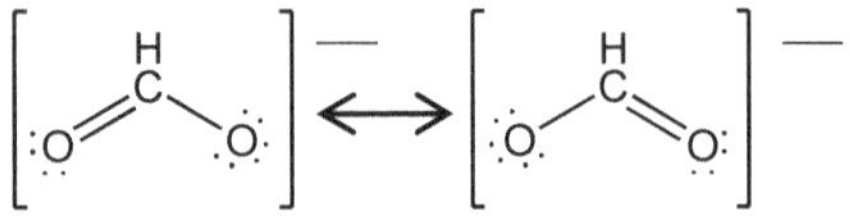

[formate resonance structures shown]

will always exist in one form or the other.

54. What is the chemical composition of magnesium nitrate?

A. 11.1% Mg, 22.2% N, 66.7% O
B. 16.4% Mg, 18.9% N, 64.7% O
C. 20.9% Mg, 24.1% N, 55.0% O
D. 28.2% Mg, 16.2% N, 55.7% O

55. The IUPAC name for Cu₂SO₃ is:

A. Dicopper sulfur trioxide
B. Copper (II) sulfate
C. Copper (I) sulfite
D. Copper (II) sulfite

56. Household "chlorine bleach" is sodium hypochlorite. Which of the following best represents the production of sodium hypochlorite, sodium chloride, and water by bubbling chlorine gas through aqueous sodium hydroxide?

A. $4Cl(g) + 4NaOH(aq) \rightarrow NaClO_2(aq) + 3NaCl(aq) + 2H_2O(l)$

B. $2Cl_2(g) + 4NaOH(aq) \rightarrow NaClO_2(aq) + 3NaCl(aq) + 2H_2O(l)$

C. $2Cl(g) + 2NaOH(aq) \rightarrow NaClO(aq) + NaCl(aq) + H_2O(l)$

D. $Cl_2(g) + 2NaOH(aq) \rightarrow NaClO(aq) + NaCl(aq) + H_2O(l)$

57. Balance the equation for the neutralization reaction between phosphoric acid and calcium hydroxide by filling in the blank stoichiometric coefficients.

___H_3PO_4 + ___$Ca(OH)_2$ →

___$Ca_3(PO_4)_2$ + ___H_2O

A. 4, 3, 1, 4
B. 2, 3, 1, 8
C. 2, 3, 1, 6
D. 2, 1, 1, 2

58. Write an equation showing the reaction between calcium nitrate and lithium sulfate in aqueous solution. Include all products.

A. $CaNO_3(aq) + Li_2SO_4(aq) \rightarrow CaSO_4(s) + Li_2NO_3(aq)$

B. $Ca(NO_3)_2(aq) + Li_2SO_4(aq) \rightarrow CaSO_4(s) + 2LiNO_3(aq)$

C. $Ca(NO_3)_2(aq) + Li_2SO_4(aq) \rightarrow 2LiNO_3(s) + CaSO_4(aq)$

D. $Ca(NO_3)_2(aq) + Li_2SO_4(aq) + 2H_2O(l) \rightarrow 2LiNO_3(aq) + Ca(OH)_2(aq) + H_2SO_4(aq)$

59. Find the mass of CO_2 produced by the combustion of 15 kg of isopropyl alcohol in the reaction:

$$2C_3H_7OH + 9O_2 \rightarrow 6CO_2 + 8H_2O$$

A. 33 kg
B. 44 kg
C. 50 kg
D. 60 kg

60. What is the density of nitrogen gas at STP? Assume an ideal gas and a value of 0.08206 L·atm/(mol·K) for the gas constant.

A. 0.62 g/L
B. 1.14 g/L
C. 1.25 g/L
D. 2.03 g/L

61. Find the volume of methane that will produce 12 m³ of hydrogen in the reaction:

$$CH_4(g) + H_2O(g) \rightarrow CO(g) + 3H_2(g)$$

Assume temperature and pressure remain constant.

A. 4.0 m³
B. 32 m³
C. 36 m³
D. 64 m³

62. A 100. L vessel of pure O_2 at 500. kPa and 20.° C is used for the combustion of butane:

$$2C_4H_{10} + 13O_2 \rightarrow 8CO_2 + 10H_2O$$

Find the mass of butane that consumes all the O_2 in the vessel. Assume O_2 is an ideal gas and use a value of R = 8.314 J/(mol•K).

A. 183 g
B. 467 g
C. 1.83 kg
D. 7.75 kg

63. Consider the reaction between iron and hydrogen chloride gas:

$$Fe(s) + 2HCl(g) \rightarrow FeCl_2(s) + H_2(g)$$

7 moles of iron and 10 moles of HCl react until the limiting reagent is consumed. Which statements are true?

I. HCl is the excess reagent
II. HCl is the limiting reagent
III. 7 moles of H_2 are produced
IV. 2 moles of the excess reagent remain

A. I and III
B. I and IV
C. II and III
D. II and IV

64. 32.0 g of hydrogen and 32.0 grams of oxygen react to form water until the limiting reagent is consumed. What is present in the vessel after the reaction is complete?

A. 16.0 g O_2 and 48.0 g H_2O
B. 24.0 g H_2 and 40.0 g H_2O
C. 28.0 g H_2 and 36.0 g H_2O
D. 28.0 g H_2 and 34.0 g H_2O

65. The reaction:

$$(CH_3)_3CBr(aq) + OH^-(aq) \rightarrow (CH_3)_3COH(aq) + Br^-(aq)$$

occurs in three elementary steps:

$(CH_3)_3CBr \rightarrow (CH_3)_3C^+ + Br^-$ is slow

$(CH_3)_3C^+ + H_2O \rightarrow (CH_3)_3COH_2^+$ is fast

$(CH_3)_3COH_2^+ + OH^- \rightarrow (CH_3)_3COH + H_2O$ is fast

What is the rate law for this reaction?

A. Rate = $k\left[(CH_3)_3CBr\right]$
B. Rate = $k\left[OH^-\right]$
C. Rate = $k\left[(CH_3)_3CBr\right]\left[OH^-\right]$
D. Rate = $k\left[(CH_3)_3CBr\right]^2$

66. Which statements about reaction rates are true?

   I. Catalysts shift an equilibrium to favor product formation.
   II. Catalysts increase the rate of forward and reverse reactions.
   III. A greater temperature increases the chance that a molecular collision will overcome a reaction's activation energy.
   IV. A catalytic converter contains a homogeneous catalyst.

   A. I and II
   B. II and III
   C. II, III, and IV
   D. I, III, and IV

67. Write the equilibrium expression K_{eq} for the reaction:

   $CO_2\ (g) + H_2\ (g) \leftrightarrow CO\ (g) + H_2O\ (l)$

   A. $\dfrac{[CO][H_2O]}{[CO_2][H_2]^2}$

   B. $\dfrac{[CO_2][H_2]}{[CO][H_2O]}$

   C. $\dfrac{[CO][H_2O]}{[CO_2][H_2]}$

   D. $\dfrac{[CO]}{[CO_2][H_2]}$

68. What could cause this change in the energy diagram of a reaction?

   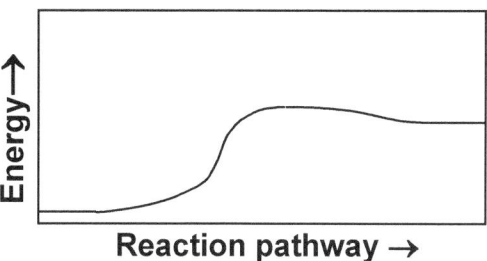
   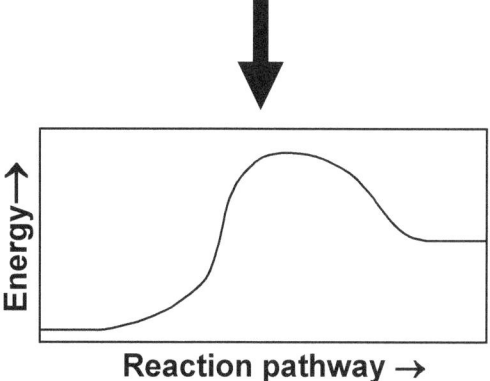

   A. Adding a catalyst to an endothermic reaction
   B. Removing a catalyst from an endothermic reaction
   C. Adding a catalyst to an exothermic reaction
   D. Removing a catalyst from an exothermic reaction

69. $BaSO_4$ ($K_{sp} = 1 \times 10^{-10}$) is added to pure H_2O. How much is dissolved in 1 L of saturated solution?

   A. 2 mg
   B. 10 μg
   C. 2 μg
   D. 100 pg

70. The exothermic reaction
2NO (g) + Br$_2$ (g) ↔ 2NOBr (g)
is at equilibrium. According to
Le Chatelier's principle:

A. Adding Br$_2$ will increase [NO].
B. An increase in container volume (with T constant) will increase [NOBr].
C. An increase in pressure (with T constant) will increase [NOBr].
D. An increase in temperature (with P constant) will increase [NOBr].

71. At a certain temperature, T, the equilibrium constant for the reaction 2NO (g) ↔ N$_2$ (g) + O$_2$ (g) is $K_{eq} = 2 \times 10^3$. If a 1.0 L container at this temperature contains 90 mM N$_2$, 20 mM O$_2$, and 5 mM NO, what will occur?

A. The reaction will make more N$_2$ and O$_2$.
B. The reaction is at equilibrium.
C. The reaction will make more NO.
D. The temperature, T, is required to solve this problem.

72. Which statement about acids and bases is *not* true?

A. All strong acids ionize in water.
B. All Lewis acids accept an electron pair.
C. All Brønsted bases use OH⁻ as a proton acceptor
D. All Arrhenius acids form H⁺ ions in water.

73. NH$_4$F is dissolved in water. Which of the following are conjugate acid/base pairs present in the solution?

I. NH$_4$⁺/NH$_4$OH
II. HF/F⁻
III. H$_3$O⁺/H$_2$O
IV. H$_2$O/OH⁻

A. I, II, and III
B. I, III, and IV
C. II and IV
D. II, III, and IV

74. What are the pH and the pOH of 0.010 M HNO$_3$ (aq)?

A. pH = 1.0, pOH = 9.0
B. pH = 2.0, pOH = 12.0
C. pH = 2.0, pOH = 8.0
D. pH = 8.0, pOH = 6.0

75. What is the pH of a buffer solution made of 0.128 M sodium formate (HCOONa) and 0.072 M formic acid (HCOOH)? The pK_a of formic acid is 3.75.

A. 2.0
B. 3.0
C. 4.0
D. 5.0

76. A sample of 50.0 ml KOH is titrated with 0.100 M HClO$_4$. The initial buret reading is 1.6 ml and the reading at the endpoint is 22.4 ml. What is [KOH]?

A. 0.0416 M
B. 0.0481 M
C. 0.0832 M
D. 0.0962 mM

CHEMISTRY 7-12

77. Rank the following from lowest to highest pH. Assume a small volume for the component given in moles:

   I. 0.01 mol HCl added to 1 L H_2O
   II. 0.01 mol HI added to 1 L of an acetic acid/sodium acetate solution at pH 4.0
   III. 0.01 mol NH_3 added to 1 L H_2O
   IV. 0.1 mol HNO_3 added to 1 L of a 0.1 M $Ca(OH)_2$ solution

   A. I < II < III < IV
   B. I < II < IV < III
   C. II < I < III < IV
   D. II < I < IV < III

78. Which statement about thermochemistry is true?

   A. Particles in a system move about less freely at high entropy.
   B. Water at 100° C has the same internal energy as water vapor at 100° C.
   C. A decrease in the order of a system corresponds to an increase in entropy.
   D. At its sublimation temperature, dry ice has higher entropy than gaseous CO_2.

79. What is the standard heat of combustion of CH_4 (g)? Use the following data:

Standard heats of formation	
CH_4 (g)	−74.8 kJ/mol
CO_2 (g)	−393.5 kJ/mol
H_2O (l)	−285.8 kJ/mol

   A. −890.3 kJ/mol
   B. −604.6 kJ/mol
   C. −252.9 kJ/mol
   D. −182.5 kJ/mol

80. Which statement about reactions is true?

   A. All spontaneous reactions are exothermic and cause an increase in entropy.
   B. An endothermic reaction that increases the order of the system cannot be spontaneous.
   C. A reaction can be non-spontaneous in one direction and also non-spontaneous in the opposite direction.
   D. Melting snow is an exothermic process.

81. 10. kJ of heat are added to one kilogram of iron at 10.° C. What is its final temperature? The specific heat of iron is 0.45 J/g·° C.

   A. 22° C
   B. 27° C
   C. 32° C
   D. 37° C

82. Which reaction is not a redox process?

   A. Combustion of octane:
   $2C_8H_{18} + 25O_2 \rightarrow 16CO_2 + 18H_2O$

   B. Depletion of a lithium battery:
   $Li + MnO_2 \rightarrow LiMnO_2$

   C. Corrosion of aluminum by acid:
   $2Al + 6HCl \rightarrow 2AlCl_3 + 3H_2$

   D. Taking an antacid for heartburn:
   $CaCO_3 + 2HCl \rightarrow CaCl_2 + H_2CO_3$
   $\rightarrow CaCl_2 + CO_2 + H_2O$

83. Given the following heats of reaction:

   $\Delta H = -0.3$ kJ / mol for
   $Fe(s) + CO_2(g) \rightarrow FeO(s) + CO(g)$

   $\Delta H = 5.7$ kJ / mol for
   $2Fe(s) + 3CO_2(g) \rightarrow Fe_2O_3(s) + 3CO(g)$

   and $\Delta H = 4.5$ kJ / mol for
   $3FeO(s) + CO_2(g) \rightarrow Fe_3O_4(s) + CO(g)$

   use Hess' Law to determine the heat of reaction for:

   $3Fe_2O_3(s) + CO(g) \rightarrow 2Fe_3O_4(s) + CO_2(g)$

   A. −10.8 kJ/mol
   B. −9.9 kJ/mol
   C. −9.0 kJ/mol
   D. −8.1 kJ/mol

84. Given:

   $E° = -2.37$V for
   $Mg^{2+} (aq) + 2e^- \rightarrow Mg (s)$
   and
   $E° = 0.80$ V for
   $Ag^+ (aq) + e^- \rightarrow Ag (s)$

   what is the standard potential of a voltaic cell composed of a piece of magnesium dipped in a 1 M Ag^+ solution and a piece of silver dipped in 1 M Mg^{2+}?

   A. 0.77 V
   B. 1.57 V
   C. 3.17 V
   D. 3.97 V

85.

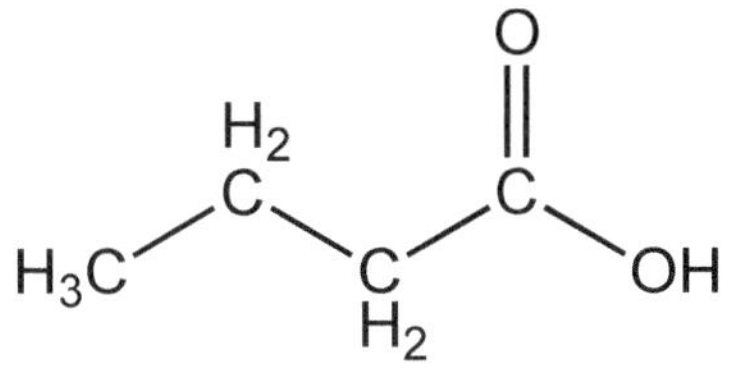

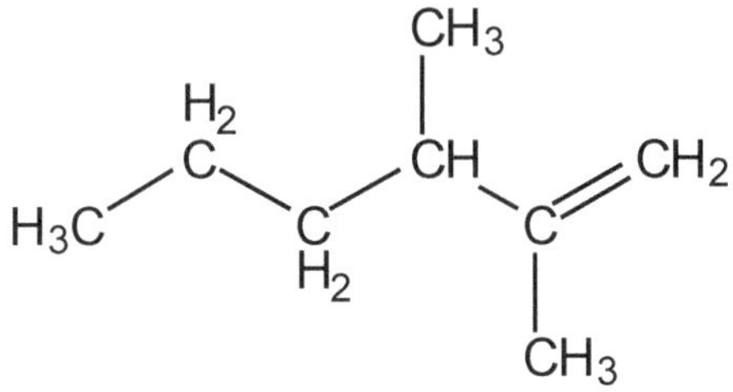

[Structure: CH3-CH2-CH(CH3)-C(CH3)=CH2 type hydrocarbon shown]

A proper name for this hydrocarbon is:

A. 4,5-dimethyl-6-hexene
B. 2,3-dimethyl-1-hexene
C. 4,5-dimethyl-6-hexyne
D. 2-methyl-3-propyl-1-butene

86. An IUPAC approved name for this molecule is:

A. butanal
B. propanal
C. butanoic acid
D. propanoic acid

87. Which molecule has a systematic name of methyl ethanoate?

A. H3C-C(=O)-O-CH3

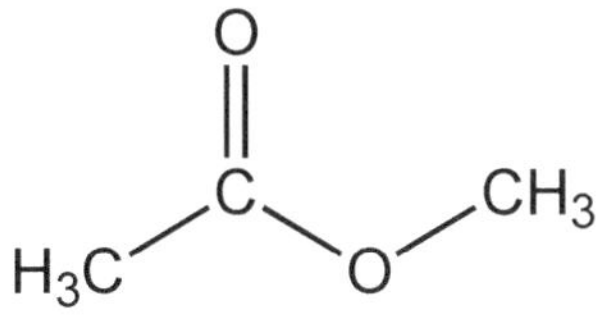

B. HC(=O)-O-CH2-CH3

C. H3C-C(=O)-CH2-CH3

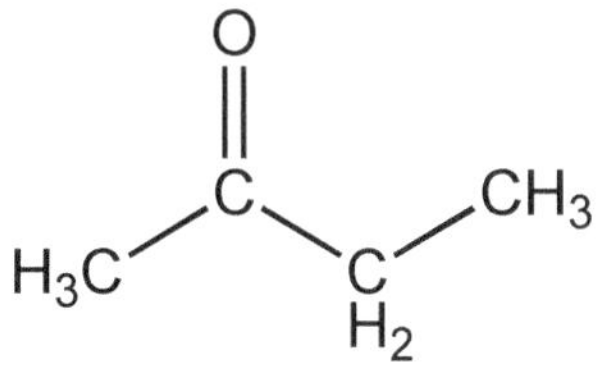

D. HC(=O)-O-C(=O)-CH3

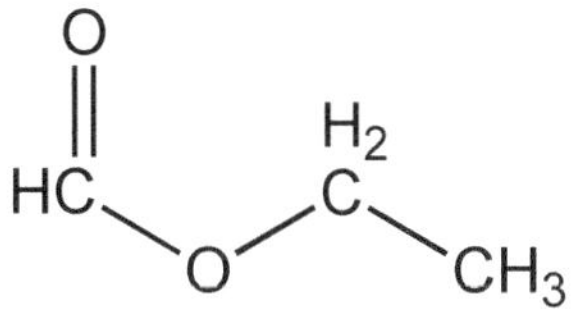

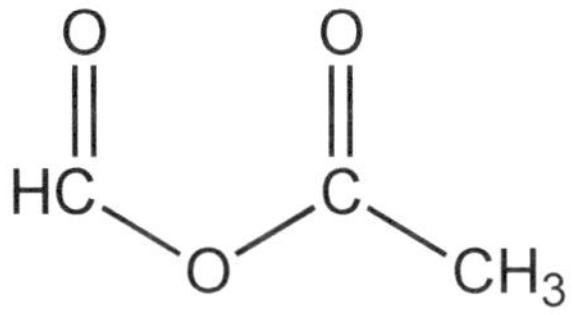

88. This compound:

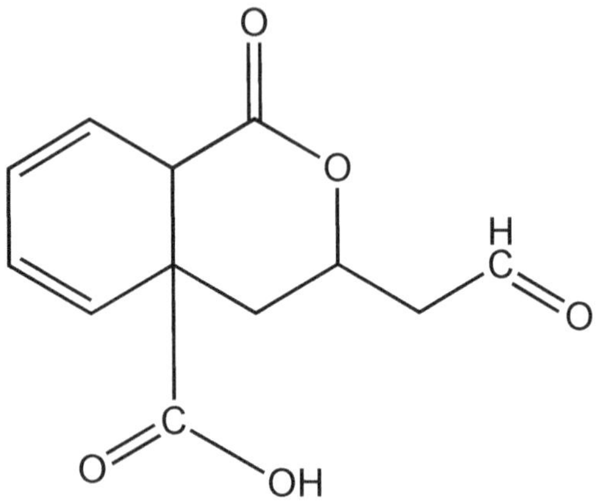

contains an:

A. alkene, carboxylic acid, ester, and ketone
B. aldehyde, alkyne, ester, and ketone
C. aldehyde, alkene, carboxylic acid, and ester
D. acid anhydride, aldehyde, alkene, and amine

89. Which of the following pairs are isomers?

I.

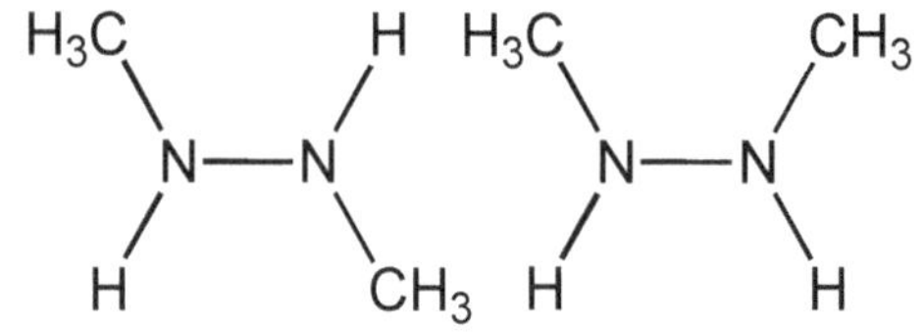

II. pentanal, 2-pentanone

III.

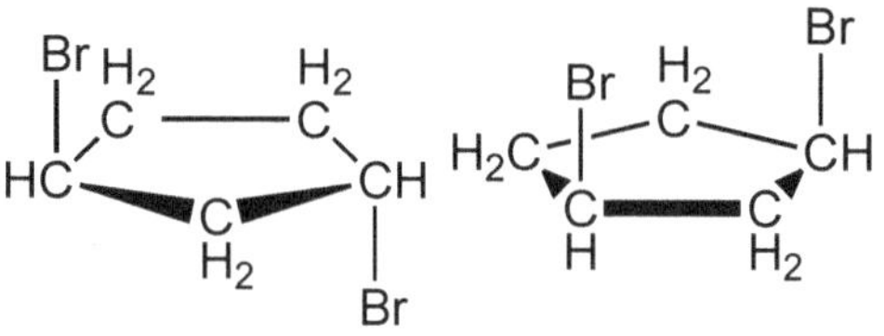

IV.

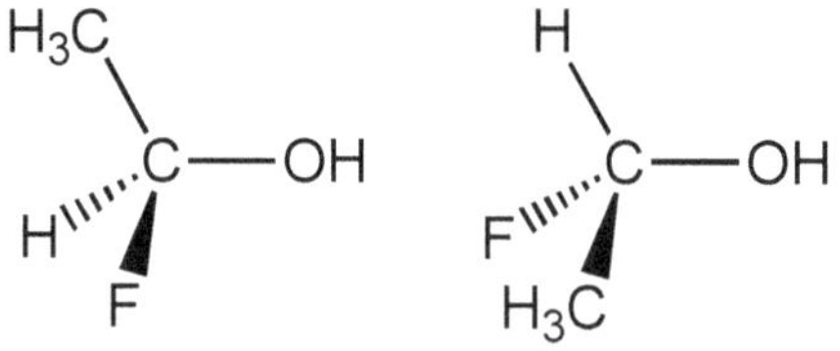

A. I and IV
B. II and III
C. I, II, and III
D. I, II, III, and IV

90. Which instrument would be most useful for separating two different proteins from a mixture?

A. UV/vis spectrophotometer
B. Mass spectrometer
C. Gas chromatograph
D. Liquid chromatograph

91. Classify these biochemicals:

I. [structure of a nucleotide with phosphate, ribose sugar, and cytosine base]

II. [structure of a cyclic sugar with multiple OH groups]

III. [structure of a tripeptide with serine, alanine, and tyrosine residues]

IV. [structure of a triglyceride/fat with long hydrocarbon chains and ester linkages]

A. I - nucleotide, II - sugar, III - peptide, IV - fat
B. I - disaccharide, II - sugar, III - fatty acid, IV - polypeptide
C. I - disaccharide, II - amino acid, III - fatty acid, IV - polysaccharide
D. I - nucleotide, II - sugar, III - triglyceride, IV - DNA

92. You create a solution of 2.00 µg/ml of a pigment and divide the solution into 12 samples. You give four samples each to three teams of students. They use a spectrophotometer to determine the pigment concentration. Here is their data:

Team	Concentration (µg/ml)			
	sample 1	sample 2	sample 3	sample 4
1	1.98	1.93	1.92	1.88
2	1.70	1.72	1.69	1.70
3	1.78	1.99	2.87	2.20

Which of the following is true?

A. Team 1 has the most precise data.
B. Team 3 has the most accurate data in spite of having low precision.
C. The data from Team 2 is characteristic of a systematic error.
D. The data from Team 1 is more characteristic of random error than the data from Team 3.

93. Which pair of measurements has identical meanings?

A. 32 micrograms and 0.032 g
B. 26 nm and 2.60×10^{-8} m
C. 3.01×10^{-5} m^3 and 30.1 ml
D. 0.0020 L and 20 cm^3

94. Match the instrument with the quantity it measures

   I. eudiometer
   II. calorimeter
   III. manometer
   IV. hygrometer

   A. I - volume, II - mass, III - radioactivity, IV - humidity
   B. I - volume, II - heat, III - pressure, IV - humidity
   C. I - viscosity, II - mass, III - pressure, IV - surface tension
   D. I - viscosity, II - heat, III - radioactivity, IV - surface tension

95. Four nearly identical gems from the same mineral are weighed using different balances. Their masses are:

   3.4533 g, 3.459 g, 3.4656 g, 3.464 g

   The four gems are then collected and added to a volumetric cylinder containing 10.00 ml of liquid, and a new volume of 14.97 ml is read. What is the average mass of the four stones and what is the density of the mineral?

   A. 3.460 g and 2.78 g/ml
   B. 3.460 g and 2.79 g/ml
   C. 3.4605 g and 2.78 g/ml
   D. 3.461 g and 2.79 g/ml

96. Which list includes equipment that would not be used in vacuum filtration?

   A. Rubber tubing, Florence flask, Büchner funnel
   B. Vacuum pump, Hirsch funnel, rubber stopper with a single hole
   C. Aspirator, filter paper, filter flask
   D. Lab stand, clamp, filter trap

97. Which of the following statements about lab safety is not true?

   A. Corrosive chemicals should be stored below eye level.
   B. A chemical splash on the eye or skin should be rinsed for 15 minutes in cold water.
   C. MSDS means "Material Safety Data Sheet."
   D. A student should "stop, drop, and roll" if their clothing catches fire in the lab.

98. Which of the following lists consists entirely of chemicals that are considered safe enough to be in a high school lab?

   A. hydrochloric acid, lauric acid, potassium permanganate, calcium hydroxide
   B. ethyl ether, nitric acid, sodium benzoate, methanol
   C. cobalt (II) sulfide, ethylene glycol, benzoyl peroxide, ammonium chloride
   D. picric acid, hydrofluoric acid, cadmium chloride, carbon disulfide

99. The following procedure was developed to find the specific heat capacity of metals:

    1. Place pieces of the metals in an ice-water bath so their initial temperature is 0° C.
    2. Weigh a Styrofoam cup.
    3. Add water at room temperature to the cup and weigh it again
    4. Add a cold metal from the bath to the cup and weigh the cup a third time.
    5. Monitor the temperature drop of the water until a final temperature at thermal equilibrium is found.

    _____ is also required as additional information in order to obtain heat capacities for the metals. The best control would be to follow the same protocol except to use _____ in step 4 instead of a cold metal.

    A. The heat capacity of water, a metal at 100° C
    B. The heat of formation of water, ice from the 0° C bath
    C. The heat of capacity of ice, glass at 0° C
    D. The heat capacity of water, water from the 0° C bath

100. Which statement about the impact of chemistry on society is not true?

    A. Partial hydrogenation creates *trans* fat.
    B. The Haber process incorporates nitrogen from the air into molecules for agricultural use.
    C. The CO_2 concentration in the atmosphere has decreased in the last ten years.
    D. The concentration of ozone-destroying chemicals in the stratosphere has decreased in the last ten years.

Answer Key

1. C	30. B	59. A	88. C
2. B	31. D	60. C	89. B
3. D	32. A	61. A	90. D
4. A	33. C	62. A	91. A
5. C	34. C	63. D	92. C
6. D	35. A	64. C	93. C
7. C	36. D	65. A	94. B
8. B	37. C	66. B	95. B
9. B	38. B	67. D	96. A
10. D	39. B	68. B	97. D
11. A	40. B	69. A	98. A
12. D	41. D	70. C	99. D
13. B	42. B	71. A	100. C
14. D	43. C	72. C	
15. B	44. D	73. D	
16. C	45. A	74. B	
17. A	46. C	75. C	
18. B	47. C	76. A	
19. D	48. A	77. A	
20. A	49. D	78. C	
21. D	50. B	79. A	
22. D	51. C	80. B	
23. A	52. B	81. C	
24. C	53. D	82. D	
25. C	54. B	83. B	
26. B	55. C	84. C	
27. A	56. D	85. B	
28. A	57. C	86. C	
29. B	58. B	87. A	

TEACHER CERTIFICATION STUDY GUIDE

Rationales with Sample Questions

Note: The first insignificant digit should be carried through intermediate calculations. This digit is shown using *italics* in the solutions below.

1. **A piston compresses a gas at constant temperature. Which gas properties increase?**

   II. Average speed of molecules
   III. Pressure
   IV. Molecular collisions with container walls per second

   A. I and II
   B. I and III
   C. II and III
   D. I, II, and III

   Answer C. A decrease in volume (*V*) occurs at constant temperature (*T*). Average molecular speed is determined only by temperature and will be constant. *V* and *P* are inversely related, so pressure will increase. With less wall area and at higher pressure, more collisions occur per second.

2. **The temperature of a liquid is raised at atmospheric pressure. Which liquid property increases?**

   A. critical pressure
   B. vapor pressure
   C. surface tension
   D. viscosity

   Answer B. The critical pressure of a liquid is its vapor pressure at the critical temperature and is always a constant value. A rising temperature increases the kinetic energy of molecules and decreases the importance of intermolecular attraction. More molecules will be free to escape to the vapor phase (vapor pressure increases), but the effect of attractions at the liquid-gas interface will fall (surface tension decreases) and molecules will flow against each other more easily (viscosity decreases).

3. Potassium crystallizes with two atoms contained in each unit cell. What is the mass of potassium found in a lattice 1.00×10^6 unit cells wide, 2.00×10^6 unit cells high, and 5.00×10^5 unit cells deep?

   A. 85.0 ng
   B. 32.5 µg
   C. 64.9 µg
   D. 130. µg

Answer D. First we find the number of unit cells in the lattice by multiplying the number in each row, stack, and column:

1.00×10^6 unit cell lengths $\times\, 2.00 \times 10^6$ unit cell lengths $\times\, 5.00 \times 10^5$ unit cell lengths
$= 1.00 \times 10^{18}$ unit cells

Avogadro's number and the molecular weight of potassium (K) are used in the solution:

$$1.00 \times 10^{18} \text{ unit cells} \times \frac{2 \text{ atoms of K}}{\text{unit cell}} \times \frac{1 \text{ mole of K}}{6.02 \times 10^{23} \text{ atoms of K}} \times \frac{39.098 \text{ g K}}{1 \text{ mole of K}}$$
$$= 1.30 \times 10^{-4} \text{ g}$$
$$= 130. \text{ µg}$$

4. A gas is heated in a sealed container. Which of the following occur?

   A. gas pressure rises
   B. gas density decreases
   C. the average distance between molecules increases
   D. all of the above

Answer A. The same material is kept in a constant volume, so neither density nor the distance between molecules will change. Pressure will rise because of increasing molecular kinetic energy impacting container walls.

TEACHER CERTIFICATION STUDY GUIDE

5. How many molecules are in 2.20 pg of a protein with a molecular weight of 150 kDa?

   A. 8.83×10^9
   B. 1.82×10^9
   C. 8.83×10^6
   D. 1.82×10^6

   Answer C. The prefix "p" for "pico-" indicates 10^{-12}. A kilodalton is 1000 atomic mass units.

   $$2.20 \text{ pg protein} \times \frac{10^{-12} \text{ g}}{1 \text{ pg}} \times \frac{1 \text{ mole protein}}{150 \times 10^3 \text{ g protein}} \times \frac{6.02 \times 10^{23} \text{ molecules protein}}{1 \text{ mole protein}} =$$
   $$= 8.83 \times 10^6 \text{ molecules}$$

6. At STP, 20. µL of O_2 contain 5.4×10^{16} molecules. According to Avogadro's hypothesis, how many molecules are in 20. µL of Ne at STP?

   A. 5.4×10^{15}
   B. 1.0×10^{16}
   C. 2.7×10^{16}
   D. 5.4×10^{16}

   Answer D. Avogadro's hypothesis states that equal volumes of different gases at the same temperature and pressure contain equal numbers of molecules.

7. An ideal gas at 50.0° C and 3.00 atm is in a 300. cm³ cylinder. The cylinder volume changes by moving a piston until the gas is at 50.0° C and 1.00 atm. What is the final volume?

   A. 100. cm³
   B. 450. cm³
   C. 900. cm³
   D. 1.20 dm³

   Answer C. A three-fold decrease in pressure of a constant quantity of gas at constant temperature will cause a three-fold increase in gas volume.

8. **Which gas law may be used to solve the previous question?**

   A. Charles' law
   B. Boyle's law
   C. Graham's law
   D. Avogadro's law

   Answer B. The inverse relationship between volume and pressure is Boyle's law.

9. **One mole of an ideal gas at STP occupies 22.4 L. At what temperature will 1 mole of an ideal gas at 1 atm occupy 31.0 L?**

   A. 34.6° C
   B. 105° C
   C. 378° C
   D. 442° C

   Answer B. Either Charles' law, the combined gas law, or the ideal gas law may be used with temperature in Kelvin. Charles' law or the combined gas law with $P_1 = P_2$ may be manipulated to equate a ratio between temperature and volume when P and n are constant:

   $$V \propto T \text{ or } \frac{P_1 V_1}{T_1} = \frac{P_2 V_2}{T_2} \Rightarrow \frac{T_1}{V_1} = \frac{T_2}{V_2} \Rightarrow T_2 = V_2 \frac{T_1}{V_1}$$

   $$T_2 = 31.0 \text{ L} \frac{273.15 \text{ K}}{22.4 \text{ L}} = 378 \text{ K} = 105 \text{ °C}.$$

   The ideal gas law may also be used with the appropriate gas constant:

   $$PV = nRT \Rightarrow T = \frac{PV}{nR}$$

   $$T = \frac{(1 \text{ atm})(31.0 \text{ L})}{(1 \text{ mol})\left(0.08206 \frac{\text{L-atm}}{\text{mol-K}}\right)} = 378 \text{ K} = 105 \text{ °C}.$$

10. Why does CaCl$_2$ have a higher normal melting point than NH$_3$?

   A. London dispersion forces in CaCl$_2$ are stronger than covalent bonds in NH$_3$.
   B. Covalent bonds in NH$_3$ are stronger than dipole-dipole bonds in CaCl$_2$.
   C. Ionic bonds in CaCl$_2$ are stronger than London dispersion forces in NH$_3$.
   D. Ionic bonds in CaCl$_2$ are stronger than hydrogen bonds in NH$_3$.

   Answer D. London dispersion forces are weaker than covalent bonds, eliminating choice A. A higher melting point will result from stronger intermolecular bonds, eliminating choice B. CaCl$_2$ is an ionic solid resulting from a cation on the left and an anion on the right of the periodic table. The dominant attractive forces between NH$_3$ molecules are hydrogen bonds.

11. Which intermolecular attraction explains the following trend in straight-chain alkanes?

Condensed structural formula	Boiling point (°C)
CH$_4$	-161.5
CH$_3$CH$_3$	-88.6
CH$_3$CH$_2$CH$_3$	-42.1
CH$_3$CH$_2$CH$_2$CH$_3$	-0.5
CH$_3$CH$_2$CH$_2$CH$_2$CH$_3$	36.0
CH$_3$CH$_2$CH$_2$CH$_2$CH$_2$CH$_3$	68.7

   A. London dispersion forces
   B. Dipole-dipole interactions
   C. Hydrogen bonding
   D. Ion-induced dipole interactions

   Answer A. Alkanes are composed entirely of non-polar C-C and C-H bonds, resulting in no dipole interactions or hydrogen bonding. London dispersion forces increase with the size of the molecule, resulting in a higher temperature requirement to break these bonds and a higher boiling point.

TEACHER CERTIFICATION STUDY GUIDE

12. List NH₃, PH₃, MgCl₂, Ne, and N₂ in order of increasing melting point.

   A. N_2 < Ne < PH_3 < NH_3 < $MgCl_2$
   B. N_2 < NH_3 < Ne < $MgCl_2$ < PH_3
   C. Ne < N_2 < NH_3 < PH_3 < $MgCl_2$
   D. Ne < N_2 < PH_3 < NH_3 < $MgCl_2$

   Answer D. Higher melting points result from stronger intermolecular forces. MgCl₂ is the only material listed with ionic bonds and will have the highest melting point. Dipole-dipole interactions are present in NH₃ and PH₃ but not in Ne and N₂. Ne and N₂ are also small molecules expected to have very weak London dispersion forces and so will have lower melting points than NH₃ and PH₃. NH₃ will have stronger intermolecular attractions and a higher melting point than PH₃ because hydrogen bonding occurs in NH₃. Ne has a molecular weight of 20 and a spherical shape and N₂ has a molecular weight of 28 and is not spherical. Both of these factors predict stronger London dispersion forces and a higher melting point for N₂. Actual melting points are: Ne (25 K) < N₂ (63 K) < PH₃ (140 K) < NH₃ (195 K) < MgCl₂ (987 K).

13. 1-butanol, ethanol, methanol, and 1-propanol are all liquids at room temperature. Rank them in order of increasing viscosity.

   A. 1-butanol < 1-propanol < ethanol < methanol
   B. methanol < ethanol < 1-propanol < 1-butanol
   C. methanol < ethanol < 1-butanol < 1-propanol
   D. 1-propanol < 1-butanol < ethanol < methanol

   Answer B. Higher viscosities result from stronger intermolecular attractive forces. The molecules listed are all alcohols with the -OH functional group attached to the end of a straight-chain alkane. In other words, they all have the formula $CH_3(CH_2)_{n-1}OH$. The only difference between the molecules is the length of the alkane corresponding to the value of *n*. With all else identical, larger molecules have greater intermolecular attractive forces due to a greater molecular surface for the attractions. Therefore the viscosities are ranked: methanol (CH_3OH) < ethanol (CH_3CH_2OH) < 1-propanol ($CH_3CH_2CH_2OH$) < 1-butanol ($CH_3CH_2CH_2CH_2OH$).

14. Which gas has a diffusion rate of 25% the rate for hydrogen?

   A. helium
   B. methane
   C. nitrogen
   D. oxygen

Answer D. Graham's law of diffusion states:

$$\frac{r_1}{r_2} = \sqrt{\frac{M_2}{M_1}}$$

Hydrogen (H_2) has molecular weight of 2.0158 u. Using the unknown for material #1 and hydrogen for material #2 in the equation for Graham's law, the ratio of rates is:

$$\frac{r_{unknown}}{r_{hydrogen}} = \sqrt{\frac{2.0158 \text{ u}}{M_{unknown}}} = 0.25. \text{ Squaring both sides yields } \frac{2.0158 \text{ u}}{M_{unknown}} = 0.0625$$

Solving for $M_{unknown}$ gives:

$$M_{unknown} = \frac{2.0158 \text{ u}}{0.0625} = 32 \text{ u}$$

The given possibilities are: He (4.0 u), CH_4 (16 u), N_2 (28 u), and O_2 (32 u).

15. Which substance is most likely to be a gas at STP?

   A. SeO_2
   B. F_2
   C. $CaCl_2$
   D. I_2

Answer B. A gas at STP has a normal boiling point under 0° C. The substance with the lowest boiling point will have the weakest intermolecular attractive forces and will be the most likely gas at STP. F_2 has the lowest molecular weight, is not a salt, metal, or covalent network solid, and is non-polar, indicating the weakest intermolecular attractive forces of the four choices. F_2 actually is a gas at STP, and the other three are solids.

16. What pressure is exerted by a mixture of 2.7 g of H2 and 59 g of Xe at 0° C on a 50. L container?

   A. 0.69 atm
   B. 0.76 atm
   C. 0.80 atm
   D. 0.97 atm

Answer C. Grams of gas are first converted to moles:

$$2.7 \text{ g H}_2 \times \frac{1 \text{ mol H}_2}{2 \times 1.0079 \text{ g H}_2} = 1.33 \text{ mol H}_2 \quad \text{and} \quad 59 \text{ g Xe} \times \frac{1 \text{ mol H}_2}{131.29 \text{ g H}_2} = 0.449 \text{ mol Xe}$$

Dalton's law of partial pressures for an ideal gas is used to find the pressure of the mixture:

$$P_{total}V = (n_{H_2} + n_{Xe})RT \Rightarrow P_{total} = \frac{(n_{H_2} + n_{Xe})RT}{V}$$

$$P_{total} = \frac{(1.33 \text{ mol} + 0.449 \text{ mol})\left(0.08206 \frac{\text{L-atm}}{\text{mol-K}}\right)(273.15 \text{ K})}{50. \text{ L}} = 0.80 \text{ atm}.$$

17. A few minutes after opening a bottle of perfume, the scent is detected on the other side of the room. What law relates to this phenomenon?

   A. Graham's law
   B. Dalton's law
   C. Boyle's law
   D. Avogadro's law

Answer A. Graham's law describes the rate of diffusion (or effusion) of a gas, in this instance, the rate of diffusion of molecules in perfume vapor.

18. Find the partial pressure of N_2 in a container holding H_2O and N_2 at 150. kPa and 50° C. The vapor pressure of H_2O at 50° C is 12 kPa.

A. 12 kPa
B. 138 kPa
C. 162 kPa
D. The value cannot be determined.

Answer B. The partial pressure of H_2O vapor in the container is its vapor pressure. The partial pressure of N_2 may be found by manipulating Dalton's law:

$$P_{total} = P_{H_2O} + P_{N_2} \Rightarrow P_{N_2} = P_{total} - P_{H_2O}$$
$$P_{N_2} = P_{total} - P_{H_2O} = 150. \text{ kPa} - 12 \text{ kPa} = 138 \text{ kPa}$$

19. The normal boiling point of water on the Kelvin scale is closest to:

A. 112 K
B. 212 K
C. 273 K
D. 373 K

Answer D. Temperature in Kelvin is equal to the temperature in Celsius plus 273.15. Since the normal boiling point of water is 100° C, it will boil at 373.15 K, corresponding to answer D.

20. Which phase may be present at the triple point of a substance?

   I. Gas
   II. Liquid
   III. Solid
   IV. Supercritical fluid

   A. I, II, and III
   B. I, II, and IV
   C. II, III, and IV
   D. I, II, III, and IV

   Answer A. Gas, liquid, and solid may exist together at the triple point.

21. In the following phase diagram, _____ occurs as P is decreased from A to B at constant T and _____ occurs as T is increased from C to D at constant P.

   A. deposition, melting
   B. sublimation, melting
   C. deposition, vaporization
   D. sublimation, vaporization

   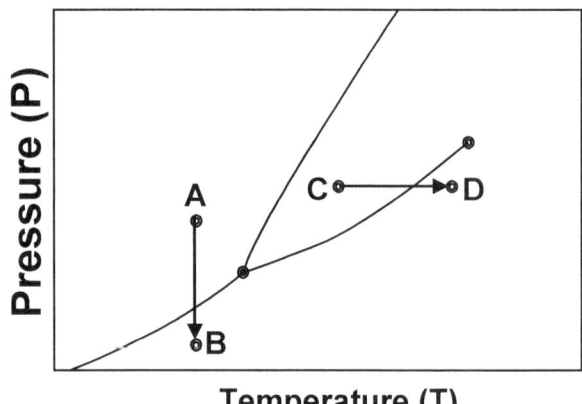

   Answer D. Point A is located in the solid phase; point C is located in the liquid phase. Points B and D are located in the gas phase. The transition from solid to gas is sublimation and the transition from liquid to gas is vaporization.

22. Heat is added to a pure solid at its melting point until it all becomes liquid at its freezing point. Which of the following occur?

   A. Intermolecular attractions are weakened.
   B. The kinetic energy of the molecules does not change.
   C. The freedom of the molecules to move about increases.
   D. All of the above.

   Answer D. Intermolecular attractions are lessened during melting. This permits molecules to move about more freely, but there is no change in the kinetic energy of the molecules because the temperature has remained the same.

23. Which of the following occurs when NaCl dissolves in water?

    A. Heat is required to break bonds in the NaCl crystal lattice.
    B. Heat is released when hydrogen bonds in water are broken.
    C. Heat is required to form bonds of hydration.
    D. The oxygen end of the water molecule is attracted to the Cl⁻ ion.

    Answer A. The lattice does break apart, H-bonds in water are broken, and bonds of hydration are formed, but the first and second processes require heat while the third process releases heat. The oxygen end of the water molecule has a partial negative charge and is attracted to the Na⁺ ion.

24. The solubility of $CoCl_2$ is 54 g per 100 g of ethanol. Three flasks each contain 100 g of ethanol. Flask #1 also contains 40 g $CoCl_2$ in solution. Flask #2 contains 56 g $CoCl_2$ in solution. Flask #3 contains 5 g of solid $CoCl_2$ in equilibrium with 54 g $CoCl_2$ in solution. Which of the following describes the solutions present in the liquid phase of the flasks?

    A. #1 - saturated, #2 - supersaturated, #3 - unsaturated.
    B. #1 - unsaturated, #2 - miscible, #3 - saturated.
    C. #1 - unsaturated, #2 - supersaturated, #3 - saturated.
    D. #1 - unsaturated, #2 - not at equilibrium, #3 - miscible.

    Answer C. Flask #1 contains less solute than the solubility limit, and is unsaturated. Flask #2 contains more solute than the solubility limit, and is supersaturated and also not at equilibrium. Flask #3 contains the solubility limit and is a saturated solution. The term "miscible" applies only to liquids that mix together in all proportions.

25. The solubility at 1.0 atm of pure CO_2 in water at 25° C is 0.034 M. According to Henry's law, what is the solubility at 4.0 atm of pure CO_2 in water at 25° C? Assume no chemical reaction occurs between CO_2 and H_2O.

    A. 0.0085 M
    B. 0.034 M
    C. 0.14 M
    D. 0.25 M

    Answer C. Henry's law states that CO_2 solubility in M (mol/L) will be proportional to the partial pressure of the gas. A four-fold increase in pressure from 1.0 atm to 4.0 atm will increase solubility four-fold from 0.034 M to 0.14 M.

TEACHER CERTIFICATION STUDY GUIDE

26. Carbonated water is bottled at 25° C under pure CO_2 at 4.0 atm. Later the bottle is opened at 4° C under air at 1.0 atm that has a partial pressure of 3×10^{-4} atm CO_2. Why do CO_2 bubbles form when the bottle is opened?

    A. CO_2 leaves the solution due to a drop in solubility at the lower total pressure.
    B. CO_2 leaves the solution due to a drop in solubility at the lower CO_2 pressure.
    C. CO_2 leaves the solution due to a drop in solubility at the lower temperature.
    D. CO_2 is formed by the decomposition of carbonic acid.

    Answer B. A is incorrect because if the water were bottled under a different gas at a high pressure, it would not be carbonated. CO_2 partial pressure is the important factor in solubility. C is incorrect because a decrease in temperature will increase solubility, and the change from 298 K to 277 K is relatively small. D may occur, but this represents a small fraction of the gas released.

27. When KNO_3 dissolves in water, the water grows slightly colder. An increase in temperature will _____ the solubility of KNO_3.

    A. increase
    B. decrease
    C. have no effect on
    D. have an unknown effect with the information given on

    Answer A. The decline in water temperature indicates that the net solution process is endothermic (requiring heat). A temperature increase supplying more heat will favor the solution and increase solubility according to Le Chatelier's principle.

28. An experiment requires 100. mL of a 0.500 M solution of $MgBr_2$. How many grams of $MgBr_2$ will be present in this solution?

    A. 9.21 g
    B. 11.7 g
    C. 12.4 g
    D. 15.6 g

    Answer A.

    $$0.100 \text{ L solution} \times \frac{0.500 \text{ mol MgBr}_2}{\text{L}} \times \frac{(24.305 + 2 \times 79.904) \text{ g MgBr}_2}{\text{mol MgBr}_2} = 9.21 \text{ g MgBr}_2$$

29. 500. mg of RbOH are added to 500. g of ethanol (C_2H_6O) resulting in 395 mL of solution. Determine the molarity and molality of RbOH.

A. 0.0124 M, 0.00488 m
B. 0.0124 M, 0.00976 m
C. 0.0223 M, 0.00488 m
D. 0.0223 M, 0.00976 m

Answer B. First we determine the moles of solute present:

$$0.500 \text{ g RbOH} \times \frac{1 \text{ mol RbOH}}{(85.468 + 15.999 + 1.0079) \text{ g RbOH}} = 0.004879 \text{ mol RbOH}$$

This value is used to calculate molarity and molality:

$$\frac{0.04879 \text{ mol RbOH}}{0.395 \text{ L solution}} = 0.0124 \text{ M RbOH}$$

and

$$\frac{0.04879 \text{ mol RbOH}}{0.500 \text{ kg ethanol}} = 0.00976 \; m \text{ RbOH.}$$

30. Which of the following would make the best solvent for Br_2?

A. H_2O
B. CS_2
C. NH_3
D. Molten NaCl

Answer B. The best solvents for a solute have intermolecular bonds of similar strength to the solute ("like dissolves like"). Bromine is a non-polar molecule with intermolecular attractions due to weak London dispersion forces. The relatively strong hydrogen bonding in H_2O and NH_3 and the very strong electrostatic attractions in molten NaCl would make each of them a poor solvent for Br_2 because these molecules would prefer to remain attracted to one another. CS_2 is a fairly small non-polar molecule.

TEACHER CERTIFICATION STUDY GUIDE

31. Which of the following is most likely to dissolve in water?

A. H_2
B. CCl_4
C. $(SiO_2)_n$
D. CH_3OH

Answer D. The best solutes for a solvent have intermolecular bonds of similar strength to the solvent. H_2O molecules are connected by fairly strong hydrogen bonds. H_2 and CCl_4 are molecules with intermolecular attractions due to weak London dispersion forces. $(SiO_2)_n$ is a covalent network solid and is essentially one large molecule with bonds that are much stronger than hydrogen bonds. CH_3OH (methanol) is miscible with water because it contains hydrogen bonds between molecules.

32. Which of the following is not a colligative property?

A. Viscosity lowering
B. Freezing point lowering
C. Boiling point elevation
D. Vapor pressure lowering

Answer A. Vapor pressure lowering, boiling point elevation, and freezing point lowering may all be visualized as a result of solute particles interfering with the interface between phases in a consistent way. This is not the case for viscosity.

33. List the following aqueous solutions in order of increasing boiling point.

   I. 0.050 m AlCl$_3$
   II. 0.080 m Ba(NO$_3$)$_2$
   III. 0.090 m NaCl
   IV. 0.12 m ethylene glycol (C$_2$H$_6$O$_2$)

   A. I < II < III < IV
   B. I < III < IV < II
   C. IV < III < I < II
   D. IV < III < II < I

Answer C. The number of particles in solution determine colligative properties; the greater the number of dissolved particles, the greater the boiling point elevation. The first three materials are strong electrolyte salts, and C$_2$H$_6$O$_2$ is a non-electrolyte and will not dissociate, so it will have the lowest boiling point.

AlCl$_3$(aq) is Al^{3+} +3 Cl$^-$. So $0.050 \dfrac{\text{mol AlCl}_3}{\text{kg H}_2\text{O}} \times \dfrac{4 \text{ mol particles}}{\text{mol AlCl}_3} = 0.200 \ m$ particles

Ba(NO$_3$)$_2$(aq) is Ba^{2+} +2 NO$_3^-$. So $0.080 \dfrac{\text{mol Ba(NO}_3)_2}{\text{kg H}_2\text{O}} \times \dfrac{3 \text{ mol particles}}{\text{mol Ba(NO}_3)_2} = 0.240 \ m$ particles

NaCl(aq) is Na$^+$ +Cl$^-$. So $0.090 \dfrac{\text{mol NaCl}}{\text{kg H}_2\text{O}} \times \dfrac{2 \text{ mol particles}}{\text{mol NaCl}} = 0.180 \ m$ particles

C$_2$H$_6$O$_2$(aq) is not an electrolyte. So $0.12 \dfrac{\text{mol C}_2\text{H}_6\text{O}_2}{\text{kg H}_2\text{O}} \times \dfrac{1 \text{ mol particles}}{\text{mol C}_2\text{H}_6\text{O}_2} = 0.12 \ m$ particles

Ba(NO$_3$)$_2$ dissociates to create the most particles, so C is correct.

34. Osmotic pressure is the pressure required to prevent _____ from flowing from low to high _____ concentration across a semipermeable membrane.

A. solute, solute
B. solute, solvent
C. solvent, solute
D. solvent, solvent

Answer C. Osmotic pressure is the pressure required to prevent osmosis, which is the flow of solvent across the membrane from low to high solute concentration. This is also the direction from high to low solvent concentration.

35. A solution of NaCl in water is heated on a mountain in an open container until it boils at 100.° C. The air pressure on the mountain is 0.92 atm. According to Raoult's law, what mole fraction of Na⁺ and Cl⁻ are present in the solution?

A. 0.04 Na⁺, 0.04 Cl⁻
B. 0.08 Na⁺, 0.08 Cl⁻
C. 0.46 Na⁺, 0.46 Cl⁻
D. 0.92 Na⁺, 0.92 Cl⁻

Answer A. The vapor pressure of H₂O at 100.° C is exactly 1 atm. Boiling point decreases with external pressure, so the boiling point of pure H₂O at 0.9 atm will be less than 100.° C. Adding salt raises the boiling point at 0.92 atm to 100.° C by decreasing vapor pressure to 0.92 atm. According to Raoult's law:

$$P^{vapor}_{solution} = P^{vapor}_{pure\ solvent} (\text{mole fraction})_{solvent} \Rightarrow (\text{mole fraction})_{solvent} = \frac{P^{vapor}_{solution}}{P^{vapor}_{pure\ solvent}}$$

$$\text{Therefore, } (\text{mole fraction})_{H_2O} = \frac{0.92 \text{ atm at } 100.°C}{1.0 \text{ atm at } 100.°C} = 0.92 \frac{\text{mol H}_2\text{O}}{\text{mol total}}$$

The remaining 0.08 mole fraction of solute is evenly divided between the two ions:

$$(\text{mole fraction})_{solute} = 1 - (\text{mole fraction})_{H_2O} = 1 - 0.92 = 0.08 \frac{\text{mol solute particles}}{\text{mol total}}$$

$$(\text{mole fraction})_{Na^+} = 0.08 \frac{\text{mol solute particles}}{\text{mol total}} \times \frac{1 \text{ mol Na}^+}{2 \text{ mol solute particles}} = 0.04 \frac{\text{mol Na}^+}{\text{mol total}}$$

$$(\text{mole fraction})_{Cl^-} = 0.08 \frac{\text{mol solute particles}}{\text{mol total}} \times \frac{1 \text{ mol Cl}^-}{2 \text{ mol solute particles}} = 0.04 \frac{\text{mol Cl}^-}{\text{mol total}}.$$

36. Write a balanced nuclear equation for the emission of an alpha particle by polonium-209.

A. $^{209}_{84}Po \rightarrow \, ^{205}_{81}Pb + \, ^{4}_{2}He$
B. $^{209}_{84}Po \rightarrow \, ^{205}_{82}Bi + \, ^{4}_{2}He$
C. $^{209}_{84}Po \rightarrow \, ^{209}_{85}At + \, ^{0}_{-1}e$
D. $^{209}_{84}Po \rightarrow \, ^{205}_{82}Pb + \, ^{4}_{2}He$

Answer D. The periodic table shows that polonium has an atomic number of 84. The emission of an alpha particle, $^{4}_{2}He$ (eliminating choice C), will leave an atom with an atomic number of 82 and a mass number of 205 (eliminating choice A). The periodic table identifies this element as lead, $^{205}_{82}Pb$, not bismuth (eliminating choice B).

37. Write a balanced nuclear equation for the decay of calcium-45 to scandium-45.

A. $^{45}_{20}Ca \rightarrow \, ^{41}_{18}Sc + \, ^{4}_{2}He$
B. $^{45}_{20}Ca + \, ^{0}_{1}e \rightarrow \, ^{45}_{21}Sc$
C. $^{45}_{20}Ca \rightarrow \, ^{45}_{21}Sc + \, ^{0}_{-1}e$
D. $^{45}_{20}Ca + \, ^{0}_{1}p \rightarrow \, ^{45}_{21}Sc$

Answer C. All four choices are balanced mathematically. "A" leaves scandium-41 as a decay product, not scandium-45. "B" and "D" require the addition of particles not normally present in the atom. If these reactions do occur, they are not decay reactions because they are not spontaneous. "C" involves the common decay mechanism of beta emission.

38. $^{3}_{1}H$ decays with a half-life of 12 years. 3.0 g of pure $^{3}_{1}H$ were placed in a sealed container 24 years ago. How many grams of $^{3}_{1}H$ remain?

A. 0.38 g
B. 0.75 g
C. 1.5 g
D. 3.0 g

Answer B. Every 12 years, the amount remaining is cut in half. After 12 years, 1.5 g will remain. After another 12 years, 0.75 g will remain.

39. Which of the following isotopes is commonly used for medical imaging in the diagnosis of diseases?

A. cobalt-60
B. technetium-99m
C. tin-117m
D. plutonium-238

Answer B. The other three isotopes have limited medical applications (tin-117m has been used for the relief of bone cancer pain), but only Tc-99m is used routinely for imaging.

40. List the following scientists in chronological order from earliest to most recent with respect to their most significant contribution to atomic theory:

I. John Dalton
II. Niels Bohr
III. J. J. Thomson
IV. Ernest Rutherford

A. I, III, II, IV
B. I, III, IV, II
C. I, IV, III, II
D. III, I, II, IV

Answer B. Dalton founded modern atomic theory. J.J. Thomson determined that the electron is a subatomic particle, but he placed it in the center of the atom. Rutherford discovered that electrons surround a small dense nucleus. Bohr determined that electrons may only occupy discrete positions around the nucleus.

41. Match the theory with the scientist who first proposed it:

   I. Electrons, atoms, and all objects with momentum also exist as waves.
   II. Electron density may be accurately described by a single mathematical equation.
   III. There is an inherent indeterminacy in the position and momentum of particles.
   IV. Radiant energy is transferred between particles in exact multiples of a discrete unit.

   A. I - de Broglie, II - Planck, III - Schrödinger, IV - Thomson
   B. I - Dalton, II - Bohr, II - Planck, IV - de Broglie
   C. I - Henry, II - Bohr, III - Heisenberg, IV - Schrödinger
   D. I - de Broglie, II - Schrödinger, III - Heisenberg, IV - Planck

   Answer D. Henry's law relates gas partial pressure to liquid solubility. Schrödinger's equation is the equation that describes electron density, so D is the correct answer.

42. How many neutrons are in $^{60}_{27}Co$?

   A. 27
   B. 33
   C. 60
   D. 87

   Answer B. The number of neutrons is found by subtracting the atomic number (27) from the mass number (60).

43. The terrestrial composition of an element is: 50.7% as a stable isotope with an atomic mass of 78.9 u and 49.3% as a stable isotope with an atomic mass of 80.9 u. Calculate the atomic mass of the element.

   A. 79.0 u
   B. 79.8 u
   C. 79.9 u
   D. 80.8 u

   Answer C.
   Atomic mass of element = (Fraction as 1st isotope) (Atomic mass of 1st isotope)
   +
   (Fraction as 2nd isotope) (Atomic mass of 2nd isotope)
   = (0.507) (78.9 u) + (0.493) (80.9 u) = 79.89 u = 79.9 u

44. Which of the following is a correct electron arrangement for oxygen?

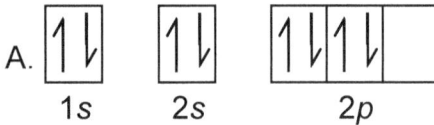

B. $1s^2 1p^2 2s^2 2p^2$
C. 2, 2, 4
D. none of the above

Answer D. Choice A violates Hund's rule. The two electrons on the far right should occupy the final two orbitals. B should be $1s^2 2s^2 2p^4$. There is no $1p$ subshell. C should be 2, 6. Number lists indicate electrons in shells.

45. Which of the following statements about radiant energy is <u>not</u> true?

A. The energy change of an electron transition is directly proportional to the wavelength of the emitted or absorbed photon.
B. The energy of an electron in a hydrogen atom depends only on the principle quantum number.
C. The frequency of photons striking a metal determines whether the photoelectric effect will occur.
D. The frequency of a wave of electromagnetic radiation is inversely proportional to its wavelength.

Answer A. The energy change (ΔE) is <u>inversely</u> proportional to the wavelength (λ) of the photon according the equation:

$$\Delta E = \frac{hc}{\lambda}$$

where h is Planck's constant and c is the speed of light.

Choice B is true for hydrogen. Atoms with more than one electron are more complex. The frequency of individual photons, not the number of photons determines whether the photoelectric effect occurs, so choice C is true. Choice D is true. The proportionality constant is the speed of light according to the equation:

$$\nu = \frac{c}{\lambda}$$

46. Match the orbital diagram for the ground state of carbon with the rule/principle it violates:

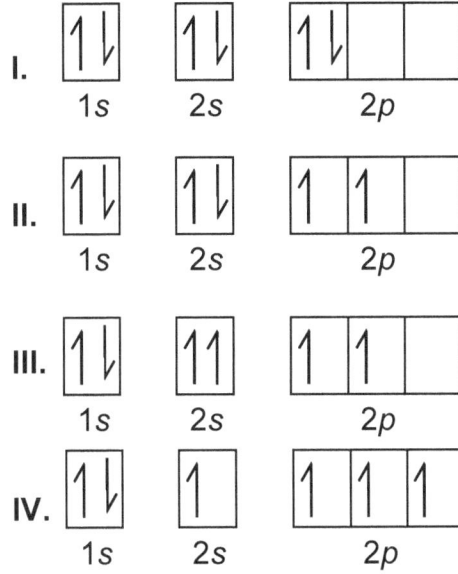

A. I - Pauli exclusion, II - Aufbau, III - no violation, IV - Hund's
B. I - Aufbau, II - Pauli exclusion, III - no violation, IV - Hund's
C. I - Hund's, II - no violation, III - Pauli exclusion, IV - Aufbau
D. I - Hund's, II - no violation, III - Aufbau, IV - Pauli exclusion

Answer C. Diagram I violates Hund's rule because a second electron is added to a degenerate orbital before all orbitals in the subshell have one electron. Diagram III violates the Pauli exclusion principle because both electrons in the 2s orbital have the same spin. They would have the same 4 quantum numbers. Diagram IV violates the Aufbau principle because an electron occupies the higher energy 2p orbital before the 2s orbital has been filled; this configuration is not at the ground state.

47. Select the list of atoms that are arranged in order of increasing size.

A. Mg, Na, Si, Cl
B. Si, Cl, Mg, Na
C. Cl, Si, Mg, Na
D. Na, Mg, Si, Cl

Answer C. These atoms are all in the same row of the periodic table. Size increases further to the left for atoms in the same row.

48. Based on trends in the periodic table, which of the following properties would you expect to be greater for Rb than for K?

I. Density
II. Melting point
III. Ionization energy
IV. Oxidation number in a compound with chlorine

A. I only
B. I, II, and III
C. II and III
D. I, II, III, and IV

Answer A. Rb is underneath K in the alkali metal column (group 1) of the periodic table. There is a general trend for density to increase lower on the table for elements in the same row, so we select choice I. Rb and K experience metallic bonds for intermolecular forces, and the strength of metallic bonds decreases for larger atoms further down the periodic table resulting in a lower melting point for Rb, so we do not choose II. Ionization energy decreases for larger atoms further down the periodic table, so we do not choose III. Both Rb and K would be expected to have a charge of +1 and therefore an oxidation number of +1 in a compound with chlorine, so we do not choose IV.

49. Rank the following bonds from least to most polar:

C-H, C-Cl, H-H, C-F

A. C-H < H-H < C-F < C-Cl
B. H-H < C-H < C-F < C-Cl
C. C-F < C-Cl < C-H < H-H
D. H-H < C-H < C-Cl < C-F

Answer D. Bonds between atoms of the same element are completely non-polar, so H-H is the least polar bond in the list, eliminating choices A and C. The C-H bond is considered to be non-polar even though the electrons of the bond are slightly unequally shared. C-Cl and C-F are both polar covalent bonds, but C-F is more strongly polar because F has a greater electronegativity.

50. At room temperature, CaBr₂ is expected to be:

   A. a ductile solid
   B. a brittle solid
   C. a soft solid
   D. a gas

Answer B. Ca is a metal because it is on the left of the periodic table, and Br is a non-metal because it is on the right. The compound they form together will be an ionic salt, and ionic salts are brittle solids (choice B) at room temperature. NaCl is another example.

51. Which of the following is a proper Lewis dot structure of CHClO?

Answer C. C has 4 valence shell electrons, H has 1, Cl has 7, and O has 6. The molecule has a total of 18 valence shell electrons. This eliminates choice B which has 24. Choice B is also incorrect because has an octet around a hydrogen atom instead of 2 electrons and because there are only six electrons surrounding the central carbon. A single bond connecting all atoms would give choice A. This is incorrect because there are only 6 electrons surrounding the central carbon. A double bond between C and O gives the correct answer, C. A double bond between C and O and also between C and Cl would give choice D. This is incorrect because there are 10 electrons surrounding the central carbon.

52. In C_2H_2, each carbon atom contains the following valence orbitals:

A. p only
B. p and sp hybrids
C. p and sp^2 hybrids
D. sp^3 hybrids only

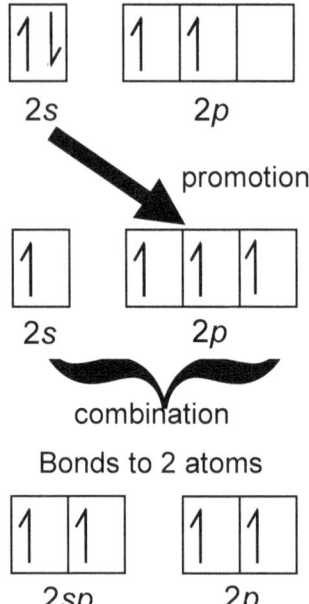

Answer B. An isolated C has the valence electron configuration $2s^22p^2$. Before bonding, one s electron is promoted to an empty p orbital. In C_2H_2, each C atom bonds to 2 other atoms. Bonding to two other atoms is achieved by combination into two p orbitals and two sp hybrids.

53. Which statement about molecular structures is false?

A. ![structure] is a conjugated molecule.

B. A bonding σ orbital connects two atoms by the straight line between them.
C. A bonding π orbital connects two atoms in a separate region from the straight line between them.
D. The anion with resonance forms will always exist in one form or the other.

Answer D. A conjugated molecule is a molecule with double bonds on adjacent atoms such as the molecule shown in A. Choices B and C give the definition of sigma and pi molecular orbitals. D is false because a resonance form is one of multiple equivalent Lewis structures, but these structures do not describe the actual state of the molecule. The anion will exist in a state between the two forms.

TEACHER CERTIFICATION STUDY GUIDE

54. What is the chemical composition of magnesium nitrate?

A. 11.1% Mg, 22.2% N, 66.7% O
B. 16.4% Mg, 18.9% N, 64.7% O
C. 20.9% Mg, 24.1% N, 55.0% O
D. 28.2% Mg, 16.2% N, 55.7% O

Answer B. First find the formula for magnesium nitrate. Mg is an alkali earth metal and will always have a 2+ charge. The nitrate ion is NO_3^-. Two nitrate ions are required for each Mg^{2+} ion. Therefore the formula is $Mg(NO_3)_2$

Determine the chemical composition:

1) Determine the number of atoms for each element in $Mg(NO_3)_2$:
   1 Mg, 2 N, 6 O.

2) Multiply by the molecular weight of the elements to determine the grams of each in one mole of the formula:

$$\frac{1 \text{ mol Mg}}{\text{mol Mg(NO}_3)_2} \times \frac{24.3 \text{ g Mg}}{\text{mol Mg}} = 24.3 \text{ g Mg/mol Mg(NO}_3)_2$$

$$2(14.0) = 28.0 \text{ g N/mol Mg(NO}_3)_2$$

$$6(16.0) = 96.0 \text{ g O/mol Mg(NO}_3)_2$$

3) Determine the formula mass: $148.3 \text{ g Mg(NO}_3)_2/\text{mol Mg(NO}_3)_2$

4) Divide to determine % composition:

$$\%Mg = \frac{24.3 \text{ g Mg/mol Mg(NO}_3)_2}{148.3 \text{ g Mg(NO}_3)_2/\text{mol Mg(NO}_3)_2} = 0.164 \text{ g Mg/g Mg(NO}_3)_2 \times 100\% = 16.4\%$$

$$\%N = \frac{28.0}{148.3} \times 100\% = 18.9\% \qquad \%O = \frac{96.0}{148.3} \times 100\% = 64.7\%$$

Answer B is correct. Answer A is the fractional representation of the presence of each atom in the formula. Composition is based on mass percentage. Answer C is the chemical composition of $Mg(NO_2)_2$, magnesium nitrite. Answer D is the chemical composition of "$MgNO_3$," a formula that results from not balancing charges.

TEACHER CERTIFICATION STUDY GUIDE

55. The IUPAC name for Cu_2SO_3 is:

A. Dicopper sulfur trioxide
B. Copper (II) sulfate
C. Copper (I) sulfite
D. Copper (II) sulfite

Answer C. Cu_2SO_3 is an ionic compound containing two Cu cations and the SO_3 anion. Choice A is wrong because it uses the naming system for molecular compounds. The SO_3 anion is 2– and is named sulfite. It takes two copper cations to neutralize this charge, so Cu has a charge of 1+, and the name is copper (I) sulfite.

56. Household "chlorine bleach" is sodium hypochlorite. Which of the following best represents the production of sodium hypochlorite, sodium chloride, and water by bubbling chlorine gas through aqueous sodium hydroxide?

A. $4Cl(g) + 4NaOH(aq) \rightarrow NaClO_2(aq) + 3NaCl(aq) + 2H_2O(l)$
B. $2Cl_2(g) + 4NaOH(aq) \rightarrow NaClO_2(aq) + 3NaCl(aq) + 2H_2O(l)$
C. $2Cl(g) + 2NaOH(aq) \rightarrow NaClO(aq) + NaCl(aq) + H_2O(l)$
D. $Cl_2(g) + 2NaOH(aq) \rightarrow NaClO(aq) + NaCl(aq) + H_2O(l)$

Answer D. Chlorine gas is a diatomic molecule, eliminating choices A and C. The hypochlorite ion is ClO^- eliminating choices A and B. All of the equations are properly balanced.

TEACHER CERTIFICATION STUDY GUIDE

57. Balance the equation for the neutralization reaction between phosphoric acid and calcium hydroxide by filling in the blank stoichiometric coefficients.

$$\_\_H_3PO_4 + \_\_Ca(OH)_2 \rightarrow \_\_Ca_3(PO_4)_2 + \_\_H_2O$$

A. 4, 3, 1, 4
B. 2, 3, 1, 8
C. 2, 3, 1, 6
D. 2, 1, 1, 2

Answer C. We are given the unbalanced equation. Next we determine the number of atoms on each side. For reactants (left of the arrow): 5 H, 1 P, 6 O, and 1 Ca. For products: 2 H, 2 P, 9 O, and 3 Ca.

We assume that the molecule with the most atoms – $Ca_3(PO_4)_2$ – has a coefficient of one, and find the other coefficients required to have the same number of atoms on each side of the equation. Assuming $Ca_3(PO_4)_2$ has a coefficient of one means that there will be 3 Ca and 2 P on the right because H_2O has no Ca or P. A balanced equation would also have 3 Ca and 2 P on the left. This is achieved with a coefficient of 2 for H_3PO_4 and 3 for $Ca(OH)_2$. Now we have:

$$2H_3PO_4 + 3Ca(OH)_2 \rightarrow Ca_3(PO_4)_2 + ?H_2O$$

The coefficient for H_2O is found by balancing H or O. Whichever one is chosen, the other atom should be checked to confirm that a balance actually occurs. For H, there are 6 H from $2H_3PO_4$ and 6 from $3Ca(OH)_2$ for a total of 12 H on the left. There must be 12 H on the right for balance. None are accounted for by $Ca_3(PO_4)_2$, so all 12 H must be associated with H_2O. It has a coefficient of 6:

$$2H_3PO_4 + 3Ca(OH)_2 \rightarrow Ca_3(PO_4)_2 + 6H_2O$$

This is choice C, but if time is available, it is best to check that the remaining atoms are balanced. There are 8 O from $2H_3PO_4$ and 6 from $3Ca(OH)_2$ for a total of 14 on the left, and 8 O from $Ca_3(PO_4)_2$ and 6 from $6H_2O$ for a total of 14 on the right. The equation is balanced.

Multiplication by a whole number is not required because the stoichiometric coefficients from step 3 already are whole numbers.

An alternative method would be to try the coefficients given for answer A, answer B, etc. until we recognize a properly balanced equation.

CHEMISTRY 7-12

TEACHER CERTIFICATION STUDY GUIDE

58. Write an equation showing the reaction between calcium nitrate and lithium sulfate in aqueous solution. Include all products.

   A. $CaNO_3(aq) + Li_2SO_4(aq) \rightarrow CaSO_4(s) + Li_2NO_3(aq)$
   B. $Ca(NO_3)_2(aq) + Li_2SO_4(aq) \rightarrow CaSO_4(s) + 2LiNO_3(aq)$
   C. $Ca(NO_3)_2(aq) + Li_2SO_4(aq) \rightarrow 2LiNO_3(s) + CaSO_4(aq)$
   D. $Ca(NO_3)_2(aq) + Li_2SO_4(aq) + 2H_2O(l) \rightarrow 2LiNO_3(aq) + Ca(OH)_2(aq) + H_2SO_4(aq)$

   Answer B. When two ionic compounds are in solution, a precipitation reaction should be considered. We can determine from their names that the two reactants are the ionic compounds $Ca(NO_3)_2$ and Li_2SO_4. The compounds are present in aqueous solution as their four component ions Ca^{2+}, NO_3^-, Li^+, and SO_4^{2-}. Solubility rules indicate that nitrates are always soluble but sulfate will form a solid precipitate with Ca^{2+}, forming $CaSO_4$ (s). Choice A results from assuming that the nitrate anion has a 2– charge instead of its 1– charge. B is correct. C assumes lithium nitrate is the precipitate. Choice D includes the reverse of a neutralization reaction. Water would not decompose due to the addition of these salts.

59. Find the mass of CO_2 produced by the combustion of 15 kg of isopropyl alcohol in the reaction:

   $$2C_3H_7OH + 9O_2 \rightarrow 6CO_2 + 8H_2O$$

   A. 33 kg
   B. 44 kg
   C. 50 kg
   D. 60 kg

   Answer A. Remember "grams to moles to moles to grams." Step 1 converts mass to moles for the known value. In this case, kg and kmol are used. Step 2 relates moles of the known value to moles of the unknown value by their stoichiometry coefficients. Step 3 converts moles of the unknown value to a mass.

   $$15 \times 10^3 \text{ g } C_4H_8O \times \underbrace{\frac{1 \text{ mol } C_4H_8O}{60 \text{ g } C_4H_8O}}_{\text{step 1}} \times \underbrace{\frac{6 \text{ mol } CO_2}{2 \text{ mol } C_4H_8O}}_{\text{step 2}} \times \underbrace{\frac{44 \text{ g } CO_2}{1 \text{ mol } CO_2}}_{\text{step 3}} = 33 \times 10^3 \text{ g } CO_2$$

   $$= 33 \text{ kg } CO_2$$

60. What is the density of nitrogen gas at STP? Assume an ideal gas and a value of 0.08206 L-atm/(mol-K) for the gas constant.

    A. 0.62 g/L
    B. 1.14 g/L
    C. 1.25 g/L
    D. 2.03 g/L

Answer C. The molecular mass M of N_2 is 28.0 g/mol:

$$d = \frac{nM}{V} = \frac{PM}{RT} = \frac{(1\text{ atm})\left(28.0\,\frac{g}{mol}\right)}{\left(0.08206\,\frac{L\cdot atm}{mol\cdot K}\right)(273.15\text{ K})} = 1.25\,\frac{g}{L}$$

Choice A results from forgetting that nitrogen is a diatomic gas. Choice B results from using a value of 25° C for standard temperature. This is the thermodynamic standard temperature, but not STP.

A faster method is to recall that one mole of an ideal gas at STP occupies 22.4 L.

$$d\,(\text{in }\tfrac{g}{L}) = \frac{M\,(\text{in }\tfrac{g}{mol})}{22.4\,\tfrac{L}{mol}} = \frac{28.0\,\tfrac{g}{mol}}{22.4\,\tfrac{L}{mol}} = 1.25\,\tfrac{g}{L}.$$

61. Find the volume of methane that will produce 12 m³ of hydrogen in the reaction: $CH_4(g) + H_2O(g) \rightarrow CO(g) + 3H_2(g)$. Assume temperature and pressure remain constant.

    A. 4.0 m³
    B. 32 m³
    C. 36 m³
    D. 64 m³

Answer A. Stoichiometric coefficients may be used directly for ideal gas volumes at constant T and P because of Avogadro's Law:

$$12\text{ m}^3\,H_2 \times \frac{1\text{ m}^3\,CH_4}{3\text{ m}^3\,H_2} = 4.0\text{ m}^3\,CH_4$$

12 g of H_2 will be produced from 32 g of CH_4 (incorrect choice B).

62. A 100. L vessel of pure O₂ at 500. kPa and 20.° C is used for the combustion of butane:

$$2C_4H_{10} + 13O_2 \rightarrow 8CO_2 + 10H_2O$$

Find the mass of butane that consumes all the O₂ in the vessel. Assume O₂ is an ideal gas and use a value of $R = 8.314$ J/(mol·K).

A. 183 g
B. 467 g
C. 1.83 kg
D. 7.75 kg

Answer A. We are given a volume and asked for a mass. The steps will be "volume to moles to moles to mass."

"Volume to moles…" requires the ideal gas law, but first several units must be altered:

Units of joules are identical to m³·Pa
500 kPa is 500×10³ Pa
100 L is 0.100 m³
20° C is 293.15 K

$PV = nRT$ is rearranged to give:

$$n = \frac{PV}{RT} = \frac{(500 \times 10^3 \text{ Pa})(0.100 \text{ m}^3 \text{ O}_2)}{\left(8.314 \frac{\text{m}^3 \cdot \text{Pa}}{\text{mol} \cdot \text{K}}\right)(293.15 \text{ K})} = 20.51 \text{ mol O}_2$$

"…to moles to mass" utilizes stoichiometry. The molecular weight of butane is 58.1 u:

$$20.51 \text{ mol O}_2 \times \frac{2 \text{ mol C}_4H_{10}}{13 \text{ mol O}_2} \times \frac{58.1 \text{ g C}_4H_{10}}{1 \text{ mol C}_4H_{10}} = 183 \text{ g C}_4H_{10}$$

63. Consider the reaction between iron and hydrogen chloride gas:

$$Fe(s) + 2HCl(g) \rightarrow FeCl_2(s) + H_2(g)$$

7 moles of iron and 10 moles of HCl react until the limiting reagent is consumed. Which statements are true?

I. HCl is the excess reagent
II. HCl is the limiting reagent
III. 7 moles of H₂ are produced
IV. 2 moles of the excess reagent remain

A. I and III
B. I and IV
C. II and III
D. II and IV

Answer D. The limiting reagent is found by dividing the number of moles of each reactant by its stoichiometric coefficient. The lowest result is the limiting reagent:

$$7 \text{ mol Fe} \times \frac{1 \text{ mol reaction}}{1 \text{ mol Fe}} = 7 \text{ mol reaction if Fe is limiting}$$

$$10 \text{ mol HCl} \times \frac{1 \text{ mol reaction}}{2 \text{ mol HCl}} = 5 \text{ mol reaction if HCl is limiting.}$$

Therefore, HCl is the limiting reagent (II is true) and Fe is the excess reagent.

5 moles of the reaction take place, so 5 moles of H₂ are produced, and of the 7 moles of Fe supplied, 5 are consumed, leaving 2 moles of the excess reagent (IV is true).

64. **32.0 g of hydrogen and 32.0 grams of oxygen react to form water until the limiting reagent is consumed. What is present in the vessel after the reaction is complete?**

A. 16.0 g O_2 and 48.0 g H_2O
B. 24.0 g H_2 and 40.0 g H_2O
C. 28.0 g H_2 and 36.0 g H_2O
D. 28.0 g H_2 and 34.0 g H_2O

Answer C. First the equation must be constructed:

$$2H_2 + O_2 \rightarrow 2H_2O$$

A fast and intuitive solution would be to recognize that:

1) One mole of H_2 is about 2.0 g, so about 16 moles of H_2 are present.
2) One mole of O_2 is 32.0 g, so one mole of is O_2 is present.
3) Imagine the 16 moles of H_2 reacting with one mole of O_2. 2 moles of H_2 will be consumed before the one mole of O_2 is gone. O_2 is limiting. (Eliminate choice A.)
4) 16 moles less 2 leaves 14 moles of H_2 or about 28 g. (Eliminate choice B.)
5) The reaction began with 64.0 g total. Conservation of mass for chemical reactions forces the total final mass to be 64.0 g also. (Eliminate choice D.)

A more standard solution is presented next. First, mass is converted to moles:

$$32.0 \text{ g } H_2 \times \frac{1 \text{ mol } H_2}{2.016 \text{ g } H_2} = 15.87 \text{ mol } H_2 \quad \text{and} \quad 32.0 \text{ g } O_2 \times \frac{1 \text{ mol } O_2}{32.00 \text{ g } O_2} = 1.000 \text{ mol } O_2$$

Dividing by stoichiometric coefficients gives:

$$15.87 \text{ mol } H_2 \times \frac{1 \text{ mol reaction}}{2 \text{ mol } H_2} = 7.935 \text{ mol reaction if } H_2 \text{ is limiting}$$

$$1.000 \text{ mol } O_2 \times \frac{1 \text{ mol reaction}}{1 \text{ mol } O_2} = 1.000 \text{ mol reaction if } O_2 \text{ is limiting.}$$

O_2 is the limiting reagent, so no O_2 will remain in the vessel.

$$1.000 \text{ mol O}_2 \text{ consumed} \times \frac{2 \text{ mol H}_2\text{O produced}}{1 \text{ mol O}_2} \times \frac{18.016 \text{ g H}_2\text{O}}{1 \text{ mol H}_2\text{O}} = 36.0 \text{ g H}_2\text{O produced}$$

$$1.000 \text{ mol O}_2 \text{ consumed} \times \frac{2 \text{ mol H}_2 \text{ consumed}}{1 \text{ mol O}_2} \times \frac{2.016 \text{ g H}_2}{1 \text{ mol H}_2} = 4.03 \text{ g H}_2 \text{ consumed}$$

The remaining H_2 is found from: 32.0 g H_2 initially − 4.03 g H_2 consumed = 28.0 g H_2 remain

65. The reaction: $(CH_3)_3CBr(aq) + OH^-(aq) \rightarrow (CH_3)_3COH(aq) + Br^-(aq)$
occurs in three elementary steps:

$(CH_3)_3CBr \rightarrow (CH_3)_3C^+ + Br^-$ is slow
$(CH_3)_3C^+ + H_2O \rightarrow (CH_3)_3COH_2^+$ is fast
$(CH_3)_3COH_2^+ + OH^- \rightarrow (CH_3)_3COH + H_2O$ is fast

What is the rate law for this reaction?

A. Rate $= k\left[(CH_3)_3CBr\right]$
B. Rate $= k\left[OH^-\right]$
C. Rate $= k\left[(CH_3)_3CBr\right]\left[OH^-\right]$
D. Rate $= k\left[(CH_3)_3CBr\right]^2$

Answer A. The first step will be rate-limiting. It will determine the rate for the entire reaction because it is slower than the other steps. This step is a unimolecular process with the rate given by answer A. Choice C would be correct if the reaction as a whole were one elementary step instead of three, but the stoichiometry of a reaction composed of multiple elementary steps cannot be used to predict a rate law.

66. Which statements about reaction rates are true?

I. A catalyst will shift an equilibrium to favor product formation.
II. Catalysts increase the rate of forward and reverse reactions.
III. A greater temperature increases the chance that a molecular collision will overcome a reaction's activation energy.
IV. A catalytic converter contains a homogeneous catalyst.

A. I and II
B. II and III
C. II, III and IV
D. I, III, and IV

Answer B. Catalysts provide an alternate mechanism in both directions, but do not alter equilibrium (I is false, II is true). The kinetic energy of molecules increases with temperature, so the energy of their collisions increases also (III is true). Catalytic converters contain a heterogeneous catalyst (IV is false).

67. Write the equilibrium expression K_{eq} for the reaction:

$CO_2\ (g) + H_2\ (g) \leftrightarrow CO\ (g) + H_2O\ (l)$

A. $\dfrac{[CO][H_2O]}{[CO_2][H_2]^2}$

B. $\dfrac{[CO_2][H_2]}{[CO][H_2O]}$

C. $\dfrac{[CO][H_2O]}{[CO_2][H_2]}$

D. $\dfrac{[CO]}{[CO_2][H_2]}$

Answer D. Product concentrations are multiplied together in the numerator and reactant concentrations in the denominator, eliminating choice B. The stoichiometric coefficient of H_2 is one, eliminating choice A. For heterogeneous reactions, concentrations of pure liquids or solids are absent from the expression because they are constant, eliminating choice C. D is correct.

TEACHER CERTIFICATION STUDY GUIDE

68. What could cause this change in the energy diagram of a reaction?

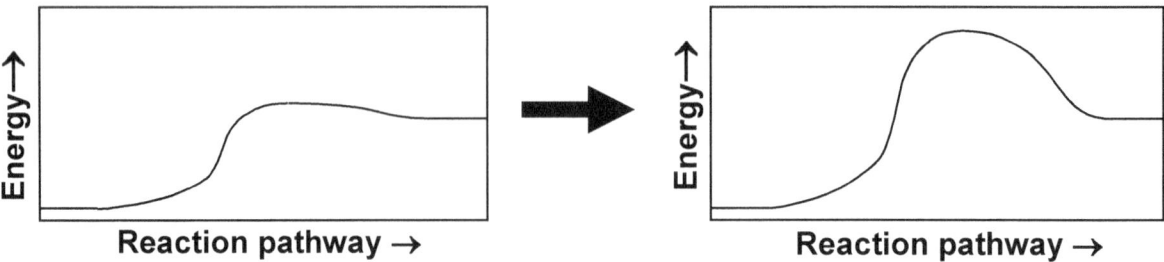

A. Adding a catalyst to an endothermic reaction
B. Removing a catalyst from an endothermic reaction
C. Adding a catalyst to an exothermic reaction
D. Removing a catalyst from an exothermic reaction

Answer B. The products at the end of the reaction pathway are at a greater energy than the reactants, so the reaction is endothermic (narrowing down the answer to A or B). The maximum height on the diagram corresponds to activation energy. An increase in activation energy could be caused by removing a heterogeneous catalyst.

69. $BaSO_4$ (K_{sp} = 1x10^{-10}) is added to pure H_2O. How much is dissolved in 1 L of saturated solution?

A. 2 mg
B. 10 μg
C. 2 μg
D. 100 pg

Answer A. $BaSO_4$ (s) → Ba^{2+} (aq) + SO_4^{2-} (aq), therefore,
$K_{sp} = \left[Ba^{2+}\right]\left[SO_4^{2-}\right]$.

In a saturated solution: $\left[Ba^{2+}\right] = \left[SO_4^{2-}\right] = \sqrt{1 \times 10^{-10}} = 1 \times 10^{-5}$ M.

The mass in one liter is found from the molarity:

$$1 \times 10^{-5} \frac{\text{mol } Ba^{2+} \text{ or } SO_4^{2-}}{L} \times \frac{1 \text{ mol dissolved } BaSO_4}{1 \text{ mol } Ba^{2+} \text{ or } SO_4^{2-}} \times \frac{(137+32+4 \times 16)\text{g } BaSO_4}{1 \text{ mol } BaSO_4}$$

$$= 0.002 \frac{g}{L} BaSO_4 \times 1 \text{ L solution} \times \frac{1000 \text{ mg}}{g} = 2 \text{ mg } BaSO_4$$

70. The exothermic reaction 2NO (g) + Br₂ (g) ↔ 2NOBr (g) is at equilibrium. According to Le Chatelier's principle:

A. Adding Br₂ will increase [NO].
B. An increase in container volume (with T constant) will increase [NOBr].
C. An increase in pressure (with T constant) will increase [NOBr].
D. An increase in temperature (with P constant) will increase [NOBr].

Answer C. Le Chatelier's principle predicts that equilibrium will shift to partially offset any change. Adding Br₂ will be partially offset by reducing [Br₂] and [NO] via a shift to the right (not Choice A). For the remaining possibilities, we may write the reaction as: 3 moles ↔ 2 moles + heat. An increase in container volume will decrease pressure. This change will be partially offset by an increase in the number of moles present, shifting the reaction to the left (not Choice B). An increase in pressure will be offset by a decrease in the number of moles present, shifting the reaction to the right (Choice C, correct). Raising the temperature by adding heat will shift the reaction to the left (not Choice D).

71. At a certain temperature, T, the equilibrium constant for the reaction 2NO (g) ↔ N₂ (g) + O₂ (g) is $K_{eq} = 2 \times 10^3$. If a 1.0 L container at this temperature contains 90 mM N₂, 20 mM O₂, and 5 mM NO, what will occur?

A. The reaction will make more N₂ and O₂.
B. The reaction is at equilibrium.
C. The reaction will make more NO.
D. The temperature, T, is required to solve this problem.

Answer A. Calculate the reaction quotient at the actual conditions:

$$Q = \frac{[N_2][O_2]}{[NO]^2} = \frac{(0.090 \text{ M})(0.020 \text{ M})}{(0.005 \text{ M})^2} = 72$$

This value is less than K_{eq} (72 < 2×10³), therefore $Q < K_{eq}$. To achieve equilibrium, the numerator of Q must be larger relative to the denominator. This occurs when products turn into reactants. Therefore NO will react to make more N₂ and O₂.

72. Which statement about acids and bases is not true?

   A. All strong acids ionize in water.
   B. All Lewis acids accept an electron pair.
   C. All Brønsted bases use OH⁻ as a proton acceptor.
   D. All Arrhenius acids form H⁺ ions in water.

Answer C. Choice A is the definition of a strong acid, Choice B is the definition of a Lewis acid, and Choice D is the definition of an Arrhenius acid. By definition, all Arrhenius bases form OH⁻ ions in water, and all Brønsted bases are proton acceptors. But not all Brønsted bases use OH⁻ as a proton acceptor. For example, NH_3 is a Brønsted base.

73. NH_4F is dissolved in water. Which of the following are conjugate acid/base pairs present in the solution?

   I. NH_4^+/NH_4OH
   II. HF/F^-
   III. H_3O^+/H_2O
   IV. H_2O/OH^-

   A. I, II, and III
   B. I, III, and IV
   C. II and IV
   D. II, III, and IV

Answer D. NH_4F is soluble in water and completely dissociates to NH_4^+ and F^-. F^- is a weak base with HF as its conjugate acid (**II**). NH_4^+ is a weak acid with NH_3 as its conjugate base. A conjugate acid/base pair must have the form HX/X (where X is one lower charge than HX). NH_4^+/NH_4OH (**I**) is <u>not</u> a conjugate acid/base pair, eliminating Choices A and B. H_3O^+/H_2O and H_2O/OH^- (**III** and **IV**) are always present in water and in all aqueous solutions as conjugate acid/base pairs. All of the following equilibrium reactions occur in $NH_4F(aq)$:

$$NH_4^+ (aq) + OH^- (aq) \leftrightarrow NH_3 (aq) + H_2O (l)$$
$$F^- (aq) + H_3O^+ (aq) \leftrightarrow HF (aq) + H_2O (l)$$
$$2H_2O (l) \leftrightarrow H_3O^+ (aq) + OH^- (aq)$$

TEACHER CERTIFICATION STUDY GUIDE

74. What are the pH and the pOH of 0.010 M HNO₃ (aq)?

A. pH = 1.0, pOH = 9.0
B. pH = 2.0, pOH = 12.0
C. pH = 2.0, pOH = 8.0
D. pH = 8.0, pOH = 6.0

Answer B. HNO₃ is a strong acid, so it completely dissociates:

$$[H^+] = 0.010 \text{ M} = 1.0 \times 10^{-2} \text{ M}.$$

$$pH = -\log_{10}[H^+] = -\log_{10}(1.0 \times 10^{-2}) = 2.0 \text{ (choices B or C)}.$$

From $pH + pOH = 14$: $pOH = 12.0$ (choice B).

75. What is the pH of a buffer made of 0.128 M sodium formate (HCOONa) and 0.072 M formic acid (HCOOH)? The pK_a of formic acid is 3.75.

A. 2.0
B. 3.0
C. 4.0
D. 5.0

Answer C. From the pK_a, we may find the K_a of formic acid:

$$K_a = 10^{-pK_a} = 10^{-3.75} = 1.78 \times 10^{-4}$$

This is the equilibrium constant:

$$K_a = \frac{[H^+][HCOO^-]}{[HCOOH]} = 1.78 \times 10^{-4} \text{ for the dissociation:}$$

$$HCOOH \rightleftharpoons H^+ + HCOO^-$$

The pH is found by solving for the H⁺ concentration:

$$[H^+] = K_a \frac{[HCOOH]}{[HCOO^-]} = (1.78 \times 10^{-4})\frac{0.072}{0.128} = 1.0 \times 10^{-4} \text{ M}$$

$$pH = -\log_{10}[H^+] = -\log_{10}(1.0 \times 10^{-4}) = 4.0 \text{ (choice C)}$$

76. A sample of 50.0 ml KOH is titrated with 0.100 M HClO₄. The initial buret reading is 1.6 ml and the reading at the endpoint is 22.4 ml. What is [KOH]?

A. 0.0416 M
B. 0.0481 M
C. 0.0832 M
D. 0.0962 M

Answer A. HClO₄ and KOH are both strong electrolytes. If you are good at memorizing formulas, solve the problem this way:

$$C_{unknown} = \frac{C_{known}(V_{final} - V_{initial})}{V_{unknown}} = \frac{0.100 \text{ M } (22.4 \text{ ml} - 1.6 \text{ ml})}{50.0 \text{ ml}} = 0.0416 \text{ M}$$

The problem may also be solved by finding the moles of known substance:

$$0.100 \frac{\text{mol}}{\text{L}} \times \frac{1 \text{ L}}{1000 \text{ mL}} \times (22.4 \text{ mL} - 1.6 \text{ mL}) = 0.00208 \text{ mol HClO}_4$$

This will neutralize 0.00208 mol KOH, and $\frac{0.00208 \text{ mol}}{0.0500 \text{ L}} = 0.0416 \text{ M}$

TEACHER CERTIFICATION STUDY GUIDE

77. Rank the following from lowest to highest pH. Assume a small volume for the added component:

I. 0.01 mol HCl added to 1 L H_2O
II. 0.01 mol HI added to 1 L of an acetic acid/sodium acetate solution at pH 4.0
III. 0.01 mol NH_3 added to 1 L H_2O
IV. 0.1 mol HNO_3 added to 1 L of a 0.1 M $Ca(OH)_2$ solution

A. I < II < III < IV
B. I < II < IV < III
C. II < I < III < IV
D. II < I < IV < III

Answer A. HCl is a strong acid. Therefore Solution I has a pH of 2 because:

$$pH = -\log_{10}\left[H^+\right] = -\log_{10}(0.01) = 2$$

HI is also a strong acid and would have a pH of 2 at this concentration in water, but the buffer will prevent the pH from dropping this low. Solution II will have a pH above 2 and below 4, eliminating choices C and D.

If a strong base were in Solution III, its pOH would be 2. Using the equation pH + pOH = 14, its pH would be 12. Because NH_3 is a weak base, the pH of Solution III will be greater than 7 and less than 12.

A neutralization reaction occurs in Solution IV between 0.1 mol of H^+ from the strong acid HNO_3 and 0.2 mol of OH^- from the strong base $Ca(OH)_2$. Each mole of $Ca(OH)_2$ contributes two base equivalents for the neutralization reaction. The base is the excess reagent and 0.1 mol of OH^- remains after the reaction. This resulting solution will have a pOH of 1 and a pH of 13.

A is correct because: 2 < between 2 and 4 < between 7 and 12 < 13.

78. **Which statement about thermochemistry is true?**

A. Particles in a system move about less freely at high entropy.
B. Water at 100° C has the same internal energy as water vapor at 100° C.
C. A decrease in the order of a system corresponds to an increase in entropy.
D. At its sublimation temperature, dry ice has higher entropy than gaseous CO_2.

Answer C. At high entropy, particles have a large freedom of molecular motion (A is false). Water and water vapor at 100° C contain the same translational kinetic energy, but water vapor has additional internal energy in the form of resisting the intermolecular attractions between molecules (B is false). We also know water vapor has a higher internal energy because heat must be added to boil water. Entropy may be thought of as the disorder in a system (C is correct). Sublimation is the phase change from solid to gas, and there is less freedom of motion for particles in solids than in gases. Solid CO_2 (dry ice) has a lower entropy than gaseous CO_2 because entropy decreases during a phase change that prevents molecular motion (D is false).

79. What is the standard heat of combustion of CH₄ (g)? Use the following data:

A. −890.3 kJ/mol
B. −604.5 kJ/mol
C. −252.9 kJ/mol
D. −182.5 kJ/mol

Standard heats of formation

$CH_4(g)$	−74.8 kJ/mol
$CO_2(g)$	−393.5 kJ/mol
$H_2O(l)$	−285.8 kJ/mol

Answer A. First we must write a balanced equation for the combustion of CH₄. The balanced equation is:

$$CH_4(g) + 2O_2(g) \rightarrow CO_2(g) + 2H_2O(l).$$

The heat of combustion may be found from the sum of the productions minus the sum of the reactants of the heats of formation:

$$\Delta H_{rxn} = H_{product\,1} + H_{product\,2} + \ldots - H_{reactant\,1} - H_{reactant\,2} \ldots$$

$$= \Delta H_f^\circ(CO_2) + 2\Delta H_f^\circ(H_2O) - \left(\Delta H_f^\circ(CH_4) + 2\Delta H_f^\circ(O_2)\right)$$

The heat of formation of an element in its most stable form is zero by definition, and the other heats of formation are found in the table, so:

$$\Delta H_{rxn} = -393.5\,\frac{kJ}{mol} + 2(-285.8\,\frac{kJ}{mol}) - \left(-74.8\,\frac{kJ}{mol} + 2(0)\right) = -890.3\,\frac{kJ}{mol} \quad \text{(choice A)}$$

80. Which statement about reactions is true?

A. All spontaneous reactions are exothermic and cause an increase in entropy.
B. An endothermic reaction that increases the order of the system cannot be spontaneous.
C. A reaction can be non-spontaneous in one direction and also non-spontaneous in the opposite direction.
D. Melting snow is an exothermic process.

Answer B. All reactions that are both exothermic and cause an increase in entropy will be spontaneous, but the converse (Choice A) is not true. Some spontaneous reactions are exothermic but decrease entropy and some are endothermic and increase entropy. Choice B is correct. The reverse reaction of a non-spontaneous reaction (Choice C) will be spontaneous. Melting snow (Choice D) requires heat. Therefore it is an endothermic process.

81. 10. kJ of heat are added to one kilogram of Iron at 10.° C. What is its final temperature? The specific heat of iron is 0.45 J/g·° C.

A. 22° C
B. 27° C
C. 32° C
D. 37° C

Answer C. The expression for heat as a function of temperature change:

$$q = n \times C \times \Delta T$$

may be rearranged to solve for the temperature change:

$$\Delta T = \frac{q}{n \times C}$$

In this case, n is a mass and C is the specific heat of iron:

$$\Delta T = \frac{10000 \text{ J}}{1000 \text{ g} \times 0.45 \frac{\text{J}}{\text{g °C}}} = 22 \text{ °C}$$

This is not the final temperature (choice A is incorrect). It is the temperature difference between the initial and final temperature:

$$\Delta T = T_{final} - T_{initial} = 22 \text{ °C}$$

Solving for the final temperature gives us:

$$T_{final} = \Delta T + T_{initial} = 22 \text{ °C} + 10 \text{ °C} = 32 \text{ °C} \text{ (Choice C)}$$

TEACHER CERTIFICATION STUDY GUIDE

82. Which reaction is not a redox process?

   A. Combustion of octane: $2C_8H_{18} + 25O_2 \rightarrow 16CO_2 + 18H_2O$
   B. Depletion of a lithium battery: $Li + MnO_2 \rightarrow LiMnO_2$
   C. Corrosion of aluminum by acid: $2Al + 6HCl \rightarrow 2AlCl_3 + 3H_2$
   D. Taking an antacid for heartburn:
      $CaCO_3 + 2HCl \rightarrow CaCl_2 + H_2CO_3 \rightarrow CaCl_2 + CO_2 + H_2O$

Answer D. The oxidation state of atoms is altered in a redox process. During combustion (Choice A), the carbon atoms are oxidized from an oxidation number of -4 to +4. Oxygen atoms are reduced from an oxidation number of 0 to -2. All batteries (Choice B) generate electricity by forcing electrons from a redox process through a circuit. Li is oxidized from 0 in the metal to +1 in the LiMnO$_2$ salt. Mn is reduced from +4 in manganese (IV) oxide to +3 in lithium manganese (III) oxide salt. Corrosion (Choice C) is due to oxidation. Al is oxidized from 0 to +3. H is reduced from +1 to 0. Acid-base neutralization (Choice D) transfers a proton (an H atom with an oxidation state of +1) from an acid to a base. The oxidation state of all atoms remains unchanged (Ca at +2, C at +4, O at -2, H at +1, and Cl at -1), so D is correct. Note that Choices C and D both involve an acid. The availability of electrons in aluminum metal favors electron transfer but the availability of CO$_3^{2-}$ as a proton acceptor favors proton transfer.

83. Given the following heats of reaction:

$\Delta H = -0.3$ kJ/mol for $\quad Fe(s) + CO_2(g) \to FeO(s) + CO(g)$

$\Delta H = 5.7$ kJ/mol for $\quad 2Fe(s) + 3CO_2(g) \to Fe_2O_3(s) + 3CO(g)$

and $\Delta H = 4.5$ kJ/mol for $\quad 3FeO(s) + CO_2(g) \to Fe_3O_4(s) + CO(g)$

use Hess' Law to determine the heat of reaction for:

$$3Fe_2O_3(s) + CO(g) \to 2Fe_3O_4(s) + CO_2(g)?$$

A. −10.8 kJ/mol
B. −9.9 kJ/mol
C. −9.0 kJ/mol
D. −8.1 kJ/mol

Answer B. We are interested in $3Fe_2O_3$ as a reactant. Only the second reaction contains this molecule, so we will take three times the opposite of the second reaction. We are interested in $2Fe_3O_4$ as a product, so we will take two times the third reaction. An intermediate result is:

$3Fe_2O_3(s) + 9CO(g) \to 6Fe(s) + 9CO_2(g) \quad\quad \Delta H = -3 \times 5.7$ kJ/mol $= -17.1$ kJ/mol

$6FeO(s) + 2CO_2(g) \to 2Fe_3O_4(s) + 2CO(g) \quad\quad \Delta H = 2 \times 4.5$ kJ/mol $= 9.0$ kJ/mol

---

$3Fe_2O_3(s) + 6FeO(s) + 7CO(g) \to$
$\quad\quad 2Fe_3O_4(s) + 6Fe(s) + 7CO_2(g)$ $\quad\quad \Delta H = (-17.1 + 9.0)$ kJ/mol $= -8.1$ kJ/mol

However, D is not the correct answer because it is not ΔH for the reaction of the problem statement. We may use six times the first reaction to eliminate both FeO and Fe from the intermediate result and obtain the reaction of interest:

$3Fe_2O_3(s) + 6FeO(s) + 7CO(g) \to$
$\quad\quad 2Fe_3O_4(s) + 6Fe(s) + 7CO_2(g)$ $\quad\quad \Delta H = -8.1$ kJ/mol

$6Fe(s) + 6CO_2(g) \to 6FeO(s) + 6CO(g) \quad\quad \Delta H = 6 \times (-0.3$ kJ/mol$) = -1.8$ kJ/mol

---

$3Fe_2O_3(s) + CO(g) \to 2Fe_3O_4(s) + CO(g)$ $\quad\quad \Delta H = (-8.1 + -1.8)$ kJ/mol
$\quad\quad\quad\quad\quad\quad\quad\quad\quad\quad\quad\quad\quad\quad\quad\quad\quad\quad = -9.9$ kJ/mol (choice B)

84. Given $E° = -2.37$ V for Mg^{2+} (aq) $+ 2e^- \rightarrow$ Mg (s) and $E° = 0.80$ V for Ag^+ (aq) $+ e^- \rightarrow$ Ag (s), what is the standard potential of a voltaic cell composed of a piece of magnesium dipped in a 1 M Ag^+ solution and a piece of silver dipped in a 1 M Mg^{2+} solution?

A. 0.77 V
B. 1.57 V
C. 3.17 V
D. 3.97 V

Answer C. Ag^+ (aq) $+ e^- \rightarrow$ Ag (s) has a larger value for $E°$ (reduction potential) than Mg^{2+} (aq) $+ 2e^- \rightarrow$ Mg (s). Therefore, in the cell described, reduction will occur at the Ag electrode and it will be the cathode. Using the equation:

$$E°_{cell} = E°(\text{cathode}) - E°(\text{anode})$$, we obtain:

$$E°_{cell} = 0.80 \text{ V} - (-2.37 \text{ V}) = 3.17 \text{ V (Answer C)}$$

Choice D results from the incorrect assumption that electrode potentials depend on the amount of material present. The balanced net reaction for the cell is:

$$Mg(s) \rightarrow Mg^{2+}(aq) + 2e^- \qquad E°_{ox} - 2.37 \text{ V}$$
$$\underline{2Ag^+(aq) + 2e^- \rightarrow 2Ag(s)} \qquad E°_{red} - 0.80 \text{ V (not 1.60 V)}$$
$$Mg(s) + 2Ag^+(aq) \rightarrow 2Ag(s) + Mg^{2+}(aq) \qquad E°_{cell} - 3.17 \text{ V (not 3.97 V)}$$

TEACHER CERTIFICATION STUDY GUIDE

85. A proper name for this hydrocarbon is:

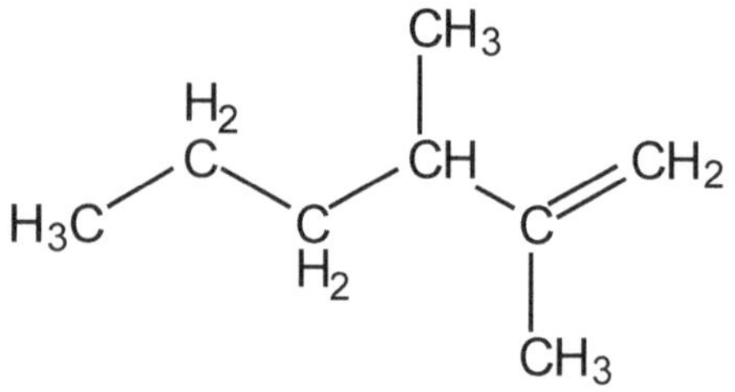

A. 4,5-dimethyl-6-hexene
B. 2,3-dimethyl-1-hexene
C. 4,5-dimethyl-6-hexyne
D. 2-methyl-3-propyl-1-butene

Answer B. The hydrocarbon contains a double bond and no triple bonds, so it is an alkene. Choice C describes an alkyne. The longest carbon chain is six carbons long, corresponding to a parent molecule of 1-hexene (circled to the left). Choice D is an improper name because it names the molecule as a substituted butane, using a shorter chain as the parent molecule. Finally, the lowest possible set of locant numbers must be used. Choice A is an improper name because the larger possible set of locant numbers is chosen.

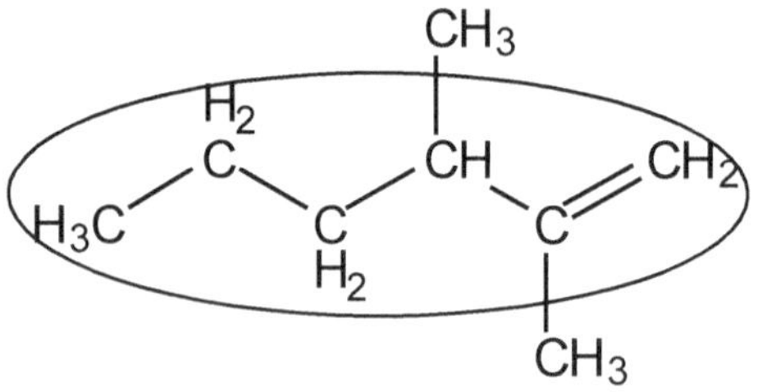

86. An IUPAC approved name for this molecule is:

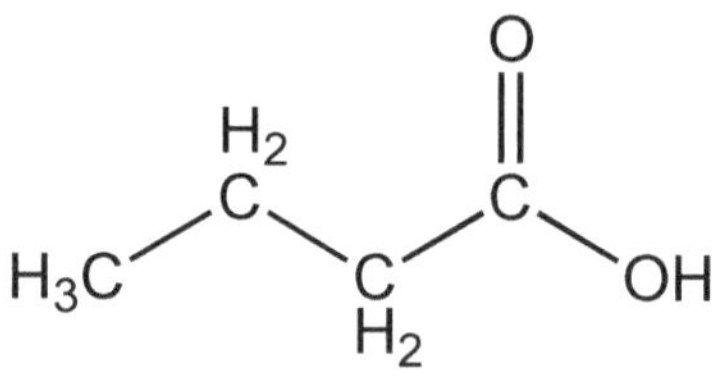

A. butanal
B. propanal
C. butanoic acid
D. propanoic acid

AnswerC. The COOH group means that the molecule is a carboxylic acid and its name will use the suffix –*oic acid*. The presence of 4 carbon atoms means the prefix *butan*- will be used. An alternate name for the molecule is butyric acid. Choices A and B would be used for aldehydes (CHO group). Choices B and D would be used for 3 carbon atoms:

butanal (also called butyraldehyde):

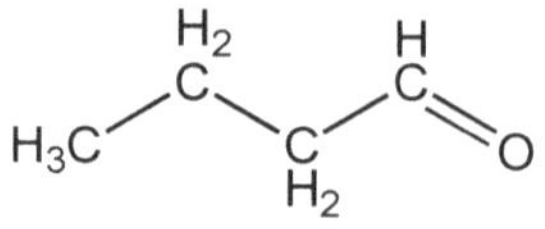

propanal (also called propionaldehyde):

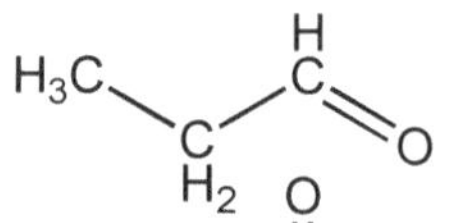

propanoic acid (also called propionic acid):

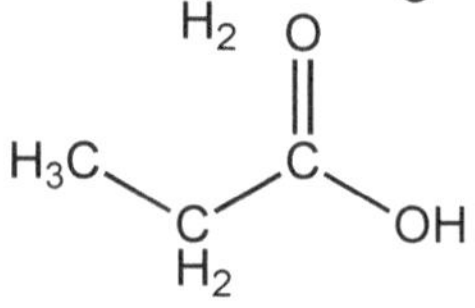

CHEMISTRY 7-12   372

87. Which molecule has a systematic name of methyl ethanoate?

A. 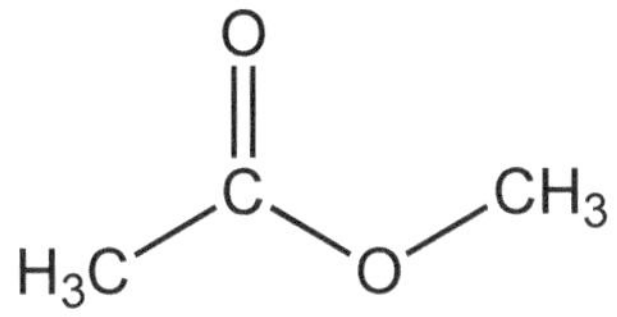 H₃C–C(=O)–O–CH₃

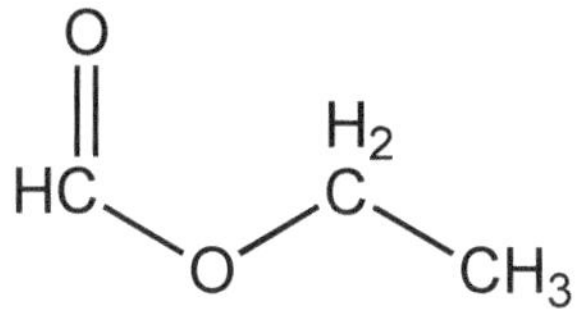

B. HC(=O)–O–C(H₂)–CH₃

C. H₃C–C(=O)–C(H₂)–CH₃

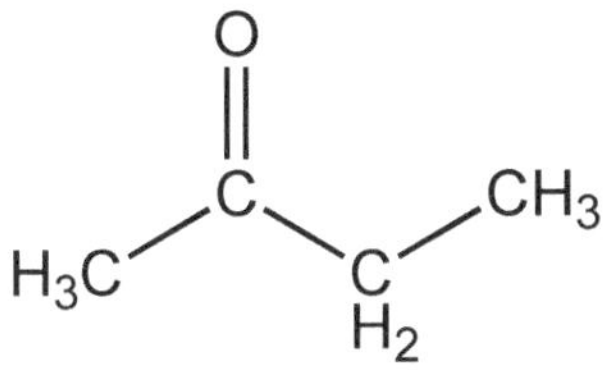

D. 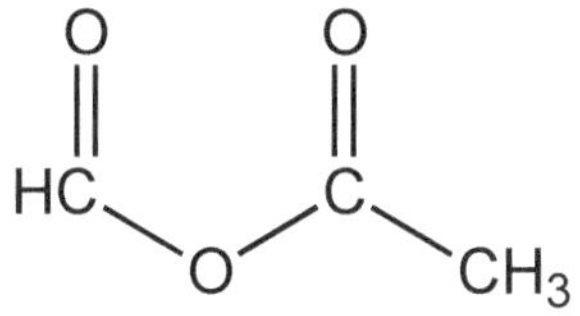 HC(=O)–O–C(=O)–CH₃

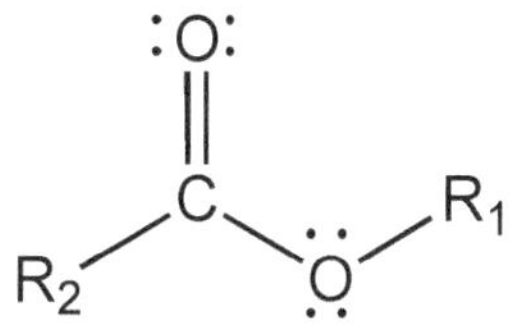

Answer A. The suffix –*oate* is used for esters. The ester group is shown to the right. Choice C is a ketone (ethyl methyl ketone or 2-butanone). The ketone group is shown to the left. Choice D is an acid anhydride (ethanoic methanoic anhydride). The acid anhydride group is shown below to the right. A and B are both esters. The hydrocarbon R₂ with the carbonyl group receives the –*oate* suffix and the hydrocarbon R₁ with the -*yl* suffix is attached to the other oxygen. Choice B is ethyl methanoate and A is correct.

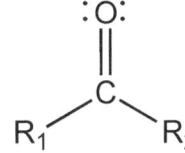

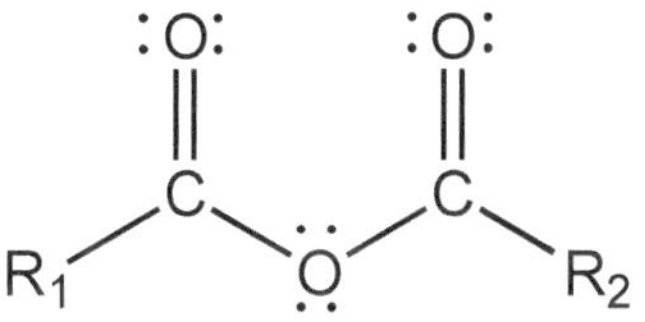

88. This compound contains an:

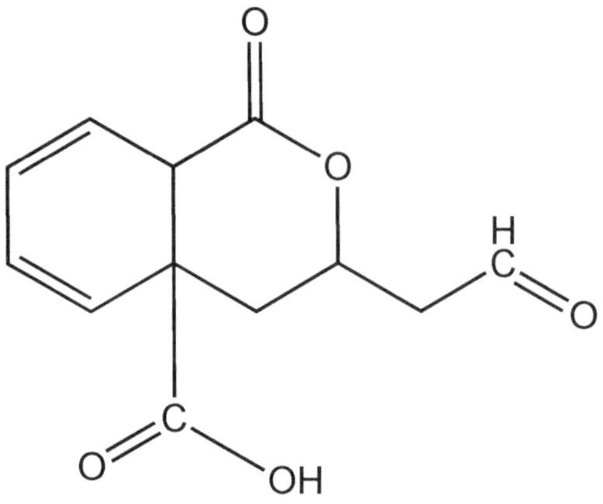

A. alkene, carboxylic acid, ester, and ketone
B. aldehyde, alkyne, ester, and ketone
C. aldehyde, alkene, carboxylic acid, and ester
D. acid anhydride, aldehyde, alkene, and amine

Answer C. The derivatives are circled below:

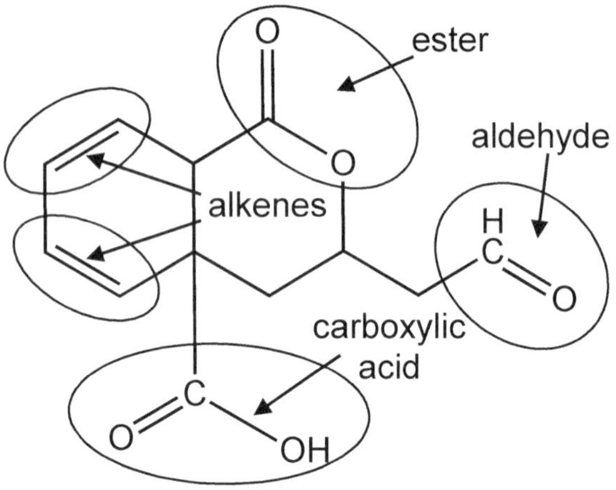

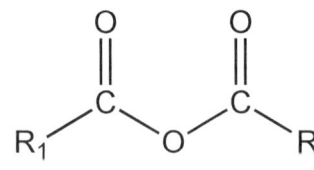

Choice A is wrong because there are no ketones in the molecule. A ketone has a carbonyl group linked to two hydrocarbons as shown to the right. All the carbonyls in the molecule are linked to at least one oxygen atom. Choice B is wrong because there are no ketones and no alkynes in the molecule. An alkyne contains a C≡C triple bond. Choice D is wrong because there are no acid anhydrides (shown to the left) and no amines (shown to the right). Amines require at least one N-C bond and there are no nitrogen atoms in the molecule.

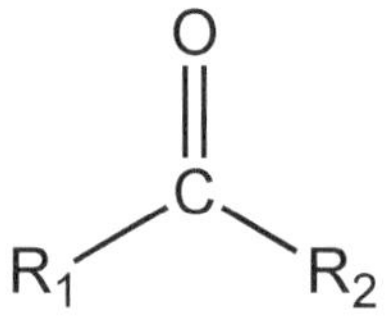

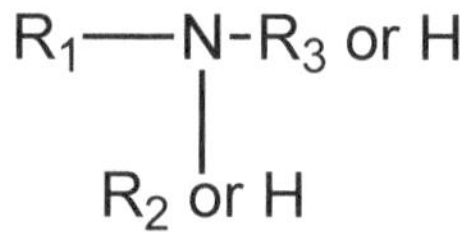

89. Which of the following pairs are isomers?

I. 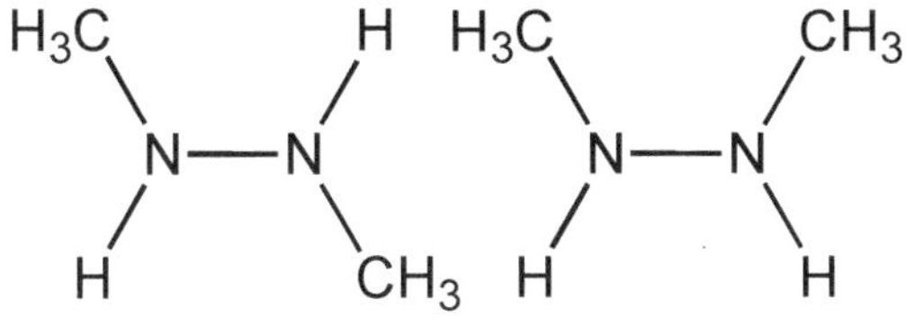 [structure: H₃C-N(H)-N(H)-CH₃ and H₃C-N(CH₃)-N(H)-H]

II. pentanal, 2-pentanone

III. 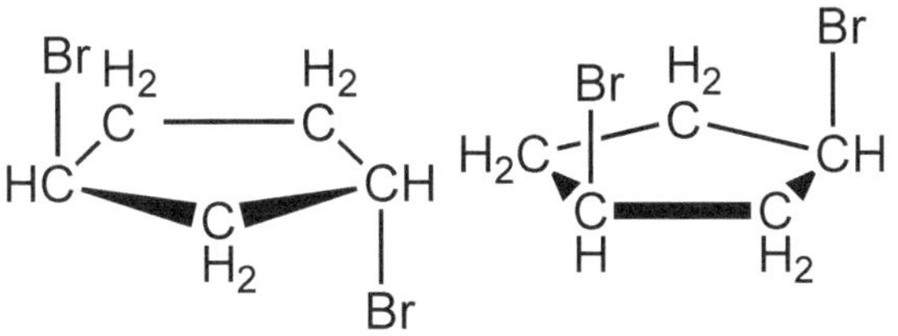 [structures: 1,3-dibromocyclopentane, trans and cis]

IV. 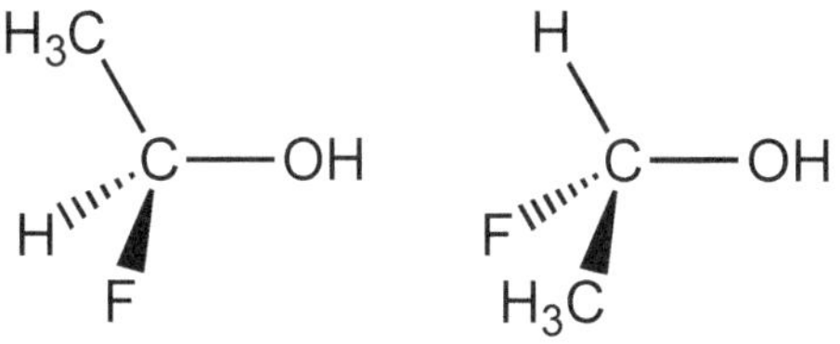 [structures: 1-fluoroethanol stereoisomers]

A. I and IV
B. II and III
C. I, II, and III
D. I, II, III, and IV

Answer B. In Pair I, the N—N bond may freely rotate in the molecule because it is not a double bond. The identical molecule is represented twice.

For Pair II, pentanal is [structure shown] and 2-pentanone is: [structure shown]

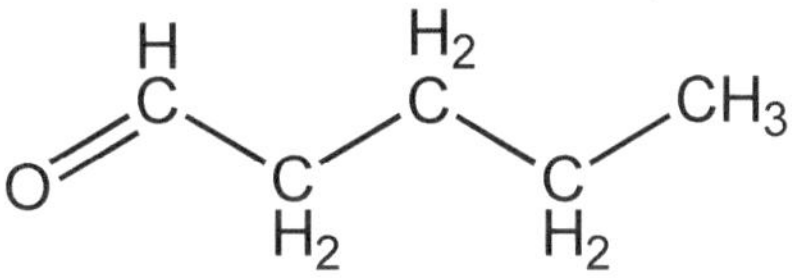

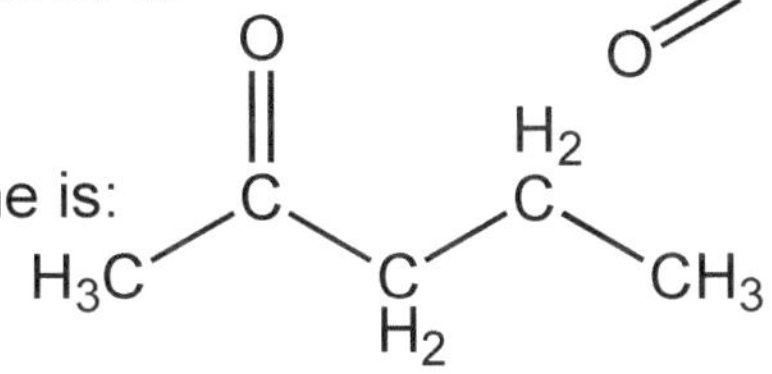

Both molecules are $C_5H_{10}O$, and they are isomers because they have the same formula with a different arrangement of atoms.

In Pair III, both molecules are 1,3-dibromocyclopentane, $C_5H_8Br_2$. In the first molecule, the bromines are in a *trans* configuration, and in the second molecule, they are *cis*. The two molecules are also viewed from different perspectives. Unlike Pair I, no bond rotation may occur because the intervening atoms are locked into place by the ring, so they are different arrangements and are isomers.

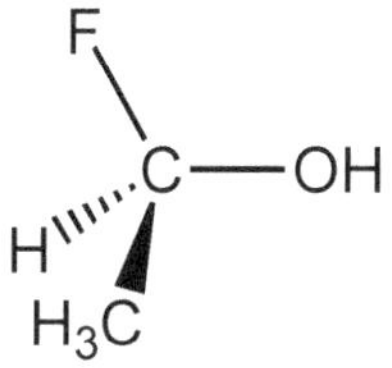

In Pair IV (1-fluoroethanol), there is a chiral center, so stereoisomers are possible, but as in Pair I, the same molecule is represented twice. Rotating the C-O bond indicates that the two structures are superimposable. The molecule shown to the right is a stereoisomer to the molecule represented in IV. The answer is B (Pairs II and III).

TEACHER CERTIFICATION STUDY GUIDE

90. Which instrument would be most useful for separating two different proteins from a mixture?

   A. UV/vis spectrophotometer
   B. Mass spectrometer
   C. Gas chromatograph
   D. Liquid chromatograph

   Answer D. UV/vis spectrophotometry measures the light at ultraviolet and visible wavelengths that can pass through the mixture, and mass spectrometry determines molecular weights. Both might be used to find the concentration of each protein, but neither is a separation technique. Gas chromatography is used for small molecules in the gas phase. Proteins are too large to exist in the gas phase. Liquid chromatography (Choice D) is used to separate large molecules.

91. Classify these biochemicals:

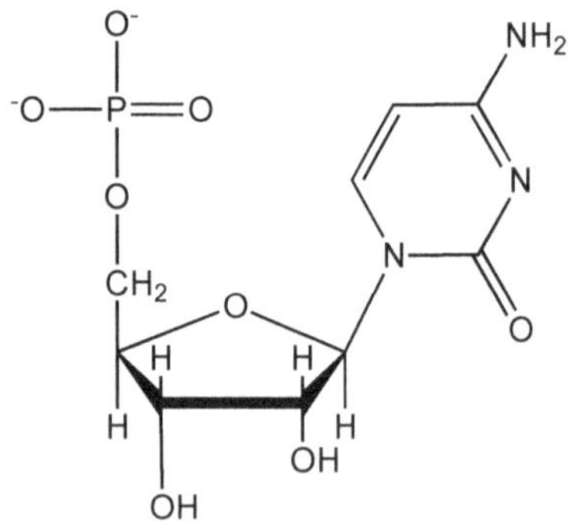

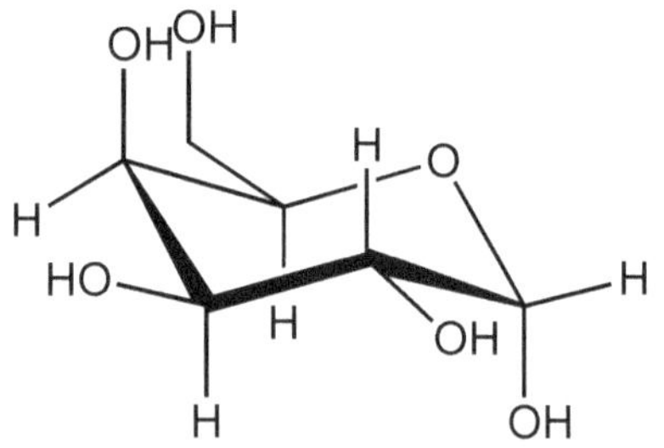

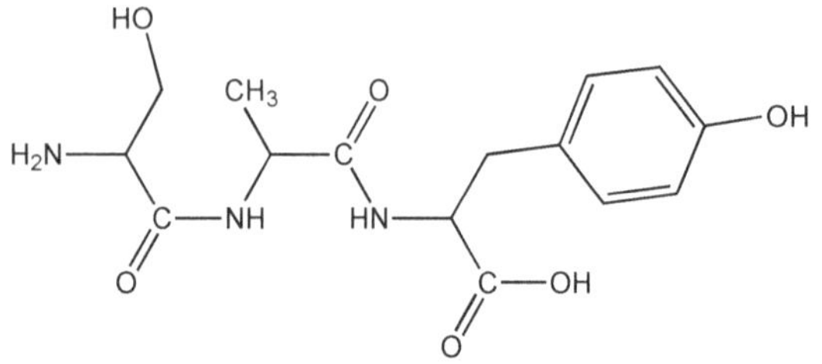

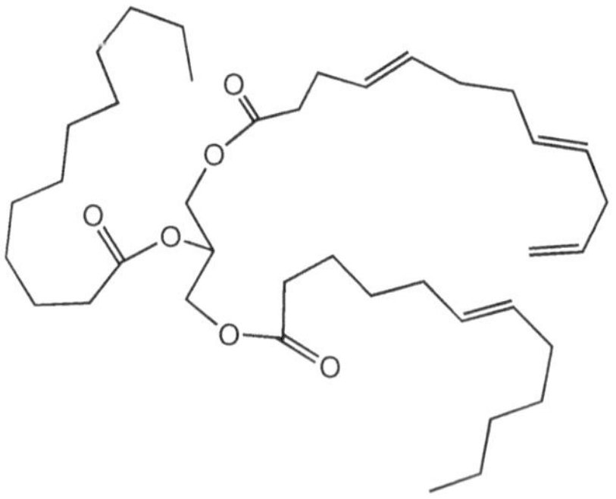

   A. I-nucleotide, II-sugar, III-peptide, IV-fat
   B. I-disaccharide, II-sugar, III-fatty acid, IV-polypeptide
   C. I-disaccharide, II-amino acid, III-fatty acid, IV-polysaccharide
   D. I-nucleotide, II-sugar, III-triglyceride, and IV-DNA

   Answer A. I is a phosphate (PO_4) linked to a sugar and an amine: a nucleotide. II has the formula $C_nH_{2n}O_n$, indicative of a sugar. III contains three amino acids linked with peptide bonds. It is a tripeptide. IV is a triglyceride, a fat molecule.

TEACHER CERTIFICATION STUDY GUIDE

92. You create a solution of 2.00 µg/ml of a pigment and divide the solution into 12 samples. You give four samples each to three teams of students. They use a spectrophotometer to determine the pigment concentration. Here is their data:

Team	Concentration (µg/ml)			
	sample 1	sample 2	sample 3	sample 4
1	1.98	1.93	1.92	1.88
2	1.70	1.72	1.69	1.70
3	1.78	1.99	2.87	2.20

Which of the following is true?

A. Team 1 has the most precise data.
B. Team 3 has the most accurate data in spite of it having low precision.
C. The data from Team 2 is characteristic of a systematic error.
D. The data from Team 1 is more characteristic of random error than the data from Team 3.

Answer C. For Choice A, the data from Team 2 are closer to the mean for Team 2 than the data from Team 1 are to their mean. Therefore, Team 1's data do not have the most precision.

For Choice B, the mean from Team 1 is near 1.9 µg/ml (we don't need to calculate exact values). It differs from the actual value by 0.1 µg/ml. The mean from Team 2 is near 1.7 µg/ml and is inaccurate by 0.3 µg/ml. The mean from Team 3 is not obvious, but it may be calculated as 2.21 µg/ml, differing from the actual value by about 0.2 µg/ml. Team 3's data are less accurate than the data from Team 1.

The data from Team 2 are clustered close to a central value but this value is wrong. Low accuracy with high precision is indicative of a systematic error. (C is correct).

For Choice D, a lack of precision is indicative of random error, and the data from Team 1 are more precise than the data from Team 3.

TEACHER CERTIFICATION STUDY GUIDE

93. Which pair of measurements has identical meanings?

A. 32 micrometers and 0.032 g
B. 26 nm and 2.60×10^{-8} m
C. 3.01×10^{-5} m^3 and 30.1 ml
D. 0.0020 L and 20 cm^3

Answer C. For A, the prefix *micro-* indicates 10^{-6}. 32 micrograms is 0.000032 g. For B, the two measurements do not have the same meaning because they differ in the number of significant figures. 26 nm is 2.6×10^{-8} m. The symbol "n" for *nano-* indicates 10^{-9}. For C and D, unit conversions between cubic meters and liters are required:

For C: 3.01×10^{-5} m$^3 \times \dfrac{1000 \text{ L}}{1 \text{ m}^3} \times \dfrac{1000 \text{ ml}}{1 \text{ L}} = 30.1$ ml (C is correct).

For D: $0.0020 \text{ L} \times \dfrac{1 \text{ m}^3}{1000 \text{ L}} \times \dfrac{(100)^3 \text{ cm}^3}{1 \text{ m}^3} = 2.0$ cm^3 (D is incorrect).

94. Match the instrument with the quantity it measures

I. eudiometer
II. calorimeter
III. manometer
IV. hygrometer

A. I - volume, II - mass, III - radioactivity, IV - humidity
B. I - volume, II - heat, III - pressure, IV - humidity
C. I - viscosity, II - mass, III - pressure, IV - surface tension
D. I - viscosity, II - heat, III - radioactivity, IV - surface tension

Answer B. A eudiometer is a straight tube used to measure gas volume by liquid exclusion. A calorimeter is a device used to measure changes in heat. A manometer is a U-shaped tube used to measure pressure. A hygrometer measures humidity (Choice B). Mass is measured with a balance, radioactivity is measured with a Geiger counter or scintillation counter. Viscosity is measured with a viscometer, surface tension is measured by several different techniques.

TEACHER CERTIFICATION STUDY GUIDE

95. Four nearly identical gems from the same mineral are weighed using different balances. Their masses are: 3.4533 g, 3.459 g, 3.4656 g, 3.464 g. The four gems are then collected and added to a volumetric cylinder containing 10.00 ml of liquid, and a new volume of 14.97 ml is read. What is the average mass of the four stones and what is the density of the mineral?

A. 3.460 g, and 2.78 g/ml
B. 3.460 g and 2.79 g/ml
C. 3.4605 g and 2.78 g/ml
D. 3.461 g and 2.79 g/ml

Answer B. The average mass is the sum of the four readings divided by four:

$$(3.4533 \text{ g} + 3.459 \text{ g} + 3.4656 \text{ g} + 3.464 \text{ g})/4 = 3.460475 \text{ g (caculator value)}$$

This value must be rounded off to three significant digits <u>after the decimal point</u> because this is the lowest precision of the added values. The 4 is an exact number. This means rounding downwards to 3.460 g, eliminating Choices C and D. The volume of the collected stones is found from the increase in the level read off the cylinder:

$$14.97 \text{ ml} - 10.00 \text{ ml} = 4.97 \text{ ml}$$

The density is found by dividing the sum of the masses by this volume:

$$\frac{3.4533 \text{ g} + 3.459 \text{ g} + 3.4656 \text{ g} + 3.464 \text{ g}}{4.97 \text{ ml}} = \frac{13.8419 \text{ g}}{4.97 \text{ ml}} = 2.7850905 \text{ g/ml (caculator value)}$$

This value must be rounded off to three <u>total</u> significant digits because this is the lowest precision of the numerator and the denominator. The first insignificant digit is a 5. In this case there are additional non-zero digits after the 5, so rounding occurs upwards to 2.79 g/ml (Choice B).

96. Which list includes equipment that would not be used in vacuum filtration?

A. Rubber tubing, Florence flask, Büchner funnel
B. Vacuum pump, Hirsch funnel, rubber stopper with a single hole
C. Aspirator, filter paper, filter flask
D. Lab stand, clamp, filter trap

Answer A. Florence flasks are round-bottomed and are used for uniform heating. They do not have the hose barb or the thick wall needed to serve as a filter flask during vacuum filtration. Only a designated filter flask should be used during vacuum filtration. Every other piece of equipment could be used in filtration. A spatula is often used to scrape dried product off of filter paper.

97. Which of the following statements about lab safety is not true?

A. Corrosive chemicals should be stored below eye level.
B. A chemical splash on the eye or skin should be rinsed for 15 minutes in cold water.
C. MSDS means "Material Safety Data Sheet."
D. A student should "stop, drop, and roll" if their clothing catches fire in the lab.

Answer D. In the lab, the safety shower should be used.

98. Which of the following lists consists entirely of chemicals that are considered safe enough to be in a high school lab?

A. hydrochloric acid, lauric acid, potassium permanganate, calcium hydroxide
B. ethyl ether, nitric acid, sodium benzoate, methanol
C. cobalt (II) sulfide, ethylene glycol, benzoyl peroxide, ammonium chloride
D. picric acid, hydrofluoric acid, cadmium chloride, carbon disulfide.

Answer A. Hydrochloric acid (HCl) is a common acid reagent in high school chemistry. Lauric acid is the fatty acid $CH_3(CH_2)_{10}COOH$ also known as dodecanoic acid. Potassium permanganate ($KMnO_4$) is a strong oxidizer. Calcium hydroxide ($Ca(OH)_2$) is a strong base. These chemicals in their pure state are hazardous, but they are considered safe enough to be in high schools. Ethyl ether (Choice B) should not be in high schools because it may form highly explosive organic peroxides over time. Benzoyl peroxide (Choice C) at low concentrations in gel form is an acne medication, but the pure compound is highly explosive. Choice D consists entirely of chemicals that are too dangerous for high schools. Picric acid is highly explosive, hydrofluoric acid is very corrosive and very toxic, all cadmium compounds are highly toxic, and carbon disulfide is explosive and toxic.

99. The following procedure was developed to find the specific heat capacity of metals:

1. Place pieces of the metals in an ice-water bath so their initial temperature is 0° C.
2. Weigh a Styrofoam cup.
3. Add water at room temperature to the cup and weigh it again.
4. Add a cold metal from the bath to the cup and weigh the cup a third time.
5. Monitor the temperature drop of the water until a final temperature at thermal equilibrium is found.

_____ is also required as additional information in order to obtain heat capacities for the metals. The best control would be to follow the same protocol except to use _____ in Step 4 instead of a cold metal.

A. The heat capacity of water / a metal at 100° C
B. The heat of formation of water / ice from the 0° C bath
C. The heat of capacity of ice / glass at 0° C
D. The heat capacity of water / water from the 0° C bath

Answer D. The equation:
$$q = n \times C \times \Delta T$$

is used to determine what additional information is needed. The specific heat, C, of the metals may be found from the heat added, the amount of material, and the temperature change. The amount of metal is found from the difference in weight between Steps 3 and 4, and the temperature change is found from the difference between the final temperature and 0° C. The additional value required is the heat added, q. This may be found from the heat removed from the water if the amount of water, the heat capacity of water, and the temperature change of water are known. The amount of water is found from the difference in weight between Steps 2 and 3, and the temperature change is found from the difference between the final temperature and room temperature. The only additional information required is the heat capacity of water, eliminating Choices B and C. Heat of formation (choice B) is only used for chemical reactions.

A good control simplifies only the one aspect under study without adding anything new. Metal at 100° C (Choice A) would alter the temperature of the experiment and glass (Choice C) would add an additional material to the study. Ice (Choice B) would require consideration of the heat of fusion. Choice D is an ideal control because the impact of water at 0° C on room temperature water is simpler than the impact of metals at 0° C on room temperature water, and nothing new is added.

100. Which statement about the impact of chemistry on society is not true?

A. Partial hydrogenation creates *trans* fat.
B. The Haber process incorporates nitrogen from the air into molecules for agricultural use.
C. The CO_2 concentration in the atmosphere has decreased in the last ten years.
D. The concentration of ozone-destroying chemicals in the stratosphere has decreased in the last ten years.

Answer C. CO_2 concentrations in the atmosphere continue to increase (Choice C), but the concentration of ozone destroying chemicals has fallen (Choice D) due to international agreements.

CPSIA information can be obtained
at www.ICGtesting.com
Printed in the USA
BVHW011103120419
545355BV00013B/797/P